EUROPEAN ANTHROPOLOGIES

ANTHROPOLOGY OF EUROPE

General Editors:
Monica Heintz, University of Paris Nanterre
Patrick Heady, Max Planck Institute for Social Anthropology

Europe is the latest region to attract anthropological research and a region whose variety and speed of change constitutes the strongest challenge to classical anthropology. Situated at the frontier with other social sciences and humanities, the anthropology of Europe has been bred by ethnology, anthropology, folklore, cultural studies, before engaging in innovative interdisciplinary approaches. 'Anthropology of Europe' publishes fieldwork monographs by young or established scholars, as well as collective or edited volumes on particular regions or aspects of European society. The series pays special attention to studies with a strong comparative component – addressing theoretical questions of interest both to anthropologists and to other scholars working in the general field of social science and the humanities.

EUROPEAN ANTHROPOLOGIES

Edited by
Andrés Barrera-González, Monica Heintz
and Anna Horolets

berghahn
NEW YORK · OXFORD
www.berghahnbooks.com

First published in 2017 by

Berghahn Books

www.berghahnbooks.com

Library of Congress Cataloging-in-Publication Data

A C.I.P. cataloging record is available from the Library of Congress

British Library Cataloguing in Publication Data

A catalogue record for this book is available from the British Library

ISBN 978-1-78533-607-2 (hardback)
ISBN 978-1-78920-764-4 (paperback)
ISBN 978-1-78533-608-9 (ebook)

CONTENTS

FIGURES AND TABLES

FIGURES

TABLES

ACKNOWLEDGEMENTS

This volume has been made possible by a series of scholarly endeavors (workshops, panels, conferences) carried out in the framework of the Europeanist network of EASA (European Association of Social Anthropologists). We would like to thank the successive executive committees of EASA and the following institutions, which have given generous support to the above-mentioned academic pursuits over the years: The European Science Foundation (ESF), Standing Committee for the Social Sciences; The Wenner-Gren Foundation for Anthropological Research, Inc New York, USA; Maison René-Ginouvès d'Archéologie et d'Ethnologie (and in particular Professor Martine Segalen); Spain's Ministerio de Educación y Ciencia, Secretaría de Estado de Universidades e Investigación; Universidad Complutense de Madrid and Consejo Superior de Investigaciones Científicas; and The Institut Universitaire de France. We would also like to thank John Eidson for his generous comments and suggestions regarding the introduction, and Deborah Pope and Megan Caine for careful language editing.

STRENGTH FROM THE MARGINS

Restaging European Anthropologies

ANDRÉS BARRERA-GONZÁLEZ, MONICA
HEINTZ AND ANNA HOROLETS

❧

In what ways did Europeans interact with the diversity of people they encountered on other continents in the context of colonial expansion, and with the peasant or ethnic 'Other' at home? How did anthropologists and ethnologists make sense of the diversity of people and societies during the nineteenth and twentieth centuries, when the discipline was progressively being established in academia? This volume aims to sketch an intellectual and institutional portrait of a discipline that was originally oriented towards the study of the 'Other', by assessing the diversity of European intellectual histories within sociocultural anthropology. It aims to give more visibility to the 'smaller' European traditions of scholarly endeavour in the differentiated fields of sociocultural anthropology and ethnology, between which dialogue has sometimes been difficult due to each field's lack of awareness of the other's background of intellectual and academic engagement. It suggests that anthropology could find renewed strength by interrogating these 'anthropologies from the margins', which have distinct intellectual genealogies and histories and whose approaches to the study of culture are more sensitive to history, for instance, or to other related disciplines.

The term 'anthropology' in this volume is used as shorthand for both sociocultural anthropology and for what is labelled ethnology, ethnography or folklore studies, in particular national traditions and specific historical and academic contexts. It was only through considering these two fields together that we were able to engage a dialogue, on an equal footing, between distinct national traditions.[1] We chose to address the contours of 'Europeanness' in order to contribute to the dialogue that had already begun around the harmonization of higher education in Europe in the framework of the Bologna Process. It is customary in this context to speak about the goal of achieving a competitive 'European science'. However, we insist on the necessary plurality of these traditions and nowhere in this volume is the aim to produce one single 'European anthropology' in the future mentioned. Through a description of past developments, we suggest that if European anthropologies are in any way scientifically 'competitive', it is because of their mutual breeding and cross-fertilization and not because of their homogenization. Thus, alongside their inspection of the past lineages and entanglements of diverse scholarly traditions and schools, the authors in this volume contemplate the present-day situation of European anthropologies and ethnologies. They reveal the new challenges facing the discipline in the context of the harmonization of European higher education and of the increased liberalization of the management of universities. They point out the difficulties encountered by a discipline known for its reflexivity, in making its results available for what could sometimes be uncritical public use.

In order to follow the rationale of the volume, this introductory chapter is organized in two parts. In the first part we will consider the diversity of anthropology's traditions in Europe through their association with the project of societal modernization, which took different forms at its early stages depending on whether anthropology accompanied the unfolding of a national identity or the discovery of the richness of an empire. In the second part we will look towards the future, and caution against the ongoing existence of inequalities in the production and diffusion of anthropological knowledge, and against the too rigid new European standards in teaching and research. Imposed by a similar project of societal modernization, these standards lead to new forms of power differentiation in the academy and the impulse to build a global science could paradoxically result in new academic inequalities.

REMEMBERING THE PAST

In a notable book on the history of anthropology, George Stocking Jr makes a useful distinction (even if he somewhat simplifies the complexity of particular cases) between nation-building and empire-building anthropologies (Stocking 1984). This is a categorization of the discipline that is based on its socio-historical mode of implementation, which reflects, in turn, on the relation between the anthropologist and the Other. These two distinct ways of doing anthropology appear to share a common goal: the understanding and modernization of society. Focusing on the common goal of societal modernization contributes to reducing the perceived differences between ethnology (*Volkskunde*, the study of 'the people', of one's own national traditions) and sociocultural anthropology (*Völkerkunde*, the study of 'other peoples', particularly non-European peoples). This approach will equally allow us to emphasize the current challenges and dangers of building European anthropology in response to the imperative of social usefulness.

Rescuing 'Small' Traditions

One of the first questions to emerge in the process of writing an inclusive[2] social history of the discipline is: on what remarkable facts and events should it be constructed? This is followed by a consideration of who chooses, and when, what is deemed to be meaningful for its development.

The received wisdom is that anthropology was established in the academy at some point during the second half of the nineteenth century, through initiatives taken and institutions set up either in the United States (Hinsley 1994 [1981]; Bieder 1986) or in Victorian Britain (Stocking 1984, 1991; Kuklick 1993 [1991], 2008). However, in a well-documented and thoroughly researched book, Han F. Vermeulen (2008, 2015) takes the beginnings of the discipline (under the names of *Ethnographie* and *Ethnologie*) back to the eighteenth century. It was in the context of the German Enlightenment, and in relation to extensive ethnographic work carried out by German scholars participating in Russian expeditions to Siberia, that these disciplines were established and received a decisive impulse in their practice and theory.[3] We can, of course, take the history back further, to antiquity, as some history of anthropology textbooks do, pointing out the relevance for *anthropos-logos* of works such as Herodotus' *The History*.[4] Accounts of prodigious journeys of travel and trade may also be considered precedents for anthropology. In this regard, there are certainly many authors and works that could be recalled as part of anthropology's intellectual lineage and heritage (see, for example, Hodgen 1964). In this volume, the chapter by Wolf-Knuts and Hakamies mentions such a relevant precedent in Finland and describes a case of discontinuity and overlooked 'ethnographic occasion' (a term forged by Pels and Salemink, 2002 [1999]). The beginnings of Finnish folklore collection, including institutional efforts to 'preserve memories from bygone times', date back to as early as the sixteenth and seventeenth centuries. But due to geopolitical circumstances, as well as to cultural influences, it was not until much later that studying Finnish culture became a recognized discipline.

In this volume we have explicitly aimed to rescue these forgotten opportunities, which have indirectly shaped the discipline of anthropology but of which its practitioners today are not necessarily aware. This rewriting of the history of the discipline in Europe demanded an integration of ethnology and anthropology as two facets of the same pursuit. But also, through the presentation of 'big' or 'great' traditions, such as those of Germany or France, alongside 'small' or 'little' traditions, such as Croatia's or Finland's, we aimed to draw readers' attention to overlooked similarities and differences between variously situated and grounded European anthropologies. For the sake of clarity, in what follows we will use Stocking's categorization of empire-building and nation-building anthropologies, while at the same time pointing out the historical elements that run beyond this categorization.

The Ideal of Societal Modernization in the Anthropologies Associated with Imperial and Neocolonial Governance

It has been sufficiently demonstrated that anthropology is inextricably associated with colonial and imperial endeavours (Asad 1973). This historical context relates to the commonplace assumption that anthropological inquiry arises from the (peaceful or violent) encounter with the Other: the distant and far apart Other, be it in time, space, culture and/or social organization. In this sense, anthropology would be understood as stemming, in practice, from intellectual and moral reflection, not on a generic human being, but on human beings other than us. At the different historical junctures these would be the barbarians, pagans, savages or primitives situated beyond the political and civilizational boundaries of the colonial metropolis, or alternatively the rural folk, peasants, ethnic minorities and outcasts at home.

It should be remembered that anthropology has made substantial progress in the academic establishment, primarily and mostly where and when it has demonstrated its usefulness for incorporating these 'Others' into the dominant national or colonial civility: as a tool of empire in colonial or neocolonial contexts, or as part of nation-building and/or statecraft pursuits. British social anthropology at the turn of the century (from the nineteenth to the twentieth century) is a case in point, considering its close association with the politics and policies of 'indirect rule', and in more general terms with the governing of the colonies (Kuper 1996 [1983]; L'Estoile, Neiburg and Sigaud 2005). In North America the establishment of the Bureau of American Ethnology in 1879 was also part and parcel of the conquest, 'pacification' and colonization of the Western frontier, and a useful means for the better government and administration of 'Indian affairs' in particular (Hinsley 1994 [1981]; Mark 1988).

Looking back at the beginnings of academic anthropology, the project of societal modernization appears to have fuelled the development of anthropology as a discipline. This is epitomized in the role played by scientific and anthropological expeditions in the establishment of a science of anthropology. The ideals of the Enlightenment promoted the incorporation of academic-scientific goals into expeditions of geographic and strategic military exploration undertaken in the fifteenth and sixteenth centuries, which were sponsored and carried out by countries with colonizing ambitions and interests. Scientific expeditions in the eighteenth century had a predominantly geographical and naturalist character. However, the range of interests gradually widened to account not only for the geography, flora and fauna of the explored lands, but also their diverse peoples and cultures, adding to the naturalist scientific endeavour the resources of disciplines such as ethnography and ethnology. Throughout the nineteenth century there was continuity in this tradition of great exploratory undertakings, with an increase in the number of expeditions bearing strictly scientific-academic contents. As pointed out above, these endeavours were promoted and carried out by countries with substantial colonial possessions (the United Kingdom and France, for example) or countries like the United States and Russia, which had embarked on vast processes of expansion of their metropolitan frontiers towards the west and east respectively.

Among the expeditions guided exclusively or predominantly by anthropological concerns and carried out between the end of the nineteenth century and the middle of the twentieth century, there are some whose direct and decisive impact on the consolidation and expansion of academic anthropology is widely acknowledged. This is certainly the case of Cambridge University's 1898 anthropological expedition to the Torres Strait led by Alfred Haddon (Hart 1998; Herle and Rouse 1998) and the North Pacific expeditions (1897–1902) under Franz Boas' intellectual aegis (Krupnik and Fitzhugh 2001). But there are other 'ethnographic occasions', which, if reconsidered, would illustrate the diversity of academic lineages and intellectual genealogies that converge in the history of anthropology. One of these is the significant case of Russian ethnographies, ethnologies and more canonical past and present sociocultural anthropologies, described by Sergey Sokolovskiy in this volume. Russia's tradition in the practice of the anthropological and ethnological sciences is characterized by sharp discontinuities and ruptures, and by the radical interference of state-government agendas and political ideologies. There was a very promising start back in the eighteenth and nineteenth centuries, when the country opened up to Western influence. The direct involvement of German scholars from the Enlightenment period in the researching and writing of the ethnography of Siberian peoples and cultures motivated local scholars to get involved in the task themselves (Vermeulen 2008, 2015). In the context of the great expansion of Russia's frontiers towards the east, the exploratory endeavours of people like Captain Vladimir Arsenyev,[5] carried out in the far eastern confines of the Russian Empire at the end of the nineteenth century, also set a very promising precedent, but this unfortunately did not have continuity or consolidate into a national tradition of ethnology-anthropology, as happened in similar circumstances in the United States. Such opportunities as those opened up for U.S. anthropology by the joint North Pacific expeditions (1897–1902) were lost to Russia due to political developments in the first decades of the twentieth century (revolutionary uprisings and tsarist autocratic setbacks; a devastating civil war; the triumph of the Bolshevik revolution and the consolidation of the Soviet regime). The above-mentioned radical political and ideological interferences, and the discontinuities that took place in Russia's history during the twentieth century, have had a very negative effect as regards the consolidation of an academic tradition in ethnology/anthropology in Russia[6] (Sokolovskiy in this volume).

... and the Resulting Vulnerability of the Discipline

When imperial projects were disrupted, the discipline was weakened. Here Russia is a case in point, but it is not the only one. One of the most striking examples of the history of anthropology's response to historical events is that of German and German-language anthropologies discussed by John Eidson in this volume, which went through a twentieth century marked by ruptures, to arrive at today's vigorous internationalizing impulse. One need only recall the disrepute the Volkskunde was brought into by its involvement with racialist and eugenic policies and the political and ideological agenda of National Socialism. The thorough critique of this school's legacy carried out by Hermann Bausinger, and the reformulation of its central purpose as an 'empirical science of culture', was an adequate point of departure for its renovation into the future (Bausinger 1993 [1971]). But, during this time, new powerful actors had come onto the scene, forcing German-speaking anthropology to yield to the dominance of Anglo-Saxon anthropologies. Today, change in the German anthropological-ethnological landscape is in full swing, and the discipline is overcoming a highly controversial past, including with regard to Völkerkunde – the imperial and colonial kind of German anthropology (Barth et al. 2005) – and reinventing its future.

If John Eidson's overview chapter on German-speaking anthropologies draws our attention to the dynamic character of processes of empires rising and empires crumbling, the chapters by Pier Paolo Viazzo on Italy and by Susana de Matos Viegas and João de Pina- Cabral on Portugal equally show the sensitivity of the discipline to historical evolutions, though in a less dramatic way. Portugal treasures a short but very fertile history in the practice of the anthropological and ethnological sciences: nation-building anthropologies inward oriented, and colonial or neocolonial anthropologies outward oriented (Ferraz de Matos 2013). There is a rich and diversified tradition of anthropology at home, as well as many substantial contributions by foreign social and cultural anthropologists from England, France and the United States. To these could be added the more recent contributions by social anthropologists from the former colony of Brazil (an example of what may be labelled 'reciprocal anthropology') and by a few Spanish anthropologists who are developing their fieldwork and professional careers in Portugal. But the deep and prolonged economic crisis threatens to undo the remarkable accomplishments of Portugal's sociocultural anthropology over the last few decades, as it forces a number of prominent anthropologists to migrate in order to make a new start or advance in their professional careers.

With regard to Italy, the schools of ethnology and sociocultural anthropology have incorporated a broad range of traditions and practices, some of them going back to the nineteenth century: intellectual traditions associated with nation-building processes, home and foreign contributions to the anthropology of Italy, and some colonial or neocolonial veins. Italy has the particularity of being one of the countries favoured by Europeanist and Mediterraneanist U.S. and British anthropologists. This is both a positive and a negative trait, as sometimes foreign anthropologists have 'either ignored local anthropological traditions or dismissed them as mere folklore studies' (Viazzo, in this volume). But locally, government interference, with incongruent and sometimes contradictory policy measures, reforms and counter-reforms, does not provide an environment where this rich blending of traditions can bear fully grown fruit (Viazzo, in this volume).

France represents a sort of 'third way' among the schools of anthropology that stem from an empire, as the development of French anthropology has been touched less by the disintegration of the French empire and more by the recent globalization trend that has pushed Anglo-Saxon anthropologies forward. One can observe that France (and in this regard also the other Francophone countries in Europe: Belgium and Switzerland) is where the differing traditions of ethnology, social anthropology and folkloristics (bearing the local denomination *arts et traditions populaires*) have taken more time to find a common ground for collaboration, or at any rate for intercommunication and cohabitation at the institutional and intellectual level. Moreover, the history of academic sociocultural anthropology (in the terms outlined at the beginning of this introduction) features many renowned French scholars who have become widely reputed ancestors and intellectual beacons for the discipline, in more than their fair share measured in purely demographic terms.

Empire-building anthropologies are as diverse as the empires they were helping to govern:[7] empires reaching out to territories far beyond the metropolis (e.g. Italy) and those ruling over adjacent territories (e.g. Russia). The chapters devoted to French, Italian, German, Portuguese and Russian traditions of sociocultural anthropology and ethnology are illustrative of this. They demonstrate how the production of anthropological knowledge contributed to and was fuelled by imperial ambitions; the impulses that have arisen from the need to tame these ambitions; and the consequences that ensued for the discipline when they failed.

Societal Modernization and the Anthropologies Associated with Nation-Building and Statecraft Pursuits

Asserting that the emergence of 'national' traditions of ethnology and sociocultural anthropology in countries like Poland or Finland was part of nation- and state-building projects sounds like a tautology. Yet, this tautology is worth articulating, since both nation-building and national traditions of the disciplines can be unfolded in a number of directions. Paying attention at this stage to the existing associations between nation-building and the disciplines of anthropology and ethnology is meaningful because of the emergence or reinstatement of new countries and independent states in Europe and also because of the constant development and renovation of these disciplines.

The most significant intellectual (and aesthetical) impulse for this type of engagement comes from the ideals of Romanticism and its concern with the common people and popular national cultures, notably from authors such as Johann G. Herder (1744–1803). Paradoxically, Herder's works, which have been widely influential in continental schools of ethnology, and the Volkskunde in particular, date from the peak years of the German Enlightenment, rather than from the Romantic period sensu strictu. Herder was very influential in the formation of folklore studies in Germany, and also in Scandinavia and Central and Eastern Europe (Bausinger 1993 [1971]: 26–39; Bendix 1997; Vermeulen 2008: 226–28; and Wolf-Knuts and Hakamies; Bitušíková; Čapo and Zrnić; Ciubrinskas; and Eidson's chapters in this volume). An independent source of intellectual inspiration for the study of folklore, and a distinctive tradition in practice, stems from Greece's *laografia* (see Aliki Angelidou's chapter in this volume). Moreover, the Greek school of laografia has influenced ethnological practices in other countries in the Balkan region, for instance in Bulgaria.

One way or another, most, if not all, the anthropological schools and traditions in Europe (with the exception of the already mentioned case of British social anthropology) are or have at some point been associated with nation-building pursuits and their ideological justification, as well as with the substantiation of the respective nation's cultural and historical foundation. For instance, Finland's schools and traditions in doing anthropology-ethnology appear during the struggle for independence from its powerful neighbours Sweden and Russia. The Finish people and their national institutions found a key ally in this struggle in scholars of ethnology and folkloristics, who, armed with innovative methods, made substantial scientific and empirical contributions. Finland's tradition in the ethnological sciences is highly original and rich, for instance in its associations with linguistics and ethnolinguistics, history and oral history, literary criticism and mythology (see Wolf-Knuts and Hakamies in this volume).

A special case is that of the new anthropologies that are emerging or re-emerging in countries that have become independent since the fall of communist regimes in Eastern Europe and beyond, namely following the dissolution of Yugoslavia, Czechoslovakia and the Soviet Union. As the discipline is rapidly changing in these areas, it is interesting to continue to monitor the establishment or re-establishment of specific schools and traditions and watch whether 'the nation' and national-state pursuits remain their catalyser. Substantial work on this topic has been carried out in the last twenty years by scholars such as Peter Skalník (Skalník 2000, 2002, 2004), Chris Hann (Hann, Sárkány and Skalník 2005; Boškovic and Hann 2013), and others (Mihailescu, Iliev and Naumovic 2008; Boškovic 2008; Kürti and Skalník 2009). Chapters on Croatia, Slovakia and Lithuania in this volume converge on the importance given to the building or recovery of national identity in the recent development of ethnology and social anthropology in these countries.

The nation-state can be seen as a vehicle for modernization or, rather, it is the need to step up modernization processes that favoured the flourishing of nation-states. As part of this driving force, ethnology was concerned with studying the soul of the nation: its customs, culture, values and identity. The modernization process is also understood as a particular kind of rationalization: the emergence of new modes of knowledge and its secularization, a distancing from religion, and the concomitant development of new modes of production and ownership. Modernization met with criticism (e.g. from the standpoint of Romanticism), but without the process of modernization would we have seen the growing nostalgia for the past, the rural, the exotic and the irrational that provided the interest for popular 'traditions'? The project of sociocultural anthropology, including ethnography and ethnology, when it is part and parcel of emerging political and cultural identities, becomes enmeshed in the modernization project and its criticism. And a possible explanation for the inherent split between the motivations for doing anthropology and those for doing ethnology might be that while some students of the rural and the irrational considered it their duty to help eradicate them (Buchowski in this volume describes such a case, when referring to 'the tribe' of positivists in Polish academia), others fought to preserve them.

... and the Complex Relationship between Anthropology and the other Social Sciences

The distinction between anthropology and ethnology is a constant reality in the history of European anthropologies, especially in Eastern Europe. If in recent years the frontiers between the two fields were blurred, many practitioners of the discipline still consider them relevant. The national traditions of the discipline in Croatia, Slovakia, Lithuania and Poland, as reflected in this volume, show ethnology and anthropology in opposition, or at any rate not in collaboration: a 'two-pronged discipline'. Only the chapter on Finland reveals a quieter and more productive relation between these two fields. Moving further to the east, we note that during the Soviet period 'ethnography' was used as a synonym for ethnology, and at times for sociocultural anthropology. With the 'Soviet era' being a loose category, as revealed by the chapter on Slovakia, the use of the discipline's name and the focus on objects of research varies over time and space as in Western countries.

The chapters on Finland, Lithuania, France and Greece, and partly that on Poland, analyse also the relation of anthropology/ethnology to other disciplines such as sociology, folklore or history. It is interesting to note that these relations are either unequal or are characterized by blurred boundaries. Susana de Matos Viegas and João de Pina-Cabral broach the matter more obliquely in their chapter on Portugal, a country that saw the development of a unique combination of empire-building and nation-building anthropologies, but struggles to assert its privileged relations to countries such as Brazil and China (its 'empire' components) in order to get noticed and be acknowledged in the national context. It is as if the concept of collaborative or complementary science was unknown to an anthropology that had to assert itself to find its own voice among the social sciences.

We also need to acknowledge today's constitution and fast expansion of new area studies like the anthropology of Eastern Europe, postsocialist studies and the anthropology of Eurasia (Barrera-González et al. 2013; chapters by Buchowski and Ciubrinskas in this volume). The aforementioned new study areas have been established, nurtured and peopled mostly by U.S., British, German and French professional anthropologists working in the region (Barrera-González et al. 2013), as funding for these fast-growing research endeavours has come from new foreign-inspired universities established in these countries; private entities like the Wenner-Gren

Foundation; and specific research programmes focused on the region set up by the Max Planck Society (mostly via the Max Planck Institute for Social Anthropology) or the French Centre National de la Recherche Scientifique (via the Centre Marc Bloch), for instance.[8] Through these external influences, we also see the looming hierarchies of knowledge and academic authority, and the unawareness or blatant mutual ignorance between local and foreign practices within the discipline of sociocultural anthropology in the European field.

Overall, what the chapters in the volume show is the occurrence of multiple crossings in the formation of most European antropologies: juxtapositions, overlaps, convergences and divergences of traditions in the development of anthropological theory, method and practice. Many of these intersections testify to the existence of unequal power relations during the past two centuries, which have ended up being reflected in the formation of the discipline. Today, the emergence of a new common scientific playground makes the European field a true laboratory for experimenting with new methods, theories and subject matters for the discipline.

LOOKING TOWARDS THE FUTURE: GOING BEYOND POWER RELATIONS

How we trace intellectual genealogies, what we quote and which lines of reflection we pursue today is likely to influence the shape of tomorrow's anthropology. Today's unequal visibility of distinct European anthropological traditions prompt us to rescue small traditions of anthropology that are bound to disappear if not interrogated and re-evaluated. The 'global' science could become a better science, one in which efforts are joint, or a colonial science, one in which traditions that are not mainstream are erased on the basis of non-conformity to the most successful standards of science. How are intellectual traditions created, and what are the power relations that exist between them? Anthropology, a science of the margins, should be particularly keen not to neglect its own mission. However, this militant argument of academic justice should be complemented by the more utilitarian argument of scientific interest. Understanding different approaches to anthropology is a helpful exercise in cultural relativism and gives a strong impulse to the paradigm change towards a historically sensitive and socially engaged anthropology. In this second section we take up this issue against the background of recent changes in the evaluation of science and academia, and warn about the thin line between the imperative of societal usefulness and the barriers to scientific freedom.

Circulation of Ideas: Who Was First and Who is Borrowing from Whom?

Scholars who were developing ethnology/anthropology worked under influences of extra-national traditions. To study these influences, we need to consider the circulation of ideas and borrowing, and even the eventuality of intellectual theft. The resulting picture is fascinating. Each chapter of this book invites the reader to plunge into the specificity of a different European country. In the introduction we will limit ourselves to raising a few questions that stem from this overview itself.

In most of the chapters on nation-building anthropologies we see that the transmission of anthropological knowledge took place mostly from empire anthropologies to more peripheral non-imperial ones. But one could wonder whether this perception was formed a posteriori on the basis of what remained more visible in theory due to current power relations within academia. If smaller traditions borrowed from 'greater' ones, was it because the national ones were less developed (underdeveloped or backward) or not dominant (i.e., not visible and influential, not able to 'talk to' more powerful traditions) in the hegemonic, notably Anglo-Saxon, academic discourse? At the beginning of the twentieth century, national intellectuals were mostly educated in the imperial metropolises of the time; this trend was resumed at the end of the twentieth century due to the increased circulation of scholars and their attraction to prestigious Western universities. These intellectuals carried throughout their career the influence of their initial training, but this did not prevent them from innovating.

One could ask why such debates between traditions are still important today. The first answer would be that maybe they should be part of the crystallization of the discipline's identity, as they resonate clearly with the difficulties identified by postmodern anthropology in relation to the thin subject/object demarcation line. But maybe these debates are simply due to academics' pragmatic need for getting published or getting a fair amount of academic recognition. These issues are referred to in a number of the chapters, and there are several proposed 'ways out' of the peripheral position: a cosmopolitan anthropology (Jasna Čapo and Valentina Gulin Zrnić in this volume); an eclectic (cross-fertilizing) anthropology, incorporating ethnological and historicist contributions (Alexandra Bitušíková in this volume); and a hybridity of theories (Jasna Čapo and Valentina Gulin Zrnić in this volume).

In this competition for recognition, figures like Malinowski and Boas, who gained fame as anthropologists based in the universities of imperial metropolises, are interesting cases. They remained important figures for the anthropological traditions of the countries to which they migrated and where they served as mediators, but did they reciprocally become agents of legitimation for their peripheral traditions of origin? People who were influential within a national tradition carried on the dialogue with the traditions of empire, even if this was in the form of rejection – as in the case of Bromley in Russia. The contrary is seldom true. National traditions do not seem to succeed in superseding their limitations and imposing 'original theory'. The Moscow-Tartu semiotic school is often cited as one of the unique paradigms that 'have made it' to the West. Because of the Western recognition, it is more likely to be considered a great theoretical contribution, as if Western validation was needed to legitimize local reputation. What is valued at some point in scholarly knowledge in the humanities, whether it is generality-universality-systematicity or novel groundbreaking paradigm freshness, prevents or leads to the recognition of intellectuals such as Eliade, Lotman and Bakhtin in the West (these last being valued according to the second criterion). In general it is considered that the periphery has to be twice as knowledgeable, twice as erudite, etc., as the centre to be allowed to speak to the centre critically.

But change often comes from the margins, and this can be applied to anthropology as a whole. Its peripheral character boosted the discipline at times when 'marginal' countries/groups became the forerunners of historic change (decolonization, emancipation and, later, postmodernism). Today, when historical processes are again driven by the centre (a Marxist view would say 'by capital'), the role of anthropology is diminishing. Anthropology could retrieve its 'marginal' vocation by exploring its own diverse voices.

Supporting Societal Modernization Today: Facing the New European Union Standards in Teaching and Research

Over the last decade, changes in European academia have aimed at creating a common European research space (Bellier 2007). This is what makes our reconsideration of the multiplicity of traditions in anthropology still relevant. The European policymakers come with a particular concept of science and the university, a different version of the requirement of the social relevance (usefulness) of science, as part of a new project of societal modernization. The university is imagined today as a place where students are made 'immune' to unemployment by their being provided with marketable skills. The academy is thus conceptualized as a reservoir of knowledge that is usable for economic development and can directly affect the affluence and wellbeing of people. It is also considered part of nationalist (or European Unionist) politics of securing oneself the best place in the international (global) competition for economic and political domination. Thus there is some continuity between EU-commissioned and empire-commissioned research in the colonial period.

The idea of preparing students to enter the job market is not faulty, yet it creates false expectations at two levels: first, that the job market generally needs the skills that should be developed at university level; and second, that students, in the course of their studies, acquire 'useful' knowledge that has overtones of 'true' knowledge. The margin of uncertainty, reflexivity and doubt present in social science and humanities knowledge shrinks dramatically. The arguments that the academy – anthropology in particular – should become more engaged with the real world and acquire more prosocial stances are well grounded (e.g. Eriksen 2005; Ribeiro and Escobar 2006). Viazzo's chapter on Italy in this volume points out that 'autistic survival' is not a viable option, that anthropology should be directed to the needs of its students and to the needs of societies. Yet, the wish to serve society and to cater for students' needs is not equivalent to the claims of contemporary neoliberal political and corporate actors, who, by and large, postulate that the university shall serve the market. Advocates of 'public anthropology' distance themselves from the statement that anthropology (or any other humanities discipline) could be a panacea for repairing the malfunctioning of the late capitalist world. Rather, they look for ways of making anthropology a more integral part of today's society. As for sociology, Michael Burawoy (2011) argued that economic and political institutions had a disproportionally large influence on the outlook of the discipline, and suggested that civil society institutions should be given more opportunities to shape the research agenda. How anthropologists might act in order to engage with the public sphere, without being absorbed by ideologically loaded projects they do not want to be part of, are procedures that are still to be written down. The tradition of searching for such formulas is rich; among other sources, the journal *Anthropology in Action* provides a great deal of insight into the endeavours of applied anthropology in Europe.

The difficulties experienced by the humanities in attempting to preserve their identity and their very existence have been well described. On the one hand, insecurities related to the specificity of method (participant observation), the postmodernist turn (Clifford and Marcus 1986) and the need to face the colonial entanglements of anthropology (Pels 2008) have inserted hesitation, reflexivity and avoidance of self-glorification at the disciplines' core (Descola 2005). On the other hand, the change brought from the outside under the name of university reform (Romano 2010) or 'audit culture' (Shore and Wright 1999) has been contributing to the marginalization of all humanities, including anthropology.

However, the situation across Europe is asymmetrical. The countries with shorter or more troubled traditions of institutional development of the discipline, such as Bulgaria and Poland, face more severe pressures than those where anthropology has existed as a fully fledged academic discipline for a longer period. For instance, when quantitative measurements of academic excellence are developed in a haphazard and non-transparent fashion (cf. Brenneis 2009), national anthropologies that use 'smaller' languages (such as Lithuanian or Slovak) automatically find themselves in a disadvantageous position compared with those whose language base is wider (such as English or Portuguese) (Wagner 2012).

Generally, institutional change is driving anthropology/ethnology to become a new type of science, which is inadequately built on the model of hard sciences in which all communications and publications are in English, and all publishing is in peer-reviewed journals rather than in books and is signed by whole teams of researchers. None of these criteria are favourable to anthropology, with its monographs, its literary style and its individually performed in-depth fieldwork. There is some resistance to this trend, but the possibility of resisting is more open to those scholars who are from the 'bigger' traditions, supported by richer economies. Scholars from the 'new' Europe often have to be more complacent out of fear of being excluded from European funding opportunities that are not adequately paralleled by national funding.

The issue of how academic knowledge is produced and disseminated is crucial today, when publications are the first means of evaluating science and the first token of prestige. Publishing is pivotal: whose hands are on the levers of publishing? What are the processes for getting into good publishing houses? What is the gap between the written rules and the practical (tacit) knowledge or practice as such? This matter is very much related to the issue of access to audiences, and the internal differentiation of audiences in anthropological writing: audiences that evaluate and enable, or not, career development; audiences that speak or do not speak the same 'language' as the author. By 'language' we refer here to the language of constructing the scholarly argument, the 'canon' of literature one refers to as well as a set of ethical and epistemological sensibilities that members of a discursive community share. We add to this the importance of embeddedness in networks of academic practice, which could be central or peripheral. Scholarly cooperation is starting to bear the signs of business monopoly and it is extremely difficult for a new player to enter the game. In the context of rapid technological development that makes information, including anthropological knowledge, ever more vast and seemingly ever more available, marketing and networking mechanisms often define what will be noticed, selected for scholarly debate and recognized – not academic excellence. Many scholars in peripheral universities publish a lot of books in local publishing houses, and are not able to 'market' them properly. Some of them do not even undergo a fully-fledged review process. In these cases, publication is no longer a vehicle of scientific advancement; it is a dead end.

These changes – however minuscule or particular they may seem – are a sign of the continued and perhaps increasing (or increasingly obvious) dependence of science (academy) on politics and the economy. It may be that they signal a shift in modernization perceptions. The Enlightenment ideal of science that is ruled by its internal logic gives way to a project of science that is financially efficient and serves particular political or economic goals. This can also be seen as a particular backlash of modernization rhetoric, since the overarching goal of a rational actor controlling the external environment has come full circle and ended up being executed on science itself. The criteria that are used in the evaluation of science today come from different and incompatible social fields (be it economics or politics).

More particularly, the neoliberal rhetoric of European research policy results in a changing outlook for sciences and humanities. It positions scholars so that they need to constantly prove their usefulness and their ability to positively influence national and European economies in a bureaucratic fashion. The case of the Research Assessment Exercises in the United Kingdom described by Shore and Wright (1999) is representative of European science in general. The possibilities of resistance are limited, since research funding is heavily dependent on these evaluations, as Shore (2010) demonstrates in his analysis of the Performance Based Research Fund introduced in New Zealand. The emphasis on efficiency puts inadequate pressure on researchers' productivity and compromises the significance of their findings (e.g. more innovative, 'risky' and less predictable research designs are avoided, longer-term projects are pursued less often, etc.). A few chapters in the volume devote space to this new predicament (notably those on Greece and Portugal). The regard towards the future of anthropology is sometimes optimistic, sometimes pessimistic. The optimistic view comes from discipline practitioners in countries where anthropology has succeeded in finding a niche. The pessimistic view is often linked to institutional pressure to join with other humanities disciplines, to dismantle departments, and to secure more students to justify their existence.

Science and the Market: Ethnographic Notes on the Entrepreneurial University

The above state of affairs is neither new nor unique to the practice of anthropology, but it is worth mentioning, given its impact on the content of science. Due to either academic capitalism (Hoffman 2011) or the schizophrenic university (Shore 2010), depending on the interpretation we favour, anthropology does change. The way in which Hoffman uses Bourdieu's terminology to explain the workings of academic capitalism is instructive. He suggests that 'an increase in market-orientation has not displaced more traditional academic practices and values but facilitated the development of new conceptual vocabularies that are subtly remaking academic practice and culture' (Hoffman 2011: 441). Hoffman distinguishes four such domains: market-oriented entrepreneurialism, external consulting work, consumer-oriented research and interdisciplinarity (cf. Strathern 2005). The tensions between these domains and the contradictory priorities that they set for scholars contribute to the new divisions in the academy. One of these is a division between disciplines that are close to and those that are 'far removed from market potential' (Hoffman 2011: 457), like biochemistry and art history respectively. When a discipline that is further distanced from the market (as anthropology is) is made to adopt the vocabulary of entrepreneurialism, it causes a greater and more painful stretching of the discipline's identity than in the case of one that is closer. In Chevalier's chapter on French anthropology, the issue of dependence on the economic sphere acquires an interesting twist. She writes about the role museums play in the development of the profession. As increasingly commercial institutions, museums need to follow the aesthetics of mass consumption in their endeavours. This forces anthropologists who cooperate with museums to direct their research or their display of results in the direction of 'mass digestible' aesthetic objects. This is one example of how various domains (market, consumption, aesthetics and materiality) interact to shape the scientific discipline.

Paradoxically, these processes also give rise to new sensitivities and imperatives that are not necessarily detrimental to science but rather bring it into new societal contexts. Hoffman gives an example of a 'wide variety of civic engagement and community collaboration' resulting from the influence of 'external consulting work' vocabulary (Hoffman 2011). Since in Bourdieu's original theory the issue of a given field's autonomy is pivotal, the issue of autonomy also surfaces in the discussion of the dependence of science and the academy on other fields: do they have autonomy now; have they ever had autonomy; should they have it; is it feasible that they will have it at least partially; and what logics and vocabularies will be at work, if a degree of autonomy is achieved?

In one important sense, however, science cannot completely divorce itself from the market: it is a field of professional activity; scholars live off their profession. Thus, when considering how anthropology is practised today in Europe we could not overlook the fact that the academy is a 'place' where anthropologists work. It is important, therefore, to consider how their workload is distributed between academic and administrative tasks in the context of the grant-based funding of science. Employment conditions have to be analysed in conjunction with research-funding conditions. In her chapter, Bitušíková tries to explain why most Slovak anthropologists do not work in faraway lands, by pointing to the low level of funding available for overseas research, or for any research activities in fact. Doing online ethnography or anthropology at home becomes a matter of necessity rather than a choice.

We can also look at how precarious employment influences the type of research that is carried out (i.e., what kind of ethnography can be carried out if a researcher is employed on a one or two-year contract with no prospect of extension?). The rising numbers of anthropology graduates increase competition for university positions in the discipline, even in such established traditions as the British one (Kuper 2005). University employment has become notoriously precarious in Germany, where many anthropologists with qualifications as high as that of Habilitated Doctor can count on only short-term contracts, and where many decide to quit academia due to the impossibility of attaining longer-term posts.

The wider availability of higher education across Europe during the last decades of the twentieth century caused university student numbers to swell. In the countries of Eastern and Central Europe, the demand for higher education increased after 1989; the establishment of numerous private universities met this demand. This niche was saturated, however. In the second decade of the twenty-first century, demographic factors (the lower numbers of prospective students) threaten the existence of many departments and institutes, especially in the humanities and social sciences. This is the case in Poland and Bulgaria, for instance, where anthropology departments in private but also public universities are experiencing hardships, and academics who work there fear unemployment.

Universities have always been dependent on politics and the economy in one way or another, but we may be witnessing the end of a unique arrangement in Western Europe, in which universities have enjoyed a considerable amount of autonomy. In the chapter on Portuguese anthropology, the authors suggest that this may be an effect of the recession in Europe. It has also been voiced that it might be linked to bureaucratization and centralization caused by European integration (Bellier 2008). Yet again, we need to differentiate at the European scale, because the relative autonomy from the political field (e.g. in terms of curriculum development) that has been the rule for French and Italian universities since the late 1960s and early 1970s was achieved in Lithuania, Poland and Croatia only in the early 1990s. While the increased freedom of theorizing after 1989 is indisputable, the postcolonial critique of transformations in the Eastern and Central European academy demonstrates that speaking of limitless freedom would be naive, since Western thought has an added symbolic value compared to the others, which is unrelated to its academic merit (Buchowski 2006; Warczok and Zarycki 2014). In places where anthropology departments are only just emerging, academic freedom is being achieved at the very moment when the existence of the academy is under an immense threat because of a dramatic lack of funds.

CONCLUSION

The volume that we are presenting to readers is not being thought of as an exhaustive catalogue of all traditions in European sociocultural anthropology and ethnology. Rather, we see our goal as that of juxtaposing traditions 'big' and 'small', developed as part of the processes of nation-building and/or empire-building and concerned with the proximate or with the distant other. The chapters collected in this volume demonstrate that national traditions of sociocultural anthropology and ethnology are hardly ever independent of other traditions; they are usually hybrids that have grown out of borrowings and mutual influences. It appears that the disciplines would benefit greatly from viewing this latter feature as their strength. Yet the socio-economic context of academic knowledge remains by and large hostile to hybridity. Research on what is hybrid and mobile in national traditions could become a future venue for research in the history of anthropology.

We share the view that anthropology and ethnology should attempt to find ways of actively engaging with the world outside of the academy (cf. Hann 2009) and stop being 'autistic' (Viazzo, this volume). Yet, on the basis of the collected evidence we humbly acknowledge that the roads to public anthropology and to applying ethnological knowledge to social practice are bumpy. To start with, the epistemological commitment to avoiding ethnocentrism dictates that the ways of defining 'public good' should be treated as 'neither common nor sensible', to paraphrase Herzfeld's definition of common sense (2001: 1). It is, therefore, obvious that anthropology and ethnology – more than any other academic discipline – should care about being reflexive. In a recent essay, Johannes Fabian (2014) suggested that this reflexivity should be intersubjective rather than critical. We thus propose considering this volume as an exercise in various traditions of anthropology and ethnology speaking and listening to each other.

Andrés Barrera-González, has received a Ph.D. in Political Science and Sociology and is Associate Professor of Social Anthropology at the University Complutense of Madrid. He has published on issues of inheritance and family systems, language politics and policies, and cultural identities in Spain. At present he is involved in research and writing in the history of anthropology and ethnology in Spain and the Hispanic world.

Monica Heintz (Ph.D. Cambridge) is Associate Professor in Social Anthropology at the University of Paris Nanterre. She is the author of *"Be European, Recycle Yourself!": Changing Work Ethic in Romania*, editor of *Weak State, Uncertain Citizenship: Moldova*, and *The Anthropology of Moralities*, and co-editor of the volume *Transitions Historiques*.

Anna Horolets is an Assistant Professor at the Institute of Ethnology and Cultural Anthropology at the University of Warsaw. She has recently published a monograph on niche tourism from Poland to the former Soviet Union (2013) and articles on migrants' leisure. She is an editor for social anthropology of the Polish peer-reviewed journal *Studia Socjologiczne*.

NOTES

1. 'National' is used here as shorthand for a far more complex state of affairs, which each chapter will consider in more detail. For instance, it quickly became clear to us that it was irrelevant to consider German anthropology as restricted to the anthropology practised within the country of Germany, and that the unit that would make sense intellectually today for the development of the discipline included all German-speaking countries in Europe (Germany, Austria and Switzerland).
2. 'Inclusive' refers here to considering Volkskunde and Völkerkunde, major and minor national traditions, equally. Nevertheless, the concept is also relevant in other contexts and senses (Handler 2000, 2006).
3. It is interesting to note that imperial authorities commissioned the ethnographic surveys and ethnological research carried out in Russia's eastern confines via the Russian Academy of Sciences (Vermeulen 2008: 1–23). On the contributions made by German-speaking countries to the development of anthropology *(Ethnologie)* see also: Stocking (1996); Barth et al. (2005); and John Eidson in this volume.
4. The supporting argument is that *The History* from the time of the Greco-Persian wars in the fifth century BC incorporates descriptions of the diversity of the nations, peoples, customs and cultures that Herodotus encountered on his travels, or came to know about from either oral (including folklore and myth) or written sources. *The History* is also a dramatic account of the epic confrontation between the perceived Greek civility and Persian despotism.
5. Captain Vladimir K. Arsenyev carried out several military-exploratory expeditions to the far east, north of Vladivostok. As a result of these expeditions he wrote travel and exploration narratives (some of them published posthumously in 1937 under the title *In the Sikhote-Alin Mountains*), as well as books about the geography and ethnography of the lands he explored. Arsenyev's most famous and justly acclaimed work is the narrative of his expeditions to the Ussurian taiga, with a small party of soldiers, and with Dersu Uzala, a local hunter, as his guide and close collaborator.
6. An illustration of the unfavourable environment in which Russian scholars have had to work and develop their careers at different times in history is the law passed by the Duma in 2013, which imposed a thorough reorganization of the Russian Academy

of Sciences, in which anthropology (in its diverse local denominations) has had a significant institutional presence since the eighteenth century.

7. We refer here to both the actual and the projected/attempted empires, to compare Portuguese and French colonial empires with the late colonial ambitions of Germany.

8. The Max Planck Institute for Social Anthropology was founded in 1999 in Halle (Saale), former East Germany. The inauguration of its permanent buildings a few years later was marked by the convening of a series of lectures delivered by prominent anthropologists, entitled 'Four Traditions in Anthropology' (Barth et al. 2005).

REFERENCES

Asad, T. (ed.). 1973. *Anthropology and the Colonial Encounter*. Amherst, NY: Humanity Books.

Barrera-González, A., M. Caldwell, M. Heintz and A. Horolets. 2013. 'The Anthropology of Europe', in Carrier, J. and D.B. Gewertz (eds), *Handbook of Sociocultural Anthropology*. London: Bloomsbury, pp. 506–522.

Barth, F., A. Gingrich, R. Parkin and S. Silverman. 2005. *One Discipline, Four Ways: British, German, French, and American Anthropology (Halle Lectures)*. Chicago, IL: University of Chicago Press.

Bausinger, H. 1993 [1971]. *Volkskunde, ou l'ethnologie allemande*. Paris: Editions de la Maison des Sciences de l'Homme.

Bellier, I. 2007. 'L'anthropologie dans la politique européenne de recherche', *Séminaire AFA-APRAS, Actualités de l'anthropologie 12 June 2007*.

———. 2008. 'L'anthropologie dans l'Espace Européen de la Recherche, un monde à construire', *Madrid Symposium*, plenary speech.

Bendix, R. 1997. *In Search of Authenticity: The Formation of Folklore Studies*. Madison, WI: University of Wisconsin Press.

Bieder, R.E. 1986. *Science Encounters the Indian, 1820–1880: The Early Years of American Ethnology*. Norman, OK: University of Oklahoma Press.

Boškovic, A. (ed.). 2008. *Other People's Anthropologies: Ethnographic Practice on the Margins*. Oxford: Berghahn.

Boškovic, A. and C. Hann (eds). 2013. *The Anthropological Field on the Margins of Europe, 1945–1991*. Berlin: LIT Verlag.

Brenneis, D. 2009. 'Anthropology in and of the Academy: Globalization, Assessment and our Field's Future', *Social Anthropology/Anthropologie Sociale* 17(3): 261–75.

Buchowski, M. 2006. 'The Specter of Orientalism in Europe: From Exotic Other to Stigmatized Brother', *Anthropological Quarterly* 79(3): 463–82.

Burawoy, M. 2011. 'The Last Positivist', *Contemporary Sociology* 40(4): 396–404.

Clifford, J. and G. Marcus. 1986. *Writing Cultures: Poetics and Politics of Ethnography*. University of California Press.

Descola, P. 2005. 'On Anthropological Knowledge', *Social Anthropology/Anthropologie Sociale* 13(1): 65–73.

Eriksen, T.H. 2005. *Engaging Anthropology*. Oxford: Berg Publishers.

Fabian, J. 2014. 'Ethnography and Intersubjectivity: Loose Ends', *HAU: Journal of Ethnographic Theory* 4(1): 199–209.

Ferraz de Matos, P. 2013. *The Colours of the Empire: Racialized Representations During Portuguese Colonialism*. New York and Oxford: Berghahn.

Handler, R. (ed.). 2000. *Excluded Ancestors, Inventible Traditions: Essays Toward a More Inclusive History of Anthropology*. Madison, WI: University of Wisconsin Press.

———. 2006. *Central Sites, Peripheral Visions: Cultural and Institutional Crossings in the History of Anthropology*. Madison, WI: University of Wisconsin Press.

Hann, C. 2009. 'Poznan Manifesto for a Public Anthropology in the European Public Sphere', *EASA Newsletter* no. 50, December. Retrieved 24 September 2016 from http://www.easaonline.org/downloads/newsletters/easa_news_50.pdf

Hann, C., M. Sárkány and P. Skalník (eds). 2005. *Studying Peoples in the People's Democracies: Socialist Era Anthropology in East-Central Europe*. Berlin: LIT Verlag.

Hart, K. [1998] (n.d.). 'The Place of the 1898 Cambridge Anthropological Expedition to the Torres Straits (CAETS) in the History of British Social Anthropology', *Science as Culture*. Retrieved 24 September 2016 from http://www.human-nature.com/science-as-culture/hart.html

Herle, A. and S. Rouse (eds). 1998. *Cambridge and the Torres Strait: Centenary Essays on the 1898 Anthropological Expedition*. Cambridge: Cambridge University Press.

Herodotus. 1987. *The History*, trans. D. Grene. Chicago, IL: University of Chicago Press.

Herzfeld, M. 2001. *Anthropology: Theoretical Practice in Culture and Society*. Malden, MA: Blackwell.

Hinsley, C.M. 1994 [1981]. *[Savages and Scientists] The Smithsonian and the American Indian: Making a Moral Anthropology in Victorian America*. Washington, D.C.: Smithsonian Institution Press.

Hodgen, M.T. 1964. *Early Anthropology in the Sixteenth and Seventeenth Centuries*. Philadelphia, PA: University of Pennsylvania Press.

Hoffman, S.G. 2011. 'The New Tools of the Scientific Trade: Contested Knowledge Production and the Conceptual Vocabularies of Academic Capitalism', *Social Anthropology/Anthropologie Sociale* 19(4): 439–62.

Krupnik, I. and W.W. Fitzhugh (eds). 2001. *Gateways: Exploring the Legacy of the Jesup North Pacific Expedition, 1897–1902*. Washington, D.C.: Arctic Studies Center, NMNH, SI.

Kuklick, H. 1993 [1991]. *The Savage Within: The Social History of British Anthropology, 1885–1945*. Cambridge: Cambridge University Press.

Kuklick, H. (ed.). 2008. *A New History of Anthropology*. Malden, MA: Blackwell.

Kuper, A. 1996 [1983]. *Anthropology and Anthropologists: The Modern British School*, 3rd revised and enlarged edition. London: Routledge.

———. 2005. 'Alternative Histories of British Social Anthropology', *Social Anthropology/Anthropologie Sociale* 13(1): 47–64.

Kürti, L. and P. Skalník (eds). 2009. *Postsocialist Europe: Anthropological Perspectives from Home*. New York: Berghahn.

L'Estoile, B.D., F. Neiburg and L. Sigaud. 2005. 'Anthropology and the Government of "Natives": A Comparative Approach', in B.D. L'Estoile, F. Neiburg and L. Sigaud (eds), *Empires, Nations, and Natives: Anthropology and State-Making*. Durham, NC: Duke University Press, pp. 1–29.

Mark, J. 1988. *A Stranger in Her Native Land: Alice Fletcher and the American Indians*. Lincoln and London: University of Nebraska Press.

Mihailescu, V., I. Iliev and S. Naumovic (eds). 2008. *Studying Peoples in the People's Democracies II: Socialist Era Anthropology in South-East Europe*. Berlin: LIT Verlag.

Pels, P. 2008. 'What Has Anthropology Learned from the Anthropology of Colonialism?', *Social Anthropology/Anthropologie Sociale* 16(3): 280–99.

Pels, P. and O. Salemink (eds). 2002 [1999]. *Colonial Subjects: Essays on the Practical History of Anthropology*. Ann Arbor, MI: University of Michigan Press.

Ribeiro, G.L. and A. Escobar (eds). 2006. *World Anthropologies: Disciplinary Transformations in Systems of Power*. Oxford: Berg.

Romano, A. 2010. 'Studying Anthropology in the Age of University Reform', *Social Anthropology/Anthropologie Sociale* 18(1): 57–73.

Shore, C. 2010. 'Beyond the Multiversity: Neoliberalism and the Rise of the Schizophrenic University', *Social Anthropology/Anthropologie Sociale*, special issue 'Anthropologies of University Reform' 18(1): 15–29.

Shore, C. and S. Wright. 1999. 'Audit Culture and Anthropology: Neo-Liberalism in British Higher Education', *The Journal of the Royal Anthropological Institute* 5(4): 557–75.

Skalník, P. (ed.). 2000. *Sociocultural Anthropology at the Turn of the Century: Voices from the Periphery*. Prague: Set Out-Roman Mísek.

———. 2002. *The Struggles for Sociocultural Anthropology in Central and Eastern Europe*. Prague: Set Out-Roman Mísek.

———. 2004. *Anthropology of Europe: Teaching and Research, 3*. Prague: Set Out-Roman Mísek.

Stocking, G.W. Jr (ed.). 1984. *Functionalism Historicized: Essays on British Social Anthropology*. Madison, WI: University of Wisconsin Press.

———. 1991. *Colonial Situations: Essays on the Contextualization of Ethnographic Knowledge*. Madison, WI: University of Wisconsin Press.

———. 1996. *Volkgeist as Method and Ethic: Essays on Boasian Ethnography and the German Ethnological Tradition*. Chicago, IL: University of Chicago Press.

Strathern, M. 2005. 'Experiments in Interdisciplinarity', *Social Anthropology/Anthropologie Sociale* 13(1): 75–90.

Vermeulen, H.F. 2008. 'Early History of Ethnography and Ethnology in the German Enlightenment: Anthropological Discourse in Europe and Asia, 1710–1808', Doctoral dissertation. Leiden: University of Leiden.

———. 2015. *Before Boas: The Genesis of Ethnography and Ethnology in the German Enlightenment*. Lincoln, NE: University of Nebraska Press.

Wagner, I. 2012. 'Selektywna analiza problemu publikacji humanistów i przedstawicieli nauk społecznych w języku angielskim' ['Selective analysis of the problem of English language publications in humanities and social sciences'], *Przegląd Socjologii Jakościowej* [Qualitative Sociology Review] 8(1): 166–87. Retrieved 1 October 2014 from http://www.przegladsocjologiijakosciowej.org

Warczok, T. and T. Zarycki. 2014. 'Bourdieu Recontextualized: Redefinitions of Western Critical Thought in the Periphery', *Current Sociology* 62(3): 334–51, DOI: 10.1177/0011392114523974.

1

AT THE PORTUGUESE CROSSROADS

Contemporary Anthropology and its History

Susana de Matos Viegas and João de Pina-Cabral

INTRODUCTION

In this chapter, we argue that anthropology in Portugal at the beginning of the twenty-first century is a diverse and successful discipline that has found its distinctive voice. The path that led to this state of affairs can be traced back to the late nineteenth century. In order to understand the discipline's substantive development, we suggest that one has to be attentive to two orders of phenomena – we call them the political and the epistemic axes.

The epistemic axis has its opposite poles in the humanist and the positivist traditions as they developed in nineteenth century Europe. The political axis stretches the discipline (albeit at times under different names) between two large-scale State projects. In the Portuguese case, these were mutually dependent: nation-building and empire-building. Over the century, political circumstances dictated which of these State projects gained more currency; however both successfully coexisted throughout the history of the discipline.

The singular position in which Portuguese anthropology finds itself today is the product, among other factors, of a particular linguistic situation that marked its development. Academic writing in Portuguese has increased enormously over the decades, since a number of vibrant anthropological traditions, notably the Brazilian one, use this language for establishing their conceptual and methodological frameworks. This does not exclude Portuguese anthropology from the broader international dialogue but it does create a viable alternative to the domination of English-language anthropology – thus allowing it to exercise a 'non-hegemonic cosmopolitanism'. The shift of interest towards a focus on the Portuguese-speaking world (alongside with an increased interest in urban as well as historical and archival research) is one of the outcomes of this process. Having said this, however, the overall optimistic picture of the discipline's development that we present in this chapter is tainted by the spectre of the 'austerity' crisis that has affected negatively all the social sciences and humanities in the peripheral countries of Europe.

As stressed above, ever since its inception in the second half of the nineteenth century, academic anthropology (broadly defined as the study of the human condition) has had to integrate two tensional axes of polarization: one relating to preoccupations of an epistemic nature, the other to matters of political representation. Concerning the political axis, anthropology was asked to provide the intellectual ground for the existence of human collective entities: peoples (folk), nations, ethnicities. European anthropology was called to address the constitution of the nation as much as that of the empire.[1] Here, particularly in continental Europe, where the national bourgeoisie was in power, a group of intellectuals that defined itself as cosmopolitan needed to capture the essence of those in whose name it ruled: either the folk or the natives of the empire.[2] These were always perceived as differentiated voices, whose only chance of being generalized in terms of a national or an imperial voice was through the mediation of the ruling bourgeoisie. The possibility of imperial rule required a capacity to describe those one ruled at home quite as much as those one ruled abroad. As a discourse on the nature of humanity, throughout late nineteenth and twentieth centuries, academic anthropology always found itself caught up between these two poles of the political axis. At times and in places where an extra-European empire was less relevant, the call of folklore and ethnology made itself felt in stronger terms; at other times and in places where an extra-European empire became more relevant, the anthropology of remote peoples came to dominate the discipline.

Concerning the epistemic axis, anthropology faced more universalistic preoccupations. Whilst divine causation had been abandoned within the academic enterprise from the mid nineteenth century, the philosophical underpinnings upon which academic anthropology built itself at the time of the Belle Époque were solidly neo-Cartesian and later neo-Kantian. The separation between man's bodily condition and man's mental condition was taken for granted. Whilst the two were ultimately supposed to be co-derived, they required different modes of apprehension and different forms of analysis.

From the beginning, therefore, the emergent field of the scientific study of mankind found itself divided between those who gave a greater emphasis to values, meanings and narratives and those who gave greater emphasis to rules, functions and institutions. Humanistically inspired anthropology, based on philology and cultural ethnology, found itself confronted by scientifically inspired positivist anthropology. The relationship between the two tendencies was ever one of tension and interdependency. For as long as they remained within the modernist worldview, Darwinian naturalism united the two undertakings in spite of the fact that they were pulled apart by Cartesian epistemology, where body and mind never fully resolved themselves into each other. The general universalist framework – that is, the intellectual investment in formulating a common human condition – is what kept the two poles of each of the axes from ever splitting asunder giving rise to a disciplinary field (albeit under different designations).

In light of this (see Figure 1.1), we can observe that, in the political axis, empire-building and nation-building (*volkerkunde* and *volkskunde*) have tended permanently towards subdisciplinary specialization without ever fully achieving it; whilst, at the same time, in the epistemic axis, the positivistic endeavour to find the determination of social behaviour within a rule-oriented framework never fully abandoned the engagement with philological and interpretative approaches. Anthropology as an academic enterprise over the past two centuries has found itself often in a dilemma,

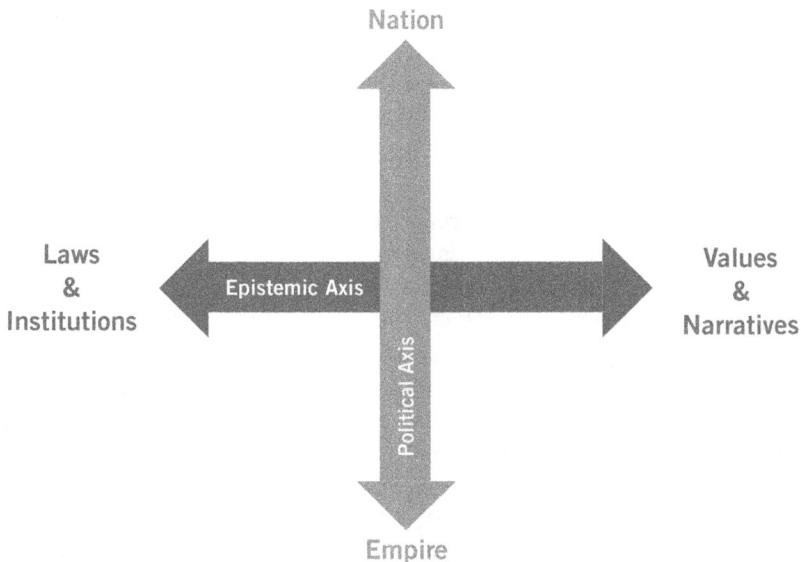

FIGURE 1.1. The two axes of definition of the anthropological endeavour

where each practitioner and each local school have been challenged by the particular mix of the four drives that other practitioners and other schools have advocated. Something, however, did come to unite the field and that was what we might call, in continuation of Adam Kuper's well-known argument (1988), *the primitivist paradigm*. Primitivism emerged as a methodological strategy for the broader project of identifying a human condition round about the 1860s (Pina-Cabral 2017a: 27, 47). As has often been observed, this position postulated that something that is elemental (i.e., it cannot be further reduced) is necessarily simple and, since human society was supposed to have evolved from a simpler condition towards a more sophisticated, civilized condition, what was primitive was also anterior. Thus, if one studied forms of human life that were simpler, one would also be able to identify the analytical elements of human life and one would have access to the past. Anthropology could, therefore, reach to the past. It could overcome the limitations of coevalness (see Fabian 1983) and achieve universality.

The paradigm of primitive society, thus, succeeded in integrating preoccupations with both law and institutions, on the one hand, and values and narratives, on the other, through theories of the joint evolution of family and religion (see Kuper 1988). By reference to the political axis, however, the matter positioned itself differently depending on the particular political and social conditions of each European society where anthropology was being developed. In particular, in continental Europe, as in Portugal, the integration between nation and empire was carried out under the aegis of a national ruling bourgeoisie, which was not the case in England. The ultimate separation between an ethnological (nation-building) project and an anthropological (empire-building) project, which occurred at the Royal Anthropological Institute in the late 1930s, never occurred throughout continental Europe, where the two modes of anthropology remain deeply intertwined to this day.

In this chapter, we suggest a reading of the formation of anthropology in Portugal that develops on this observation that 'nation-building' and 'empire-building' were never very far from each other and tended to fade into one another. In fact, in the Portuguese case, at the end of the nineteenth century and up to the 1970s, possessing an empire was a defining condition for the survival of a European nationhood project (cf. Pina-Cabral and Feijó 2002). In this sense, we distance ourselves slightly from the more polarized interpretations that have been inspired by the work of George Stocking Jr. (1982). For the Portuguese case, João Leal's historical analysis has broadly represented this position (2000, 2001, 2006, 2008). He subsumes the history of anthropology in Portugal under the driving force of the 'nation-building' process:

In fact, despite the existence of an empire and the absence of a national problem in the classical sense, Portuguese anthropology emerged and developed from 1870 until 1960 as a 'nation-building anthropology', that is, an anthropology that favoured, not only the study of local folk traditions, but also conducted that study as part of a search for Portuguese national identity. (Leal 2001: 646; 2006: 112–13)

For this author, the prevalence of this national disposition in an imperial country is not paradoxical in view of the fragile nature of the Portuguese imperial undertaking: 'the absence of an anthropological tradition of "empire-building" in Portugal must be related to the weakness of Portuguese colonialism, as exercised by a peripheral country, itself dependent on the larger European powers, particularly England' (Leal 2001: 646; 2006: 113). More recently, however, other authors who have further researched the history of science in Portugal have come to moderate this view. For example, in his study of the collection of human skulls from the then colony of Timor, Ricardo Roque argues, 'in Portugal, the anthropology of nation-building coexisted with empire-building anthropologies' (2010: 148). If we distance ourselves from the confusion resulting from the existence of a myriad of subdisciplinary headings whose meanings in the past were never quite the same as they are today, this observation must surely prevail.

In this chapter, we will examine the present situation of anthropology in Portugal in relation to this background history. We will conclude that the changes in trends and research agendas that we have been witnessing over the past thirty years of a democratic regime, much like in the past, are associated with Portugal's situation within a global order. In fact, from a broader perspective, we see anthropology in Portugal as part of what might be called a 'fifth tradition' – that is, one that places itself beyond the four main imperial traditions of anthropology (German, French, British and American). In this sense, their non-hegemonic cosmopolitanism places Portuguese social scientists in a position that is akin to that of the Japanese, the Indians or the Brazilians (e.g. Pina-Cabral 2004: 262). In particular, Portugal's place at a crossroads of the Euro-American routes and the south Atlantic routes of intellectual exchange has recently reaffirmed its importance in the way Portuguese social sciences intervene in the global scientific debate.

AT THE PORTUGUESE CROSSROADS

Portuguese social sciences emerge in the late nineteenth century out of two previous inputs corresponding to different combinations of the polar terms referred to above: on the one hand, an original romantic movement in the first half of the century that attempted to formulate Portuguese nationalism at a time of invasion and civil war (1807–1850s) and, on the other hand, a preoccupation with laying the groundwork for the imperial occupation of Africa at a time when the European powers were carving out the continent (1870s–1890s). These latter efforts, mostly associated with the Society of Geography of Lisbon (*Sociedade de Geografia de Lisboa*), only came to have practical relevance after 1890, when colonial territorial administration was finally generalized.

After the opening of the railway line from Lisbon to Paris (*Sud Express* 1887), a new impetus towards academic and scholarly renewal was felt throughout the country. New formulations emerged around a small group of young scholars in Oporto, both of positivistic anthropology – and the name of Oliveira Martins is a central marker here (1881) – and of philological and ethnological studies – where names like A.A. Rocha Peixoto and José Leite de Vasconcellos stand out (cf. Pina-Cabral 1991: 26–27; Leal 2006: 63–81). At this time, for obvious reasons, the questions of empire were less central than the engagement with a reformulation of nationhood that accompanies the change of regime to a republic (1910). For public figures such as Bernardino Machado and Teófilo Braga, both of whom were Presidents of the Republic, their scholarly interests in physical anthropology and philology, respectively, were part of their engagement with renewing the nation in the face of deep crisis.

Considering the subsequent evolution of social and cultural anthropology in Portugal, the work of Leite de Vasconcellos, Adolfo Coelho and Rocha Peixoto deserves special attention (cf. Pina-Cabral 1991: 24–26; Leal 2006: 114). Leite de Vasconcellos' (1933–1985) major unfinished oeuvre *Ethnologia Portuguesa* maps out the country and remained a central inspiration until the 1970s. His vision of ethnology as a science, associated with his museological preoccupations, was to have considerable repercussions in the second half of the century.

The theoretical mind of greatest reach, however, was Rocha Peixoto (1866–1909), whose thinking concerning *comunitarismo agro-pastoril* (rural communitarianism) was going to launch a century-long debate surrounding the notions of 'Portuguese house' and of 'community'.[3] This conception of the forms of rural settlement and their metaphorization in terms of both nation and empire was to continue to echo right to this day.[4] It was Rocha Peixoto who identified the loci of primitiveness that supported a bourgeois conception of the naturalness of the Portuguese nation and its rights of autochthony throughout the twentieth century. Rocha Peixoto's early death in 1909 stopped in its tracks one of the greatest minds of his period.

From the 1930s up to the 1970s a number of prestigious Portuguese and foreign anthropologists were going to follow in Rocha Peixoto's steps, choosing as field sites those that he had identified for special attention as primary exemplars of Portuguese primitiveness. Vilarinho da Furna, studied earlier in the century by Tude de Souza, would turn into Jorge Dias' first study (Dias 1981 [1948]). Later still, in 1971, it would be chosen by António Campos as the site of a very well-known anthropological documentary. This film, made at a time when the village was literally disappearing under a dam, continues to have a considerable impact today.[5] In turn, Rio de Onor was the site of Abade do Baçal's famous essays (Alves 1908–1948) and would be Dias' second field site (1981 [1953]). Later, this village and nearby sites were also revisited by a number of colleagues such as Brian Juan O'Neill (2007 [1987]) and Joaquim Pais de Brito (1996), among others. In fact, even in cases where Rocha Peixoto's impetus was not fully acknowledged, one cannot help but observe that José Cutileiro's groundbreaking monograph on inequality in Alentejo (1971) or Sally Cole's study of Vila do Conde's fishing community (1991) follow in the steps of works inspired by Rocha Peixoto, such as Silva Picão's study of Alentejo's rural proletariat or Santos Graça's study of fishing folk (Picão 1983 [1903]; Graça 1992), respectively.

At the end of the Second World War, Salazar's dictatorship had managed to create minimal conditions for a relaunch of scholarly institutions. This manifested itself both in relation to the ethnological discourse on Portugal and in the investment in colonial institutions and their respective ideology. In fact, the main figures in the anthropological discourse of the time – namely, the anthropobiologist A. Mendes Corrêa – underwent a transition from nationalist concerns (see his famous racialist study of Nuno Álvares Pereira, the saintly general of the fourteenth century) to imperial matters (Corrêa 1924, 1949). In the early 1950s, Mendes Corrêa moved to Lisbon to integrate the newly re-established school of colonial administration – then renamed ISCPU (cf. Pina-Cabral 1991: 30–33; Roque 2010: 163). From then onwards, Mendes Corrêa worked explicitly at building a school of colonial anthropology that, as Ricardo Roque argues, 'should contribute to empire-building. Simply put, its objects of knowledge were the "natives" inhabiting the colonies under Portuguese rule' (2010: 164).[6]

By mid century, therefore, ruralist 'ethnology' was increasingly side-stepped for the project of empire-building ('anthropology'). The colonial exhibitions of 1934 in Oporto and 1940 in Lisbon laid out an important ideological framework that was to have reverberations right until the end of the dictatorship in the 1970s (cf. Thomaz 2002: 205–87; Porto 2009: 92–102). This museological tradition was going to have a considerable impact both in Portugal and in the new cities of the African colonies during the 1950s: museums such as the Museum of Natural History of Lourenço Marques or the Diamang Museum of Dundo (Porto 2009) were new loci for anthropological practice, where physical anthropology and sociocultural anthropology were in constant co-relation.

In the late 1940s and 1950s, the modernist intellectuals that had sided with
Salazar in the efforts both to modernize Portugal and to lay out new bases
for the African colonies started to distance themselves increasingly from
the regime. For instance, one of the central actors in the organization of the
colonial exhibitions, Henrique Galvão, eventually became one of the bitterest
enemies of Salazar's colonial policies (cf. Pina-Cabral 2001; Thomaz 2002:
159–65). His thinking as a contributor to the colonial process constitutes
an excellent example of the establishment of continuities in primitiveness
between Portuguese ruralist identities and those of colonial natives. As
Omar Ribeiro Thomaz demonstrates, 'Henrique Galvão makes it amply clear
that his "Africanist" option does not distance him from his "Lusitanism";
on the contrary, it transforms it into a denser and deeper experience, since
his conception of the nation depends necessarily on Portugal's African
experience' (Thomaz 2002: 159). This continuity between the Portuguese
'traditional' world and that of the Empire's natives is expressed by Galvão as
by many anthropologists of the period, both those who were for and those
who were against the dictatorial regime:[7] by the mid 1950s, 'for Galvão –
as for many of Salazar's opponents – the African and the Oriental natives
of the Portuguese colonies were not victims of colonialism, but of fascism'
(Thomaz 2002: 165).

At the time, Salazar's regime moved increasingly towards an ideological
posture in which the people of the 'Portuguese Overseas' *(Ultramar
Português)* were seen as essentially Portuguese, thus manifesting forms
of autochthony, tradition and community that were phantasmatically
interpreted in primitivist fashion as co-constitutive of the imperial nation
(cf. Thomaz 2002: 165). During this period (1950s and 1960s) various
'scientific expeditions' to the 'overseas territories' were subsidized by the
regime, and involved intellectuals of note such as Ruy Cinatti in the case of
Timor (a poet and anthropologist trained in Oxford) and Jorge Dias in the
case of Mozambique.[8]

A major ideological figure in this process turns out to have been
Brazil's foremost anthropologist, Gilberto Freyre. His attempt to provide
an ideological framework for Brazilian society as an example of 'racial
democracy' came to constitute an indispensable ideological crutch for
Salazar's beleaguered regime during the late colonial period (1961–1974).
The notion of *Lusotropicalism* operated a mediation between being
Portuguese and being 'tropical' in ways that would continue to reverberate
to this day in forms of Portuguese self-Orientalization (cf. Freyre 1940;
Castelo 1999; Pina-Cabral 2017b).

This was a time of increasing international isolation, in view of the fact
that, contrary to Portugal, other European nations were moving towards
democracy and decolonization. By 1961, Portugal's ideological isolation

was demanding a decisive response, particularly in the light of the Indian occupation of Goa and Diu in that year and the launching of guerrilla wars in Guiné, Angola and Mozambique (1961/1964). The newly reformed colonial school (ISCSPU) was the site where this effort to rebuild the intellectual foundations of Portugueseness (both internally and overseas) was to be established.

In terms of anthropology, however, oddly enough, it was Jorge Dias (who was in fact trained in Germany during the war – Munich and Berlin) who embodied the renewal of Portuguese anthropological thinking at mid century (cf. Oliveira 1974: 14; Pina-Cabral 1991: 12, 28–29; Leal 2006: 149–66). He founded the Museum of Ethnology, whose central collection was based on his earlier Portuguese ruralist interests but was integrated with valuable collections from all the corners of the Portuguese empire (Africa, India and the Far East). Much like the more direct disciples of Leite de Vasconcellos (Viegas Guerreiro among them), during the late colonial period, Portuguese anthropologists directed their attention predominantly towards imperial subject matters, using Freyre's anthropology as a kind of intellectual mould.

The democratic revolution of 1974 was a major watershed. Dias had died shortly before it (1973) and his Museum entered into a prolonged period of recess. At first, the old colonial school was taken over by left-leaning students, among whom were a number of anthropologists, but soon enough the scholars associated to Salazarism came back again.[9] Throughout the 1980s it was directed by an Africanist anthropologist who had been a counter-insurgent specialist during the late days of the dictatorship (José Júlio Gonçalves).

By the early 1980s Portuguese universities were restructuring themselves and vigorously adopting more international styles of academic practice. This was a decade of intense institution-building. Two new departments of anthropology were founded (at University Institute of Lisbon – ISCTE-IUL and at Universidade Nova – UNL) by a group of scholars trained abroad (predominantly in France and the United Kingdom). By the end of the decade the new undergraduate degrees in Anthropology were fully consolidated and a new Portuguese Association of Anthropology (APA) had been founded (cf. Pina-Cabral 1989).

The work of the anthropologists carrying out research in the post-revolutionary decade (1976–1986) responded to the central challenge of reformulating Portugueseness. The democratic revolution had been carried out in the name of the *povo* (the folk) but, by the late 1970s, it was becoming increasingly obvious that the category was vacuous and highly problematic. By then, anthropologists had to face two apparent contradictions: (a) the received conception of Portugueseness was ruralist, in a country that aimed at being modern and democratic and (b) being Portuguese was deeply associated to an imperialist, Catholic ideology of Lusotropicalism that was perceived as a dead-end and as antagonistic to Portugal's then desired future, as a member of the European Community.

The only anthropological inspiration available at the time was José Cutileiro's monograph on class conflict in Alentejo, which had been published in English in 1971 and had broken with a century-old tradition of primitivist readings of Portugal. Cutileiro's anti-communitarian reading was, however, oddly ambiguous (cf. Fernandes 2006) – as the author's later career came to highlight – but, at the time, it provided an important framework for a debate concerning the meaning of rurality and Portugueseness that can also be traced in the work of the first monographs written after the revolution: Pina-Cabral (1986) and Brian O'Neill (2007 [1987]). The 1980s was a period of intense internal questioning, which is reflected in the work of colleagues whose fieldwork was carried out at this time (e.g. Cristiana Bastos, João Leal, Jorge Freitas Branco, José Manuel Sobral, Miguel Vale de Almeida, Paula Godinho). By the early 1990s a new approach to non-European ethnography was also starting to emerge in the work of people like Rosa Perez (Gujerat, India), Amélia Frazão and Clara Carvalho (Guiné-Bissau), and Maria Cardeira da Silva (Morocco).[10]

TEACHING, PUBLISHING AND INTERACTING

Founded in 1989, the Portuguese Association of Anthropology (APA) has witnessed the ups and downs of the discipline. APA has constituted a voice for the discipline whenever there have been matters of common concern, and since 2005 it has been a member of the World Council of Anthropological Associations.[11] Presently it has around 300 registered members and, over the past decade, it has organized five congresses. Anthropologists played a significant and visible role in the growth of Portuguese social sciences that occurred during the 1990s and 2000s, and participated in the constitution of a national system of scientific research that developed after Portugal's entry into the European Community, led by the charismatic figure of José Mariano Gago.[12]

We will now come to an overview of the present institutional context of anthropology in Portugal in terms of teaching, research, publishing activities and participation in the public domain (see Viegas 2009). The 1990s and 2000s were periods of intense growth in university-level teaching, in response to a generally perceived need on the part of both the public and the political authorities to overcome a legacy of backwardness. This is decidedly clarified by comparing the figures of students that were studying BA and MA degrees. In 1993, there were only 17,700 BA students and 5,287 MA students in all of Portugal, whilst in 2003 the figure almost doubles, to 30,012 and 11,106 respectively (Dima 2005: 29, 30). Anthropology fully accompanied these trends. Whilst in the early 1990s there were no MA degrees in Anthropology and around 60 students enrolled annually in undergraduate degrees, we estimate that, at present, around 180 students enrol annually in anthropology at undergraduate level and 70 at Master's level.

Unfortunately, most departments of Anthropology are concentrated in Lisbon: the Department of Anthropology of UNL (founded in 1970), the Department of Anthropology at ISCTE-IUL (created in 1982), and ISCSP (University of Lisbon) give BA, MA and Ph.D. courses. The Institute of Social Science (University of Lisbon – ICS) – a research and postgraduate institute dedicated to the study of the Social Sciences – has a Ph.D. course in Social and Cultural Anthropology. Postgraduate teaching reflects the areas of main thematic interest in the discipline: visual anthropology – e.g. 'Visual Cultures', 'Material Culture and Consumption', 'Tourism and Heritage' and 'Digital Visual Culture'; issues of contemporary political relevance – e.g. 'Human Rights and Social Movements' or 'Migrations'; and issues of regional relevance – e.g. Islamic Studies, African Studies or Indian Studies.

Aside from these departments, there are also BA and MA courses in Anthropology at the University of Coimbra.[13] Anthropology is also being taught at the University of Minho; at the University of Trás-os-Montes and Alto Douro; and there are anthropologists working in a number of universities and polytechnic institutes. In 2017 we estimate that permanent academic staff in Anthropology in Portugal amounted to a total of around ninety anthropologists. Aside from these, of course, there is a large group of posts-doctoral scholars with temporary contracts working in research centres funded by the governmental funding agency (FCT).

The research centres specializing in anthropology developed in close articulation with university teaching. They have grown exponentially over the past twenty years in line with the growth in other areas of science. In fact, by comparison with other social sciences, Portuguese anthropology has given signs of singular energy and collective purpose both in terms of organization and productivity.[14] An example of this was the consolidation in 2008 of a group of smaller research centres into a Centro em Rede de Investigação em Antropologia (CRIA) – a national inter-institutional network of research centres. This was a response to a call for rationalization of means by the FCT.

CRIA integrates around eighty Ph.D. level researchers with projects in areas such as Social Movements and Human Rights, Migration and Transnationalism, Heritage and Tourism, Material Culture and Visual Anthropology and Nature Conservation, and it has links with the postgraduate programmes at ISCTE-IUL and UNL.[15] At ICS – an institution that integrates in roughly equal terms sociologists, anthropologists, historians and political scientists – there are twenty anthropologists, six of whom are doctoral level research assistants. At present, CRIA and ICS together represent the bulk of research being carried out in social and cultural anthropology in Portugal: 80 per cent of the funding awarded by the FCT to anthropology was to CRIA and ICS.[16] Since 1995, these research centres have been evaluated regularly by international committees appointed by the FCT, receiving the classifications of very good and excellent respectively.

Furthermore, a number of smaller research units have been relevant. Among them, we note: IICT (Instituto de Investigação Científica Tropical – more recently integrated into other institutions), a research centre where anthropology is part of an interdisciplinary Program of Global Development geared at countries of the CPLP (Community of Portuguese-Speaking Countries); the Centre of African Studies at ISCTE-IUL with special emphasis on the Portuguese-speaking African countries (renamed in 2012 as the Centre for International Studies – Centro de Estudos Internacionais); and Coimbra's CIAS (Centre for Anthropology and Health), which lately has been geared away from the social sciences towards genetics and palaeontology.

These research centres also undertake collaborative research related to themes of public concern. Since 2005, CRIA has had partnerships with governmental and non-governmental organizations, such as ACIDI (High Commissioner for Immigration and Intercultural Dialogue); GIS (Group for Immigration and Health); CPR (Portuguese Council for the Refugees); UNITWIN-UNESCO; Dundo Museum (Angola); Musée du Quai Branly; and the Musée Ethnologique de Salagon (France). In turn, ICS has developed a number of such partnerships, for example, with ACIDI; with Brazil's federal agency for Indian affairs (FUNAI); with the urban police (PSP); and a number of other agencies.

Ethnological museums have played an important role in the past in opening anthropology to the wider public. Dias' research group at the National Museum of Ethnology (Ernesto Veiga de Oliveira, Fernando Galhano and Benjamim Enes Pereira) left a significant museological heritage, which, during the late 1990s, was given a new lease of life under the direction of Joaquim Pais de Brito. Exhibitions such as those on the end of rurality, on African masks, on fado or on Brazil's Amerindian cultures had a noted public impact. Similarly, the Anthropological Museum of the University of Coimbra, based on the Brazilian eighteenth-century collections and the African collections of the university, came alive for the short period in which undergraduate teaching in social and cultural anthropology was carried out there. Unfortunately, today, for a number of reasons, both institutions find it hard to keep active. Benjamim Enes Pereira and a number of younger colleagues largely inspired by him have invested in local museums and collections, giving rise to some important museological sites of which the Village Museum of Luz is perhaps the one that had greater public impact. Finally, anthropology has been very visible to the wider public through documentary film production. From the early 1990s, a group of anthropological documentarists, initially influenced by the Granada Centre at the University of Manchester, created a considerable body of work.[17]

Publishing in anthropology in Portugal also grew. At CRIA, the journal *Etnográfica* (founded in 1995) has managed to achieve a good level of international recognition. *Análise Social*, an interdisciplinary journal founded in 1963 and affiliated with ICS, is also active in the area of social anthropology. Other journals played a role in previous decades, such as *Ethnologica* or *Antropologia Portuguesa*. In the 1980s and 1990s, a number of publishing houses were active in anthropology; for example, the Gulbenkian Foundation and Edições 70 with collections of translated textbooks; D. Quixote, with its "Portugal de Perto" collection; and Celta, with a number of important monographs; Livros Horizonte, Colibri, Difel and Almedina have also published in the area. More recently, Imprensa de Ciências Sociais at ICS, the only university press active in Portuguese social sciences, has been very active in anthropology.

As this brief overview has hopefully highlighted, Portuguese anthropology continues to exist at a crossroads between the extra-European thematic pole and the national thematic pole. In fact, since 1976, empire-building has been out of the question altogether and yet teaching and research agendas have continued to move backwards and forwards between the two poles.

ANTHROPOLOGY'S CROSSINGS

From the mid 1990s, Portuguese social sciences and humanities were integrated in the EU-subsidised programmes of promotion of science. As part of the political commitments of the socialist government, the first truly competitive research and doctoral grants started to be awarded by 1995. This had a tremendous impact on standards of research (which were now being competitively evaluated by committees integrating international scholars) and led to the constitution of a new generation of anthropologists that, for the first time, could afford to carry out research in all corners of the world.

The period going up to 2012 was, therefore, one of continued growth and consolidation in all of the social sciences. This had a decisive impact in terms of internationalization and overall quality and variety of anthropological research. Figure 2.1 provides us with an overview of the evolution of funding distributed by the government's research agency (FCT) and the numbers of active doctoral and postdoctoral grants between 1994 and 2015. In this period the number of active Ph.D. grants increased twentyfold (from 466 to 8,676 in 2012), and while postdoctoral grants were almost non-existent in 1994 (only 23 active grants) there were in 2012 2,561 (these are three-year grants, renewable for a further three years).

In fact, what these figures show is that, from the mid 1990s to the mid 2000s, the country was fast recovering from the scene of utter devastation left by the dictatorship (1928–1974) and then the financial crisis of the early 1980s. The problem was both that up to 1994 there were no doctoral and research grants but also that there were very few doctoral candidates, as the first generation of Ph.D. students after the 1974 Revolution were hired as assistant professors immediately after obtaining their undergraduate degrees. In fact, in most areas, such as anthropology, it was only by the mid 1990s that most MA programmes were launched.

Furthermore, there was a noticeable change in the matter of international degrees. We do not have figures for anthropology only, but we have reasons to believe that our discipline followed the general national trend. From 2000 onwards there is a noticeable decrease in the number of people taking their Ph.D.s abroad (from 43% in 1995 to 20% in 2010). To the contrary, there is a corresponding increase in the number of 'mixed doctorates' – that is, resulting from international collaboration (8% in 1995 to 27% in 2010).[18] By the early 2000s, many of the Ph.D. programmes were internationally recognized and started receiving their first foreign students. Again, this also applies to anthropology and some of the other social sciences.

Academics trained abroad could now carry out their research in Portugal and started to develop new postgraduate programmes. Competition for research funds increased accordingly: whilst, in 2000, 1,961 projects were submitted to the FCT in all areas of science, by 2008 the figure was three times higher (5,697). In the social sciences, there was an equivalent increase: (c. 200 in 2000 and c. 700 in 2008). Concerning approved grants in the subdisciplinary area of anthropology, figures show that, from 2000 to 2009, there was a large increase in funding available: from an average of 250,000 € per year in the beginning of the 2000s to an average of 700,000 € per year at the end of that decade.[19] However, it must be noted that competition became much stronger. Whilst in 2000, 39 per cent of the research projects received funding, in 2008 this percentage decreased to 25 per cent.[20]

In order to be able to respond to the funding possibilities afforded by the FCT, anthropology had to affirm itself as a distinct discipline within the broader field of the social sciences. Contrary to many other European countries, we managed to preserve the subdisciplinary title of 'Anthropology' in the awarding of research grants and the appointment of evaluation committees. This was not always an easy task, both for endogenous and exogenous reasons. In order to ensure the survival of the distinct intellectual

Nº of underway PhD Grants.

Nº of underway Post-doc Grants.

■ Total

PhD Grants

Post-doc Grants

Funding year

Funding (million euros)

Year	Total	PhD Grants	Post-doc Grants
1994		466	23
1995		1220	79
1996		1177	90
1997	1750		225
1998	2296		298
1999	2614		357
2000	3032		468
2001	3233		580
2002	3451		689
2003	3764		836
2004	4094		998
2005	4060		1183
2006	4671		1363
2007	5591		1749
2008	6736		1925
2009	7831		1851
2010	8636		2044
2011	8676		2275
2012	8335		2528
2013	7520		2722
2014	5806		2561
2015	4714		2581

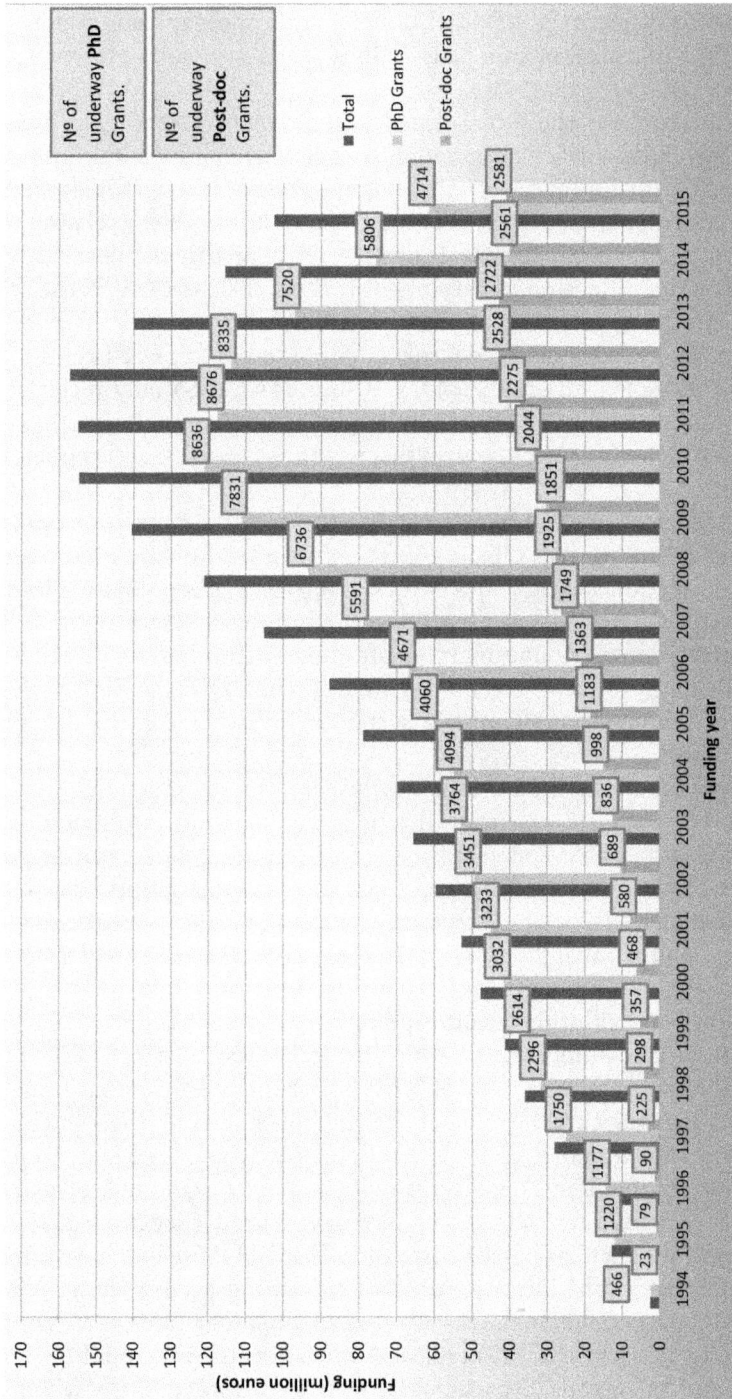

FIGURE 1.2. Evolution of the funding and number of active doctoral and postdoctoral grants, 1994–2015

Source: Fundação para a Ciência e a Tecnologia, FCT Board, May 2016. http://www.fct.pt/estatisticas/bolsas/

and scientific concerns of its practitioners, anthropology had to affirm its singularity in the face of other disciplines while internally preserving its plurality.

In particular, over these two decades, the relation to the more policy-oriented trends that became hegemonic in sociology obliged anthropologists to fight systematically for the epistemological value of ethnographic research when faced with quantitative surveys. Internally, however, the relation with 'biological anthropology' was at times complex, in particular because what is meant by that title is often very unclear. From 2000 to 2009, 33 per cent of the FCT's funding in the disciplinary title of 'Anthropology' was awarded to projects in genetics or palaeontology. Yet, the one research centre that lays claim to biological anthropology (Coimbra's CIAS) only received 12 per cent of this, with most of the funding being attributed to geneticists in prestigious medical research centres that have practically no anthropological concerns.[21]

In spite of such ambiguities, the insistence of Portuguese anthropology on its own disciplinary specificity for the purposes of funding was centrally important for anthropology both in preserving the methodological plurality of the best practices and in preserving the interdisciplinary outlook that characterizes our discipline when confronted with other social sciences, such as sociology or social psychology. Being recognized as a subdisciplinary title was essential in maintaining a sustained investment in the discipline over the years.

Finally, concerning the evolution of research topics, a general drift can be observed during this period. The previous focus on Portuguese rural society was largely abandoned in favour, firstly, of studies of urban sites and problems of modernity in Portugal (55% of attributed grants); secondly, of field sites that included the vast area of the Portuguese-speaking world (33%); and, thirdly, an interest in archival research, museology and historical anthropology (12%).[22]

The internationalization of anthropological debate is, of course, a situated issue. Peter Fry's comments concerning the internationalization of Brazilian anthropology are apposite here. He shows that the countries that Brazilian academics visit most are the same ones that publish their journals and books (2004: 239). Furthermore, he notes that France and the United States remain very important, but that 'there is a growing importance of Portugal and the countries of Latin America in this pattern of visitation' (Fry 2004: 232).

In the decade that has passed since the writing of these comments, there has been a significant increase in relations among academics writing in Portuguese, particularly in the social sciences and humanities. For example, in the congresses of the Portuguese Association of Anthropology since 2009, around half of the 500 participants were from abroad, 140 of whom are

Brazilians. Most of the remainder are colleagues who work in Portuguese-speaking contexts around the world. Anthropology in Portuguese has visibly exploited these possibilities over the past decade, which can be seen in the disciplinary journals, both in Portugal (esp. *Etnográfica* and *Análise Social*) and in Brazil, where journals such as *Mana, Horizontes Antropológicos, Novos Estudos CEBRAP, Revista de Antropologia* and others have started to publish regularly contributions by Portuguese colleagues. Furthermore, Brazilian publishing houses have had a great impact in Portugal, particularly since the mid 1990s, when the two academic communities came to develop more intense links.

In fact, at a global level, the sharing of a scientific language creates the conditions for the institution of intermediary areas of negotiation (cf. Pina-Cabral 2007: 234). This means that scholars writing and reading in Portuguese come to develop mutual understandings in terms of concepts used, authors referred to and shared knowledge. These do not counter their participation in the more global scientific debate in English but they do increase the possibility of questioning the more dominant global views and fashions, allowing for increased innovativeness and critical distancing.

A further aspect of the internationalization of science that occurred in this period was that research centres in Portugal started receiving postdoctoral researchers from abroad. In 2010, in particular, as the result of the programme entitled 'A Compromise with Science', a number of scholars from various European countries were hired with five-year contracts. This was especially marked at CRIA, where seventeen new anthropologists from abroad (thirteen of these from Europe) were hired, as well as at ICS.[23]

CONCLUDING IN CRISIS

In this chapter, we have traced the way in which anthropology has evolved in Portugal in the twentieth century, with particular reference to the past three decades. We have argued that the original tensions that marked our disciplinary project since its inception in the mid nineteenth century have remained alive throughout the twentieth century. Today, however, we are faced with new challenges that correspond to a world where the primitivist paradigm no longer holds sway; and where the opposition between nation and empire is as inoperable as the opposition between subjective meaning and objective behaviour.

We believe that we have shown that, in their peripheral condition, Portuguese social scientists have been quite successful at addressing the challenges of contemporary science. They have managed to produce a distinct voice, not only marked by the global nature of the use of the

Portuguese language, but also marked by their multiple networks both in Europe and in the Atlantic world. Together with Brazilian anthropologists and with the budding communities of social scientists emerging in Africa, they have produced a body of work and a distinctive canon that will be a reference for some time to come.

As an intellectual effort, anthropology no longer responds to the two axes identified above. On the one hand, new approaches that resolved the old Cartesian dilemmas that determined the epistemic axis are quickly imposing themselves (see Pina-Cabral 2017a); on the other hand, the political choice between nation and empire is no longer applicable. Portugal, as well as most other peripheral European nations, has to face brutally the challenge of understanding what Europe can mean in political terms for the future, now that the political consensus behind the European Union has been irremediably shattered.

Over the past decade, the recessive 'austerity' regime imposed by the European Union in the interests of the international financial institutions has affected Portuguese academia very severely. These were certainly years of desperation and gloom. The sudden break in the development of academic funding will leave its marks for decades to come. The ecumenical values that emerged in the aftermath of the Second World War and that carried along the project of European political integration seem to have lost some of their appeal during the postcolonial period. The imposition of 'austerity' left a whole new generation of Europeans, among them the newly trained Portuguese social scientists, with a lacklustre future. The outstanding work of the previous decades that we outlined above might well turn out to have a troubled sequel, as happened long ago when the First World War broke the back of a whole generation of very creative Portuguese intellectuals; or at the end of the Second World War, when the dictatorship, supported by the imperial forces at work during the Cold War, managed to smother yet another generation of Portuguese scholars. Some of the more capable Portuguese anthropologists had to search abroad for the means to continue their careers. Similarly, most of the young anthropologists from Europe and Brazil who had found in Portugal a welcome environment for their research, contributing decisively to the dynamism of the local anthropological project, have had to leave once again.

It must be noted that the change in government in early 2016 has allowed for a return to a less incompetent management of scientific funding. Nevertheless, the number of grants both for postgraduate teaching and for research continues to decrease. This tendency is supported by the direct attacks against the humanities and the social sciences arising from other scientific fields – themselves also threatened by the overall reduction in scientific funding. Backed up by implicit pseudo-truths concerning what is called in neoliberal lingo 'impact', these attacks find an echo in the characteristic disparagement against intellectual endeavour. In spite of that, research and teaching continues and, in the hard years of 'austerity' still to come, Portuguese anthropology will surely be able to rely on its accumulated strengths in order to survive. Nevertheless, we trust that the cosmopolitan outlook of Portuguese anthropologists and the steadfastness of the local institutions of learning will hopefully carry forward the impetus acquired in the 1990s into the mid decades of our century.

Susana de Matos Viegas is Research Fellow at the Institute of Social Sciences – University of Lisbon. She was the President of the Portuguese Association of Anthropology and member of the Directory Board of the Association of Social Sciences in Portuguese. Her research interests include kinship, place and territorial belonging, both among Amerindian peoples (Brazil) and the Fataluku (Timor-Leste).

João de Pina-Cabral is Professor of Social Anthropology at the University of Kent and Research Professor at the Institute of Social Sciences of the University of Lisbon. Among his academic monographs in English are *Between China and Europe: Person, Culture and Emotion in Macao* (2002) and *World: An Anthropological Examination* (2017).

NOTES

1. Differing, in this way, from North American anthropology: 'Studies of Native Americans ... took shape ... in 1879. But the anthropological study of African Americans would remain of minimal interest, at least to white scholars, for another half century. Still, a profound difference between the history of our discipline in Europe, on the one hand, and in the Western Hemisphere on the other, inheres in the simple fact that our subjects of study, our "primitive" peoples, were our neighbours – our ill-treated, indeed often persecuted, neighbours. In this instance as in others, the anthropology we do and have done is conditioned by the history and social complexion of the society whence we come' (Mintz 1996: 290).
2. See Pina-Cabral (1991: 19–22); Herzfeld (1986); Leal (2000).
3. See Peixoto (1967, vol. I: 330–47); also Peixoto (1990).
4. Rocha Peixoto's essays on votive offerings (e.g. Pina-Cabral et al. 1997), on the 'Portuguese house' *(casa portuguesa)* and on temporary dune dwellings (e.g. Oliveira, Galhano and Pereira 1988) etc., constitute points of reference to many of the debates in the second half of the twentieth century in Portuguese anthropology, architecture and archaeology. One of the most vivid impacts is the notion of the 'traditional Portuguese house' in the Portuguese school of architecture, from the

times of Raul Lino in the 1930s through to the generation of the 1960s, and even to present day (Távora and Roseta 2004 [1961]). Popular forms of architecture continue to repeat unwittingly the characteristic features identified by Rocha Peixoto – cf. Pais de Brito's essay on the competition concerning 'Portugal's most Portuguese village' (Brito 1982).

5. See Catarina Alves Costa *Falamos de António Campos*, documentary film, Lisbon 2009.

6. Concerning Mendes Corrêa and his relation to the colonial effort, see also Roque (2003, 2006).

7. Concerning Henrique Galvão, see Pina-Cabral (2001) and Thomaz (2002: 157–90). As cultural historians have noted, this was the period of development of an intellectual movement associated with the support of the Salazarist dictatorship that stressed the importance of folklore towards furthering national identity (cf. Branco 1994, 1999; Melo 2001).

8. For recent researches on the Timorese case see: Marques, Roque and Roque (2011); Hicks (2017); Viegas and Feijó (2017).

9. Now called ISCSP, the school dropped the reference to overseas at the time of the Revolution.

10. From the mid 1990s onwards the production by Portuguese anthropologists was so vast and differentiated that we would not be able to include here a representative and fair sample. Unfortunately, therefore, bound by the limits of the present chapter, we were obliged to limit the references to a minimum after this period.

11. See www.apantropologia.net

12. See the interview of José Mariano Gago published in *Análise Social* 46, 200 (2011).

13. A department of anthropology was created at Coimbra in 1995, but it was closed in 2010, and the members of staff (twelve palaeontologists and biologists and five social and cultural anthropologists) were integrated into the Department of Life Sciences. Their present undergraduate degree in Anthropology is geared towards the study of 'the biological, social and cultural variability of human groups' and they offer BA, MA and Ph.D. degrees in Anthropology and Palaeontology.

14. See the assessment of this made by António Barreto, *Análise Social* 46, 200 (2011).

15. For further information on CRIA, see www.cria.org.pt

16. Data gathered from approved research grants by the FCT under the subdisciplinary field of anthropology from 2000 to 2009 – http://www.fct.pt/apoios/projectos/consulta/projectos.phtml.pt

17. Note the role of APORDOC – the documentarists' association – in this development.

18. Cf. Ph.D. Grants given by the FCT (http://www.fct.pt/estatisticas/bolsas).

19. Data gathered from approved research grants by the FCT in the subdisciplinary area of anthropology from 2000 to 2009 – http://www.fct.pt/apoios/projectos/consulta/projectos.phtml

20. Cf. http://www.fct.pt/apoios/projectos/estatisticas/index.phtml.pt#cg

21. Centro de Investigação em Biopatologia e Oncobiologia, Universidade do Porto; Centro de Patologia e Imunologia Molecular, IPATIMUP-Universidade do Porto; Instituto Nacional de Medicina Legal.

22. Data gathered from approved research grants by the FCT in the subdisciplinary area of anthropology from 2000 to 2009 – http://www.fct.pt/apoios/projectos/consulta/projectos.phtml.pt

23. We are grateful to Antónia Pedroso de Lima and Catarina Mira at CRIA for their help in compiling this information.

REFERENCES

Alves, F.M. 1908–1948. *Memórias Arqueológico-Historicas do Distrito de Bragança*, 11 vols. Various publishers (republished by Abade de Baçal Museum).

Branco, J.F. 1994. 'Portugal e as suas Etnografias: Para uma Análise da Herança Leitiana (Compilação Bibliográfica)', *Revista Lusitana* 12: 95–110.

———. 1999. 'A Fluidez dos limites: discurso etnográficos e movimento foclórico em Portugal', *Etnográfica* 3(1): 23–48.

Brito, J.P.D. 1982. 'O Estado Novo e a aldeia mais portuguesa de Portugal', in A. Costa Pinto (ed.), *O Fascismo em Portugal: Actas do Colóquio Realizado na Faculdade de Letras de Lisboa em Março de 1980*. Lisboa: A Regra do Jogo, pp. 511–32.

———. 1996. *Retrato de Aldeia com Espelho: Ensaio sobre Rio de Onor*. Lisboa: Dom Quixote. Colecção Portugal de Perto.

Castelo, C. 1999. *"O modo português de estar no mundo": o luso-tropicalismo e a ideologia colonial portuguesa: 1933–1961*. Porto: Edições Afrontamento.

Cole, S. 1991. *Women of the Praia: Work and Lives in a Portuguese Coastal Community*. Princeton, NJ: Princeton University Press.

Corrêa, A.A.M. 1924. *Os povos primitivos da Lusitânea*. Porto: A. Figueirinhas.

———.1949. *Ultramar Português*. Lisboa: Agencia Geral das Colónias.

Cutileiro, J. 1971. *A Portuguese Rural Society*. Oxford: Clarendon Press.

Dias, J. 1981 [1948]. *Vilarinho da Furna, uma Aldeia Comunitária*. Lisboa: INCM.

———. 1981 [1953]. *Rio de Onor: Comunitarismo Agro-Pastoril*. Lisboa: Presença.

Dima, A.M. 2005. 'Higher Education in Portugal: Country Report'. Center for Higher Education Policy studies (Chapter – Higher Education Monitor). Texas. Retrieved 12 June 2012 from http://doc.utwente.nl/53331

Fabian, J. 1983. *Time and the Other: How Anthropology Makes its Object*. New York: Columbia University Press.

Fernandes, M. 2006. *Terra de Catarina: Do latifúndio à Reforma Agrária: Ocupação de Terras e Relações Sociais em Baleizão*. Lisboa: Celta.

Freyre, G. 1940. *O mundo que o português criou; aspectos das relações sociais e de cultura do Brasil com Portugal e as colónias portuguesas*, 1st ed. Lisboa: Livros do Brasil.

Fry, P. 2004. 'Internacionalização da disciplina', in W. Trajano and G. Lins Ribeiro (eds), *O Campo da Antropologia no Brasil*. Rio de Janeiro: Contra Capa ABA, pp. 227–48.

Graça, A.S. 1992. *O Poveiro: usos, costumes, tradições, lendas*. Lisboa: Coleccão Portugal de Perto/D. Quixote.

Herzfeld, M. 1986. *Ours Once More: Folklore, Ideology, and the Making of Modern Greece*. Londres: Pella.

Hicks, D. 2017. 'Research Past and Research Present: Doing Fieldwork in Portuguese Timor and Timor-Leste' in M. Nygaard-Christensen and A. Bexley (eds), *Fieldwork in Timor-leste: Understanding Social Change Through Practice*. Copenhagen: NIAS Press, pp. 32–57.

Kuper, A. 1988. 'The Idea of Primitive Society', in A. Kuper, *The Invention of Primitive Society: Transformations of an Illusion*. London and New York: Routledge, pp. 1–14.

Leal, J. 2000. *Etnografias Portuguesas (1870–1970): Cultura Popular e Identidade Nacional*. Lisboa: D. Quixote.

_____. 2001. '"Tylorian Professors" and "Japanese Corporals": Anthropological Theory and National Identity in Portuguese Ethnography', in A. Blok, C. Bromberger and D. Albera (eds), *L'Anthropologie de la Mediterranée/Anthropology of the Mediterranean*. Paris: Maison méditerranéenne des sciences de l'homme, pp. 645–62.

_____. 2006. *Antropologia em Portugal: Mestres, Percursos, Transições*. Lisboa: Livros Horizonte.

_____. 2008. 'The Hidden Empire: Peasants, Nation Building, and the Empire in Portuguese Anthropology', in S.R. Roseman and S. Parkhurst (eds), *Recasting Culture and Space in Iberian Contexts*. Albany, NY: University of New York Press, pp. 35–53.

Marques, V.R., A. Roque and R. Roque (eds). 2011. *Timor: Missões Científicas e Antropologia Colonial: Actas do Colóquio*. Lisboa: IICT/ICS-UL, Electronic Edition. Retrieved 12 June 2012 from http://www2.iict.pt/?idc=102&idi=17321

Martins, J.P.O. 1881. *Elementos da Antropologia*, 2nd ed. Lisboa: Bertrand.

Melo, D. 2001. *Salazarismo e cultura popular*. Lisboa: Imprensa de Ciências Sociais.

Mintz, S. 1996. 'Enduring Substances, Trying Theories: The Caribbean Region as Oikoumene', *Journal of the Royal Anthropological Institute* 2(2): 289–311.

Oliveira, E.V.D. 1974. 'António Jorge Dias: Biography and Bibliography', in *Memoriam António Jorge Dias* (Vol. I). Lisboa: Instituto de Alta Cultura. Junta de Investigações do Ultramar.

Oliveira, E.V.D., F. Galhano and B. Pereira. 1988. *Construções Primitivas em Portugal*. Lisboa: Colecção Portugal de Perto/Dom Quixote.

O'Neill, B.J. 2007 [1987]. *Social Inequality in a Portuguese Hamlet: Land, Late Marriage, and Bastardy 1870–1978*. Cambridge: Cambridge University Press.

Peixoto, A.A.R. 1967–1975. *Obras*, 3 vols. Póvoa do Varzim. Câmara Municipal da Póvoa do Varzim.

_____. 1990. *Etnografia Portuguesa: Obra Etnográfica completa*. Lisboa: Colecção Portugal de Perto/Dom Quixote.

Picão, J.D.S. 1983 [1903]. *Através dos campos: Usos e costumes agrícola-alentejanos (Concelho de Elvas)*. Lisboa: Colecção Portugal de Perto/Dom Quixote.

Pina-Cabral, J. 1986. *Sons of Adam, Daughters of Eve: The Peasant Worldview of the Alto Minho*. Oxford: Clarendon Press.

_____. 1989. 'Breves considerações sobre o estado da antropologia em Portugal', *Antropologia Portuguesa* 7: 29–36.

_____. 1991. 'A Antropologia em Portugal hoje', *Os Contextos da Antropologia* 11–41.

_____. 2001. 'Galvão among the Cannibals: The Emotional Constitution of Colonial Power', *Identities* 8(4): 483–515.

_____. 2004. 'Uma história de sucesso: a antropologia brasileira vista de longe', in W. Trajano and G. Lins Ribeiro (eds), *O Campo da Antropologia no Brasil*. Rio de Janeiro: Contra Capa/ABA, pp. 249–63.

_____. 2007. 'Língua e hegemonia nas ciências sociais', *Análise Social* XLII (182): 233–37.

Pina-Cabral, J. et al. 1997. *Milagre que Fez*. Coimbra: Museu Antropológico.

_____. 2017a. *World: An Anthropological Examination*. Chicago: HAU Books.

_____. 2017b. 'An Ecumenist Anthropology', *American Anthropologist* 119(2), in print.

Pina-Cabral, J. and R.G. Feijó. 2002. 'Do Ultimato à morte de Amália: Notas sobre a sociedade e a identidade portuguesas no século XX', in F. Pernes (ed.), *Século*

XX: Panorama da Cultura Portugesa, vol. 1. Porto: Fundação Serralves/Edições Afrontamento, pp. 61–80.

Porto, N. 2009. *Modos de Objectificação da dominação colonial: o caso do Museu do Dundo, 1940–1970*. Lisboa: Fundação Calouste Gulbenkian/Fundação para a Ciência e Tecnologia.

Roque, R. 2003. 'Correia, António Augusto Esteves Mendes', in A. Nóvoa (ed.), *Dicionário de Educadores Portugueses: 900 Biografias de Homens e Mulheres que se Dedicaram ao Ensino e à Educação nos Séculos XIX e XX*. Porto: ASA, pp. 389–92.

———. 2006. 'A Antropologia Colonial Portuguesa (1911–1950)', in D. Curto Ramada (ed.), *Estudos de Sociologia da Leitura em Portugal no Século XX*. Lisboa: Fundação Calouste Gulbenkian, pp. 789–822.

———. 2010. *Headhunting and Colonialism: Anthropology and the Circulation of Human Skulls in the Portuguese Empire, 1870–1930*. Hampshire: Palgrave Macmillan.

Stocking Jr., G.W. 1982. 'Afterword: A View from the Center', *Ethnos* 47: 172–86.

Távora, F. and H. Roseta (eds). 2004 [1961]. *Arquitectura Popular em Portugal*. Lisboa: Centro Editor Livreiro da Ordem dos Arquitectos.

Thomaz, O.R. 2002. *Ecos do Atlântico Sul: representações sobre o terceiro império português*. Rio de Janeiro: UFRJ/FAPESP.

Vasconcellos, J.L.D. 1933–1985. *Etnografia Portuguesa*, 9 vols. Lisboa: Imprensa Nacional.

Viegas, S.M. 2009. 'O Ensino, a Investigação e a Divulgação da Antropologia em Portugal', in *Livro do IV Congresso da Associação Portuguesa de Antropologia: Classificar o Mundo*. Lisboa: APA, pp. 327–43.

———. 2011. 'Três etnografias nas décadas de 1960–1970: os Fataluku', in V.R Marques, A. Roque and R. Roque (eds), *Timor: Missões Científicas e Antropologia Colonial: Actas do Colóquio*. Lisboa: IICT/ICS-UL, Electronic Edition. Retrieved 12 June 2012 from http://www2.iict.pt/?idc=102&idi=17321

Viegas, S. de Matos and R. Graça Feijó (eds). 2017. *Transformations in Independent Timor-Leste. Dynamics of Social and Cultural Cohabitations*. London and New York: Routledge.

CHAPTER

2

WHEN A GREAT SCHOLARLY TRADITION MODERNIZES

German-Language Ethnology in the Long Twentieth Century

JOHN R. EIDSON

INTRODUCTION

This chapter offers an overview of the history and current situation of sociocultural anthropology in Germany, Austria and the German-speaking portion of Switzerland. In these countries, sociocultural anthropology is currently subject to far-reaching processes of internationalization, given, among other things, the marginal status that the German language has in the international scientific community today. Yet it also retains a distinctive profile insofar as international trends must be reconciled with a distinctive intellectual heritage, with particular traditions of higher education and with the inherited division of labour between sociocultural anthropology and various sister disciplines. The chapter reviews the intellectual and institutional history of German-language sociocultural anthropology from the 1860s to the present, commenting on its development as a science and situating it within the larger context of German social history.

GERMAN-LANGUAGE ETHNOLOGY
FROM PROMINENCE TO OBSCURITY

In the decades before and after 1900, German-speaking ethnologists were recognized internationally as representatives of one of the great scholarly traditions of the colonial powers. They were cited prominently by British, French and American colleagues, such as Edward B. Tylor (1871), Bronislaw Malinowski (1922), Marcel Mauss (1925), Alfred L. Kroeber (1935), Clyde Kluckhohn (1936), Robert H. Lowie (1937) and Franz Boas (1940); and their influence radiated widely in Eastern Europe and Russia (Slezkine 1991; Sárkány 2002). By the mid-twentieth century, however, they had largely lost their international standing, descending into apparent insignificance and neglect. Why?

The decline of German-language ethnology can be explained in large part with reference to twentieth-century political history. During the First World War, anti-German sentiment swept the allied nations, resulting in the devaluation of German as a foreign language (e.g. Gilbert 1981) and, ultimately, as an international language of scholarship (Schlee 1990). When, in the course of the war, Germany lost its colonies in Africa and the Pacific, ethnologists were deprived of their fields of research and relegated to archives and museums. The rise of the National Socialist state in the 1930s disrupted links to foreign colleagues (Proctor 1988: 157, 163–66). Some German ethnologists embraced the new order, some were corrupted, some retreated into niches, and others emigrated, usually never to return (Fischer 1990; Hauschild 1995a; Streck 2000a). Finally, the Second World War, together with Germany's genocidal campaigns, completed the isolation of the land and its inhabitants, including its ethnologists (Métraux 1948; Westphal-Hellbusch 1959: 853).

The consequences of twentieth-century political history for German-language ethnology can hardly be overestimated. Nevertheless, some have argued that the negative effects of the two World Wars and of Nazi crimes were augmented by factors intrinsic to ethnology in the German language area; namely, the peculiarities of its institutional bases, its theories and its methods. While such arguments cannot be assessed adequately in this brief overview, we return to them in conclusion, offering some insight into contrasting perspectives and competing explanations.

THE OBJECT OF INVESTIGATION

This chapter is devoted to the branch of scholarship in the German language area that corresponds most closely to sociocultural anthropology, as this term is currently understood in the international scientific community. The German language area includes not only Germany – by far the greatest part, both geographically and demographically – but also Austria and much of Switzerland. Divided politically, these countries are linked by geography, language and history. Thus, as two Austrian colleagues have noted, it is 'almost impossible', when considering the field of sociocultural anthropology, to treat them separately (Dostal and Gingrich 1996: 263; see also Lowie 1937; Heine-Geldern 1964; Mühlmann 1968; Braukämper 1979; Turner and Paproth 1989; Geisenhainer 2002; Petermann 2004; Gingrich 2005, 2007; Rössler 2007).

The German equivalent of sociocultural anthropology is not *Anthropologie* but *Ethnologie* or *Völkerkunde*. First coined in the sixteenth century, the term Anthropologie had, by the late eighteenth century, come to denote either philosophical speculation about human nature or the natural history of humanity and its subdivisions (Marquard 1971; Vermeulen 2006). The terms Ethnologie and Völkerkunde – respectively, Greek-based and German-based neologisms for the study of diverse peoples – were coined in the mid to late eighteenth century, first, by German-speaking field researchers in the Russian empire, who were documenting the characteristics of populations in Siberia (Vermeulen 2006, 2015), and, second, by scholars at the University of Göttingen, where reports from Siberia and elsewhere were being synthesized according to the newly established principles of Enlightenment historiography (Fischer 1970; Schlesier and Urban 1994 [1987]; Stagl 1995: 233–68, 1998; Vermeulen 1995, 2015).

Many modern commentators on developments in the eighteenth century have viewed Anthropologie as an overarching category, encompassing Ethnologie (e.g. Herzog 1965; Mühlmann 1968; Petermann 2004: 278–300; Haller 2012: 31–58). Recently, Han Vermeulen (2006, 2015) has challenged this view, arguing that Anthropologie was developed primarily by physicians and philosophers as a science of *Rassen* (races), whereas Ethnologie was developed primarily by historians as a science of *Völker* (peoples). However that may be, it is clear that the two terms have, since their appearance, designated distinct but interrelated approaches (Fischer 1983: 30–33; Proctor 1988; Massin 1996; Geisenhainer 2002, 2009, 2014; Laukötter 2007). Therefore, further investigation might focus most fruitfully on variations in their interrelationship in different national traditions of scholarship (Eidson 2000, 2008).

The terms *Volkskunde* and *Völkerkunde*, based on the singular and plural forms, respectively, of the German word for 'people', were used interchangeably when first coined in the eighteenth century; but by the mid nineteenth century Volkskunde had come to denote the branch of scholarship devoted to the folk culture of German-speaking peoples (especially, peasants, farmhands, artisans, miners, day labourers and domestic servants), while Völkerkunde was used to refer to the study of non-European peoples (Lutz 1969; Vermeulen 2006). This distinction is still perceptible in the terms currently favoured for these two disciplines: for Volkskunde, *Europäische Ethnologie* and for Völkerkunde, simply, *Ethnologie*. We return to the relationship between Volkskunde and Völkerkunde in conclusion.

Most recently, some German-speaking colleagues have begun to use German equivalents of Anglo-American terms for their discipline; namely, *Sozialanthropologie* and *Kulturanthropologie* – despite the fact that each has potentially misleading precedents in German language history.[1] Nevertheless, Völkerkunde and, especially, Ethnologie are still the most common designations for sociocultural anthropology in the German language area. This use of the word Ethnologie corresponds to the older American usage, as kept alive in the title of the journal *American Ethnologist*; but it contrasts with common usage in many of the other countries included in this volume, where cognates of ethnology are used to refer to disciplines that are equivalent to Volkskunde.

THE INSTITUTIONALIZATION OF ETHNOLOGY IN THE GERMAN LANGUAGE AREA

Conceived in the latter half of the eighteenth century as subfields of philosophy, medicine or history, Anthropologie and Ethnologie first emerged as separate academic disciplines over a century later. Important impulses came, for anthropology, from natural scientists and medical doctors and, for ethnology, from giants of humanist scholarship such as Johann Gottfried Herder, Wilhelm von Humboldt and Alexander von Humboldt, who are credited with contributing decisively to the development of modern conceptions of culture, language and comparative studies (Boas 1904; Mühlmann 1968: 62–66; Berg 1984, 1990; Broce 1986; Bunzl 1996; Gingrich 2005: 64–75). No less important, however, were the activities of lesser known scholars and also amateur enthusiasts among the educated bourgeoisie.

Examination of German university curricula shows, for example, that lectures with the words Anthropologie and Ethnologie in the title were held by professors of established disciplines, beginning in the early nineteenth century (Geisenhainer 2009, 2014). Simultaneously, educated laypersons, whether individually or as members of learned societies, engaged in scholarly pastimes, often amassing collections of various objects and eventually inducing local administrators to found museums – principally in the latter half of the nineteenth century – by donating their collections to the commune or municipality.[2] In cities that had not only amateur archaeologists, historians and naturalists but also collectors of exotic artefacts, or connections to them, the donation or purchase of such artefacts resulted in the founding of ethnological museums – or, initially, of ethnological departments within already existing archaeological or natural historical museums (Laukötter 2007: 32–35).

Beginning in about the mid nineteenth century, ethnological museums were founded in over a dozen cities in the German language area.[3] Clearly, such museums were products of the colonial era, in which German-speaking people participated imaginatively and – especially in Eastern Europe and Russia – in fact, even before the acquisition of overseas colonies in the 1880s (e.g. Gothsch 1983; Zantop 1997; Zimmerman 2001; Ther 2004; Speitkamp 2005; Conrad 2012). Ethnological museums can also be understood, however, as expressions of municipal cultural policy in a politically divided land with a long history of independent cities and multiple royal or princely courts – each of which had to have its own cabinet of curiosities. H. Glenn Penny (2002, 2008) has written of competition among cities with museums in displaying their 'worldliness' and their commitment to cultivation.

Early developments in universities and museums were followed by further steps in the process of institutionalization, as may be illustrated with reference to Adolf Bastian (1826–1905) – a physician, gentleman scholar, world traveller and collector of artefacts, who was well versed in the humanist tradition of Herder and the brothers Humboldt. Often cited as the founding father of German ethnology, Bastian was responsible for a whole series of 'firsts' (von den Steinen 1905; Baldus 1968; Fiedermutz-Laun 1970, 1986; Koepping 1983; Bunzl 1996: 46–52; Buchheit and Koepping 2001; Fischer, Bolz and Kamel 2007).[4] In 1867, after having spent years as a ship's surgeon, Bastian became the first to complete the Habilitation (the postdoctoral dissertation required of candidates for a professorship) in the field of Ethnologie. In 1868, he was appointed assistant curator of the ethnographic and prehistoric collections of the Königliches Museum (Royal Museum) in Berlin, and in 1873 he presided, as director, over the founding of the Museum für Völkerkunde. In 1869, the year he began lecturing on ethnology at the university in Berlin, he founded the journal *Zeitschrift für Ethnologie* (together with Robert Hartmann) and the local-level Berliner Gesellschaft für Anthropologie, Ethnologie und Urgeschichte, or Society for Anthropology, Ethnology and Prehistory (with Rudolf Virchow and others). In 1870, Bastian also played a leading role in founding the national-level Deutsche Gesellschaft für Anthropologie, Ethnologie und Urgeschichte.[5]

'More than any other ethnologist', writes one authority on Bastian, 'the founder of ethnology in Germany has been understood in diametrically opposed ways' (Fiedermutz-Laun 1986: 167)[6] – a fact that is often attributed to his labyrinthine prose.[7] With his famous collaborator, Virchow, Bastian is said to have shared a principled avoidance of 'the classification of data according to predetermined categories' (Penny 2008: 85). Aside from his well-known rejection of Darwinism, at least in the form propagated by his contemporary, Ernst Haeckel, Bastian's relation to popular ideas regarding social evolution and diffusion was ambivalent. His emphasis both on 'uniform laws of growth and a general psychic unity of mankind' and on 'the diversity ... of cultures' (Baldus 1968: 23) found expression in the distinction between *Elementargedanken* and *Völkergedanken* – the former being categories of thought common to all humans and the latter being the particular form these take under varying geographical and historical circumstances (Bastian 1860).[8] Despite the ambiguities of his thought, Bastian's influence was far-reaching (Penny 2008). Those younger colleagues whom he influenced most strongly included Boas and Karl von den Steinen (Gingrich 2005: 90).

Friedrich Ratzel (1844–1904), who articulated a very different and perhaps even more influential research programme, might be viewed as a second founding father of German-language ethnology.[9] He began his career as a natural scientist cum journalist, travelling widely and publishing prolifically on various peoples and places around the globe. Before long, his publications transcended mere journalism (Ratzel 1882–1891, 1885–1888), earning him an appointment as professor of geography in Leipzig in 1886. In contrast to Bastian, Ratzel assumed that humankind is basically uninventive – an assumption that led him to reject notions of parallel development and to search instead for specific origins and for evidence of the ways in which devices, ideas and institutions are spread through migration, trade or conquest (Lowie 1937: 119–27; Smith 1991: 140–54). Ethnologists within Ratzel's immediate sphere of influence included Heinrich Schurtz, Leo Frobenius and Fritz Graebner (Westphal-Hellbusch 1959: 849; Smith 1991: 154–61; Gingrich 2005: 91, 108).

In founding the *Berliner Gesellschaft*, Bastian and Virchow brought anthropology and ethnology into close association but treated them as separate fields, largely eschewing causal arguments bridging the gap between the natural history and the cultural history of humankind. Beginning around 1900, however, many scholars began seeking to establish even closer ties between anthropology and ethnology and to subordinate the latter to the former (Proctor 1988; Massin 1996; Laukötter 2007). This trend coincided with the rise of eugenics, internationally, and with the founding in the German language area of influential new societies in which a number of ethnologists participated –for example, the Gesellschaft für Rassenhygiene (Society for Racial Hygiene or Eugenics), founded in 1905.

During the first half of the twentieth century, most professional ethnologists were employed in museums, though some also taught at universities or other educational institutions (Westphal-Hellbusch 1959:

849–50).[10] Full professorships were created first in the field of anthropology, which, however, was understood to include ethnology: in Berlin, one of Bastian's assistants, Felix von Luschan, became full professor of anthropology in 1909 (Laukötter 2007a: 154); and, in Vienna, Rudolf Pöch became full professor of anthropology and ethnography in 1919 (Szilvássy, Spindler and Kritscher 1980).[11] The first university chair created exclusively for ethnology went to Karl Weule, who had gotten his doctoral degree in geography under Ratzel and his training as an ethnologist and anthropologist under Bastian and von Luschan. In 1920, Weule became full professor of ethnology in Leipzig, after having spent twenty years working at the local ethnological museum (Reche 1929).[12]

Although anthropology and ethnology were closely linked, the feeling of distinctiveness among ethnologists was strong enough to motivate the founding of the Gesellschaft für Völkerkunde (Society for Ethnology) in 1929 (Streck 2009; Geisenhainer 2011). Renamed the Deutsche Gesellschaft für Völkerkunde (German Society for Ethnology) in 1938, this is still the national association of ethnologists in Germany.[13]

DOMINANT TRENDS IN THE EARLY TWENTIETH CENTURY

Science is international. Nevertheless, distinct national traditions take shape due to the combined effects of a number of factors (cf. Stichweh 1996): language communities and their corresponding media and public spheres; publishing history; the national climate of opinion; the institutional bases of scholarship and teaching; the politics of academic appointment and research funding; and the exemplary accomplishments or entrepreneurial activities of ambitious figures during processes of institutionalization. Since these factors are just beginning to be explored in the history of German-language ethnology, we focus in the following on the distinctive profile that resulted from their interaction, while pointing occasionally to paths that might be followed in seeking causal explanations.

Recent Austrian and German commentators have rightly emphasized the variety of approaches that characterized German-language ethnology before and after the First World War. For example, Andre Gingrich (2005: 63, 94–110) differentiates between the 'hegemonic traditions' of the 'academic schools' and various 'peripheral and subaltern traditions', arguing that the latter represent a more fitting heritage from our contemporary point of view. Similarly, Bernhard Streck (2009: 268–69) emphasizes the 'pluralism' of interwar German-language ethnology, which, he suggests, transcended 'the tripartite division of German ethnology ... which is favoured in the historiography of the discipline'. In our overview of developments in the early twentieth century, however, it may be deemed legitimate to focus on the three main schools, because they were, in important ways, dominant at home and influential abroad. What is more, they served as bases for the revival of research and teaching following the Second World War. These three schools are *Kulturgeschichte* (cultural history), *Kulturmorphologie* (cultural morphology) and *Ethnosoziologie* (ethno-sociology).

Of the various approaches to Kulturgeschichte, three are selected for comment; namely, those of Fritz Graebner and Bernhard Ankermann, of Wilhelm Schmidt and of Hermann Baumann (cf. Haller 2012: 52–56). Each of these approaches may be understood as a variant form of what has come to be known as the *Kulturkreislehre*, or the Doctrine of Cultural Provinces.[14] As such, they differed, to greater or lesser degrees, even from those varieties of cultural history with which they shared common roots, such as those espoused by Boas and his students.[15]

The concept of *Kulturkreise*, or cultural provinces, was inspired by Bastian and especially Ratzel, named by Frobenius (1897, 1898), formalized by Ankermann (1905) and Graebner (1905, 1911), and further developed in different directions by Schmidt (Schmidt and Koppers 1924; Schmidt 1939) and, somewhat later, Baumann (1934, 1940).[16] Research in this tradition went beyond mere diffusionism in attempting to trace the geographical distribution, origins and migratory paths not only of individual cultural traits but of complexes of traits and even of whole integrated cultures, which were thought, under certain conditions, to maintain their integrity as they spread out in space. Specified criteria (especially, of form and quantity) were supposed to help determine whether cultural resemblances were reliable indicators of common origins (Graebner 1911: 98–99, 108–9; Johansen 1992; Vajda 1993). The concept of Kulturkreise was supplemented by the concept of *Kulturschichten*, or cultural strata (Graebner 1911: 125–51), so that any part of the surface of the globe could be seen to have been inhabited by a succession of distinct cultures, which overlapped and partially displaced or mixed with one another. Ankermann and Graebner were museum ethnologists (both, initially, in Berlin, though Graebner moved later to Cologne), who referred to artefacts in attempting to reconstruct cultural provinces, cultural strata and paths of diffusion – and, so, to contribute to the reconstruction of the cultural history of humankind (Leser 1977, 1977/1978).

Schmidt was an empire builder who developed the Kulturkreislehre in a particular direction (Conte 1987; Brandewie 1990; Marchand 2003). As a young Roman Catholic priest of German origin, he was appointed in 1895 to a seminary near Vienna, where in 1906 he founded the journal *Anthropos* (with the subtitle, *Internationale Zeitschrift für Völker- und Sprachenkunde*, i.e., International Journal of Ethnology and Linguistics) and in 1931 a research institute of the same name. Schmidt became a lecturer at the University of

Vienna in 1921, then full professor at the University of Fribourg, Switzerland, in 1942, after having been forced by the National Socialists to close shop in Vienna in 1938. Combining his own brand of cultural history with the thesis of original monotheism, Schmidt arrived at historical reconstructions of distinct cultural provinces and strata that soon became doubtful even to his closest colleagues, who included his fellow clerics and ethnologists, Wilhelm Koppers, Martin Gusinde and Paul Schebesta (Haekel 1959: 867; Marchand 2003: 309).

Baumann, who was trained as a museum ethnologist under Ankermann in Berlin, developed a version of the Kulturkreislehre that was restricted to continental Africa and that postulated a link between culture and a corresponding 'racial substratum' (Baumann 1934: 137, 1940; Braun 1995).[17]

Kulturmorphologie – a variant form of Kulturgeschichte – was the brainchild of the academic outsider and scientific entrepreneur Frobenius. Like his erstwhile collaborator, Oswald Spengler, Frobenius believed that cultures are living entities, each with a distinctive essence that makes itself manifest – in varying ways, depending on the stage in the life cycle of the culture in question – in art, symbols, everyday behaviour, ritual, world view and so on (Straube 1990; Streck 1995, 1999; Marchand 1997; Kohl 2010). Frobenius's (1921) word for this unifying cultural force was the Greek neologism, *Paideuma*, which may be compared with Kroeber's (1917) much-criticized notion of the 'superorganic' (Kramer 1995: 98), though it seems to have been conceived with an even higher degree of reification. Like Schmidt, Frobenius created a research infrastructure where none had previously existed, seeking sponsors, leading several research expeditions into the African interior from 1904 to 1932, founding the Forschungsinstitut für Kulturmorphologie (Research Institute for Cultural Morphology) in Munich in 1920, moving house with his whole operation to Frankfurt am Main in 1925 and founding the journal *Paideuma* in 1938.

Ethnosoziologie is a term coined by Richard Thurnwald, another Austrian who studied in Berlin before doing fieldwork in Micronesia, Melanesia and, later, East Africa. In his analyses, Thurnwald combined a social psychological approach with a variety of functionalist sociology bearing some resemblance to that of his British contemporaries (Thurnwald 1931–1935; see also Lowie 1937: 242–49; Melk-Koch 1989, 1995). Of the ethnologists mentioned in this section, Thurnwald had the closest ties to British and American colleagues; but he was also among those who were most involved in developing ethnology as an applied colonial science, even after the Nazi seizure of power (Thurnwald 1935, 1940). Unlike Schmidt and Frobenius, Thurnwald was not a successful institution builder, although he founded the journal *Zeitschrift für Völkerpsychologie und Soziologie* (1925), which was later renamed *Sociologus* (1932). Among academic ethnologists in the German language area, he remained – until shortly before his death – a marginal, if outspoken, figure, who did, however, train students who later became quite influential.

ETHNOLOGY UNDER NATIONAL SOCIALISM

With the shift to racial determinism and eugenics, beginning around 1900, the field of anthropology became increasingly appealing to participants in *völkisch* (radical nationalist) movements (Proctor 1988; Smith 1991; Massin 1996). Then, in the Third Reich, anthropologists did, in fact, provide ideological and practical support to the Nazi regime (Proctor 1988: 156–66; Schafft 2004; Sachse 2010). What of ethnology?

Early research on the history of ethnology under National Socialism suggested that the discipline suffered under or benefited from official neglect (Fischer 1990). While this view was not entirely unfounded, especially with regard to particular universities or museums (Gingrich 2005: 134–35), subsequent research painted a different picture: 'There were National Socialist ideologues and practitioners who used ethnology, and there were many ethnologists who wanted to participate in National Socialist ideology and praxis' (Streck 2000: 8).

No attempt will be made here to summarize the (by now) sizable body of literature and the corresponding debates regarding German ethnology during the National Socialist period (e.g. Hauschild 1987, 1995a; Fischer 1990; Mosen 1991; Michel 1992, 1995; Dostal 1994; Linimayr 1994; Braun 1995; Spöttel 1995; Streck 2000a; Geisenhainer 2002; Kreide-Damani 2010). A brief review of the roles played by selected figures is enough to indicate that ethnologists, like representatives of other disciplines, included in their ranks enthusiastic Nazis, opportunists, not so innocent bystanders, passive and active opponents and victims (Gingrich 2005: 111–36; Haller 2012: 67–69).

While ideologically close to the völkisch orientation of the Nazis, Frobenius – who during the First World War had been sent to East Africa and the Middle East by 'Berlin ... to stir up jihad ... against the Allies' (Hastings 2010: 43; see also McMeekin 2010: 145–53) – was too old and perhaps too noncompliant to play a major role during the Third Reich (Marchand 1997; Kohl 2010). Frobenius's student and successor, Adolf Jensen, did not support the Nazis and was dismissed from his position as director of the Institut für Kulturmorphologie (Gingrich 2005: 116–17).

Thurnwald was not a Nazi party member and was later described as a regime critic by Leonhard Adam (1955: 151), a colleague of partial Jewish descent who was dismissed from his position in 1933 and emigrated in 1938 (Massola 1961). But Thurnwald's support for a doctoral candidate who did applied research on Roma and Sinti – whom Heinrich Himmler had already identified as a 'menace' – was consistent with his attempts to promote Ethnosoziologie as a colonial science in the service of the state (Gingrich 2005: 106, 121–22). In this spirit, he participated in a public debate with members of the cultural-historical school, including Baumann, in which each party attempted to prove its superior loyalty to National Socialist power-holders (Turner and Paproth 1989: 131, 141; Müller 1993: 220–21, footnote 22). Wilhelm Mühlmann, one of Thurnwald's most distinguished students, is now held to have been one of the most active supporters of the Nazi regime among German ethnologists (Michel 1992, 1995).

In Austria, Schmidt – who is said to have been a dogmatic tyrant, a fascist and an anti-Semite (Gingrich 2005: 109) – openly opposed the National Socialists and, with the incorporation of Austria into Germany in 1938, was, along with some of his colleagues, dismissed from his posts. Schmidt shifted his base of operations to a location near Fribourg, Switzerland, where a university professorship was created for him. Meanwhile, the department at the University of Vienna was entrusted to Baumann, who, aside from representing a less daringly speculative form of cultural history, was also a Nazi party member (Gingrich 2005: 116, 2007: 16).

Those ethnologists who were forced to flee or who chose to emigrate, because of either Jewish ancestry, Jewish spouses, socialist inclinations, moral outrage or a combination of these factors, included Leonard Adam, Herbert Baldus, Robert von Heine-Geldern, Paul Kirchhoff, Paul Leser, Julius Lips and Franz Steiner, among others (Kramer 1995: 101; Riese 1995; Gingrich 2005: 117–19). Some émigrés –for example, Kirchhof in Mexico and Baldus in Brazil – were subsequently influential in promoting the discipline of ethnology in their host countries.[18]

THE LATTER HALF OF THE TWENTIETH CENTURY IN WEST GERMANY, AUSTRIA AND SWITZERLAND

From the desolate conditions of the post-war years to the present day, the field of ethnology has grown dramatically in Germany, Austria and Switzerland (Kohl 1997: 102–3; Fillitz 2003; Waldis 2003; Haller 2012; Bierschenk, Krings and Lentz 2013). In 1946, ethnology was represented, with nine professorships and six further senior positions, at fifteen different universities in the German language area (Streck 2009: 275–76). In 2012, while still a relatively small discipline in comparison to sociology and political science, ethnology was represented at twenty-nine different universities.

The years between 1945 and 1967 were marked by a relatively steady increase in the number of departments, professorships and students, especially after the refounding, in 1951, of the Deutsche Forschungsgemeinschaft (DFG), or German Research Foundation, which provided ample funding for ethnographic fieldwork (Haller 2012: 62–66). In the 1970s, several new professorships were added to already existing departments; but the 1980s marked a period of institutional stagnation.[19]

After the Second World War, scholarly renewal lagged behind institutional growth, as representatives of the major ethnological schools of the pre-war era stepped forward to reinstate the traditions in which they had been trained. Some former Nazis were dismissed permanently; but, in the American, British and French zones, which in 1949 became the Federal Republic of Germany, others were allowed to reappear, if with some delay, and to play a prominent role in research and teaching (Gingrich 2005: 138–39; Haller 2012: 102–4).

In Fribourg and once again in Vienna, Schmidt continued to promote his programme until his death in 1954. Thereafter, Schmidt's successors rejected the particular historical reconstructions that he had proposed but continued to pursue a modified cultural-historical approach for some years to come (Haekel 1956, 1959; Fillitz 2003: 104; Gingrich 2005: 141). Despite his Nazi past, Baumann played a key role in re-establishing cultural history in West Germany (Gingrich 2005: 139–41; Haller 2012: 103–4). The cultural morphological tradition was carried forward by Jensen, who, in addition to becoming a university professor and director of the ethnological museum in Frankfurt, also regained official control of the Forschungsinstitut für Kulturmorphologie (soon to be renamed the Frobenius Institut) (Haller 2012: 50). In Berlin, the elderly Thurnwald finally became a full professor and, during the few years that remained to him, revived the journal *Sociologus* (Melk-Koch 1989: 281; Gingrich 2005: 139, 142). Thurnwald's student, Mühlmann, also a former member of the National Socialist party, re-emerged and eventually became a full professor and an influential teacher (Michel 1992, 1995; Gingrich 2005: 138–39, 143–45; Haller 2012: 102).

Despite – or, perhaps, because of – the revival of the three major schools of the pre-war era, many post-war scholars exhibited a sceptical attitude towards all ethnological theory, combined with a commitment to a form of empiricism that was supposedly free of presuppositions (Westphal-Hellbusch 1959: 854; Fillitz 2003: 104; Haller 2012: 87–88, 146–50). Today's commentators cite a number of reasons for this development: the discrediting of theory by dogmatists such as Schmidt; the ideological deformation and political instrumentalization of theory under the Nazis; the prevalence of a non-utilitarian conception of science, with an emphasis on the value of facts in and of themselves; the new emphasis on (DFG-funded) fieldwork as the central mission of ethnology; and even a defensive reaction to the rise of theory-oriented social science in the 1960s (see, for example,

Haller 2012: 40, 88, 149). Those who have read the German-language ethnological literature of this era might recall the sometimes odd mixture of dry description, eccentricity and unexamined assumption (cf. Hinz 1969; Vossen 1969). This has prompted Dieter Haller (2012: 146), author of a recent history of ethnology in West Germany from 1945 to 1990, to call for examination of 'the theories that might lie below the surface of theory-skepticism' – a task that has yet to be accomplished.[20]

Among German-speaking ethnologists, members of the generation of 1968 write of a break with national traditions and a turn towards British, French and American models in that year of international upheaval – a break instigated, at least in part, by 'critically oriented students who were tired of the stale dishes that were being fed to them' (Petermann 2004: 642; see also Kohl 1997: 105–7; Streck 1997: 44, 2009: 277; Gingrich 2005: 145–46). The supposed break might best be seen as a dramatic – or dramatized – phase within a larger trend that first became evident in the late 1950s (Johansen 1983: 304; Treide 2005: 147), reached a new peak in the late 1960s, and continues today in an ongoing, if uneven, process of internationalization (cf. Bierschenk, Krings and Lentz 2013). The gradual attenuation of identification with national traditions of ethnological research corresponds roughly with the liberalization of West German society and the progressive integration of Germany and Austria, especially, into the 'Western World' (Haller 2012).

EAST GERMANY IN THE MID TO LATE TWENTIETH CENTURY

Following the Second World War, Soviet authorities and scholars returning from exile re-established and reformed the discipline of ethnology in the Soviet zone, concentrating ethnological research in a relatively small number of centres (Noack and Krause 2005: 28–34).[21] In Berlin, the fusion of Völkerkunde and Volkskunde in a single university department was supposed to be 'the key to reorganising the disciplines along non-racist, non-nationalist lines' (Noack and Krause 2005: 25). The new designation of the unified field was Ethnographie, which was evidently modelled on the Russian term, *etnografia* (Johansen 1983: 303; Noack and Krause 2005: 28–29; Streck 2009: 277; cf. van der Heyden 2005: 304–5 note 7).

In the German Democratic Republic (GDR), founded in 1949, the influence of Marxist-Leninist historical materialism was most evident in grand theoretical statements (e.g. Sellnow 1961; Guhr 1969) and in research on topics that were specified in the Marxist canon (e.g. Herrmann and Köhn 1988). Within Marxism-Leninism, however, there was room for conflicting viewpoints, as, for example, in the 'formations debate' concerning, among other things, the Asiatic mode of production (Johansen 1983: 307–10; Noack and Krause 2005: 37–40). Beyond that, there was a significant amount of variation in ethnological research and teaching, depending on the place, the institutional setting, the precise period in the history of the Soviet zone/ GDR and the agency of leading figures (compare Noack and Krause 2005 and Treide 2005 on university departments in Berlin and Leipzig, respectively). If, with time, the political orthodoxy prevailed, at least officially, this did not preclude the production of regional studies of lasting value (Gingrich 2005: 146–48; van der Heyden 2005; Noack and Krause 2005; Treide 2005).

Reference to the Marxist-Leninist orientation does help us to understand the dual orientation of East German ethnology towards historical, even prehistoric questions, on one hand, and towards contemporary movements of national liberation, on the other (Noack and Krause 2005: 44; Treide 2005: 148; van der Heyden 2005: 311–15): each of these topics corresponds to a particular phase in a larger evolutionary or dialectical process. Other explanations for the dominant historical orientation in East German ethnology are the legacy of early twentieth-century German-language ethnology and, more pragmatically, the severe limits on fieldwork opportunities, which led researchers to seek data in colonial archives and museum collections. Indeed, museums seem to have played an even greater role in post-war ethnological research in the east than they did in the west. Two of the three leading ethnological journals in East Germany were published by museums.[22]

After 1989, most East German scholars in the humanities and social sciences, including ethnologists, lost their jobs. At Humboldt University in Berlin, the academic unit combining Völkerkunde and Volkskunde under the heading of Ethnographie was dissolved and replaced with a new Institut für Europäische Ethnologie, with West Germans in leading positions (Noack and Krause 2005: 25–26). In Leipzig, by 1993, the Lehr- und Forschungsbereich Ethnographie was reorganized as the Institut für Ethnologie, also under West German leadership. In comparison with the university departments, however, the ethnological museums in Leipzig and Dresden displayed greater continuity in personnel in the first decade of German unification (van der Heyden 2005: 318–19).

A SURVEY OF CONTEMPORARY INSTITUTIONS

Following German unification in 1990, German ethnology experienced a new phase of growth. Most notable was the founding in Halle of the Max-Planck-Institut für ethnologische Forschung in 1999 and the Seminar für Ethnologie of the Martin Luther University in 2002.[23] Halle has remained the exception, however, as most other examples of recent growth have taken the form of single professorships or small research foci within joint departments or super-departmental programmes (Haller 2012: 317–18). Further jobs for ethnologists, or sociocultural anthropologists, have been created in interdisciplinary research centres, such as the Max-Planck-Institut für evolutionäre Anthropology, founded in Leipzig in 1998, and the Max-Planck-Institut zur Erforschung multireligiöser und multiethnischer Gesellschaften, founded in Göttingen in 2007.[24]

At this writing, ethnology is represented at twenty-nine universities in the German language area – twenty-three in Germany, five in Switzerland and one in Austria. About two thirds of these twenty-nine universities have fully-fledged *Institute* or *Seminare* (departments) of ethnology or sociocultural anthropology; but in other cases ethnology is combined with related disciplines in a joint department, in an interdisciplinary programme, or in a larger *Fakultät* – that is, an academic subdivision within a university.[25] The assignation of chairs or departments of ethnology to a particular Fakultät – for example, history, geography, philosophy or social science – varies from one university to the next.[26]

Small departments have only one full professor and large departments only a handful (Bollig 2013: 166–68). However, each department head attempts to gather an assortment of staff members to help him or her achieve departmental goals: professorial assistants with six-year contracts, junior staff with annual or per semester employment arrangements, *Privatdozenten*, staff members with third-party funding, professors emeriti, (unpaid) honorary professors and (minimally paid) by-the-course lecturers (Dracklé 2003: 61–63; Gingrich 2007: 25; Bollig 2013: 168–70).[27]

As was the case during the early history of the discipline, ethnological museums are still numerous in the German language area today. Of the forty-five German, Austrian and Swiss museums listed on the website of the Deutsche Gesellschaft für Völkerkunde, over half are independent museums of ethnology. While only a few are university museums or collections, many others have cooperative relations with local university departments, where museum staff members often serve as honorary professors or lecturers. Nevertheless, ethnologists in the German language area frequently express their concern about the gulf between university departments and museums (see Münzel 2003). The need to re-establish close connections between them is a recurring motif in the newsletter of the Deutsche Gesellschaft für Völkerkunde (e.g. Schlee 2005; Kohl and Hahn 2010).

The largest centres for ethnology in the German language area consist in clusters of institutions, including, for example, large to medium-sized university departments, museums and independent research institutes (Gingrich 2007: 25). Vienna has not only a large university department (the Institut für Kultur- und Sozialanthropologie as Schmidt's original creation is now called) but also the Weltmuseum Wien (formerly, the Museum für Völkerkunde) and a second Institut für Sozialanthropologie in the *Österreichische Akademie der Wissenschaften* (Austrian Academy of Sciences). Berlin has at least three bases for ethnology, including Bastian's Ethnologisches Museum and, at the Free University, the Institut für Ethnologie and the Lateinamerika-Institut. Some would also add the Humboldt University's Institut für Europäische Ethnologie to the list. The Max-Planck-Institut für ethnologische Forschung in Halle has three departments, each with its own director, heads of research groups, senior and junior scholars and doctoral candidates – in all, over 100 members of the scientific staff. Since the Max-Planck-Institut has a number of Ph.D. candidates but cannot grant degrees, it works closely with the university-based Seminar für Ethnologie in Halle. In Zurich, a large Ethnologisches Seminar, founded in 1971, is supplemented by the university-based Völkerkundemuseum (1889); and the city has two further museums based on private collections. Recently, however, the Institut für Sozialanthropologie in Bern, founded with the name Ethnologisches Seminar in 1966, has grown to rival Zurich as the largest university department in Switzerland.

Today, the central professional associations in the German language area include the Anthropologische Gesellschaft in Wien, or Anthropological Society of Vienna (founded in 1870), the Deutsche Gesellschaft für Völkerkunde (founded in 1929) and the Schweizerische Ethnologische Gesellschaft, or Swiss Ethnological Society (founded in 1971). These three national-level organizations hold separate biennial meetings or, occasionally, meet jointly.[28]

Leading German-language journals, which increasingly feature contributions written in English (and sometimes in French), include the *Zeitschrift für Ethnologie* (founded in 1869), the *Mitteilungen der Anthropologischen Gesellschaft in Wien* (founded in 1870), *Anthropos* (founded in 1906), *Sociologus* (founded in 1925, given its present name in 1932, shut down in 1933 and re-established in 1951), *Paideuma* (founded in 1938) and *Ethnologica Helvetica*, now called *Tsantsa* (founded in 1971 and renamed in 1997). In addition, many museums have their own journals.[29] Increasingly, however, German-speaking ethnologists want or feel compelled to publish in reputable English-language journals.

THE CHARACTER AND SITUATION OF ETHNOLOGY
IN THE GERMAN LANGUAGE AREA TODAY

The growth of the discipline of ethnology in the German language area began in the post-war years and has extended to the present. Over this same period of time, however, ethnologists have occupied a peripheral position, nationally and internationally; and, hence, they are plagued by dilemmas that are common in peripheral regions and institutions. These dilemmas concern, especially, the relationship of German-speaking ethnologists (1) to older national traditions and current international trends, (2) to their sister discipline, Volkskunde, (3) to their own language and (4) to their own traditions of higher education. In closing, we address each of these problematic relationships in turn.

German-Speaking Ethnologists between National Traditions and International Trends

When, during a meeting in 1995, Dieter Haller asked Clifford Geertz if he knew of any contemporary German ethnologists, the only name that occurred to Geertz was that of Wilhelm Schmidt – who had died in 1954 (Haller 2012: 14). This anecdote illustrates a state of affairs with which German-speaking ethnologists are all too familiar: the neglect of their contributions by their colleagues abroad. Some have observed that this international neglect is compounded when German-speaking ethnologists underestimate the significance of each other's work and overestimate that of British, French and American counterparts (Kohl 1997; Hauser-Schäublin 2001).

The perception that their discipline has lost its international standing is shared widely among German-speaking ethnologists, but there is no consensus regarding the causes of or the remedies for this condition. Some argue that international neglect is largely a function of the political isolation of Germany following the two World Wars, which resulted in the abandonment of German as an international language of scholarship and the devaluation of things German. Ideas and approaches that were characteristic of early twentieth-century German and Austrian ethnology, some suggest, are rejected in their original form but embraced when they are reformulated with only slight alterations by American scholars (Münzel 1989: 48; Schlee 1990, 2010; Hauschild 1995: 42; Kohl 1997, 2010: 16; Streck 2009: 269; Haller 2012: 325, 341).

Other German-speaking ethnologists attribute the post-war plight of their discipline not only to external circumstances but also to the peculiarities of the theories, methods and institutions of the early twentieth century, which were revived after 1945. Fritz Kramer (1995: 88, 102) has argued that German-language ethnology deviated fatally from 'international developments', beginning with Herder, whom he sees as a proponent of the 'counter-enlightenment' in Isaiah Berlin's (1979) sense. The tradition founded by Herder and leading eventually to Frobenius got its just deserts, in Kramer's view, when he and his age-mates let if fall unceremoniously at the end of the 1960s. Gingrich (2005: 92–93) and Martin Rössler (2007: 15) are no less severe in their judgement, but, in pinpointing the divergence of German-language ethnology from 'international developments', they focus less on Herderian roots than on early twentieth-century cultural history, especially the Kulturkreislehre.

Gingrich and Rössler do not provide detailed justification for their rejection of the Kulturkreislehre and related forms of cultural history. Like others writing before him, Rössler (2007: 15) merely suggests that the peculiarities of these approaches may be explained with reference to Germany's loss of its colonies during the First World War, to the corresponding absence of a fieldwork tradition and to the continuing dominance of ethnological museums as bases of comparative studies aimed at the reconstruction of protocultures (see also Westphal-Hellbusch 1959: 849–50, 859). To be convincing, however, critical assessments of the Kulturkreislehre would have to be supported by analysis of significant methodological differences among various approaches to cultural history. Such differences become evident in Max Weber's (1903, 1905, 1906, 1975) critique of the economic historian Wilhelm Roscher and the cultural historian Karl Lamprecht, who are known to have influenced Ratzel (Smith 1991: 188; Chickering 1993: 294). Further indications of methodological differences among those who value cultural history may be gleaned from the critiques that Boas (1911, 1933) and Robert Lowie (1937: 157–60, 177–95) direct at the work of Graebner, Schmidt and others.

Despite the wide variation in attitudes among contemporary German-speaking ethnologists towards their predecessors, Gingrich (2007: 15) claims with some justification that there was a 'gradual "fading out" of any specifically "national" tradition of socio-cultural anthropology in German during the 1980s and 1990s'. Most ethnologists in Germany, Austria and Switzerland, he continues, now 'represent one or the other German-speaking sub-branch of global anthropology' (Gingrich 2007: 15; see also Bierschenk, Krings and Lentz 2013). Simultaneously, however, this same author evaluates positively some continuities linking contemporary German-speaking ethnologists with the past; namely, the emphasis on historical approaches, on area studies and on corresponding language-learning (Gingrich 2005: 151).[30] Haller (2012: 328–30) places even greater emphasis on continuities with the past, citing influences of *Kulturgeschichte* and *Kulturmorphologie* even among some of their contemporary critics.

In Germany, the internationalization of research, in ethnology as in other fields, has been promoted by the DFG and the Max-Planck-Gesellschaft, the society that is responsible for founding and monitoring the many Max Planck Institutes, each with its own disciplinary focus. Not least, however, internationalization has come about at the initiative of German-speaking ethnologists themselves, particularly through the agency of scholars who have studied and taught abroad, who cooperate actively with colleagues in other countries, and for whom older forms of Völkerkunde are either irrelevant or no longer of central concern (Bierschenk, Krings and Lentz 2013: 11). At the biennial meeting of the Deutsche Gesellschaft für Völkerkunde in 1995, there was, a colleague told me, considerable resistance, particularly from some older ethnologists, to the founding of a section for the study of 'Migration, Multiculturalism and Identity' (personal communication, September 2007; cf. Haller 2012: 178, 332). Just over fifteen years later, however, these or related topics are featured prominently in the profiles of many university departments. Nevertheless, there is still a pronounced tendency among German-speaking ethnologists to define their subject as the science of 'otherness' (e.g. Kohl 2000) and to seek 'others' mainly among non-European peoples of the 'Global South' (Haller 2012: 178, 331–34; Bierschenk, Krings and Lentz 2013: 10, 20; Bollig 2013: 175–87).

Ethnologie and Volkskunde

The discipline of *Volkskunde* was institutionalized at about the same time as its sister-science, *Ethnologie*, but with an orientation towards national ethnography, 'folk' literary genres and the material culture of the lower classes (Weber-Kellermann, Bimmer and Becker 2003). Since then – with the notable exception of developments in the GDR – *Volkskunde* and *Ethnologie* have led more or less separate existences. There is, however, evidence of significant theoretical and methodological parallels between the two disciplines in the early twentieth century – parallels that have not yet been explored sufficiently.[31]

In the decades following the Second World War, scholars in the field of *Volkskunde* began to examine critically their predecessors' ideological biases and their involvement in the Third Reich – a process that led to the reorganization, the redefinition and even the renaming of the field (Dow and Lixfeld 1986; Gerndt 1987; Jacobeit, Lixfeld and Bockhorn 1994; Lixfeld 1994; Brednich 2001; Zimmermann 2005; Kaschuba 2006; Welz 2013). Names currently in use by various university departments include *Volkskunde*, *Empirische Kulturwissenschaft*, *Europäische Ethnologie* and *Kulturanthropologie*. Today, this discipline is represented at twenty-six German universities (with individual chairs or full departments), four

Austrian universities and two Swiss universities. Museums for *Volkskunde* are legion.[32]

In addition to displaying some historical similarities of theory and method, *Volkskunde* and *Ethnologie* are converging, insofar as both are assimilating to the standards of Anglo-American, Western European, or international sociocultural anthropology and cultural studies. Nevertheless, attempts at dialog – usually promoted by the few Europeanists among German-speaking ethnologists – have produced negligible results (Nixdorff and Hauschild 1982; Kirsch 2006, 2007), due, apparently, to the disciplines' separate institutional histories, to differences in their regional orientation, to lingering mutual prejudices and to fears that closer ties or fusion might lead university administrators, or the state governments to which they are beholden, to reduce personnel and save money by funding one department rather than two (Gingrich 2007: 20; Bollig 2013: 167–68).

German-Speaking Ethnologists and the German Language

In 2011, the population of the German language area – including about 81 million Germans, 8 million Austrians and 5 million German-speaking Swiss (not to mention the much smaller language communities in Liechtenstein and Luxembourg) – amounted to a total of about 94 million. These millions, taken together with the many German speakers in neighbouring countries or scattered around the globe, obviously represent a strong basis for the perpetuation of the German language. Nevertheless, German-speaking ethnologists, like their colleagues in smaller countries, are under pressure to conform to English as the international language of science (Bierschenk, Krings and Lentz 2013: 27).

In Germany, Austria and the German-speaking parts of Switzerland, the language of education and of university instruction is German; but, the further students advance in the study of the various sciences, the greater the tendency to make way for English as a second language or as the dominant language. This is true for university lectures and seminars, sometimes for doctoral dissertations, for scholarly journals, for the publishing strategies of individual scholars and even for professional meetings.

A colleague reported that 'there have been discussions about English as the language of the biennial meetings of the Deutsche Gesellschaft für Völkerkunde for as long as I can remember – at least since I first started attending in the early 1980s ... As I recall, during the meeting in Heidelberg in 1999, all of the plenary sessions were held in English. If I am not mistaken, that created some controversy' (personal communication, 7 April 2011).

Among German-speaking ethnologists, attitudes towards publishing in German range between two extremes, with, presumably, the majority falling somewhere in between: (1) publishing in German is provincial and isolating and will doom ethnology in the German language area to irrelevance; and (2) German-speaking ethnologists submit too willingly to the hegemony of the English language; they should (also) publish in German.[33]

Responses to the Reform of Higher Education in Europe

In 1999, representatives of twenty-nine European ministries of higher education met in Bologna, Italy, where they agreed to far-reaching reforms aimed at standardizing degree programmes, ensuring uniformity of university qualifications, making 'credits' transferable across international boundaries and facilitating the mobility of students and university graduates within Europe. In 1999 in Austria, 2001 in Switzerland and 2003 in Germany, the Bologna Accords were adopted officially, and, thereafter, institutions of higher learning in the German language area began to shift from older degree programmes to the new Bachelor of Arts and Master of Arts degrees. This has required the wholesale reorganization of university departments, affecting departmental structure and budgeting, the curriculum, requirements for students majoring or minoring in the field, and teaching, testing and grading.

Among ethnologists (as among faculty members of other departments), there are at least three reasons for criticism of and resistance to the 'Bologna catastrophe', as Haller (2012: 40) calls it: first, opposition to the stated goals of Bologna reforms; second, dismay that the implemented reforms and innovations have not (yet) achieved the stated goals; and, third, the suspicion that policymakers and university administrators are using the Bologna Process to push through economically or ideologically motivated restructuring, especially at the expense of small departments.

Many academics in the German language area have opposed or expressed grave reservations concerning the Bologna Process, because it represents, in their eyes, a violation of the principles of higher education that were conceived in the context of Wilhelm von Humboldt's plans for the reform of Prussian universities – which subsequently achieved the status of a national ideal (Dracklé 2003, 2005; Haller 2012: 40, 313–14). For these critics, the standardization of the curriculum and of the requirements for majors, which entails the regular repetition of introductory, intermediary and advanced courses, means a loss of the storied *Freiheit der Lehre* – the freedom of professors to teach as they see fit, in conjunction with their own research. With the pejorative term *Verschulung*, German-speaking critics of Bologna reforms refer to the 'watering down' of university study until it resembles school instruction, from which, in the Humboldtian tradition, it should be distinguished clearly. New auditing technologies, designed to measure performance quantitatively, increase administrative and teaching responsibilities; while new demands for the timely achievement of career milestones make intensive study and long-term fieldwork difficult (Haller 2012: 313–15).

A second ground for criticism of the Bologna Process is its apparent failure to achieve its stated goals. In personal communication (9 August 2007), a German colleague described it as 'an inexact copy of a supposedly Anglo-American model', which does not have the desired effect. Forms have been standardized, but not contents. Three-year Bachelor of Arts programmes do not qualify students for anything but further study. Transferring credits among universities in different countries remains difficult, which, in turn, restricts the mobility of students. And so on.

Finally, university ethnologists, especially in Germany, express their concern that the reforms accompanying the Bologna Process affect not only the curriculum but also the structure of university departments, particularly the type and number of positions (Dracklé 2005; Haller 2012: 313). What is more, some view the new limits on the maximum number of years that junior faculty members can teach at a university without achieving promotion to a professorship as a form of age discrimination that impedes career development, while threatening to deprive departments of needed personnel. 'There are many who see the current university reform as a strategy for cutting costs, which is only disguised as a reform and linked, regrettably, to the Bologna Process' (Dracklé 2005: 97–98).

The current crisis of the universities – and especially of relatively small departments such as ethnology – is situated within the larger economic crisis, which began in 2008 and threatens to linger for many years to come. The strength of the discipline of ethnology in the German language area, which was built up during the second half of the twentieth century and the first decade of the current century, may be sufficient, however, to ensure the discipline's survival in coming decades.

John R. Eidson is a Senior Research Fellow in the Department of 'Integration and Conflict' at the Max Planck Institute for Social Anthropology in Halle an der Saale, Germany. He received his BA in anthropology from Duke University in 1976 and his Ph.D. in social anthropology from Cornell University in 1983. His research interests include social theory, the history of anthropology and the social anthropological and social historical study of Germany. He is the editor of *Das anthropologische Projekt: Perspektiven aus der Forschungsland-schaft Halle/Leipzig* (Leipziger Universitätsverlag, 2008) and author, most recently, with Günther Schlee and others, of 'From Identification to Framing and Alignment: A New Approach to the Comparative Analysis of Collective Identities', in *Current Anthropology*, vol. 58, no. 3, June 2017.

NOTES

Thanks to Astrid Bochow, Aleksandar Bošković, Katja Geisenhainer, Joachim Görlich, Chris Hann, Krisztina Kehl, Thomas Kirsch, Jacqueline Knörr, Stephen P. Reyna, Mihály Sárkány, Günther Schlee, Bertram Turner, Han Vermeulen, Larissa Vetters, Uwe Wolfradt and the editors of this volume for providing information, making helpful suggestions, or commenting critically on earlier drafts of this chapter. The author retains full responsibility for any inadequacies.

1. The term Kulturanthropologie has been used by philosophers, such as Erich Rothacker (1942), to denote a field of study that is related to philosophical anthropology and to the philosophy of culture. Sozialanthropologie was coined in the late nineteenth century to designate an approach in biological anthropology that today's commentators describe as racist and social Darwinist (Proctor 1988: 143–44; Massin 1996: 132–34).

2. On the role of learned societies in the development of archaeology and historical scholarship, see Boockmann et al. 1972. With reference to the *Heimatmuseum* (a type of local museum devoted to the history of the home town), Karl Ditt (1997) shows how the artifacts collected by amateur and semi-professional researchers eventually became museum collections. All evidence suggests that ethnological museums developed similarly.

3. Ethnological museums were founded in Munich (1868), Leipzig (1869), Berlin (1873), Dresden (1875), Hamburg (1879), Stuttgart (1884), Zurich (1889), Freiburg (1895), Bremen (1896), Cologne (1901), Frankfurt am Main (1904), Basel (1917) and Vienna (1928) (Penny 2002, 2008 and Laukötter 2007). In most cases, the dates in parentheses refer to the founding of an independent ethnological museum. Often, however, earlier dates could be given for the founding of an ethnographic department within a larger museum – a department that later became the basis for an independent museum of ethnology. For example, the ethnographic collection in Vienna, based in large part on purchased materials that had been gathered during the voyages of James Cook, began in 1806 as part of the Kaiserliches Hofnaturalienkabinet, then, in 1876, became part of the Naturhistorisches Museum, before, in 1928, becoming the basis for the independent Museum für Völkerkunde. Most recently, this institution has been renamed the Weltmuseum Wien (www.weltmuseumwien.at, last accessed on 21 March 2017). In the museum in Dresden, ethnology was combined with zoology and anthropology until 1946 (Icke-Schwalbe 2010; www.voelkerkunde-dresden.de/index.php?id=50, last accessed on 18 December 2012).

4. Of course, Bastian had many predecessors deserving of recognition (see Lowie 1937; Mühlmann 1968; Petermann 2004; Vermeulen 1995, 2006, 2015; Geisenhainer 2009, 2014); nevertheless, his leading role as an institution-builder and trainer of the first generation of professional ethnologists lends some justification for beginning with him in a brief survey of this type.

5. To allow for proper identification, we leave the names of German, Austrian and Swiss institutions in German. Some names are translated in the text or in the endnotes, but those that contain recognizable cognates of words in English or in Romance languages are sometimes left untranslated.

6. All quotations from German texts or interview transcripts have been translated by the author.

7. On Bastian's eccentric writing style, see von den Steinen (1905), Lowie (1937: 32–35) and Mühlmann (1968: 88). Recently, though not necessarily very plausibly, Andrew Zimmerman (2007: 45) has attempted to rehabilitate Bastian's admittedly 'nearly unreadable' prose by describing it as a literary experiment that was intended to 'capture the non-narrative, non-interpretive, natural-scientific approach to German ethnology'.

8. While Bastian emphasized geographical and historical determinants, he was not entirely free of the widespread racial determinism of his day, as is evident in Bastian 1868.

9. Like Bastian, Ratzel had many predecessors who influenced his ethnological orientation within the field of geography (see Penny 2008 and Geisenhainer 2014). He is singled out here because, again like Bastian, he helped to train the first generation of professional ethnologists.

10. Some commentators suggest that the prominence of museums may have contributed to the development of particular research methods and theoretical orientations in the German language area (Westphal-Hellbusch 1959: 859–60; Rössler 2007: 15). Since, however, museums were also dominant in other national traditions of ethnological research, at least until the mid twentieth century (see Stocking 1992: 127 and Parkin 2005: 168–69, 195, 199–200), evaluation of the validity of this suggestion would require detailed comparative study, which, however, is still lacking.

11. Identifying the 'first' is always problematic. Here, the reference is to the first full professorship – that is, *ordentliche Professur* in each field, which is taken to indicate a definitive stage in the process of institutionalization. There were earlier incidences of the *außerordentliche Professur* – approximately equivalent to the American associate professor: Emil Schmidt became the first *außerordentlicher Professor für Anthropologie und Ethnologie* in Leipzig in 1889 (Geisenhainer 2002: 141).

12. Weule began work at Leipzig's ethnological museum in 1899 and became director in 1907. By 1901 he had become außerordentlicher (roughly, associate) professor at the local university, where, in 1914, he became director of the first university department of ethnology in the German language area (Reche 1929; Streck 1997: 55; Geisenhainer 2002: 141–47).

13. Literal translations of the name of this organization are given in the text. Currently, however, the official translation of Deutsche Gesellschaft für Völkerkunde is German Anthropological Association.

14. Kulturkreis is often translated as 'culture circle'; but the word *Kreis* is used commonly to denote not only the geometric form 'circle' but also a bounded territorial unit such as a 'county'. Hence my preference for translating Kreis as 'province' in this case, for which there is also a precedent in the relevant literature (e.g. Leser 1977/1978: 110–11). In an impassioned defence of Graebner, Leser (1963, 1977, 1977/1978) insists that there was no commonly shared definition of Kulturkreis and that Graebner himself was not a proponent of the Kulturkreislehre. Clearly, there were important differences between Graebner and others – Schmidt, for example – but such differences remain submerged in our very general introduction to the topic.

15. For critical discussions of the Kulturkreislehre from a contemporaneous American – or German-American – perspective, see Boas (1911) and Lowie (1937: 157–60, 177–95). For a recent reference to differences among various forms of cultural history in early twentieth-century ethnology, see Kan (2009: 336).

16. As Leser (1963) demonstrates, the word Kulturkreis had an interesting prehistory before becoming established in ethnological discourse; however, its technical ethnological usage was determined largely by Ratzel, Frobenius, Ankermann and Graebner. On Bastian's use of the same term or similar terms, see Fiedermutz-Laun (1970) and Wolfradt (2011: 23).

17. Other scholars, who, like Baumann, pursued a form of cultural history derived largely from Graebner and Ankermann were Walter Krickeberg (Berlin) and Hans Plischke (Göttingen); see Gingrich (2005: 116).

18. See www.germananthropology.com/short-portrait/herbert-baldus and www.germananthropology.com/short portrait/paul-kirchhoff, last accessed on 11 November 2013.

19. The 1980s also saw the emergence of *Entwicklungsethnologie* in Germany, which may be translated as development ethnology or the ethnology of development (Schlee 2008: 198–200). Within the DGV, a section for development ethnology was founded in 1985 (and officially recognized in 1989), and the corresponding periodical, called simply *Entwicklungsethnologie*, has appeared since 1992. Although promoted by recognized scholars, development ethnology remains a relatively underdeveloped subfield in the German-speaking lands. Some ethnologists have found permanent employment with national development agencies, but most involvement comes in the form of contract work, especially among Africanists. For overviews and general discussions, see Bliss (1988), Bierschenk and Elwert (1993), Prochnow (1996), Schönhuth (1998) and Schönhuth and Bliss (2004). Compare Rottenburg (2009). For an attempt to trace links between the colonial ethnology of the early twentieth century and the development ethnology of the late twentieth century, see König (1984).

20. See also Haller's website at www.germananthropology.com, which features video interviews with post-war and contemporary German-speaking ethnologists and 'short portraits' of German-speaking contributors to ethnology since Herder.

21. By the mid 1950s, East German centres for ethnological research included the Institut für Völkerkunde und deutsche Volkskunde of Humboldt University in Berlin; the Kommission für Vor- und Frühgeschichte and the Institut für Volkskunde of the Akademie der Wissenschaften in Berlin; the Institut für Ethnologie – later renamed several times, finally becoming the Lehr- und Forschungsbereich für Ethnographie – of the Karl Marx University in Leipzig; the Museum für Völkerkunde in Leipzig; and the Staatliches Museum für Völkerkunde in Dresden (Johansen 1983: 313).

22. The three East German ethnological journals were the *Abhandlungen und Berichte des Staatlichen Museums für Völkerkunde Dresden*, founded in 1952; the *Ethnographisch-Archäologische Zeitschrift*, founded in 1953 and given this name in 1960; and the *Jahrbuch des Museums für Völkerkunde Leipzig*, founded in 1962 (Johansen 1983: 304).

23. The English names of these institutions are, respectively, the Max Planck Institute for Social Anthropology and the Institute of Social and Cultural Anthropology.

24. The names of these institutes in English are, respectively, the Max Planck Institute for Evolutionary Anthropology and the Max Planck Institute for the Study of Religious and Ethnic Diversity.

25. These rough statistics are based on data drawn from observation, from personal communication and from the website of the Deutsche Gesellschaft für Völkerkunde (www.dgv-net.de, last accessed on 21 March 2017), which provides links to individual

departments and professorial chairs. For further information on professorships and departments of ethnology or sociocultural anthropology in Germany, see Bierschenk, Krings and Lentz (2013) and Bollig (2013). For the German language area as a whole, Krickau (1999) is still worth reading.

26. This scattering of chairs and departments of ethnology among different *Fakultäten* clearly has not contributed to the unity of the discipline and has, perhaps, fostered what some have called its 'eccentricity' (Vossen 1969). But the actual effects of this institutional division have not yet been investigated adequately.

27. A Privatdozent, in the German academic system, is a scholar who, having written and successfully defended the postdoctoral dissertation, or Habilitation, is qualified to become a professor and has been granted certain academic rights by the corresponding Fakultät of a particular university (to hold lectures, administer examinations and supervise doctoral candidates) but who has not yet been appointed to a professorship. In Germany, since 2002, the position of *Juniorprofessor* provides outstanding young scholars with an opportunity to follow an alternative path to full professorship – that is, one that does not necessarily require the traditional Habilitation. Unlike the *Assistent*, a Juniorprofessor or Juniorprofessorin is not appointed by a professor to whose chair he or she is then attached; rather, the position is filled by a search committee.

28. The Österreichische Ethnologische Gesellschaft, which published the *Wiener Völkerkundliche Mitteilungen* from 1953 to 1995, participated in joint biennial meetings with the Deutsche Gesellschaft für Völkerkunde and the Anthropologische Gesellschaft in Wien before dissolving in 1995.

29. Museum-based journals include the *Baessler Archiv* (founded 1910) of the Ethnologisches Museum in Berlin, the *Archiv für Völkerkunde* (founded 1946) of the Museum für Völkerkunde in Vienna, and *Tribus* (n.s. since 1951/1953), published by the Linden-Museum, the Staatliches Museum für Völkerkunde in Stuttgart.

30. Some university departments not only have strong regional foci but also advertise the fact in their names; for example, the Institut für Ethnologie und Afrika-Studien in Mainz and the Institut für Ethnologie und Afrikanistik in Munich, both of which may be translated as Department of Ethnology and African Studies.

31. For example, in the early twentieth century, Volkskunde was often linked with territorial history and dialectology in the context of projects dedicated to the mapping of cultural provinces on the basis of the distribution of traits (e.g. Aubin, Frings and Müller 1926; Ebert et al. 1936; see Oberkrome 1993 and Schmoll 2009). While focused within the German language area, this historical-geographical research, which was in turn linked to various atlas projects, was conceptually related to the Kulturkreislehre insofar as it was supposed to determine prehistoric and historic boundaries between different cultures (German and French in the west, German and Slavic in the east), to trace the development of historical landscapes under persisting conditions of German 'particularism', or to distinguish stages in a progression (or degeneration) from traditional community to modern society.

32. See the website of the Deutsche Gesellschaft für Volkskunde – www.d-g-v.org (last accessed on 29 May 2012).

33. An amusing example of 'resistance' to the 'domination' of English may be found in the following English-language abstract of a German-language article published in the *Zeitschrift für Ethnologie*: 'Abstract: The contribution discusses the limits and the limitrophe [*sic*] zone between art, literature, and scientific literature in ethnology.

The "literary turn" has layed [*sic*] open but more clear [*sic*] that German ethnology and especially ethnological reviews put more value on five lines [*sic*] summaries in pidgin English for nonexisting English readers of five lines [*sic*] summaries than on good texts in any language' (Münzel 1997: 33).

REFERENCES

Adam, L. 1955. 'In Memoriam: Richard Thurnwald', *Oceania* 25(3): 145–55.

Ankermann, B. 1905. 'Kulturkreise und Kulturschichten in Afrika', *Zeitschrift für Ethnologie* 37: 54–84.

Aubin, H., T. Frings and J. Müller. 1926. *Kulturströmungen und Kulturprovinzen in den Rheinlanden: Geschichte, Sprache, Volkskunde.* Bonn: Ludwig Röhrscheid Verlag.

Baldus, H. 1968. 'Adolf Bastian', in D.L. Sills (ed.), *International Encyclopedia of the Social Sciences*, vol. 1. New York: The Free Press, pp. 23–24.

Bastian, A. 1860. *Der Mensch in der Geschichte: Zur Begründung einer psychologischen Weltanschauung*, three vols. Leipzig: Otto Wigand.

———. 1868. *Das Beständige in den Menschenrassen und die Spielweite ihrer Veränderlichkeit: Prolegomena zu einer Ethnologie der Culturvölker.* Berlin: Dietrich Reimer Verlag.

Baumann, H. 1934. 'Die afrikanischen Kulturkreise', *Africa: Journal of the International Institute of African Languages and Cultures* 7(2): 129–39.

———. 1940. 'Völker und Kulturen Afrikas', in H. Baumann, R. Thurnwald and D. Westermann (eds), *Völkerkunde von Afrika: Mit besonderer Berücksichtigung der kolonialen Aufgabe.* Essen: Essener Verlagsanstalt, pp. 1–371.

Berg, E. 1984. 'Die Nachwirkungen des Bildes vom "Homme naturel" auf den ethnologischen Kulturbegriff: Überlegungen zu Herders Kulturanthropologie', in E.W. Müller et al. (eds), *Ethnologie als Sozialwissenschaft, Kölner Zeitschrift für Soziologie und Sozialpsychologie*, Special issue 26. Opladen: Westdeutscher Verlag, pp. 85–100.

———. 1990. 'Johann Gottfried Herder (1744–1803)', in W. Marschall (ed.), *Klassiker der Kulturanthropologie von Montaigne bis Margaret Mead.* Munich: Verlag C.H. Beck, pp. 51–68.

Berlin, I. 1979. *Against the Current: Essays in the History of Ideas.* London: Hogarth Press.

Bierschenk, T. and G. Elwert (eds). 1993. *Entwicklungshilfe und ihre Folgen: Ergebnisse empirischer Untersuchungen in Afrika.* Frankfurt am Main: Campus Verlag.

Bierschenk, T., M. Krings and C. Lentz. 2013. 'Was ist ethno an der deutschsprachigen Ethnologie der Gegenwart?', in T. Bierschenk, M. Krings and C. Lentz (eds), *Ethnologie im 21. Jahrhundert.* Berlin: Dietrich Reimer Verlag, pp. 7–34.

Bliss, F. 1988. 'The Cultural Dimension in West German Development Policy and the Contribution of Ethnology', *Current Anthropology* 29(1): 101–21.

Boas, F. 1904. 'The History of Anthropology', *Science* 20(512): 513–24.

———. 1911. 'Review of Graebner, "Methode der Ethnologie"', *Science* 34: 804–10. Reprinted in Boas, F. 1940. *Race, Language and Culture.* New York: The Free Press, pp. 295–304.

————. 1933. 'Review of G. W. Locher, "The Serpent in Kwakiutl Religion: A Study in Primitive Culture"', *Deutsche Literaturzeitung*, pp. 1182–86. Reprinted in Boas, F. 1940. *Race, Language and Culture*. New York: The Free Press, pp. 446–50.

————. 1940. *Race, Language and Culture*. New York: The Free Press.

Bollig, M. 2013. 'Ethnologie in Deutschland heute: Strukturen, Studienbedingungen, Forschungsschwerpunkte', in T. Bierschenk, M. Krings and C. Lentz (eds), *Ethnologie im 21. Jahrhundert*. Berlin: Dietrich Reimer Verlag, pp. 165–88.

Boockmann, H., A. Esch, H. Heimpel, T. Nipperdey and H. Schmidt. 1972. *Geschichtswissenschaft und Vereinswesen im 19. Jahrhundert*. Göttingen: Vandenhoeck & Ruprecht.

Brandewie, E. 1990. *When Giants Walked the Earth: The Life and Times of Wilhelm Schmidt, SVD*. Fribourg: Fribourg University Press.

Braukämper, U. 1979. 'Ethnology in West Germany Today', *Royal Anthropological Institute News* 33: 6–8.

Braun, J. 1995. *Eine deutsche Karriere: Die Biographie des Ethnologen Hermann Baumann (1902–1972)*. Munich: Akademischer Verlag.

Brednich, R.W. 2001. *Grundriß der Volkskunde: Einführung in die Forschungsfelder der Europäischen Ethnologie*, 3rd ed. Berlin: Dietrich Reimer Verlag.

Broce, G.L. 1986. 'Herder and Ethnography', *Journal of the History of the Behavioral Sciences* 22(2): 150–70.

Buchheit, K.P. and K.P. Koepping. 2001. 'Adolf Philipp Wilhelm Bastian', in C.F. Feest and K.-H. Kohl (eds), *Hauptwerke der Ethnologie*. Stuttgart: Kröner, pp. 19–25.

Bunzl, M. 1996. 'Franz Boas and the Humboldtian Tradition: From *Volksgeist* und *Nationalcharakter* to an Anthropological Concept of Culture', in G.W. Stocking Jr. (ed.), *Volksgeist as Method and Ethic: Essays on Boasian Ethnography and the German Anthropological Tradition*. Madison, WI: University of Wisconsin Press, pp. 17–78.

Chickering, R. 1993. *Karl Lamprecht: A German Academic Life (1856–1915)*. Atlantic Heights, NJ: Humanities Press.

Conrad, S. 2012. *German Colonialism: A Short History*, trans. S. O'Hagan. Cambridge: Cambridge University Press.

Conte, É. 1987. 'Wilhelm Schmidt: Des letzten Kaisers Beichtvater und das "neudeutsche Heidentum"', in H. Gerndt (ed.), *Volkskunde und Nationalsozialismus, Münchner Beiträge zur Volkskunde* 7. Munich: Münchner Vereinigung für Volkskunde, pp. 261–78.

Ditt, K. 1997. 'Die westfälische Heimatbewegung 1871–1945: Eine kulturelle Bewegung zwischen Zivilisationskritik und politischer Instrumentalisierung', in K. Weigand (ed.), *Heimat: Konstanten und Wandel im 19./20. Jahrhundert*. Munich: Deutscher Alpenverein, pp. 263–84.

Dostal, W. 1994. 'Silence in the Darkness: German Ethnology during the National Socialist Period', *Social Anthropology* 2(3): 251–62.

Dostal, W. and A. Gingrich. 1996. 'German and Austrian Anthropology', in A. Barnard and J. Spencer (eds), *Encyclopedia of Social and Cultural Anthropology*. London: Routledge, pp. 263–65.

Dow, J.R. and H. Lixfeld (ed. and trans.). 1986. *German Volkskunde: A Decade of Theoretical Confrontation, Debate, and Reorientation (1967–1977)*. Bloomington, IN: Indiana University Press.

Dracklé, D. 2003. 'Farewell to Humboldt? Teaching and Learning Anthropology in Germany', in D. Dracklé, I.R. Edgar and T.K. Schippers (eds), *Educational Histories of European Social Anthropology: Learning Fields, Vol. 1.* New York, Oxford: Berghahn Books, pp. 56–68.

———. 2005. 'Der Bologna Prozess als Herausforderung für die deutsche Ethnologie', *Mitteilungen der Deutschen Gesellschaft für Völkerkunde* 34 (April): 97–98.

Ebert, W., T. Frings, K. Gleißner, R. Kötzschke and G. Streitberg. 1936. *Kulturräume und Kulturströmungen im mitteldeutschen Osten*, two vols. Halle: Max Niemeyer Verlag.

Eidson, J. 2000. 'Anthropologie', in B. Streck (ed.), *Wörterbuch der Ethnologie*, 2nd ed. Wuppertal: Edition Trickster/Peter Hammer Verlag, pp. 27–32.

———. 2008. 'Einleitung in das anthropologische Projekt', in J. Eidson (ed.), *Das anthropologische Projekt: Perspektiven aus der Forschungslandschaft Halle/Leipzig.* Leipzig: Leipziger Universitätsverlag, pp. 10–35.

Fiedermutz-Laun, A. 1970. *Der Kulturhistorische Gedanke bei Adolf Bastian.* Wiesbaden: Franz Steiner Verlag.

———. 1986. 'Adolf Bastian und die Begründung der deutschen Ethnologie im 19. Jahrhundert', *Berichte zur Wissenschaftsgeschichte* 9: 167–81.

Fillitz, T. 2003. 'From the Dictate of Theories to Discourses on Theories: Teaching and Learning Social Anthropology in Vienna', in D. Dracklé, I.R. Edgar and T.K. Schippers (eds), *Educational Histories of European Social Anthropology: Learning Fields, Vol. 1.* New York, Oxford: Berghahn Books. pp. 102–12.

Fischer, H. 1970. '"Völkerkunde", "Ethnographie", "Ethnologie": Kritische Kontrolle der frühesten Belege', *Zeitschrift für Ethnologie* 95(2): 169–82.

———. 1983. 'Anfänge, Abgrenzungen, Anwendungen', in H. Fischer (ed.), *Ethnologie: Eine Einführung.* Berlin: Dietrich Reimer Verlag, pp. 11–46.

———. 1990. *Völkerkunde im Nationalsozialismus: Aspekte der Anpassung, Affinität und Behauptung einer wissenschaftlichen Disziplin.* Berlin: Dietrich Reimer Verlag.

Fischer, M., P. Bolz and S. Kamel (eds). 2007. *Adolf Bastian and His Universal Archive of Humanity: The Origins of German Anthropology.* Hildesheim: Georg Olms Verlag.

Frobenius, L. 1897. 'Der westafrikanische Kulturkreis', *Petermanns Geographische Mitteilungen* 43: 225–36, 262–67.

———. 1898. *Ursprung der afrikanischen Kulturen.* Berlin: Gebrüder Borntraeger.

———. 1921. *Paideuma: Umrisse einer Kultur- und Seelenlehre.* Munich: Beck.

Geisenhainer, K. 2002. '*Rasse ist Schicksal': Otto Reche (1879–1966) – ein Leben als Anthropologe und Völkerkundler.* Leipzig: Evangelische Verlagsanstalt.

———. 2009. 'Ethnologie', in U. von Hehl, U. John and M. Rudersdorf (eds), *Geschichte der Universität Leipzig 1409–2009*, vol. 4 (1). Leipzig: Leipziger Universitätsverlag, pp. 367–92.

———. 2011. 'Anthropologie und Ethnologie in Leipzig Ende der 1920er Jahre: Die erste Tagung der Gesellschaft für Völkerkunde und die Expeditionen des Staatlich-Sächsischen Forschungsinstituts für Völkerkunde', *Paideuma* 57: 53–80.

———. 2014. 'Nachwort', in K. Geisenhainer, L. Bohrmann and B. Streck (eds), *100 Jahre Institut für Ethnologie der Universität Leipzig: Eine Anthologie seiner Vertreter.* Leipzig: Leipziger Universitätsverlag, pp. 295–321.

Gerndt, H. (ed.). 1987. *Volkskunde und Nationalsozialismus, Münchner Beiträge zur Volkskunde* 7. Munich: Münchner Vereinigung für Volkskunde.

Gilbert, G.G. 1981. 'French and German: A Comparative Study', in C.A. Ferguson and S.B. Heath (eds), *Language in the USA.* Cambridge: Cambridge University Press, pp. 257–72.

Gingrich, A. 2005. 'The German-Speaking Countries: Ruptures, Schools, and Nontraditions: Reassessing the History of Sociocultural Anthropology in Germany', in F. Barth, A. Gingrich, R. Parkin and S. Silverman, *One Discipline, Four Ways: British, German, French, and American Anthropology – The Halle Lectures*, with a forward by C. Hann. Chicago, IL: University of Chicago Press, pp. 59–153.

———. 2007. 'Changing Contents in Shifting Contexts: An Essay on the Status of Socio-cultural Anthropology in the German-speaking Countries', *Anthropological Yearbook of European Cultures* 16: 13–28.

Gothsch, M. 1983. *Die deutsche Völkerkunde und ihr Verhältnis zum Kolonialismus: Ein Beitrag zur kolonialideologischen und kolonialpraktischen Bedeutung der deutschen Völkerkunde in der Zeit von 1870–1975*. Baden-Baden: Nomos.

Graebner, F. 1905. 'Kulturkreise und Kulturschichten in Ozeanien', *Zeitschrift für Ethnologie* 37: 28–53.

———. 1911. *Methode der Ethnologie*. Heidelberg: Carl Winters Universitätsbuchhandlung.

Guhr, G. 1969. 'Ur- und Frühgeschichte und ökonomische Gesellschaftsformationen: ein Beitrag zum Karl-Marx-Jahr 1968', *Ethnographisch-Archäologische Zeitschrift* 10: 167–212.

Haekel, J. 1956. 'Zum heutigen Forschungsstand der historischen Ethnologie', in J. Haekel, A. Hohenwart-Gerlachstein and A. Slawik (eds), *Die Wiener Schule der Völkerkunde. Festschrift anlässlich des 25jährigen Bestandes des Institutes für Völkerkunde der Universität Wien (1929–1954)*. Horn, Vienna: Verlag Ferdinand Berger, pp. 17–90.

———. 1959. 'Trends and Intellectual Interests in Current Austrian Ethnology', *American Anthropologist* 61(5): 865–74.

Haller, D. 2012. *Die Suche nach dem Fremden: Geschichte der Ethnologie in der Bundesrepublik 1945–1990*. Frankfurt am Main: Campus Verlag.

Hastings, M. 2010. 'The Turkish-German Jihad: Review of *The Berlin-Baghdad Express: The Ottoman Empire and Germany's Bid for World Power* by S. McMeekin', *New York Review of Books*, Vol. LVII, No. 19 (Dec. 9–22), pp. 42–44.

Hauschild, T. 1987. 'Völkerkunde im Dritten Reich', in H. Gerndt (ed.), *Volkskunde und Nationalsozialismus, Münchner Beiträge zur Volkskunde* 7. Munich: Münchner Vereinigung für Volkskunde, pp. 245–59.

———. 1995. '"Dem lebendigen Geist": Warum die Geschichte der Völkerkunde im "Dritten Reich" auch für Nichtethnologen von Interesse sein kann', in T. Hauschild (ed.), *Lebenslust und Fremdenfurcht: Ethnologie im Dritten Reich*. Frankfurt am Main: Suhrkamp, pp. 13–61.

Hauschild, T. (ed.). 1995a. *Lebenslust und Fremdenfurcht: Ethnologie im Dritten Reich*. Frankfurt am Main: Suhrkamp.

Hauser-Schäublin, B. 2001. 'Wer sind die deutschen Ethnologinnen?' *Mitteilungen der Deutschen Gesellschaft für Völkerkunde* 32 (Sommer): 1.

Heine-Geldern, R. 1964. 'One Hundred Years of Ethnological Theory in the German-Speaking Countries: Some Milestones', *Current Anthropology* 5(5): 407–18.

Herrmann, J. and J. Köhn (eds). 1988. *Familie, Staat und Gesellschaftsformation/Family, State and the Formation of Society: Basic Problems of Pre-Capitalist Epochs a Hundred Years after Frederick Engels' Work 'The Origin of the Family, Private Property and the State'*. Berlin: Akademie-Verlag.

Herzog, R. 1965. 'Anthropologie und Völkerkunde in ihren sich wandelnden Beziehungen',
in H. Baitsch and H. Ritter (eds), *Bericht über die 8. Tagung der Deutschen Gesellschaft
für Anthropologie in Köln, 12. bis 14. September 1963.* Supplement to *Homo: Zeitschrift
für die vergleichende Forschung am Menschen.* Göttingen: Musterschmidt-Verlag, pp.
186–92.

Hinz, E. 1969. 'Kommentar zu: Vossen, Rüdiger (1969): Ethnologie – wie lange noch
eine Wissenschaft von Privatgelehrten?' *Sociologus* 19(1): 9–12.

Icke-Schwalbe, L. 2010. 'Das Museum für Völkerkunde in Dresden in der
Museumslandschaft Sachsens nach 1945', in I. Kreide-Damani (ed.), *Ethnologie im
Nationalsozialismus: Julius Lips und die Geschichte der "Völkerkunde".* Wiesbaden:
Reichert Verlag, pp. 399–422.

Jacobeit, W., H. Lixfeld and O. Bockhorn (eds). 1994. *Völkische Wissenschaft: Gestalten
und Tendenzen der deutschen und österreichischen Volkskunde in der ersten Hälfte des
20. Jahrhunderts,* in cooperation with J.R. Dow. Vienna, Cologne, Weimer: Böhlau
Verlag.

Johansen, U. 1983. 'Die Ethnologie in der DDR', in H. Fischer (ed.), *Ethnologie: Eine
Einführung.* Berlin: Dietrich Reimer Verlag, pp. 303–18.

———. 1992. 'Materielle oder materialisierte Kultur?', *Zeitschrift für Ethnologie* 117:
1–15.

Kan, S. 2009. *Lev Shternberg: Anthropologist, Russian Socialist, Jewish Activist.* Lincoln,
NE: University of Nebraska Press.

Kaschuba, W. 2006. *Einführung in die Europäische Ethnologie,* 3rd ed. Munich: Verlag
C.H. Beck.

Kirsch, T. 2007. 'Forum zum Verhältnis von Völkerkunde und Volkskunde', *Mitteilungen
der Deutschen Gesellschaft für Völkerkunde* 37 (Feb.): 6–7.

Kirsch, T. (ed.). 2006. 'Völkerkunde/Ethnologie und Volkskunde/Europäische
Ethnologie – Ein spannungsreiches Verhältnis?' With contributions by T. Hauschild,
D. Dracklé, K. Braun and W. Kaschuba, *Mitteilungen der Deutschen Gesellschaft für
Völkerkunde* 36 (Mai): 3–13.

Kluckhohn, C. 1936. 'Some Reflections on the Method and Theory of the Kulturkreislehre',
American Anthropologist 38(2): 157–96.

König, R. 1984. 'Richard Thurnwalds Beitrag zur Theorie der Entwicklung', in E.W.
Müller et al. (eds), *Ethnologie als Sozialwissenschaft, Kölner Zeitschrift für Soziologie
und Sozialpsychologie,* Special issue 26. Opladen: Westdeutscher Verlag, pp. 364–78.

Koepping, K.-P. 1983. *Adolf Bastian and the Psychic Unity of Mankind: The Foundations
of Anthropology in Nineteenth Century Germany.* St. Lucia: University of Queensland
Press.

Kohl, K.-H. 1997. 'Homöophobie und Allophilie als Dilemma der deutschsprachigen
Völkerkunde', *Zeitschrift für Ethnologie* 12: 101–10.

———. 2000. *Ethnologie – Die Wissenschaft vom kulturell Fremden: Eine Einführung,* 2nd
ed. Munich: Verlag C.H. Beck.

———. 2010. 'The Legacy of Frobenius in Germany', in R. Kuban and M. Hambolu
(eds), *Nigeria 100 Years Ago – Through the Eyes of Leo Frobenius and His Expedition
Team.* Frankfurt am Main: Frobenius Institut, pp. 9–16.

Kohl, K.-H. and H.P. Hahn. 2010. 'Vorwort', *Mitteilungen der Deutschen Gesellschaft für
Völkerkunde* 41 (July): 1–2.

Kramer, F. 1995. 'Einfühlung: Überlegungen zur Geschichte der Ethnologie im präfaschistischen Deutschland', in T. Hauschild (ed.), *Lebenslust und Fremdenfurcht: Ethnologie im Dritten Reich*. Frankfurt am Main: Suhrkamp, pp. 85–102.

Kreide-Damani, I. (ed.). 2010. *Ethnologie im Nationalsozialismus: Julius Lips und die Geschichte der Völkerkunde*. Wiesbaden: Reichert Verlag.

Krickau, O. (ed.). 1999. *Ethnologie im deutschsprachigen Raum: Vol. 1 Personenverzeichnis; vol. 2 Studienführer*. Göttingen: Arbeitskreis für Internationale Wissenschaftskommunikation.

Kroeber, A.L. 1917. 'The Superorganic', *American Anthropologist* 19: 163–213.

———. 1935. 'History and Science in Anthropology', *American Anthropologist* 37: 539–69.

Laukötter, A. 2007. *Von der 'Kultur' zur 'Rasse' – vom Objekt zum Körper? Völkerkundemuseen und ihre Wissenschaften zu Beginn des 20. Jahrhunderts*. Bielefeld: transcript Verlag.

———. 2007a. 'The Time after Adolf Bastian: Felix von Luschan and Berlin's Royal Museum of Ethnology', in M. Fischer, P. Bolz and S. Kamel (eds), *Adolf Bastian and His Universal Archive of Humanity: The Origins of German Anthropology*. Hildesheim: Georg Olms Verlag, pp. 153–65.

Leser, P. 1963. 'Zur Geschichte des Wortes Kulturkreis', *Anthropos* 58(1/2): 1–36.

———. 1977. 'Fritz Graebner – eine Würdigung: Zum 100. Geburtstag am 4. März 1977', *Anthropos* 72(1/2): 1–55.

———. 1977/1978. 'On the Role of Fritz Graebner in the Development of Historical Ethnology', *Ethnologia Europaea* 10(2): 107–13.

Linimayr, P. 1994. *Wiener Völkerkunde im Nationalsozialismus: Ansätze zu einer NS-Wissenschaft*. Frankfurt am Main: Peter Lang.

Lixfeld, H. 1994. *Folklore and Fascism: The Reich Institute for German Volkskunde*, J.R. Dow, ed. and trans. Bloomington, IN: Indiana University Press.

Lowie, R.H. 1937. *The History of Ethnological Theory*. New York: Rinehart & Co.

Lutz, G. 1969. 'Volkskunde und Ethnologie', *Zeitschrift für Volkskunde* 65: 65–80.

Malinowski, B. 1922. *Argonauts of the Western Pacific: An Account of Native Enterprise and Adventure in the Archipelagoes of Melanesian New Guinea*. London: George Routledge & Sons.

Marchand, S. 1997. 'Leo Frobenius and the Revolt against the West', *Journal of Contemporary History* 32(2): 153–70.

———. 2003. 'Priests among the Pygmies: Wilhelm Schmidt and the Counter-Reformation in Austrian Ethnology', in H.G. Penny and M. Bunzl (eds), *Worldly Provincialism: German Anthropology in the Age of Empire*. Ann Arbor, MI: University of Michigan Press, pp. 283–316.

Marquard, O. 1971. 'Anthropologie', in J. Ritter (ed. in chief), *Historisches Wörterbuch der Philosophie*, vol. 1. Darmstadt: Wissenschaftliche Buchgesellschaft, columns 362–74.

Massin, B. 1996. 'From Virchow to Fischer: Physical Anthropology and "Modern Race Theories" in Wilhelmine Germany', in G.W. Stocking Jr., *Volksgeist as Method and Ethic: Essays on Boasian Ethnography and the German Anthropological Tradition*. Madison, WI: University of Wisconsin Press, pp. 79–154.

Massola, A. 1961. 'In Memoriam: Leonhard Adam', *Oceania* 31(3): 161–65.

Mauss, M. 1950 [1925]. 'Essai sur le don: Forme et raison de l'échange dans les sociétés archaïques', in M. Mauss, *Sociologie et anthropologie*. Paris: Presses Universitaires de France, pp. 143–279.

McMeekin, S. 2010. *The Berlin-Baghdad Express: The Ottoman Empire and Germany's Bid for World Power*. Cambridge, MA: Harvard University Press.

Melk-Koch, M. 1989. *Auf der Suche nach der menschlichen Gesellschaft: Richard Thurnwald*. Berlin: Dietrich Reimer Verlag.

———. 1995. 'Zwei Österreicher nehmen Einfluß auf die Ethnologie in Deutschland: Felix von Luschan und Richard Thurnwald', in B. Rupp-Eisenreich and J. Stagl (eds), *Kulturwissenschaft im Vielvölkerstaat: Zur Geschichte der Ethnologie und verwandter Gebiete in Österreich, ca. 1780 bis 1918*. Vienna, Cologne, Weimer: Böhlau Verlag, pp. 132–40.

Métraux, A. 1948. 'Anthropology in Germany', *American Anthropologist* 50(4): 716–23.

Michel, U. 1992. 'Wilhelm Emil Mühlmann (1904–1988) – ein deutscher Professor. Amnesie und Amnestie: Zum Verhältnis von Ethnologie und Politik im Nationalsozialismus', in C. Klingemann, M. Neumann, K.-S. Rehberg, I. Srubar and E. Stölting (eds), *Jahrbuch für Soziologiegeschichte 1991*. Opladen: Leske & Budrich, pp. 69–118.

———. 1995. 'Neue ethnologische Forschungsansätze im Nationalsozialismus? Aus der Biographie von Wilhelm Emil Mühlmann (1904–1988)', in T. Hauschild (ed.), *Lebenslust und Fremdenfurcht: Ethnologie im Dritten Reich*. Frankfurt am Main: Suhrkamp, pp. 141–67.

Mosen, M. 1991. *Der koloniale Traum: Angewandte Ethnologie im Nationalsozialismus*. Bonn: Holos Verlag.

Mühlmann, W.E. 1968. *Geschichte der Anthropologie*, 2nd ed. Frankfurt am Main: Athenäum Verlag.

Müller, K.E. 1993. 'Grundzüge des ethnologischen Holismus', in W. Schmied-Kowarzik and J. Stagl (eds), *Grundfragen der Ethnologie: Beiträge zur gegenwärtigen Theoriediskussion*, 2nd ed. Berlin: Dietrich Reimer Verlag, pp. 197–232.

Münzel, M. 1989. 'Über den Tellerrand schauen: Ein Gespräch mit Mark Münzel', *Trickster* 17: 46–57.

———. 1997. 'Ethnologie und Inszenierung (zu den Grenzen unserer Kunst)', *Zeitschrift für Ethnologie* 122: 33–43.

———. 2003. 'Die ethnologische "Museumsdebatte"', in D. Kramer, M. Münzel, E. Raabe, A. Sibeth and M. Suhrbier (eds), *Missio, Message und Museum: Festschrift für Josef Franz Thiel zum 70. Geburtstag*. Frankfurt am Main: Verlag Otto Lembeck, pp. 35–44.

Nixdorff, H. and T. Hauschild (eds). 1982. *Europäische Ethnologie: Theorie- und Methodendiskussion aus ethnologischer und volkskundlicher Sicht*. Berlin: Dietrich Reimer Verlag.

Noack, K. and M. Krause. 2005. 'Ethnographie as a Unified Anthropological Science in the German Democratic Republic', in C. Hann, M. Sárkány and P. Skalník (eds), *Studying Peoples in the People's Democracies: Socialist Era Anthropology in East-Central Europe*. Münster: LIT Verlag, pp. 25–53.

Oberkrome, W. 1993. *Volksgeschichte: Methodologische Innovation und völkische Ideologisierung in der deutschen Geschichtswissenschaft 1918–1945*. Göttingen: Vandenhoeck & Ruprecht.

Parkin, R. 2005. 'The French-Speaking Countries', in F. Barth, A. Gingrich, R. Parkin and S. Silverman, *One Discipline, Four Ways: British, German, French, and American Anthropology – The Halle Lectures*, with a forward by C. Hann. Chicago, IL: University of Chicago Press, pp. 155–253.

Penny, H.G. 2002. *Objects of Culture: Ethnology and Ethnographic Museums in Imperial Germany*. Chapel Hill, NC: University of North Carolina Press.

———. 2008. 'Traditions in the German Language', in H. Kuklick (ed.), *A New History of Anthropology*. Oxford: Blackwell Publishing, pp. 79–95.

Petermann, W. 2004. *Die Geschichte der Ethnologie*. Wuppertal: Edition Trickster im Peter Hammer Verlag.

Prochnow, M. 1996. *Entwicklungsethnologie: Ansätze und Probleme einer Verknüpfung von Ethnologie und Entwicklungshilfe*. Hamburg: LIT Verlag.

Proctor, R. 1988. 'From Anthropologie to Rassenkunde in the German Anthropological Tradition', in G.W. Stocking Jr. (ed.), *Bones, Bodies, Behavior: Essays on Biological Anthropology*. Madison, WI: University of Wisconsin Press, pp. 138–79.

Ratzel, F. 1882–1891. *Anthropo-Geographie*, three vols. Stuttgart: J. Engelhorn.

———. 1885–1888. *Völkerkunde*, three vols. Leipzig: Verlag des Bibliographischen Instituts.

Reche, O. 1929. 'Karl Weule', in O. Reche (ed.), *In Memoriam Karl Weule: Beiträge zur Völkerkunde und Vorgeschichte*. Leipzig: R. Voigtländer Verlag, pp. 1–12.

Riese, B. 1995. 'Während des Dritten Reiches (1933–1945) in Deutschland und Österreich verfolgte und von dort ausgewanderte Ethnologen', in T. Hauschild (ed.), *Lebenslust und Fremdenfurcht: Ethnologie im Dritten Reich*. Frankfurt am Main: Suhrkamp, pp. 210–20.

Rössler, M. 2007. *Die deutschsprachige Ethnologie bis ca. 1960: Ein historischer Abriss*. Kölner Arbeitspapiere zur Ethnologie, No. 1 (April).

Rothacker, E. 1942. 'Probleme der Kulturanthropologie', in N. Hartmann (ed.), *Systematische Philosophie*. Stuttgart: W. Kohlhammer, pp. 55–198.

Rottenburg, R. 2009. *Far-Fetched Facts: A Parable of Development Aid*, trans. A. Brown and T. Lampert. Cambridge, MA: The MIT Press.

Sachse, C. 2010. 'Kaiser-Wilhelm-Institut für Anthropologie, menschliche Erblehre und Eugenik', in P. Gruss, R. Rürup and S. Kiewitz (eds), *Denkorte. Max-Planck-Gesellschaft und Kaiser-Wilhelm-Gesellschaft: Brüche und Kontinuitäten 1911–2011*. Dresden: Sandstein Verlag, pp. 230–37.

Sárkány, M. 2002. 'Cultural and Social Anthropology in Central and Eastern Europe', in M. Kaase and V. Sparschuh (eds) and A. Wenninger (co-ed.), *Three Social Science Disciplines in Central and Eastern Europe: Handbook on Economics, Political Science, and Sociology (1989–2001)*. Berlin: GESIS, pp. 558–66.

Schafft, G.E. 2004. *From Racism to Genocide: Anthropology in the Third Reich*. Champaign, IL: University of Illinois Press.

Schlee, G. 1990. 'Das Fach Sozialanthropologie/Ethnologie seit dem Zweiten Weltkrieg', in W. Prinz and P. Weingart (eds), *Die sog. Geisteswissenschaften: Innenansichten*. Frankfurt am Main: Suhrkamp, pp. 306–12.

———. 2005. 'Die DGV und die Museen', *Mitteilungen der Deutschen Gesellschaft für Völkerkunde* 35 (October): 127–128.

———. 2008. 'Ethnologie und Politikberatung – Erfahrungen mit dem Somalia-Friedensprozess', in J. Eidson (ed.), *Das anthropologische Projekt: Perspektiven aus der Forschungslandschaft Halle/Leipzig.* Leipzig: Leipziger Universitätsverlag, pp. 198–216.

―――. 2010. 'Epilogue: How do Paradigm Shifts Work in Anthropology?', in O. Zenker and K. Kumoll (eds), *Beyond Writing Culture: Current Intersections of Epistemologies and Representational Practices.* Oxford, New York: Berghahn Publishers, pp. 211–27.

Schlesier, E. and M. Urban. 1994 [1987]. 'Die Völkerkunde an der Georgia Augusta – eine historische Skizze', in H.-G. Schlotter (ed.), *Die Geschichte der Verfassung und der Fachbereiche der Georg-August-Universität zu Göttingen.* Göttingen: Vandenhoeck & Ruprecht, pp. 127–29.

Schmidt, W. 1939. *The Culture Historical Method of Ethnology: The Scientific Approach to the Racial Question,* trans. S.A. Sieber, Preface by C. Kluckhohn. New York: Fortuny's.

Schmidt, W. and W. Koppers. 1924. *Der Mensch aller Zeiten, vol. III: Völker und Kulturen.* Regensburg: Josef Habbel Verlag.

Schmoll, F. 2009. *Die Vermessung der Kultur: Der Atlas der deutschen Volkskunde und die Deutsche Forschungsgemeinschaft 1928–1980.* Stuttgart: Franz Steiner Verlag.

Schönhuth, M. 1998. 'Entwicklungsethnologie: Ein Berufsfeld für deutsche Ethnologen?', in B. Lange, M. von Itter and T. Schrör (eds), *Kursbuch Ethnologie & Beruf: Erfahrungen, Berufswege und Informationen für Studierende der Ethnologie und der Kulturwissenschaften.* Marburg: Curupira, pp. 105–13.

Schönhuth, M. and F. Bliss (eds). 2004. 'Culture for Development – Cultures of Development: 20 Years of Development Anthropology in Germany', *Entwicklungsethnologie* 13(1–2). Special issue.

Sellnow, I. 1961. *Grundprinzipien einer Periodisierung der Urgeschichte.* Berlin: Akademie-Verlag.

Slezkine, Y. 1991. 'The Fall of Soviet Ethnography, 1928–38', *Current Anthropology* 32(4): 476–84.

Smith, W.D. 1991. *Politics and the Sciences of Culture in Germany 1840–1920.* Oxford: Oxford University Press.

Speitkamp, W. 2005. *Deutsche Kolonialgeschichte.* Stuttgart: Philipp Reclam jun.

Spöttel, M. 1995. *Die ungeliebte 'Zivilisation' – Zivilisationskritik und Ethnologie in Deutschland im 20. Jahrhundert.* Frankfurt am Main: Peter Lang.

Stagl, J. 1995. *A History of Curiosity: The Theory of Travel 1550–1800.* Chur, Switzerland and New York: Harwood Academic Publishers.

―――. 'Rationalism and Irrationalism in Early German Ethnology: The Controversy between Schlözer and Herder, 1772/73', *Anthropos* 93(4–6): 521–36.

Stichweh, R. 1996. 'Science in the System of World Society', *Social Science Information* 35(2): 327–40.

Stocking, G.W. Jr. 1992 [1976]. 'Ideas and Institutions in American Anthropology: Thoughts Toward a History of the Interwar Years', in G.W. Stocking, *The Ethnographer's Magic and Other Essays in the History of Anthropology.* Madison, WI: University of Wisconsin Press, pp. 114–77.

Straube, H. 1990. 'Leo Frobenius (1873–1938)', in W. Marschall (ed.), *Klassiker der Kulturanthropologie: Von Montaigne bis Margaret Mead.* Munich: Verlag C.H. Beck, pp. 151–70.

Streck, B. 1995. 'Entfremdete Gestalt: Die Konstruktion von Kultur in den zwei Frankfurter Denkschulen', in T. Hauschild (ed.), *Lebenslust und Fremdenfurcht: Ethnologie im Dritten Reich.* Frankfurt am Main: Suhrkamp, pp. 103–20.

————. 1997. *Fröhliche Wissenschaft Ethnologie: eine Führung*. Wuppertal: Edition Trickster im Peter Hammer Verlag.

————. 1999. 'Leo Frobenius oder die Begeisterung in der deutschen Völkerkunde', *Paideuma* 45: 31–43.

————. 2000. 'Einführung', in B. Streck (ed.), *Ethnologie und Nationalsozialismus*. Gehren: Escher Verlag, pp. 7–21.

————. 2009. 'Deutsche Völkerkunde: Sonderwege des 20. Jahrhunderts', *Zeitschrift für Ethnologie* 134: 267–79.

Streck, B. (ed.). 2000a. *Ethnologie und Nationalsozialismus*. Gehren: Escher Verlag.

Szilvássy, J., P. Spindler and H. Kritscher. 1980. 'Rudolf Pöch – Arzt, Anthropologe und Ethnograph', *Annalen des Naturhistorischen Museums in Wien* 83: 743–62.

Ther, P. 2004. 'Deutsche Geschichte als imperiale Geschichte: Polen, slawophone Minderheiten und das Kaiserreich als kontinentales Empire', in S. Conrad and J. Osterhammel (eds), *Das Kaiserreich transnational: Deutschland in der Welt 1871–1914*. Göttingen: Vandenhoeck & Ruprecht, pp. 129–48.

Thurnwald, R. 1931–1935. *Die menschliche Gesellschaft in ihren ethno-soziologischen Grundlagen*, 5 vols. Berlin & Leipzig: Walter de Gruyter & Co.

————. 1935. *Black and White in East Africa: The Fabric of a New Civilization. A Study in Social Contact and Adaptation of Life in East Africa*, with a chapter on women by H. Thurnwald. London: Routledge.

————. 1940. 'Die fremden Eingriffe in das Leben der Afrikaner und ihre Folgen', in H. Baumann, R. Thurnwald and D. Westermann, *Völkerkunde von Afrika: Mit besonderer Berücksichtigung der kolonialen Aufgabe*. Essen: Essener Verlagsanstalt, pp. 453–573.

Treide, D. 2005. 'Onward, but in which Direction? Anthropology at the University of Leipzig between 1950 and 1968', in C. Hann, M. Sárkány and P. Skalník (eds), *Studying Peoples in the People's Democracies: Socialist Era Anthropology in East-Central Europe*. Münster: LIT Verlag, pp. 133–58.

Turner, B. and H.-J. Paproth. 1989. 'Hundert Jahre Völkerkunde im deutschsprachigen Raum', in T. Theye (ed.), *Der geraubte Schatten: Die Photographie als ethnographisches Dokument: Eine Ausstellung des Münchner Stadtmuseums in Zusammenarbeit mit dem Haus der Kulturen der Welt*. Munich: Verlag C.J. Bucher GmbH, pp. 120–41.

Tylor, E.B. 1871. *Primitive Culture: Researches into the Development of Mythology, Philosophy, Religion, Art, and Custom*, 2 vols. London: John Murray.

Vajda, L. 1993. 'Kommentar', *Zeitschrift für Ethnologie* 118: 185–86.

van der Heyden, U. 2005. 'Africanist Anthropology in the German Democratic Republic', in C. Hann, M. Sárkány and P. Skalník (eds), *Studying Peoples in the People's Democracies: Socialist Era Anthropology in East-Central Europe*. Münster: LIT Verlag, pp. 303–30.

Vermeulen, H.F. 1995. 'Origins and Institutionalization of Ethnography and Ethnology in Europe and the USA, 1771–1845', in H.F. Vermeulen and A. Alvarez Roldán (eds), *Fieldwork and Footnotes: Studies in the History of European Anthropology*. London: Routledge, pp. 39–59.

————. 2006. 'The German Invention of Völkerkunde: Ethnological Discourse in Europe and Asia, 1740–1798', in S. Eigen and M.J. Larrimore (eds), *The German Invention of Race*. Albany, NY: State University of New York Press, pp. 123–45.

————. 2015. *Before Boas: The Genesis of Ethnography and Ethnology in the German Enlightenment*. Lincoln, NE: University of Nebraska Press.

84

JOHN R. EIDSON

von den Steinen, K. 1905. 'Gedächtnisrede auf Adolf Bastian', *Zeitschrift für Ethnologie* 37: 236–49.

Vossen, R. 1969. 'Ethnologie – wie lange noch eine Wissenschaft von Privatgelehrten?', *Sociologus* 19(1): 1–6, 17–19.

Waldis, B. 2003. 'Rethinking Local and Global: New Perspectives among Swiss Anthropologists', in D. Dracklé, I.R. Edgar and T.K. Schippers (eds), *Educational Histories of European Social Anthropology: Learning Fields, vol. 1*. New York, Oxford: Berghahn Books, pp. 139–54.

Weber, M. 1903, 1905, 1906. 'Roscher und Knies und die logischen Probleme der historischen Nationalökonomie', *Schmollers Jahrbuch* 27: 1181–221; 29: 1323–84; 30: 81–120. Reprinted in M. Weber. 1922. *Gesammelte Aufsätze zur Wissenschaftslehre*. Tübingen: J.C.B. Mohr, pp. 1–145.

———. 1975. *Roscher and Knies: The Logical Problems of Historical Economics*, trans. G. Oakes. New York: The Free Press.

Weber-Kellermann, I., A.C. Bimmer and S. Becker. 2003. *Einführung in die Volkskunde/ Europäische Ethnologie: Eine Wissenschaftsgeschichte*, 3rd ed. Stuttgart: J.B. Metzlersche Verlagsbuchhandlung.

Welz, G. 2013. 'Europa: ein Kontinent – zwei Ethnologien?', in T. Bierschenk, M. Krings and C. Lentz (eds), *Ethnologie im 21. Jahrhundert*. Berlin: Dietrich Reimer Verlag, pp. 211–27.

Westphal-Hellbusch, S. 1959. 'Trends in Anthropology: The Present Situation of Ethnological Research in Germany', *American Anthropologist* 61(5): 848–65.

Wolfradt, U. 2011. *Ethnologie und Psychologie: die Leipziger Schule der Völkerpsychologie*. Berlin: Dietrich Reimer Verlag.

Zantop, S. 1997. *Colonial Fantasies: Conquest, Family and Nation in Precolonial Germany 1770–1870*. Durham, NC: Duke University Press.

Zimmerman, A. 2001. *Anthropology and Antihumanism in Imperial Germany*. Chicago, IL: University of Chicago Press.

———. 2007. '"Diese unendlichen, sogenannten ethnologischen Bandwürmer Don Bombastians": An Appreciation of Bastian's Writing in Light of the History of Science in Imperial Germany', in M. Fischer, P. Bolz and S. Kamel (eds), *Adolf Bastian and His Universal Archive of Humanity: The Origins of German Anthropology*. Hildesheim: Georg Olms Verlag, pp. 45–49.

Zimmermann, H.-P. (ed.). 2005. *Empirische Kulturwissenschaft – Europäische Ethnologie – Kulturanthropologie – Volkskunde: Leitfaden für das Studium einer Kulturwissenschaft an deutschsprachigen Universitäten – Deutschland - Österreich – Schweiz*. Marburg: Jonas Verlag.

3

ANTHROPOLOGY IN RUSSIA

Tradition vs. Paradigm Shift

SERGEY SOKOLOVSKIY

R epetition and innovation could be seen as the key concepts providing an insight into the particularity of anthropology/ethnology in Russia. I suggest that through most of its history Russian anthropology has been evolutionist, comparative and historical; the changes included the 'Marxification' of evolutionism in the 1930s or the introduction of structuralism in 1960s and 1970s.

This chapter problematizes the practice of borrowing from other traditions. On the one hand, I consider that the discipline during most of the periods of its history looked for inspiration to the West, a gaze that could not but produce a somewhat secondary and thus less appealing nature of the Soviet anthropological knowledge. For instance, *etnografia* owes much to German *Völkerkunde* with its focus on 'ethnic culture' and its use of comparative linguistics. This is paralleled by seemingly little inspiration coming from Russian ethnologists/anthropologists to fellow practitioners elsewhere, if one excludes figures such as Propp or Vygotsky, who could not be considered ethnologists in a strict sense. On the other hand, I uncover the specific features of the discipline, such as the 'all-embracing naturalist gaze' and close cooperation with neighbouring disciplines, particularly visible in planning and implementation of teamwork during field expeditions. There were also concepts that were specific to the Russian and Soviet anthropology, notably 'ethnos' introduced by Bromley in the 1960s and long serving as a demarcation feature of the discipline.

Similarly, while the discipline emerged as a specific system for the transfer of knowledge serving the various interests (military, fiscal, administrative, ideological, etc.) of the central government and therefore changes were predominantly induced 'from the outside', and sometimes brought on by violent measures, the practitioners of ethnology/anthropology in Russia used various strategies to adapt to or to translate these imperatives in their daily work.

In this chapter I trace patterns of anthropology's knowledge exchange with neighbouring disciplines and the emergence of cross-disciplinary research fields and hybrid disciplines along with recent thematic changes in anthropological research, and briefly cover the current problems with anthropology teaching and its institutionalization as a university discipline in the post-Soviet period.

A BRIEF HISTORY OF THE DISCIPLINE

The history of the Russian tradition of anthropological research is practically as long and eventful as that of the major European (British, Dutch, French and German) and American traditions, although admittedly much less known.[1]

Russian anthropology takes its roots in folklore studies, on the one hand, and various applied ethnographic cum geographic research, motivated to a substantial degree by colonial expansion and military effort, on the other. In subsequent periods of the discipline's development, this heritage was supplemented by other components. Thus it became a widely shared opinion that the early anthropology of the mid nineteenth century had been inspired and moulded by the example of the natural sciences. One of the 'ancestors' of Russian anthropology, Dmitry Anuchin, who was trained in zoology, physical anthropology, archaeology and geography and who became known as an ardent proponent of the so-called 'anthropological triad' (physical anthropology, ethnology and archaeology), attempted to reconstruct the 'physical and psychological development of mankind from the most ancient periods of its existence ...' (Anuchin 1880: 59) and called for the integration of data from anatomy, physiology, embryology, geology, palaeontology, archaeology, zoology, history, linguistics, ethnography, geography, psychology and statistics. This holistic approach was derived from the field method used by naturalists to observe plants and animals, in which everything from soil to physical appearance and from the sounds emitted to the form of locomotion mattered. This method had not been a specific feature of the Anglo-American tradition (Stocking 1992: 22) but was typical of German and Russian naturalists, notably Karl Baer, the founder of Russian physical anthropology and archaeology.

The history of Russian anthropology, as probably of many other social sciences within those national traditions of social research that survived in the adverse conditions of centralized state control, shows a typical pattern of changes. From the early Soviet years right through to the perestroika of the late 1980s and early 1990s, changes were regularly induced 'from the outside', sometimes brought about by violent measures[2] on the authorities' behalf, followed by a slow recovery and varied adaptation strategies, from close cooperation with the state bureaucracy to scholastic escapism. The centralized character of Russian academic research and the small number of ethnographic institutions explain why the shifts in the discipline's focus and subject were regular and synchronized. These shifts, initiated by the Communist Party and perceived as 'crises' by the discipline's practitioners, could take the form of an attack or of a mere change of the central institute's head. This would set in motion a series of reformist moves that led to a thorough transformation of the discipline's focus every twenty to twenty-five years.

Hence, an external account of the discipline's history will better explain the current situation of Russian anthropology than any history written from an internal perspective. For instance, the contemporary conflict between conservative 'traditionalists' and reformist 'modernizers' is better explained in terms of external political events than of the internal dynamics of anthropological research and theorizing. The ideological pressure on and the political control of the social sciences during Soviet times were strong forces that moulded disciplines from the outside through political decisions.

Internal accounts tend to underscore achievements and stress the drawbacks and shortcomings in anthropological research. Through most of its history, Russian anthropology has been evolutionist, comparatist and historical. These mutually contradictory projects contributed to the discipline's internal dynamics, as well as to its laxity in terms of organizational and thematic grids. In the early 1930s, the Russian version of anthropological evolutionism was heavily 'Marxified'. The late 1960s and the 1970s complicated the picture by adding structuralism and, in the late 1990s and the 2000s, post-structuralism.

With its gaze turned towards the periphery of the empire and its hierarchy of central and regional institutions, Russian and its heir Soviet ethnography are to be seen mostly as a specific system for the transfer of knowledge serving the various interests (military, fiscal, administrative, ideological, etc.) of the central government. Neither peasants nor aliens were categories of people who resided in or frequented the capitals of the Russian empire. Both in the popular and learned imagination, they had always been relegated to the exotic *glubinka* (the country's interior) or to distant localities where an urban erudite trod but rarely. The applied character of Russian anthropology (etnografia of the eighteenth to twentieth century) had been pervasive in the periods of its institutionalization and maturing (roughly the nineteenth century) and resurfaces now and then in academic and governmental collaboration projects throughout the more recent history of Russian anthropology.

Intellectually, Russian anthropology (etnografia of the eighteenth to early twentieth century) owes much to German Völkerkunde with its focus on 'ethnic culture' and its use of comparative linguistics as an instrument for pinpointing intergroup differences and mapping them as a complex hierarchy of ethnolinguistic categories or *narodnosti* (folk or ethnic units). However, the intellectual links with the German kin discipline were all but severed by the turn of the twentieth century to be replaced by broader European and later North American influences, in which French, British and U.S. traditions of anthropological research were, if not exactly emulated and followed, then closely inspected and selectively borrowed.

A detailed externalist account of the discipline's history during the Soviet period must include several crucial political events. The first was the crisis of 1929 (for details see Slezkine 1991) when Nicolai Marr and his followers launched vehement attacks on ethnologists and contributed to the demise of comparativist research programmes and to the separate institutionalization of ethnographic and linguistic studies. Marr, a philologist and archaeologist specializing in Georgian and Armenian linguistics and archaeology, had become a full member of the Russian Academy of Sciences in 1912 at the age of forty-seven and remained the holder of several leading posts in academic institutions until his death in 1934 (for details and bibliography see Slezkine 1996; Alpatov 2004 [1988]). His exercises in 'iaphetology' produced a unique fusion of comparative semantic analysis with archaeological, folklore and historical data. Popular in the 1930s and 40s, this came under heavy attack during the summer months of 1950 (9 May–4 July) when a public discussion of Marr's 'new teaching on language' took place in the pages of the national newspaper *Pravda*. This was triggered by the publication of Stalin's work, *Marxism and the Problems of Linguistics* in June 1950, in which the 'new teaching on language' of Nikolai Marr had been scathingly criticized. This caused the following major shift in research focus. In October 1951, after long preparations, an academic conference of scholars from leading anthropological, linguistic and archaeological institutes was convened with the aim of bringing the tasks of the disciplines into agreement with party guidelines. The methods of ethnogenetic studies were substantially revised.

The all-Russian conference of ethnographers, which took place the same year, put special stress on the study of the family and contemporary culture of peasants and workers. Within the next five years, a score of so-called 'collective farm monographs' had been published and more than twenty dissertations written (Tolstov 1956).

The next phase of Russian etnografia and substantive change in research subject matter came with Yulian Bromley, the director of the Institute of Ethnography, part of the Academy of Sciences of the USSR (now the Institute of Ethnology and Anthropology, Russian Academy of Sciences (IEA RAS)) from 1966 to 1989, who emphasized the definition of etnografia as the study of *etnos* (Bromley 1968).[3]

One should also bear in mind that up to the mid 1970s the main task of the Soviet social sciences, as understood both by the authorities and scholars, was the ideological support and legitimization of the regime and the critique of 'bourgeois ideology'. As repression by direct coercion and violence became unpopular after Stalin, the regime's dysfunctions had to be remedied by other means such as better information on social and political processes, the optimization of government by monitoring popular opinion and other

TABLE 3.1. The changes of focus and theoretical orientations in Soviet/Russian etnografia

Period	Main object of research	Main theoretical perspective
Up to the late 1920s	Traditional culture of tribal groups and Russian peasants	The history of 'prehistorical' or 'a-historical' social and ethnic groups
1929–1950	Class and class differentiation in various ethnic communities; ethnogenesis	The study of 'survivals' within the framework of social evolution and economic formation change; research on tribal 'primitive communism'
1950–mid 1960s	Contemporary culture of peasant and 'non-Russian' groups	Culture change and 'socialist progress'
1968–1988	Ethnos and ethnic culture	The classification and study of 'ethnic processes'; ethnogenetic studies
1988–present	Conflict and change, gender, identity politics, religion, contemporary cultural expressions	Contemporary cultural, social and political processes

methods of eliciting feedback from the population in order to exercise more effective control. All these needs required professional empirical research and better educated social researchers. However, dialogue across political borders was severely limited due to ideological constraints: only technical methods of information-collection and processing could be borrowed from the West; the theory and conceptual apparatus were treated with suspicion as conflicting with Marxist dogma. This policy substantially weakened new research opportunities and channelled research into politically safe but futile directions. One of those directions was Bromley's already mentioned theory of etnos, which put the potentially dangerous studies of 'nations' and 'nationalism' onto the track of more secure and abstract typological exercises on the forms of etnos in different historical epochs and economic formations, and the classification of ethnic processes of integration and differentiation (for details, Figure 3.1 in the Annex). The current focus on ethnic issues and identity politics is the legacy of the former preoccupations with ethnogenesis, ethnic history and ethnic processes research.

CULTURAL MEDIATION AND CONCEPTUAL DISCREPANCIES

Many observers of Russian anthropology have noticed its high degree of conceptual and terminological idiosyncrasy. Teodor Shanin observed that the term 'nationality', for instance,

> describes to the English and the French the passport one carries – that is, the relation of a person to a particular state. To a Russian speaker, the term *natsional'nost'* (the semantic closest equivalent) has nothing to do directly with a state. One's belonging to a state is denoted as citizenship (*grazhdanstvo*). Natsional'nost is a specific characteristic (together with age and the colour of one's eyes) at the top of the inventory for basic human characteristics, both in common speech and the identification papers everybody carries. It is not a matter of race; the *natsional'nost'* of an 'assimilated' Tatar like the Tsar Godunov was unquestionably Russian ... Nor is it a question of one's state or place of residence. ... Nor does 'ethnicity', as ordinarily used in English speech, catch the full meaning of the Russian term, for in English ethnicity denotes 'minorities', those who are considered as 'not yet assimilated', who thereby present 'a problem' to authorities, their neighbours or themselves. ... yet the *natsional'nost'* of the Russians in Russia is centrally important as a term of common speech, analytical discourse, and explicit political strategies. (Shanin 1989: 409)

It is worth noting that most of the time Russian etnografia (the Soviet name that roughly corresponded to sociocultural anthropology in the West) looked to the West for inspiration, which made it appear secondary and less appealing in Western eyes. Although some European and American scholars, notably Ernest Gellner (1980, 1988) in Britain, and Stephen P. Dunn and Ethel Dunn (1974) in the United States, tried to engage Soviet anthropologists in a dialogue, the results were not impressive. From the early eighteenth century to the present, Russian anthropologists have borrowed extensively from other national traditions and disciplines, adapting them according to the prevalent ideological and political demands. This cultural brokerage could be viewed as an independent, separate source, altering the face of many subfields of Russian anthropology at different periods of its existence. The theoretical transfer was, however, highly selective and determined by what was perceived as the main object of study in the field at the time.

Ernest Gellner in his preface to the publication of the proceedings of the Soviet and Western anthropologists conference cautioned Western readers against conceptual and terminological non-equivalences, reminding them that etnografia in Soviet scholarly discourse is 'the science as a whole, including its theoretical parts [... and] that "anthropology", without qualification, means physical anthropology in Soviet parlance' (1980: x). He warned as well that 'when a Soviet author prefixes the term "ethno" to another word as in "ethnogenesis" this generally means ... that ethnos is an *object* of inquiry' (1980: xi).

It is of considerable interest to ask why Russian anthropology's impact on other national traditions and its contribution to the theoretical and methodological heritage of anthropology has been so inconsequential. A straightforward and simple answer would be the existence of a language barrier and the ideological isolation during much of the twentieth century. But this answer is only partly acceptable, as Russian literature as well as literary criticism (i.e., works by Mikhail Bakhtin or Yuri Lotman) overcame the language barrier and made their way through the Iron Curtain. Does this mean that the 'belles-lettres' mimesis was more readily accepted in the West than the mimetic descriptions of social reality produced by the Soviet social sciences, comparatively more prone to ideological constraints? Or was it the geographical focus of Russian anthropological research, which reflected Russian colonial geography (as well as the weakness of moral reflection impeded by Leninist dogmas), that created insurmountable barriers for the anthropological community in the West? I am not sufficiently qualified to answer these questions, for I could only make guesses as to why the vast ethnographic literature of Soviet, and now more than two decades of post-Soviet, times is left largely unclaimed by the wider anthropological community. This is not to say that Western anthropological traditions were not influenced by different ideas and theories of Russian scholars in general. Besides the already mentioned impacts of literary criticism and semiotics, one could cite the influence of Russian formalism on the elaboration of the analytical approach of structuralism (Trubetskoy, Jakobson and Propp), the works of Vygotsky on psychological and cognitive anthropology and those of Chayanov on economic anthropology. However, all these scholars were not anthropologists in the strict sense of the term, although some of them (notably Vygotsky and Propp) had fieldwork experience and directly contributed to the development of anthropology in the country.

In a recently published survey of forty-five Russian anthropologists conducted by the editorial staff of the Russian anthropological periodical *Anthropologicheskii Forum*,[4] several participants mentioned mass borrowing of ideas and methodology from the West. In the words of Ekaterina Melnikova, 'The opening of floodgates between Western and Russian scholarship has led, as often happens in such cases, to the borrowing of terminology and sometimes ideas on a mass scale' (Melnikova 2005: 459). Another participant in the same survey, Evgeny Golovko, commenting on the research subjects and topics that were 'not considered a proper object of study' during Soviet times, made a similar observation that although such topics are currently the subject of much interesting work, 'one has to acknowledge that it consists of attempts (often very successful, indeed brilliant) to catch up with what was being done abroad much earlier' (Golovko 2005: 456).

In my opinion, the problem with current borrowing from the West is not that it is happening at an unprecedented rate and scale, but that it happens in the most haphazard, uncritical and disorderly fashion. Peter Skalník, an uncompromising critic of Soviet ethnography, once asked the question of whether 'Russian and other post-communist ethnographers ... want to become anthropologists and thereby achieve an intellectual revolution or continue hiding behind changed labels of ethnologists'. He went on to suggest that if 'the former is their goal, then they will have to translate, study, and digest the vast anthropological literature, which in turn will enable them to carry out a thorough and frank re-evaluation of the fairly large body of their own writing up till now' (Skalník 1998: 10).

Unlike Soviet translations that were carefully chosen and few, present-day translations into Russian, though more numerous, do not undergo the processes of systematic selection and rigorous editing. These translations are almost exclusively comprised of anthropological classics of the nineteenth and first half of the twentieth century – the works of Lewis H. Morgan, Edward B. Tylor, James G. Frazer, Lucien Levi-Brühl, Bronislaw K. Malinowski, Arnold Van Gennep, Marcel Mauss, M. Eliade, Edward E. Evans-Pritchard, Alfred R. Radcliffe-Brown, A. Kroeber, Clyde Kluckhorn, Paul Radin, George Murdock, Marshall Sahlins, Victor Turner, Roger Caillois, Edmund Leach, Margaret Mead, Ruth F. Benedict and Leslie White – that is, only a minor part of the world's anthropological heritage. The anthropological thought of the 1960s and 70s is represented by a few works from Claude Levi-Strauss, Clifford Geertz, Mary Douglas, Pierre Bourdieu and Maurice Godelier.

Concerning language, it is worth noting that the early stages of the discipline (eighteenth and nineteenth centuries) were multilingual, with publications of research results in Latin, German, French and Russian. During the late Soviet period, the bulk of domestic ethnographic research was published in Russian, a trend that continues today, although the number of publications in English is continuously growing; publications in French and German have become marginal.

The reception of new translations and theoretical innovations developed elsewhere suffers from ill-coordinated teaching and commenting. Lack of trained faculty in most peripheral universities and conservative reactions to innovations at the central universities of Moscow and St. Petersburg, combined with a lack of funding for the purchase of foreign books for university libraries, are additional causes of the poor quality of this reception. Large-scale borrowing from the West has contributed to the 'secondary nature' of Russian anthropology: many Western colleagues use Russian anthropological publications as raw data, not for theoretical inspiration.

RELATIONS WITH NEIGHBOURING DISCIPLINES

Let us recall that important changes, altering the research terrain in terms of disciplinary boundaries and alliances, were caused by external pressures, their subsequent suspension leading to new readjustments.

The all-embracing naturalist gaze survived in Russia till the end of the twentieth century and influenced the work of Vladimir Vernadsky, Nikolai Vavilov and Valery Alexeyev, a physical anthropologist, who on his premature death left over 600 scholarly publications in fields as diverse as palaeoanthropology, anthropogenetic and ethnogenetic studies, craniology, osteology, human palaeoecology, prehistory and medical geography. Specialists who worked on particular problem areas built networks of cooperation that cut across the boundaries of disciplines as different as social, biological, medical and 'hard' sciences. Yet, particular disciplines had their 'central' or 'typical' problem areas constituting the core of their disciplinary identity. Cooperation in the studies of these 'core' problem areas was usually between specialists from the narrower range of neighbouring disciplines and subfields.

In the case of Russian etnografia, for several generations of researchers the 'legitimate set' of such disciplines or fields had been the triad of physical anthropology, ethnology and archaeology. Even the first specialized Soviet anthropological research institution founded in 1933 as the Institute of

Anthropology and Ethnography, within a year, had been renamed the Institute of Anthropology, Ethnography and Archaeology. The word 'ethnography' in the title was a specifically Soviet terminological invention created during the early struggle with ethnology as 'bourgeois science' in the 1920s (for details see Slezkine 1991; Bertrand 2002). This happened at the conference of Moscow and Leningrad ethnographers in April 1929, which proclaimed non-Marxist ethnology 'a bourgeois surrogate for social sciences'. It signalled the end of the intellectual map of Russian anthropology formed by predominantly German and other European influences and initiated new preoccupations with the class struggle and class stratification in various ethnic groups (Soveshchanie 1929: 115–16). After another major attack from the Marxist reformers at the all-Russian conference on Archaeology and Ethnography in May 1932, the focus of ethnographic research subsequently moved, for several years, from the study of preliterate non-industrial and premodern groups to scholastic exegesis of the theory of the 'primitive communist formation', the genesis of classes and the family and the role of 'survivals' (Slezkine 1991: 481). The 'survivals' were identified not so much for purposes of reconstructing certain social institutions of the past, but more as impediments to progress that were to be abolished in the construction of socialist society.

Dogmatic interpretations of the Marxist approach to the study of social phenomena produced new themes that demanded new configurations of methods and different interdisciplinary alliances. 'Primitive peoples' history' in the view of the discipline's reformers was to be focused on the issues raised by Marxist classics, namely on the study of the origins of the family, classes, religions, arts and other 'superstructures', the ethnogenesis and geographical distribution of ethnic groups and such practical issues as the transformation of pre-capitalist societies into socialist ones and the construction of socialist culture (Rezoliutsia 1932: 12–14). From that period onwards, Russian anthropology became more and more isolated from creative dialogue with other national research traditions beyond the political borders of the country. Divorce with the classic anthropological heritage was selective and uneven in the various subfields composing the discipline, but the split initiated by the Bolshevik Cultural Revolution so thoroughly reconfigured and redrew disciplinary alliances and borders that its consequences have still not been overcome today. The 'iron curtain' policy and witch-hunting for dissidents aggravated intellectual isolation and contributed to the idiosyncratic institutionalization of the Soviet social sciences, quite different from their Western counterparts. The resultant semi-isolation from developments abroad and ideological censure inside the country produced a unique conceptual vocabulary, whose rendering into the vocabularies of other research traditions posed a considerable challenge.

Most of the main commentaries on the characteristic features of etnografia as a discipline, written by Soviet anthropologists in the pre-war period, stressed its proximity to history. At the major universities (both in Leningrad and Moscow), etnografia had been relocated from the Department of Geography to the Department of History. In 1945, Sergei Tolstov (director of the Institute of Ethnography from 1942 till 1966) wrote: 'Etnografia is a branch of history, which researches the cultural and customary distinctiveness of various peoples of the world in their historical development, which studies the problems of origin and cultural-historical relations between these peoples, and which uncovers the history of their settlements and movements' (Tolstov 1946).

The definition of the director of the central ethnological body of Soviet science was equivalent to a directive, and Soviet ethnographers busied themselves in studying the historical development of ethnic groups and cultures throughout the country's territory, often ignoring contemporary cultural phenomena. As a result, while Soviet ethnographers produced quite rich ethnohistorical accounts, works on contemporary sociocultural processes were rare until 1951. Tamara Dragadze remarked that 'a Soviet anthropologist is a historian, not a sociologist' (1987: 155). The pervasive historicism of Russian etnografia contributed to its peripheral status as a subsidiary discipline of history and has been a factor in its marginalization in the university education system.

The positioning of etnos as the central object of ethnographic research advocated by Yulian Bromley at the end of the 1960s led to the new strategy of defining boundaries with history, sociology and social anthropology and several other social sciences that were perceived as neighbouring. By positioning etnos (groups, categories, peoples as ethnic communities) and not cultures, societies or individuals as the main object of ethnographic research, Bromley put emphasis on the functions of these objects that served as demarcation features of the discipline. He designated such functions as intra-ethnic integration and inter-ethnic differentiation and grouped them under the generic heading of 'ethnic functions' (Bromley 1981: 84–85). He used 'ethnic functions' as differential markers for distinguishing the research focus of etnografia from that of cultural studies *(kulturologia)*, linguistics, history and psychology. According to his methodology, any component (a trait or feature) of a given etnos should be assessed through the lens of 'ethnic functions' (does it serve integration or differentiation purposes, is it characteristic of every constitutive part of a given etnos and is it distinctively unique to that etnos, etc.). If this component is unique to the etnos under consideration and quite common across its constitutive groups and communities, then it could be viewed as belonging to the core area of ethnographic research, for it is considered as serving 'ethnic functions'.

Hence Bromley's insistence that the core area for ethnographic research on culture was so-called 'traditional everyday culture' *(traditsionnaia bytovaia kultura)*; in the linguistic sphere, it was ordinary, commonplace language *(obikhodnyi yazyk)*; and in psychology, it was routine, common-sense notions *(obydennoe soznanie)* (Bromley 1981: 84). By setting traditional culture against its other domains ('high', modernized urban culture), Bromley drew the boundary between etnografia and kulturologia and, by focusing on habitual experience and thinking, he contrasted the 'ethnographic problematic' of ethno-psychology with mainstream psychology, which studied psychological phenomena as universal, generalized features of individuals. His differentiation between vernacular language and its literary form set the boundaries between ethnographic studies of ritual behaviour and folklore and mainstream academic linguistics and cultural critique endorsed by linguists, kulturologists and literary critics.

During all periods of Soviet and post-Soviet anthropology's history, alignment with academic linguistics has been optional and tentative. Although in the 1920s and 30s the stress on knowledge of native languages was quite strong, the lack of funds for long field research and anthropologists' frequent switches from one linguistic group to another (aggravated by the unusual richness of the linguistic composition of the country's population, divided into more than 150 different linguistic communities, even if we ignore dialects often incomprehensible to the speakers of other dialects of the same language, which could thus have been treated as separate languages) had contributed to the early disappearance of linguistics from ethnographers' curriculums. The usual way of specialization was language training 'on the side', at the linguistics department of the same university or privately (I do not mean here the foreign languages training, which has often been a factor in students' area specialization). Back in the 1930s, it had been usual for an anthropologist to learn the language of the group in the field, to work out an alphabet for an unwritten language, to describe its grammar and to write a textbook for a local aboriginal school. But already at the end of this period, field linguists had taken over this job from ethnographers, leaving them with 'extralinguistic' or 'metalinguistic' topics, such as the sociolinguistics of ethnic groups, certain linguistic issues in the study of folklore, the linguistic aspects of local classifications and terminologies (i.e., semantic and semiotic aspects of kinship terms, etc.). The Ph.D. requirements for linguists and ethnographers were always quite different and the latter's postgraduate programmes rarely included topics from the linguistics domain, except the classification of languages and linguistic composition of regions.

This is not to say that ethnographers/anthropologists have not worked quite productively together in joint teams, such as on folklore expeditions or ethnographic research on dialect borders. The Institute of Ethnography series

'Peoples of the World' of the 1950s, for example, required the preparation of detailed ethnic maps of various regions and thorough knowledge of linguistic geography. The semiotics of culture propagated and studied by Yuri Lotman and his pupils at Tartu University inspired some Leningrad ethnographers and folklorists to use semiotic methods in their research into various aspects of material culture, such as the semiotics of dwelling and house construction (Baiburin 1983). The Moscow school of semiotics (Vladimir Toporov, Vyacheslav Ivanow, Boris Uspensky, Nikita Tolstoy, Eliazar Meletinsky and others) influenced ethnographers and folklorists specializing in Slavic groups (Byelorussians, Ukrainians, Russians) and the study of rituals and mythology.

The rapprochement between linguistics and ethnology produced Russian ethnolinguistics of a very special kind, whose topics look more like a search for *Volksgeist* than contemporary cognitive anthropology.

The fragmentation of the discipline into many specialized research fields, regional specializations, subdisciplines, etc. from the 1970s to the 1990s helped to create the current situation in which many Russian ethnologists/anthropologists publish for a narrow audience of immediate colleagues with the same specialization (often only a few people), with the result that few follow developments in neighbouring areas or other national traditions. Whereas in the case of the American anthropological tradition there was a marked increase in the number of 'adjectival anthropologies', in Soviet etnografia of the period there was a similar increase in 'ethno-prefixed' disciplines (such as ethnodemography, ethnoecology, ethnopsychology, ethnoconflictology, etc.), where the prefix 'ethno-' was not the same as in ethno-botany but implied a reference to an ethnos or basic ethnic unit, for the proclaimed subject of Soviet etnografia was the ethnos, understood as:

> a social organism which had formed, over a certain territory out of a group of people with similarities of language, common traits of culture and everyday life, some common social values and traditions and a considerable blending of different social components achieved in the course of the development of economic and social cultural relations. The basic features of an ethnic community were ethnic self-identity and self-name, language, territory, specific features of psychic make-up, culture and everyday life as well as some specific forms of socio-territorial organization or a drive to create one. (Kozlov 1967: 111)

As elsewhere in Europe, physical anthropologists in their studies are more often associated with ancient and medieval history than with etnografia. The Khorezm expedition, set up by Sergei Tolstov, survived in a reduced form the directorship of Yulian Bromley and exists as a small team of ethno-archaeologists at the IEA RAS even now.

Bio-anthropological data was readily used in ethnogenetic studies and in compendiums on the history of particular ethnic groups. With the decline of academic studies in ethnogenesis, during the 1970s and 80s (now such studies are maintained mostly by archaeologists, at the Institute of Archaeology, RAS in Moscow and at its St. Petersburg twin Institute for the Study of Material Culture), archaeology became marginalized. A conservative group of ethnologists at the Omsk University Chair of Ethnography and Museology have made ethnogenetic studies and 'ethno-historical regions' their primary object of research and regularly publish works on 'ethnic archaeology', with descriptions of so-called 'ethno-archaeological complexes', but this is viewed by most of the others as a particularly 'peripheral' and outdated preoccupation.

An analogy could be drawn between the relation of ethnology with history, on the one side, and of ethnology with physical anthropology, on the other, except that institutionally the links with anthropology are stronger (there are a number of physical anthropologists among the staff of both Moscow and St. Petersburg academic ethnographical institutions IAE RAS and MAE). A special physical anthropologists panel is organized at every all-Russian congress of ethnologists.

'Ethnology plus archaeology' and 'ethnology plus physical anthropology', both quite prominent alliances in the past, fell into disfavour in liberal Russian scholarship. The virtual disappearance of these previously central synthetic fields was caused by ideological shifts. The first union produced prolific pop-science publications in local ethnonationalism, as it helped to link territory to ethnic group and enabled ethnic leaders to wage war against other 'less autochthonous' claimants. The second union of ethnology and physical anthropology is implicated, if not in outright racism, then in racialism, since on the basis of this synthesis Russian anthropologists have created what they call 'ethnic anthropology' and published a number of works with bio-anthropological profiles of all the country's ethnic groups.

There is another peculiar marriage of what has been traditionally viewed as part of physical anthropology with certain research issues from the agenda of sociocultural anthropology. I am speaking here of a small research group (both at the IEA RAS and at the Centre for Anthropological Study and Research of the Russian State University for Humanities), which is specializing in what could be called sociobiology or evolutionary behaviour studies. A primatologist who heads this group (Marina Butovskaia) ingeniously uses her training in primate ethology to research into the current urban subcultures of begging, gender-specific behaviour, human sexual behaviour, hunter-gatherer studies, etc.

Two other interdisciplinary fields of burgeoning activity are 'the contact areas' between anthropology and political science and anthropology and sociology. The first contact area started as an applied field during the perestroika years, as various ethnic mobilization movements and conflicts attracted the attention of scholars from both fields. A series of reports on applied and ethnic anthropology, now numbering almost three hundred issues, was begun in the early 1990s. The study of power and conflict, banned during the Soviet period, again became a central concern for early post-Soviet ethnology/anthropology.

Ethnic sociology, started some twenty years earlier during the disciplinary scope expansion initiated by Bromley when ethnic ecology, ethnic demography, ethnic psychology and ethnic sociology groups were formed, continues to exert some influence outside anthropology (the department at the Institute of Ethnology and Anthropology has dwindled to a small group but a new department has been organized by L. Drobizheva at the Institute of Sociology). The interdisciplinary boundaries in this case remain blurred and the division of labour unarticulated.

Sociologists equipped with qualitative methods (including ethnography) were the first to embrace the problematic of newly born social anthropology and set the standards for Ph.D. programmes and teaching requirements for the new university courses. As they were not well read in classical anthropology at the time, both the standards and programmes suffered. The institutionalization of social anthropology by sociologists and of cultural anthropology by kulturologists effectively isolated and divided these two seemingly different disciplines from each other and from mainstream ethnology. So, today, in some regions of the country there are three separate disciplines, each with a very different research focus and agenda, while in others the dividing lines are blurred or ignored as mere bureaucratic inventions. The Soviet etnografia normativity, which crystallized and emerged around the 1960s, came to an abrupt end at the turn of the century. Now the departments and chairs that cling to a Soviet-style 'traditional' ethnographic agenda are seen as hopelessly retrograde, while the new social anthropology chairs, with rare exceptions, are considered absurdly eclectic.

Thus, at different periods in the history of their discipline, Soviet scholars repeatedly redefined its main objects and subject area, establishing various alliances with 'neighbouring fields' and underlying differences with similar research programmes of other social sciences and humanities. Focus on or the necessity for the synthesis of archaeological, linguistic, bio-anthropological and ethnological data had been dictated by research agendas or by the nature of the main issues that general anthropology was addressing at the time, mainly the reconstruction of the history of mankind and the particular histories of its constitutive 'races' and 'peoples'. With the break-up of the evolutionary grand narrative and subsequent change of research focus, the synthesizing effort lost its main objective and the unity of the discipline was threatened. From this perspective, our current preoccupation with the unity or diversity of anthropological disciplines might be a corollary of the interrelationship of data from its various subfields needed for reflection on certain research issues. The question is whether we still have these problems that demand the joint efforts of all the constitutive 'subfields' on our agenda or whether we have become so specialized in our research that no such problems are in sight.

CURRENT RESEARCH

Unlike our 'hard science' colleagues, who turned away from the ideology of cumulativism, following the suggestion of Thomas Kuhn that scientific revolutions create paradigmatic shifts, ruptures and theoretic incommensurability, the moving forces of the social sciences and humanities seem to be creating, instead of revolutions, just scandals and fashions. A minor scandal engendered by a new set of arguments, data or new public sentiment and sensitivity could put an end to anthropological preoccupation with one particular theory or concept and create incentives to produce another one, as has happened at various times with 'tribe', 'race' 'assimilation' and, in the case of Soviet/Russian anthropology, is happening now with 'ethnogenetic studies' and the concept of 'ethnos'. Fashions are subtler than scandals, as the change of preferences often takes place without any proclamation of war, with no arguments pro and contra. People do not so much just 'turn away from' certain subjects, as be 'attracted to' another research agenda that promises new impressions, vistas, and, well yes, funding.

New research directions, after rapid institutionalization, often become isolated and 'compartmentalized' – that is, instead of integrating their findings and visions into the mainstream anthropology, they establish separate networks of researchers, who establish their own journal, regularly meet at specialist conventions and strategically position their subdiscipline as an addition, but not one requiring the revision of methods in other 'traditional' research areas. A case in point is the organization of a department of 'ethno-gender studies' at IEA RAS around 1995. So now, instead of gender-sensitive anthropology, we have ended up with a small group of scholars who are doing cross-cultural gender research in different ethnic communities, while others continue to ignore gender issues.

The culture wars fought currently in the Russian social sciences and humanities resemble more trench warfare than offensive operations. The decade-long debate over the status of ethnicity (constructionists vs. primordialists) is becoming stale; Russian anthropologists are starting to look apprehensively for other directions, especially those viewed as new for traditional mainstream Russian etnografia. The community of Russian ethnologists is painfully and slowly moving towards the much wider concerns of sociocultural anthropology. As an illustration I would mention only a few topics that were unthinkable as subjects of ethnographic concern only ten years ago. In the last couple of years, the *Ethnographic Review*, the anthropological journal of the Russian Academy of Sciences, which was founded in 1889 by Dmitry Anuchin and then resumed in 1926 by Soviet ethnographers as *Etnografia* (from 1930 to 1990 as *Sovetskaia etnografia*; since 1991 *Etnograficheskoe obozrenie* – that is, the *Ethnographic Review* again), has devoted special issues to the anthropology of advertising, organizations, tourism, dreaming, everyday conversations, militant Islam, Muslim headscarves, etc. Except for the last topic, which would have been considered a legitimate object in the ethnographic study of costume (all political implications would have been ignored!), all the others would not have been considered to belong to the field of ethnology. The topical profile of current research is summarized in Table 3.2 below.

The library crisis that started in the early 1990s due to inadequate funding, when even the leading academic institutions and libraries did not receive most of the anthropological journals published abroad and could not pay for online access to academic article collections, has contributed to the growing gap between the present concerns of Russian anthropology and developments in other national traditions, though trips abroad, Internet access and joint projects do somewhat alleviate the situation.

Research Institutions

Specialized anthropological research institutions were established in the USSR during the 1920s and 30s. The already mentioned IEA RAS was organized in 1933 (its Moscow branch in December 1943). Today, besides research institutes within the Russian Academy of Sciences in Moscow, St. Petersburg, Novosibirsk, Omsk, Irkutsk, Yakutsk and Vladivostok, there are a number of research centres at large universities (Moscow State University and the Russian State University for Humanities (RGGU); Kazan university; the European University in St. Petersburg), anthropological research 'laboratories' at smaller or new universities and teams of researchers at central and local ethnographical and local history museums.

In Moscow, the oldest institute for physical anthropology (the Dmitry Anuchin Research Institute and Museum of Anthropology of the Moscow State University) was organized in 1922. Its goals are 'the study of individual, age, gender and territorial diversity of Man', and its current staff comprises more than thirty bio-anthropologists specializing in anatomy, human genetics, craniology, anthropometry, osteology, human ecology and other branches of bio-anthropology and primatology. The Institute is a member of the European Anthropological Association. In terms of interdisciplinary research, the institute's anthropologists regularly contact and work in joint teams with archaeologists, medical scientists and biologists (including medical and population geneticists, primatologists).

At present, most of the research is concentrated at several institutes of the Russian Academy of Sciences (in Moscow, St. Petersburg, Novosibirsk, Omsk and Vladivostok) and at a few university research centres conducting mostly regional ethnographic research.

Teaching

Though the number of chairs and university research centres where students receive training in ethnology/sociocultural anthropology has substantially increased compared to the mid-1980s period, when there were only four or five chairs providing such training, the understanding of what should be taught as social anthropology remains highly idiosyncratic and unpredictable and ranges from art history and philosophical anthropology to physical anthropology, archaeology and local history. The oldest chairs are at Moscow University, St. Petersburg (former Leningrad) University, and Kazan University. Younger centres were established between the late 1980s and the early 1990s at Altay (Barnaul), Omsk, Novosibirsk, Tomsk, Irkutsk and Kuban (Krasnodar) universities, and between the late 1990s and the early 2000s at Saratov, Stavropol, Chelyabinsk, Dagestan (Makhachkala), Abakan, Izhevsk, Syktyvkar, Cheboksary and Ulan-Ude universities.

There are now thirty-three working chairs where students are trained either in ethnology or sociocultural anthropology (ten Ethnography and Archaeology chairs; three Ethnology and Archaeology chairs; eighteen Social and/or Cultural Anthropology chairs; two Physical Anthropology chairs). All these could be subdivided into three broad categories: 1) those where a conservative, mostly Soviet-style ethnology, with a focus on ethnic studies, is taught: Moscow and St. Petersburg (Dept. of History), Kazan, Omsk and Tomsk universities; Abakan, Barnaul, Chelyabinsk, Cheboksary, Yekaterinburg State (Dept. of History), Gorno-Altaysk, Irkutsk, Makhachkala, Novosibirsk and Syktyvkar universities; 2) European-style social anthropology chairs (St. Petersburg European University, Russian State University for Humanities in Moscow, Saratov and, to some degree, Kuban universities); 3) 'Eclectic' Anthropology chairs (universities in Chita, Urals State Technical in Yekaterinburg, Russian State Social in Moscow, Novosibirsk State Technical, St. Petersburg University (Dept. of Sociology), Far-Eastern State, Kuibyshev Far East State Technical and State University for Economics and Service in Vladivostok; Vladivostok; Tyumen, Orel, and

Izhevsk universities; Moscow City Psychology and Pedagogical University; Tomsk Branch of the Russian Social University).

While 'ethnographers' grappled with new challenges, trying to adopt their accumulated knowledge of the terrain to new circumstances, their neighbours from other social sciences and humanities departments were quicker to occupy the opening niche for sociocultural anthropology and to institutionalize it by establishing new university chairs (mainly at departments of Sociology and Political Sciences) and Ph.D. programmes. The chairs of 'Scientific Communism' and 'Economy of Socialism' ceased to exist; their personnel was prepared to take the opportunity to stay by affiliating with new departments to study ethnic conflicts and mobilization, ethnic politics, nationalism, local cultural history, etc. In the mid 1990s, with the establishment of Ph.D. programmes in Social and Cultural Anthropology (treated as a branch of Sociology) and the creation of new universities and colleges, a score of new chairs, centres and even departments of Social Anthropology appeared across the country.

In the central institutions of Moscow and St. Petersburg, where professional communities were well consolidated and institutionalized, the research innovations were processed in an additive manner. In peripheral centres and chairs, interdisciplinary boundaries had to be renegotiated; which often led to schisms and splits in groups of researchers and to fissions and fusions of various subdisciplines in order to form new partnerships. For example, in 1992 a new chair of Archaeology and Ethnography split from the chair of World History at Novosibirsk state university. In 2000, a chair of Philosophy and Social Anthropology was established at Chita State University, which was reorganized into the chair of Social and Cultural Anthropology in 2004. Most of the new chairs were quite eclectic in their curriculum choices (to cite but a few examples, courses ranging from ethno-archaeology and regional studies to intercultural communication, sociolinguistics and semiotics, social adaptation, comparative analysis of political systems, sociology and political studies are taught as main subjects).

There have been no good Russian textbooks on sociocultural anthropology so far; most of the published textbooks are either methodologically outdated, or merely reflect the authors' highly idiosyncratic views on what 'proper anthropology' should engage in. Fieldwork methods are rarely taught, and the last comprehensive textbook on ethnography was reprinted in the mid 1960s.

The recent proliferation of anthropology chairs has not had a considerable impact on current research practices. This is due to the fact that most of the graduates cannot find a job at the existing research centres. The causes are numerous: because of meagre retirement pensions most of the senior generation prefer to continue work after retirement age, thus preventing the younger generation from obtaining positions in academic institutions; the number of jobs outside academia has not substantially increased with the rising numbers of chairs; many professors work in several places due to very low salaries; public funding for science remains inadequate.

CONCLUDING REMARKS

To sum up, Russian anthropology is going through a period of transition and is suffering from all the problems of finding an identity; it has lost its previous focus on ethnic studies but has not acquired any new common focus. Many futile research fields tainted by nationalist ideology and sponsored by local political elites still survive as part of the domestic research terrain.

Various research teams and university faculty throughout the country are 'inventing' social anthropology as a discipline, often indiscriminately confusing it with art history, applied sociology, public relations and the like.

The borders of the discipline have significantly broadened, and its scope has encompassed many new topics and objects, but the lack of professional training and low standards of teaching prevent the integration of borrowed methods and ideas and fuel conservative reactions from 'old school' ethnographers. The fruits of the most recent measures whereby bachelor and master programmes in anthropology have been established to remedy the situation are yet to be seen.

Sergey Sokolovskiy is a chief editor of an academic anthropological journal *Etnograficheskoe obozrenie*, author of over 300 publications, including five monographs and several edited volumes on the issues of minority rights and indigeneity construction, identity studies and history of Russian anthropology, based on field research in Western Siberia and Russian north-west.

ANNEX

TABLE 3.2. Publications in the Russian anthropological journal *Sovetskaia Etnografia/Etnograficheskoe Obozrenie* 1975–2009 by subject/subdiscipline

Focus of articles	1975–79	1980–84	1985–89	1990–94	1995–99	2000–04	2005–09	Σ
Disciplines, traditional for Russian anthropology Σ₁	*112*	*103*	*93*	*160*	*214*	*249*	*354*	*1285*
Ethnicity and identity studies; theory of ethnos	0	2	2	4	13	12	55	88
Culture theory and cultural anthropology	30	25	24	30	44	29	47	339
Social anthropology	12	14	4	6	4	6	36	82
Methodology and research methods	4	3	10	3	5	12	13	50
Physical anthropology	8	7	3	1	3	5	6	33
Ethnogenetic and ethnic history studies	6	2	2	3	5	12	17	47
Ethnic archaeology	2	1	3	0	18	6	4	34
Folklore studies	12	10	7	17	17	18	20	101
Ethnonymics and onomastics	1	1	1	3	7	8	7	28
Studies of religion	4	3	7	19	48	47	56	184
Museum studies	0	2	9	7	3	11	5	37
Ethnic and historical demography	7	19	4	9	11	19	20	89
Archival studies and historiography	4	4	3	2	3	9	11	36
History of anthropology	16	7	8	54	32	54	55	226
Ethnic sociology	6	3	6	2	1	1	2	21
New research fields Σ₂	*224*	*7*	*19*	*30*	*74*	*44*	*78*	*266*
Ethnic ecology	1	3	2	4	7	4	6	27
Ethnic and cross-cultural psychology	3	1	9	5	3	4	9	34
Ethnic sociolinguistics	8	0	7	2	2	5	2	26
Ethno-political studies	2	1	0	14	33	11	26	87
Ethnic conflicts studies	0	0	0	1	4	4	2	11
Legal anthropology	0	1	0	0	12	5	23	41
Gender studies	0	1	0	4	10	8	8	31
Human ethology	0	0	1	0	3	3	2	9
Sum total:	126	110	112	190	288	293	432	*1551*

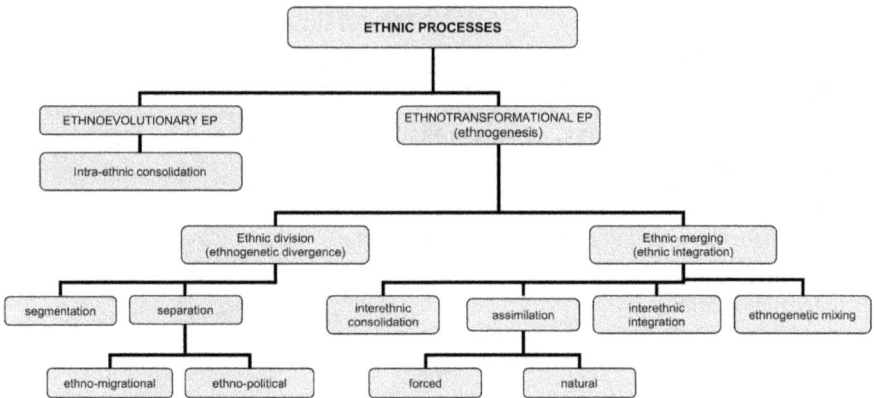

FIGURE 3.1. Typology of ethnic processes in Soviet ethnography, 1970–1980s

NOTES

1. The most recent books on the history of Russian anthropology include Mogilner (2008); Tumarkin (1999, 2003); Tishkov and Tumarkin (2004); Solovei (1998, 2004) (but see also Tokarev 1966). A sample of relevant works by Western scholars would include Banks (1996); Bertrand (2002); Chichlo (1984, 1985); Dragadze (1995); Geraci (2001); Hirsch (2005); Khazanov (1995); Martin (2001); Plotkin and Howe (1985); Olcott (1995); Skalník (1981, 1986, 1988); Slezkine (1991, 1994); and Van Meurs (2000).

2. See, inter alia, a two-volume set on repression in Soviet anthropology, compiled by Daniil Tumarkin (1999, 2003) and the article on the early Soviet ethnography crisis by Yuri Slezkine (1991), as well as the recent book by Frédéric Bertrand (2002) on the early period of Soviet etnografia. Some relevant periods of the history of Russian anthropology were also described in Martin (2001); Hirsch (2005) and Cadiot (2007).

3. In fact, this was a reiteration of a deeply entrenched view among Russian anthropologists derived from Herder and Humboldt. Nikolai Kharuzin, in one of his works, defined 'lifeways of tribes and peoples' as the subject of ethnography (1901: 37); Sergei Shirokogoroff introduced etnos as the main object of ethnographical research as early as 1922. Soviet anthropology, or as it was named after the conference of 1929 'etnografia', had been consistent in the delineation of its subject and in its identification of the main objects of research. Since its institutionalization as a separate field of research its main object had been 'peoples', designated later as 'etnoses'. From N. Kharuzin (1901), N. Mogiliansky (1908), and S. Shirokogoroff (1922, 1923) right up to L. Gumilev (1967), Yu. Bromley (1968) and V. Tishkov (1992) it had been focused on ethnic phenomena and any other object of research had been viewed as 'deviant' and treated with suspicion as 'not quite ethnographic'.

4. Special issue, 2005; published in abridged form as a special section 'The Current State of Ethnography and Anthropology in Russia' in its English edition, named 'Forum for Anthropology and Culture' 2, 2005.

REFERENCES

Alpatov, V.M. 2004 [1988]. *Istoriia odnogo mifa: Marr i marrizm*, 2nd ed. Moscow: Editorial URSS.

Anuchin, D. 1880. 'Antropologicheskie ocherki', *Russkaia mysl'* 3: 48–60.

Baiburin, A. 1983. *Zhilische v obriadakh i predstavleniakh vostochnykh slavian*. Leningrad: Nauka.

Banks, M. 1996. *Ethnicity: Anthropological Constructions*. London and New York: Routledge.

Bertrand, F. 2002. *L'anthropologie soviétique des années 20–30: Configuration d'une rupture*. Bordeaux: Presses Universitaires de Bordeaux.

Bromley, Y.V. 1968. 'Etnos i endogamia', *Sovetskaia etnografia* 6: 84–91.

———. 1981. *Sovremennye problemy etnografii: ocherki teorii i istorii*. Moscow: Nauka.

———. 1983. *Ocherki teorii etnosa*. Moscow: Nauka.

Cadiot, J. 2007. *La laboratoire imperial: Russie–l'URSS 1860–1940*. Paris: CNRS Editions.

Chichlo, B. 1984. 'L'ethnographie soviétique est-elle une anthropologie?', in B. Rupp-Eisenreich (ed.), *Histoire de l'anthropologie, XVIe–XIXe siècles*. Paris: Klincksiek.

———. 1985. 'Trente années d'anthropologie (etnografiia) soviétique', *Revue des Etudes slaves* 57(2): 309–24.

Dragadze, T. 1987. 'Fieldwork at Home: The USSR', in A. Jackson (ed.), *Anthropology at Home*. London and New York: Tavistock Publications, pp. 155–63.

———. 1995. 'Politics and Anthropology in Russia', *Anthropology Today* 11(4): 1–3.

Dunn, S.P. and E. Dunn. 1974. *Introduction to Soviet Ethnography*, 2 vols. Berkeley, CA: Highgate Road Social Science Research Station.

Elfimov, A. 1997. 'The State of the Discipline: Interviews with Russian Anthropologists', *American Anthropologist* 99(4): 775–85.

Gellner, E. 1975. 'The Soviet and the Savage', *Current Anthropology* 10(4): 595–617.

———. 1980. *Soviet and Western Anthropology*. New York: Columbia University Press.

Gellner, E. (ed.). 1988. *State and Society in Soviet Thought*. Oxford: Blackwell.

Geraci, R.P. 2001. *Window on the East: National and Imperial Identities in Late Tsarist Russia*. Ithaca: Cornell University Press.

Golovko, E. 2005. 'Comment in the Section "The Current State of Ethnography and Anthropology in Russia"', *Forum for Anthropology and Culture* 2: 454–58.

Gumilev, L.N. 1967. 'O termine etnos: Etnos kak iavlenie', *Doklady otdelenii i komissii Geograficheskogo obshchestva SSSR* 3: 90–107.

Hirsch, F. 2005. *Empire of Nations: Ethnographic Knowledge and the Making of the Soviet Union*. Ithaca and London: Cornell University Press.

Kharuzin, N. 1901. *Etnografia*, issue 1. St. Petersburg.

Khazanov, A.M. 1995. *After the USSR: Ethnicity, Nationalism, and Politics in the Commonwealth of Independent States*. Madison, WI: University of Wisconsin Press.

Kozlov, V. 1967. 'O poniatii etnicheskoi obschnosti', *Sovetskaia etnografia* 2: 100–11.

———. 1969. *Dinamika chislennosti narodov*. Moscow: Nauka.

Martin, T. 2001. *The Affirmative Action Empire: Nations and Nationalism in the Soviet Union, 1923–1939*. Ithaca: Cornell University Press.

Melnikova, E. 2005. 'Comment in the Section "The Current State of Ethnography and Anthropology in Russia"', *Forum for Anthropology and Culture* 2: 459–63.

Mogiliansky, N.M. 1908. 'Etnogafia i eio zadachi', *Yezhegodnik Russkogo antropologicheskogo obshchestva* III: 100–15.

Mogilner, M. 2008. *Homo imperii: Istoria fizicheskoi antropologii v Rossii.* Moscow: NLO.

Olcott, M.B. 1995. 'Soviet Nationality Studies between Past and Future', in D. Orlovsky (ed.), *Beyond Soviet Studies.* Washington, D.C.: The Woodrow Wilson Center Press, pp. 135–48.

Plotkin, V. 1990. 'Dual Models, Totalizing Ideology and Soviet Ethnography', *Cahiers du monde russe et soviétique* 31(2–3): 235–42.

Plotkin V. and J.E. Howe. 1985. 'The Unknown Tradition: Continuity and Innovation in the Soviet Ethnography', *Dialectical Anthropology* 9(2): 257–312.

'Rezoliutsia Vserossiiskogo Arkheologo-etnograficheskogo Soveshchania 7–11 maia 1932 goda'. 1932. *Sovetskaia etnografia* 3: 4–14.

Shanin, T. 1989. 'Ethnicity in the Soviet Union: Analytical Perceptions and Political Strategies', *Comparative Study of Society and History* 31(3): 409–24.

Shirokogoroff, S.M. 1922. *Mesto etnografii sredi nauk i klassifikatsia etnosov.* Shanghai: n.p.

———. 1923. *Etnos: Issledovanie osnovnykh printsipov etnicheskikh i etnograficheskikh iavlenij.* Shanghai: n.p.

Skalník, P. 1981. 'Community: Struggle for a Key Concept in Soviet Ethnography', *Dialectical Anthropology* 6(2): 183–91.

———. 1986. 'Towards an Understanding of Soviet Etnos Theory', *South African Journal of Ethnology* 9: 157–66.

———. 1988. 'Union Soviétique – Afrique du Sud: les "Théories" de l'etnos', *Cahiers d'Etude africaines* 28(2): 157–76.

———. 1998. 'Commentary to Tishkov's article "U.S. and Russian Anthropology"', *Current Anthropology* 39(1): 10–11.

Skalník, P. (ed.). 2001. *Sociocultural Anthropology at the Turn of the Century: Voices from the Periphery.* Prague: Set Out.

———. 2002. *A Post-Communist Millennium: The Struggles for Sociocultural Anthropology in Central and Eastern Europe.* Prague: Set Out.

Slezkine, Y. 1991. 'The Fall of Soviet Ethnography, 1928–38', *Current Anthropology* 32(4): 476–84.

———. 1994. 'The USSR as a Communal Apartment, or How a Socialist State Promoted Ethnic Particularism', *Slavic Review* 53(2): 414–52.

———. 1996. 'N. Ia. Marr and the National Origins of Soviet Ethnogenetics', *Slavic Review* 55(4): 826–62.

Solovei, T.D. 1998. *Ot burzhuaznoi 'etnologii' k sovetskoi 'etnografii': Istoria otechestvennoi etnologii pervoi treti XX veka.* Moscow: Moscow State University.

———. 2004. 'Etnologia', in *Istoricheskaia nauka v Moskovskom universitete, 1755–2004.* Moscow: Moscow State University, pp. 512–550.

Sokolovskiy, S. 1995. 'Ethnographic Research: Ideals and Reality', *Anthropology and Archeology of Eurasia* 34(2): 5–38.

'Soveshchanie etnografov Leningrada i Moskvy'. 1929. *Etnografia* 2: 110–44.

Stocking, G.W. 1992. *The Ethnographer's Magic and Other Essays in the History of Anthropology.* Madison, WI: The University of Wisconsin Press.

Tishkov, V. 1992. 'The Crisis in Soviet Ethnography', *Current Anthropology* 33(4): 371–82.

Tishkov, V. and D. Tumarkin (eds). 2004. *Vydaiushchiesia otechestvennye etnologi i antropologi XX veka.* Moscow: Nauka.

Tokarev, S.A. 1966. *Istoria russkoi etnografii (Dooktiabrskij period)*. Moscow: Nauka.

Tolstov, S.P. 1946. 'Etnografia i sovremennost', *Sovetskaia Etnografia* 1: 3–11.

———. 1956. 'Itogi i perspectivy razvitia etnograficheskoi nauki v SSSR', *Sovetskaia Etnografia* 3: 5–13.

Tumarkin, D. (ed.). 1999. *Repressirovannye etnografy*, vol. 1. Moscow: Vostochnaia literatura.

———. 2003. *Repressirovannye etnografy*, vol. 2. Moscow: Vostochnaia literatura.

Van Meurs, W. 2000. 'Ethnographie in der UdSSR: Jäger oder Sammler?', in B. Binder, W. Kaschuba and P. Niedermüller (eds), *Inszenierung des Nationalen: Geschichte, Kultur und die Politik der Identitäten am Ende des 20. Jahrhunderts*. Köln: Böhlau, pp. 107–35.

4

ANTHROPOLOGY AND ETHNOLOGY IN ITALY

Historical Development, Current Orientations, Problems of Recognition

PIER PAOLO VIAZZO

INTRODUCTION

The present state of anthropology in Italy can be properly assessed only against the backdrop of a 150-year history, which lends itself to a neat periodization, marked by two major university reforms in 1969 and 1999. For about a century, from its beginnings in the 1860s to the turning point of the late 1960s, the development of ethnological and anthropological studies in Italy was remarkably slow and quiet, both theoretically and institutionally. Since the late 1960s, however, they have gone through an unexpected and rapid acceleration, explained partly by the shift from elite to mass higher education, which entailed a sudden rise in the number of students choosing ethnological and anthropological courses as part of their curriculum, and partly by a booming interest in the social and human sciences.

The growth of cultural anthropology, initially understood in Italy as a discipline concerned almost exclusively with complex societies, greatly contributed to this success story, but it also caused tensions with ethnologists, who believed that research should focus on 'primitive' societies. On the other hand, cultural anthropology's orientation towards Italian society and culture provided a bridge with the work of students of Italian folk life and the two fields blended into a distinctive national variety of anthropology, strongly influenced by Antonio Gramsci's reflections on folklore as well as by the insights of Ernesto De Martino.

The launching of the Bologna Process in 1999 offered new opportunities and made possible the establishment of first- and second-level degree courses specifically devoted to the teaching and learning of sociocultural anthropology and ethnology, which in turn led to a further increase in the number of anthropology students. However, this expansion has proved structurally fragile and some opportunities have been missed: in view of the greatly increased number of new graduates, the need for anthropology to receive proper professional recognition has become especially acute. The new and radical university reform enacted amid furious controversy in 2010 casts shadows on Italian anthropology's prospects for the future. Much will depend on the will and ability of Italian anthropologists to invest more on a skill-based pedagogy than on the mere academic reproduction of the discipline.

A CENTURY OF SLOW AND ANTAGONISTIC DEVELOPMENT (1869–1968)

Italian anthropology was institutionally established in 1869, when a chair of *Antropologia* was inaugurated in Florence.[1] In those days, this term referred primarily to physical anthropology and the first incumbent of the new chair, Paolo Mantegazza, had been trained as a physician. Mantegazza had, however, a broader vision of the tasks of the new science than many of his contemporaries. He had travelled widely in Europe and South America and had no sympathy with those wanting to reduce anthropology to a discipline 'more interested in skulls than in thought, in races than in comparative psychology'. He was therefore a supporter of 'that branch of our science that has been called ethnology [*etnologia*], the study of peoples' (Mantegazza 1871: 26), and it is no accident that the first anthropological society, which was established in Florence and counted Mantegazza among its founders, was called the Società Italiana di Antropologia e di Etnologia.

Born in Florence, at that time the temporary capital of the recently unified Italian state, anthropology soon developed in other cities (most notably in Rome, the new capital of the kingdom since 1871) through the establishment of new chairs and the foundation of learned societies, scientific journals and museums, whose growth owed much to the ethnographic campaigns conducted by travellers and explorers (Puccini 1999). The best known among them is Lamberto Loria, who made journeys to Africa, Asia and Melanesia and donated his ethnographic collections to the museums of Rome and Florence. What makes Loria an especially interesting figure, however, is his late conversion to the study of Italian folk life *(demologia)*. In 1905, already fifty years old and just before sailing for Africa, he visited a small town in southern Italy and there, as he himself recollected, 'got the idea of abandoning the studies of exotic ethnography that had hitherto obliged me to take long and dangerous travels, and of concerning myself instead with our own people' (Loria 1912: 9). In 1906, he began to collect material for a museum of Italian ethnography and in 1911 he organized an exhibition in Rome that became the basis for the Museum of Popular Arts and Traditions (Puccini 2006). By turning from 'exotic ethnography' to Italian folklore, Loria was joining forces with scholars like Giuseppe Pitré, who had been engaged for over forty years in ethnography 'at home' in his native Sicily and whose academic achievements were recognized in 1910 when a chair of *demopsicologia* ('folk-psychology') was created for him in Palermo.

The year 1910 also saw the founding of a Society of Italian Ethnography by Loria, an ethnologist, Francesco Baldasseroni, a historian, and Aldobrandino Mochi, a physical anthropologist. The disciplinary backgrounds of the three founders show that on the eve of the First World War the spectrum of anthropological sciences in Italy still ranged from physical anthropology through prehistory and ethnology to the ethnographic study of folk traditions. However, the Society's first congress, held in Rome in 1911, laid bare a dawning disagreement between physical anthropologists and ethnologists, which started a process of separation that eventually resulted in formal divorce in the early 1930s. This was the first major schism in the history of the anthropological sciences in Italy and it had long-lasting consequences. As physical anthropologists lost interest in ethnology and emphasized the 'scientific' status of their discipline, antropologia was taught exclusively in natural science faculties, whereas etnologia ceased to be considered a branch of anthropology and was assigned, epistemologically and institutionally, to the realm of the humanities.

Etnologia's new autonomy did not, however, lead to academic growth: the first professorship would be instituted only in 1967, in Rome, nearly a century after the creation of Mantegazza's chair of Antropologia. When physical anthropology and ethnology parted ways, the latter was much the weaker academically and its interests were not advanced by the hostile attitude of the then dominant idealistic philosophy. Benedetto Croce's dislike of the social sciences is well known and he was not prepared to grant more than an ancillary position to the study of those 'primitive peoples' he resolutely placed outside the spiritual and moral progress of history. With its development thwarted in the academic world, ethnology was also given limited opportunities for professional expansion in the field of Italian colonial studies.

A distinctive feature of Italian ethnology in the period between the two world wars was the central importance given to the study of religion (Leone 1985; Alliegro 2011: 244–63). This was partly due to the influence of Father Wilhelm Schmidt, the leader of the Vienna School of *Völkerkunde*: his refutation of evolutionism, methods of diffusionist analysis and theses on the origins of religion remained part and parcel of Italian ethnological discourse until the mid 1960s. It should be noted, though, that outside the Catholic milieu Schmidt's theories did not go unchallenged. Indeed, one of his fiercest and ablest critics was an Italian, the distinguished historian of religions Raffaele Pettazzoni. Though incessantly at loggerheads with his Viennese opponent, Pettazzoni nevertheless shared Schmidt's propensity to equate ethnology with the comparative study of primitive religion. This had significant effects on the teaching of ethnology in Italy, for Pettazzoni was a key figure in ensuring the academic survival of the discipline in the difficult years that followed the separation from physical anthropology. While holding the chair of History of Religions in Rome, he also lectured in ethnology and, in 1947, he even founded a postgraduate school in ethnological studies. Around 1950, Italian ethnologists were basically divided into two camps: on the one hand, the pupils and followers of Father Schmidt and, on the other, the pupils or followers of Pettazzoni. However different their positions, both schools placed a unique emphasis on the ethnological study of religion. Similarly, they were all steeped in the theoretical tradition of the cultural-historical schools that had dominated the German-speaking world, and were mostly critical of the 'functional' approaches pioneered by Malinowski and Radcliffe-Brown (Bianchi 1971: 198–218).

If we consider terminology, we see that until 1960 the Italian usage essentially conformed to the continental European pattern in which 'anthropology' meant physical anthropology, whereas 'ethnology' referred to what in the Anglo-Saxon world was called social or cultural anthropology. While in some parts of Europe this distinction persisted until recently, in other countries things were about to change. In France, for example, *ethnologie* was partly replaced by *anthropologie sociale*, 'explicitly borrowed from British anthropology by Lévi-Strauss and others who hoped by so doing to wean [their] discipline away from the exclusive study of ethnic groups and to shore up its status as a universally applicable social science' (Godelier 1997: 3). In Italy too etnologia began to lose ground to *antropologia culturale*, a label imported from the United States by Tullio Tentori, a former pupil of Pettazzoni who had studied with Robert Redfield in Chicago. What makes the Italian case rather different from seemingly similar stories in other European countries is that the new term was not simply meant to replace etnologia, but was given by its proponents 'a special and somewhat polemical sense ... to designate a theoretical and topical orientation framed *in opposition* to that of "ethnology"' (Saunders 1984: 447). In fact, Tentori displayed a very critical attitude towards ethnology, understood as the study of 'primitive' societies, and aimed at establishing cultural anthropology as a separate discipline focused on the complex societies of the contemporary world, especially those of Italy, and envisaged as an applied social science capable of buttressing policymaking and social engineering. This attitude generated much animosity and caused the second major schism in the history of the anthropological sciences in Italy. It took place in a period in which the fall of idealist philosophy, an unprecedented interest in the social and human sciences and the shift from elite to mass university education were opening up new spaces for institutional growth.

THREE DECADES OF FRAGMENTED
INSTITUTIONAL GROWTH (1969–1999)

Until the mid 1960s, ethnology had been taught as an optional course either by professors of related disciplines or by temporary lecturers appointed each year. Cultural anthropology was also taught in a few universities by contract lecturers. The first professorship of Etnologia was established on the eve of the 1968 student unrest and of the subsequent reform in 1969, which changed the face of the Italian university system. For one thing, the reform brought about a sudden increase in the number of students by allowing all those who held a secondary school diploma to enter university. Secondly, the distinction between compulsory and optional disciplines was weakened, especially in the humanities, thereby giving formerly second-class disciplines a chance to acquire full recognition alongside philosophy, history and the classics. In this climate, cultural anthropology played no small part in giving currency to the then revolutionary view that 'subaltern' social classes had cultures worthy of recognition. This was one of several factors that contributed to its success well beyond academic circles: by the mid 1970s, in common parlance antropologia was already assumed to refer to cultural rather than to physical anthropology. The rising status of cultural anthropology encouraged its practitioners to lay claims to university positions: the first chair was established in 1970 in Bologna.

It should be stressed that not all members of the first generation of teachers of cultural anthropology were in agreement with Tentori or shared a similar background. Some of them were philosophers, whose interest in anthropological matters had been raised or heightened by Lévi-Straussian structuralism, while others had received their anthropological education abroad and were wary of terminological disputes. The latter group included Bernardo Bernardi, the incumbent of the first chair in Bologna, who had been trained as an ethnologist in Rome and had studied social anthropology with Isaac Schapera in Cape Town. Still others came from folklore studies. Tentori's contention that cultural anthropology had to deal primarily with Italy provided a bridge to the work of those Italian scholars who had practised ethnography 'at home'. As a result, the boundaries between antropologia culturale and demologia blurred and the two fields blended into a distinctive national brand of anthropology, strongly influenced by Antonio Gramsci's reflections on the study of folklore (Clemente, Meoni and Squillacciotti 1976) as well as by the insights of Ernesto De Martino, a historian of religions who had died in 1965 and had liked to call himself an 'ethnologist', even if his path-breaking fieldwork had been carried out in the south of Italy (Charuty 2011).

When Bernardi re-entered the Italian academic world to hold the chair at Bologna, he was surprised by the 'jingoistic divisions among Italian anthropologists' (Bernardi 1990: 10), which were exacerbated by the political cleavage between many of those who gathered under the banner of etnologia and the predominantly leftist cultural anthropologists. Although some fault lines are still detectable today, the contrasts and differences between the three main 'lineages' in Italian anthropology (ethnologists, cultural anthropologists, folklorists) have gradually subsided and the term antropologia is now commonly used to designate a largely unified field. The threefold origin of Italian anthropology is, however, enshrined in a portmanteau term originally proposed by Alberto Cirese – a leading exponent of demologia with a keen interest in Lévi-Strauss's work and a sophisticated grasp of the main trends in world anthropology – which is still officially adopted in ministerial vocabulary: demo-ethno-anthropological disciplines (Angioni 1994).

Taken together, in the 1970s the three anthropological disciplines experienced rapid institutional growth. In 1977 there were already twenty-one professorships at sixteen universities – six chairs for ethnology, eight for cultural anthropology and seven for folklore studies – and courses were given by temporary lecturers in other universities (Grottanelli 1977: 599). In addition, research contracts were granted to a number of younger scholars who helped with teaching as assistants. According to one estimate, in the early 1980s over 200 anthropologists were employed at some level in Italian universities (Saunders 1984: 448). The positions of many of these anthropologists were, however, highly precarious.

The following two decades were characterized more by consolidation than by further expansion: in 1998 there were thirty full professors, sixty-three associate professors and seventy-four assistant professors, with a total of 167 tenured positions (Biscione 1998: 26–30), who made up the core of a larger scientific community that included temporary lecturers, Ph.D. students and postdoctoral fellows, as well as qualified anthropologists holding positions in museums or working for international agencies and local cultural institutions. In that year, the AISEA (Associazione Italiana per le Scienze Etno-Antropologiche, a national association of academic and professional anthropologists founded in 1991) had about 400 members. While not enormous, the number of professional anthropologists in Italy was therefore comparable to that estimated at the same time for the United Kingdom in a pioneering report (Mascarenhas Keyes and Wright 1995), according to which fewer than 300 social anthropologists were employed by British universities. This report showed, however, that in Britain most anthropologists were concentrated in the twenty or so departments that awarded degrees in Social Anthropology, whereas in Italy they were scattered over a multitude of universities and faculties. It should be noted that a crucial feature of the Italian university system was a rigid division of labour between faculties and departments: undergraduate teaching was the prerogative of faculties, which were the only bodies entitled to award degrees, whereas departments were created in the 1980s with the task of coordinating research and providing common institutional and physical space to professors working in closely related fields but often belonging to different faculties. This had resulted in extreme fragmentation. As only a handful of universities could boast a 'local population' of at least ten or twelve anthropologists, the situation had changed little since the 1970s, when the freshly appointed professors of anthropological disciplines found themselves isolated and 'homeless' (Grottanelli 1977: 599). A new law promising full academic autonomy to universities had led Bernardi to 'dream of a new kind of anthropological department in Italy' (1990: 12), but in the late 1990s this dream had partly come true only where anthropologists were relatively numerous, and even there, owing to the separation of functions and prerogatives between departments and faculties, they had been given few and limited opportunities to join forces for teaching purposes. The only significant exception was postgraduate teaching. In 1986, the first Italian Ph.D. programme in anthropology was launched in Rome and others were started in the following years. A distinctive feature of doctoral programmes was that they were run by the departments rather than by the faculties. Because of the institutional and spatial fragmentation of the Italian anthropological community, they also tended to be established through university joint ventures, with the strongest departments acting as the administrative centres of the programmes and providing the core of the teaching staff.

At the turn of the new millennium, however, the Italian university system was revolutionized by the Bologna declaration of 19 June 1999. Until then,

Italian universities had offered only two degrees: the *laurea*, which in most faculties took four years to complete, and the doctorate. This two-tier system was now to be replaced by a sequence of three cycles, as established by a set of regulations mostly laid down by the government through a ministerial decree of 3 November 1999: three-year degrees providing basic instruction, to be followed by two-year courses offering specialized training in more specific fields and finally by three-year courses of advanced studies and research to achieve doctoral degrees.

While this reform offered, in principle, opportunities for change and growth, many feared that the fragmentation of the anthropological community across boundaries, which divided not only the various universities but also the various faculties of the same university, might prove a fatal structural weakness. This would have been paradoxical, as well as regrettable, in a period in which there were many signs pointing to a rising demand for anthropological training both from university students and from Italian society at large. The past fifteen years have partly confirmed that these fears were well grounded. Other developments were less predictable. To some extent, these unexpected developments have been the product of the chaotic dynamics of the university reform itself. As many pedagogic shortcomings and organizational problems soon became evident, the government was urged to promulgate a series of corrective measures, and a ministerial decree issued in 2004 effectively amounted to a 'reform of the reform'. No less importantly, the Italian political scene has also changed several times. The 1999 reform was elaborated by a centre-left government and enacted only weeks before the May 2001 elections that brought the centre-right parties back to power. The 2006 elections were won by a centre-left coalition, but after only two years new elections were called, with the victory of the centre-right. Things are now going to change even more radically because of a new sweeping and politically controversial reform that imposes the abolition of faculties and the taking over of their teaching functions by new and larger departments. Before tackling these issues, however, it is sensible to outline some of the theoretical and practical problems Italian anthropologists were forced to confront in the last decades of the twentieth century, the main research orientations that have emerged, the challenges that Italian society is posing and the answers anthropology has been able, or has failed, to provide.

RESEARCH FIELDS, THEORETICAL ORIENTATIONS AND
NEW CHALLENGES

The thorny dilemma faced by Italian anthropologists in the 1960s and 70s was whether they should emulate and catch up with what their colleagues were doing in such countries as France, Britain and the United States or, rather, look for a specifically Italian way of practising anthropology. Most of those who presented themselves as cultural anthropologists (as opposed to ethnologists) eventually opted for the latter alternative, thus running the risk not only of drifting into jingoism or theoretical 'autarky' (Remotti 1978) but also of positing a rigid partition of humankind into 'us' and 'them', the Italians studied by cultural anthropology and the 'primitives' left to ethnologists. However, the issue was complex, as Italy, like other southern European countries, had itself been the object of investigation by foreign anthropologists, who had emphasized the 'primitiveness' of Italian culture, especially in the south, and had either ignored local anthropological traditions or dismissed them as mere folklore studies (Filippucci 1996: 52). It is understandable that such notions as Banfield's (1958) 'amoral familism' may have generated diffidence towards Anglo-Saxon anthropology, all the more so since they evoked a negative image of the Italian South that had played a major role in Italy's 'Southern Question' (Gribaudi 1996; Schneider 1998). It is even more understandable that in Italy, as in other southern European countries (Leal 2001), a number of local anthropologists took offence at the disparaging attitude epitomized by John Davis's famous vignette in which 'a contemporary ethnographer from France or England or America, carrying the latest lightweight intellectual machine gun in his pack' is suddenly confronted, during his field research in Mediterranean Europe, 'by a Tylorean or Frazerian professor appearing like a Japanese corporal from the jungle to wage a battle only he knows is still on' (1977: 3–4). Besides embittering the relations between 'indigenous' anthropologists and their Anglo-American colleagues (Minicuci 2003; Hauschild 2005), the resentment caused by this attitude reinforced the tendency towards theoretical 'autarky' and had serious repercussions in the heated debate then raging between ethnologists, students of folklore and cultural anthropologists of various persuasions.

Today most practitioners would deny any essential difference between social or cultural anthropology and ethnology. Indeed, it is not uncommon for Italian anthropologists, after conducting spells of fieldwork in extra-European countries, to direct their research towards Italy, or vice versa. The collapse of these barriers has favoured contacts and exchanges between the different traditions and convergence towards common themes of discussion. This urgency to promote both theoretical confrontation and the growth of sectors of special significance led the AISEA to establish four sections specifically devoted to Historical Anthropology, Museum Anthropology, Anthropology and Literature and the Anthropology of Development. Founded in 1992, the Historical Anthropology section has played an important role in directing the attention of Italian anthropologists not only to the availability and anthropological relevance of a wide range of archival and other historical sources (Silvestrini 1999), but also to methodological and epistemological debates, which have been especially lively and fertile in Italy thanks to the stimuli provided by the 'microhistory school' (Viazzo 2000). Similar results have been achieved by the Museum Anthropology section, also created in 1992, with the aim of offering a meeting place for anthropologists working in academic contexts and their colleagues employed by ethnographic museums. This section has made a notable contribution to stimulating theoretical reflection in a field where a number of scholars are trying to combine a sophisticated and distinctive Italian approach, derived from the study of popular traditions (Cirese 1977), with the new perspectives opened up by postmodernist anthropology (Clemente 1996).[2] Although the AISEA has not been the only arena for anthropological debate in Italy, an examination of its activities and endeavours helps one to realize that, in the past decades, Italy has been the scene of one of the increasingly frequent and fruitful encounters between the hegemonic British, French and American traditions and subaltern national traditions (Gupta and Ferguson 1997: 19–32).

While the tradition stemming from De Martino and Cirese is proving alive and kicking, even a sympathetic survey of Italian folklore studies has nevertheless been forced to recognize their limitations, most notably their tendency to focus almost exclusively on pre-industrial practices and ways of life (Bravo 2001: 8). These limitations have been laid bare by a set of transformations that have profoundly changed Italian society: firstly, the depopulation of the countryside and the expansion of towns and cities; then the slowing down of urban growth itself and the first signs of a new demographic transition characterized by fertility decline and population ageing; and, finally, the arrival in those same towns and cities of large numbers of immigrants, quite often from the very parts of the world where ethnology and anthropology cut their teeth as fieldwork disciplines. If demologia has been caught on the wrong foot by these changes, it is only fair to add that the skills and expertise acquired by ethnologists and anthropologists when studying the 'remote Other' in distant and mostly rural places rarely stand up to the task of studying immigrants in domestic and mostly urban contexts. A rapid development of new skills and expertise is clearly required. Italian anthropology has been slow in reacting to these new challenges: only fifteen years ago urban anthropology could hardly be defined as a popular research field in Italy, and the attention paid to immigration was also surprisingly limited. However, the number of anthropological studies in these two fields has now grown exponentially, even if the total output still lags behind that of sociologists.

Although Italian anthropology will certainly need to turn to disciplines like sociology, economics and demography in order to overcome these limitations, it should be noted that sociologists, economists and demographers are themselves looking for help from anthropologists – not only to obtain a better understanding of immigration, but also to make sense of some elusive aspects of the 'second demographic transition' and of the related metamorphosis of family forms – and answers are finally starting to be provided (Gribaldo, Judd and Kertzer 2009; Grilli and Zanotelli 2010). Since the 1990s, calls for anthropological help have also been coming from those categories of professionals most likely to interact with immigrants and their families (school teachers, social workers, doctors and nurses). The establishment of anthropology courses by faculties of medicine has been a promising development, but so far these courses, given by contract lecturers, have only been catering for the needs of future nurses and midwives. As universities have been hard pressed to meet this new demand for some degree of anthropological training, medical staff already working in hospitals and surgeries, and other professionals, have been mostly forced to attend extramural courses organized by regional and local authorities as well as by a variety of NGOs.

One reason why, on the eve of the 1999 reform, Italian university teachers were so hard pressed was that existing courses were oversubscribed by the rising numbers of students who chose to include anthropology in their undergraduate courses and picked anthropological subjects as topics for their dissertations. Such interest was explained partly by the increased chances of meeting other cultures either abroad or at home and partly by anthropology's ability to offer unique perspectives on the interconnections and tensions between 'global villages' and 'local worlds' so characteristic of present-day society. The advent of the reform was awaited with trepidation by Italian anthropologists, who were aware of structural weaknesses in the academic organization of their discipline but also saw promises of expansion sufficient to meet the growing demand for anthropological training. The past decade has undoubtedly witnessed some expansion, but this seemingly successful story has been ridden with contradictions and hampered by serious drawbacks, and prospects for the future look uncertain. Even more so since the contested Gelmini Reform (so named after Italy's Education Minister) was finally voted in December 2010 and came into force on 29 January 2011.

A FRAGILE AND CONTRADICTORY EXPANSION (2000–2010)

By weakening or utterly abolishing the distinction between compulsory and optional courses, the 1969 reform had given formerly second-class disciplines (like ethnology and cultural anthropology, along with many others) a chance to acquire full academic credentials. Thirty years later, the new reform had similar and in many respects even more far-reaching effects on the structure of university teaching and the contents of curriculums. The decree issued by the Ministry of University and Higher Education in November 1999 did not simply establish a new system consisting of three-year degrees offering basic and broad-based instruction to be followed by more specialized two-year courses. It also encouraged the creation of innovative degree courses, not least in order to meet the new cultural, economic and technological needs of Italian society. These opportunities were taken up by all universities. Bearing in mind the great cultural but also economic importance of Italy's artistic legacy, virtually every Italian university instituted a three-year course in Cultural Heritage and virtually everywhere these new courses attracted large crowds of students. Since they often included one or more 'demo-ethno-anthropological' exam in their curriculums, their creation and numerical success turned out to be a significant factor of expansion for anthropology. But a dozen universities went one or even two steps further by launching first- and second-level courses either specifically devoted to the teaching and learning of cultural anthropology and ethnology or having anthropological disciplines at their core.[3]

The establishment of these courses means that it is now possible to obtain university degrees in Anthropology and Ethnology at the pre-doctoral level. This makes the issue of professional recognition even more urgent than before, but it also poses problems of an organizational and pedagogical nature. Although precise figures are difficult and time-consuming to collect, and often quite hard to obtain, there can be little doubt that the new courses have proved very attractive. Annual intakes of 300 or more for first-level courses have been recorded in Rome and other large Italian universities such as Bologna and Turin. As to second-level courses, the total annual intake of aspiring anthropologists for Italy rose from 168 in 2003 to over 500 in 2007.[4] These figures point to an increase that is definitely greater than that experienced by the Italian university student population as a whole, which in the first half of the last decade went up by approximately 15 per cent, with a peak around 2005 and a slight decline thereafter. Once we consider that anthropology continues to be taught in most Italian universities as part of more 'traditional' curriculums (philosophy, history, education, psychology, sociology, etc.), there can be little doubt that, if measured by the number of students, this is a huge success story. But is the anthropological profession large enough to face the new tasks? Has it grown in proportion to the increasing number of students?

Table 4.1 shows that between 2001 and 2007 the number of anthropology professors rose by a quarter, from 165 to 207 – a noticeable increase, but hardly commensurate to the greatly increased number of students – and that in the following years it has actually fallen back to 184. Adding a quick comparative perspective, Table 4.2 reveals that the size of tenured teaching staff in anthropology has increased more than the Italian professoriate taken as a whole, but also that both sociology and psychology have grown faster and more securely, which hints at a reduced ability of anthropologists (at least compared to the representatives of other social and human sciences) to convince academic authorities to create new positions for their discipline. All in all, it would thus seem that disciplinary expansion, as measured by massive annual intakes of new students, has not been mirrored by proper structural consolidation: the ratio between anthropology teachers and their students has worsened and they are more hard pressed by teaching duties and organizational burdens than they were before the reform, with

TABLE 4.1. University professors of anthropology in Italy (2001–2010)

Date	Full professors	Associate professors	Assistant professors	Total
31.12.2001	30	65	70	165
31.12.2004	44	65	77	186
31.12.2007	51	66	90	207
31.12.2010	36	54	94	184

Source: Italian Ministry of Education.

TABLE 4.2. Number of anthropologists, sociologists and psychologists in Italian universities (2001–2010)

Date	Anthropologists		Sociologists		Psychologists		Italian professoriate	
	N	Index	N	Index	N	Index	N	Index
31.12.2001	165	100	781	100	877	100	55,037	100
31.12.2004	186	113	867	111	978	112	57,556	105
31.12.2007	207	125	1,035	133	1,187	136	62,393	113
31.12.2010	184	112	1,066	136	1,244	142	59,046	107

Source: Italian Ministry of Education.

damaging effects on their ability to devote time to research and writing. Given the emphasis that is more and more placed on research assessment by governmental agencies and grant-giving bodies, this is clearly a situation that threatens to trap Italian anthropology and anthropologists in a dangerous vicious circle.

Yet these are not the only or the most important perplexing aspects of Italian anthropology's fragile expansion. Large numbers of students do not simply pose didactical and organizational problems; they also raise, far more acutely than before, the question of professional recognition. As we have seen, every year over 500 students enrol in Italian universities to receive specialized training in sociocultural anthropology and ethnology, with legitimate ambitions to become, in one way or another, professional anthropologists or, at least, to use what they have learned to get satisfactory jobs. For the many who would like to carry on with research, becoming Ph.D. students is a primary goal, but individual chances of being admitted to doctoral programmes have inevitably declined, since the number of 'slots' available has at best remained fixed, while the number of aspiring candidates has greatly increased.

For the overwhelming majority of anthropology graduates, however, the most pressing issues concern professional recognition and occupational opportunities. When in 1999 the government made specific provisions that authorized the institution of second level degrees in Cultural Anthropology and Ethnology, many hopes of formal professional recognition (similar to that enjoyed by psychologists) were attached to this innovation. These hopes were justified by, among other things, the recent official recognition of the pedagogic importance of anthropology and the other social sciences also for pre-higher education. In 1998, the social sciences had been singled out as one of the building blocks of curriculums in all kinds of secondary schools, where students could even opt for special courses with explicit emphasis on the study of the social sciences. The first textbooks specifically intended for the teaching and learning of the social sciences in secondary schools had just been published and it was significant that cultural anthropology was placed on an equal footing with psychology and sociology. In the light of this entry into secondary education, it seemed logical to expect the creation of specific university degrees in Anthropology alongside those in Sociology and Psychology. Unfortunately, these hopes have been dashed. With the advent of the centre-right government in 2001, the position accorded to the social sciences in secondary school curriculums was immediately challenged. Briefly restored after the elections of 2006, it is now under attack once again. Similarly, anthropological degrees have so far failed to receive formal recognition as a necessary or desirable prerequisite for jobs in areas where anthropological training would seem essential. Anthropology graduates are therefore left to compete in a wild, and yet often very rigidly regulated, labour market, where they may find themselves overtaken by candidates holding degrees that are far less suitable to the job but more solidly recognized.

CONCLUSION: SKILL-BASED PEDAGOGY AS AN ANTIDOTE TO AUTISTIC ANTHROPOLOGY

The sketchy picture outlined in the preceding section indicates that the expansion of anthropology after the 1999 reform, while real, has been ridden with paradoxes and contradictions. What is more, the high degree of uncertainty that surrounds Italian universities and permeates Italian society makes any forecast of the discipline's future exceedingly hazardous. The abolition of faculties imposed by the Gelmini Reform is redesigning the whole structure of the university system, and the limits to the recruitment of new teachers and researchers any government is likely to impose in times of severe economic crisis are bound to prove no less decisive. In these circumstances, it is easy to guess that anthropology will find it more difficult than other disciplines to thrive. Nevertheless, there are reasons to believe that the future of the discipline will also depend on the courses of action embarked upon by Italian anthropologists. Although the long-term consequences of the new reform cannot yet be foretold, the anthropological degree courses made possible by the previous reform should continue to exist, but their curriculums will probably need to be modified in some significant respects. An unusual anthropological study suggests that this might perhaps be for the better.

In a recent article, Angelo Romano (2010) reports the results of a field study on the effects of the 1999 reform upon the teaching and learning of anthropology in Italy, whose primary ethnographic setting was the Department of Anthropology of La Sapienza University in Rome. Besides observing the practices of both teachers and students, he collected vivid accounts that betray the genuine enthusiasm that accompanied the planning of the new anthropological degrees – in Rome (where anthropologists joined forces with social historians) and elsewhere. As Romano correctly observes, the reform appeared to provide unique opportunities and certainly required a rethinking of anthropology by professors, students and the professional world. If these opportunities have been partly missed, this is attributable to the rigid ministerial grids, which limited the possibility for anthropologists to create courses that would genuinely include other fields of academic and applied study, but also to a propensity of Italian anthropologists to aim more at reproducing the discipline than at enhancing a skill-based pedagogy. Time was therefore allocated more to the teaching and learning of anthropological theory than to practical training.

These findings echo the alarming diagnosis of the state of Portuguese anthropology made some years ago by Graça Índias Cordeiro and Ana Isabel Afonso (2003: 176), according to which 'excessively theoretical programmes' may seriously hamper the training of future anthropologists and condemn the discipline to 'an almost autistic existence, continuing as exclusively academic knowledge produced by and for university departments'. This is a risk anthropology is running everywhere, but it is probably higher in those countries where the discipline has developed within a primarily academic framework. Its confinement to secluded academic life would be a loss not simply for the corporation of professional anthropologists but for Italian society at large in which anthropological expertise is invoked in many quarters, especially to deal with the delicate problems of intercultural communication and multi-ethnic coexistence that immigration is raising. A 'less endogamic type of education' (Romano 2010: 71), focused more on skill-based pedagogy than on the academic reproduction of the discipline, might prove an antidote to merely autistic survival and should receive priority if Italian anthropologists are given a chance to modify the curriculums of their degree courses.

Pier Paolo Viazzo received his Ph.D. from University College London and is now Professor of Social Anthropology at the University of Turin, Italy. He has published extensively on European social and demographic history as well as on family and marriage patterns in the Alps and the Mediterranean region.

NOTES

1. This outline of the historical development of Italian anthropology draws largely on Viazzo (2003: 182–86, 2005: 199–205) and is based on the earlier accounts by Grottanelli (1977), Saunders (1984), Clemente et al. (1985), Filippucci (1996) and Remotti (1996) as well as on the recent, massive volume by Alliegro (2011).
2. An association of academic and other professional anthropologists with a special interest in museums and cultural heritage (SIMBDEA: Società Italiana per la Museografia e i Beni Demoetnoantropologici) was founded in 2001.
3. For detailed information see Viazzo (2008: 14–22).
4. Source: Italian Ministry of Education. Reliable figures are unfortunately unavailable for the following years.

REFERENCES

Alliegro, E.V. 2011. *Antropologia italiana: Storia e storiografia 1869–1975*. Florence: SEID Edizioni.

Angioni, G. 1994. 'Une demo-ethno-anthropologie? Des pères fondateurs aux problèmes actuels', *Ethnologie Française* 24(3): 455–73.

Banfield, E.C. 1958. *The Moral Basis of a Backward Society*. Glencoe, IL: Free Press.

Bernardi, B. 1990. 'An Anthropological Odyssey', *Annual Review of Anthropology* 19: 1–15.

Bianchi, U. 1971. *Storia dell'etnologia*. Rome: Edizioni Abete.

Biscione, M. (ed.). 1998. *Associazione Italiana per le Scienze Etno-Antropologiche: Annuario 1998*. Rome: AISEA.

Bravo, G.L. 2001. *Italiani. Racconto etnografico*. Rome: Meltemi.

Charuty, G. 2011. *Ernesto de Martino: Le precedenti vite di un antropologo*. Milan: Franco Angeli.

Cirese, A.M. 1977. *Oggetti, segni, musei: Sulle tradizioni contadine*. Turin: Einaudi.

Clemente, P. 1996. *Graffiti di museografia antropologica*. Perugia: Protagon.

Clemente, P. et al. 1985. *L'antropologia in Italia: un secolo di storia*. Rome and Bari: Laterza

Clemente, P., M.L. Meoni and M. Squillacciotti. 1976. *Il dibattito sul folklore in Italia*. Milan: Edizioni di Cultura Popolare.

Cordeiro, G.I. and A.I. Afonso. 2003. 'Cultural and Social Anthropology in the Portuguese University: Dilemmas of Teaching and Practice', in D. Dracklé, I. Elgar and T.K. Schippers (eds), *Educational Histories of European Social Anthropology*. Oxford: Berghahn Books, pp. 169–80.

Davis, J. 1977. *People of the Mediterranean: An Essay in Comparative Social Anthropology*. London: Routledge and Kegan Paul.

Filippucci, P. 1996. 'Anthropological Perspectives on Culture in Italy', in D. Forgacs and R. Lumley (eds), *Italian Cultural Studies*. Oxford: Oxford University Press, pp. 52–71.

Godelier, M. 1997. 'American Anthropology as Seen from France', *Anthropology Today* 13(1): 3–5.

Gribaldo, A., M. Judd and D.I. Kertzer. 2009. 'An "Imperfect" Contraceptive Society: Fertility and Contraception in Italy', *Population and Development Review* 35(3): 551–84.

Gribaudi, G. 1996. 'Images of the South', in D. Forgacs and R. Lumley (eds), *Italian Cultural Studies*. Oxford: Oxford University Press, pp. 72–87.

Grilli, S. and F. Zanotelli (eds). 2010. *Scelte di famiglia: Tendenze della parentela nella società contemporanea*. Pisa: Edizioni ETS.

Grottanelli, V.L. 1977. 'Ethnology and/or Cultural Anthropology in Italy', *Current Anthropology* 18(4): 593–601.

Gupta, A. and J. Ferguson. 1997. 'Discipline and Practice: "The Field" as Site, Method, and Location in Anthropology', in A. Gupta and J. Ferguson (eds), *Anthropological Locations: Boundaries and Grounds of a Field Science*. Berkeley: University of California Press, pp. 1–46.

Hauschild, T. 2005. 'Le maître, l'indigène et moi: Anthropologie réciproque en Italie du Sud', in D. Albera and M. Tozy (eds), *La Méditerranée des anthropologues*. Paris: Maisonneuve et Larose, pp. 313–34.

Leal, J. 2001. '"Tylorian Professors" and "Japanese Corporals" : Anthropological Theory and National Identity in Portuguese Ethnography', in D. Albera, A. Blok and C. Bromberger (eds), *L'anthropologie de la Méditerranée*. Paris: Maisonneuve et Larose, pp. 645–62.

Leone, A.R. 1985. 'La Chiesa, i cattolici e le scienze dell'uomo (1860–1960)', in P. Clemente et al., *L'antropologia in Italia: un secolo di storia*. Rome and Bari: Laterza, pp. 51–96.

Loria, L. 1912. 'Due parole di programma', *Lares* 1: 9–24.

Mantegazza, P. 1871. *Quadri della natura umana*. Milan: Bernardoni.

Mascarenhas-Keyes, S. and S. Wright. 1995. *Report on Teaching and Learning Social Anthropology in the United Kingdom*. London: Social Anthropology Teaching and Learning Network.

Minicuci, M. 2003. 'Antropologi e Mezzogiorno', *Meridiana* 47–48: 139–74.

Puccini, S. 1999. *Andare lontano: Viaggi ed etnografia nel secondo Ottocento*. Rome: Carocci.

———. 2006. *L'itala gente dalle molte vite: Lamberto Loria e la Mostra di Etnografia Italiana del 1911*. Rome: Meltemi.

Remotti, F. 1978. 'Tendenze autarchiche nell'antropologia culturale italiana', *Rassegna Italiana di Sociologia* 19(4): 183–226.

———. 1996. 'Antropologia', in C. Stajano (ed.), *La cultura italiana del Novecento*. Rome and Bari: Laterza, pp. 3–25.

Romano, A. 2010. 'Studying Anthropology in the Age of the University Reform', *Social Anthropology* 18(1): 57–73.

Saunders, G.R. 1984. 'Contemporary Italian Cultural Anthropology', *Annual Review of Anthropology* 13: 447–66.

Schneider, J. (ed.). 1998. *Italy's 'Southern Question': Orientalism in One Country*. Oxford: Berg.

Silvestrini, E. (ed.). 1999. *Fare antropologia storica: Le fonti*. Rome: Bulzoni.

Viazzo, P.P. 2000. *Introduzione all'antropologia storica*. Rome and Bari: Laterza.

———. 2003. 'Teaching and Learning Anthropology in Italy: Institutional Development and Pedagogic Challenges', in D. Dracklé, I. Elgar and T.K. Schippers (eds), *Educational Histories of European Social Anthropology*. Oxford: Berghahn Books, pp. 181–92.

———. 2005. 'L'anthropologie en Italie: origines, développement institutionnel et orientations actuelles', in D. Albera and M. Tozy (eds), *La Méditerranée des anthropologues*. Paris: Maisonneuve et Larose, pp. 199–213.

———. 2008. *Anthropology and Ethnology in Italy: A Preliminary Report*. Available at http://pendientedemigracion.ucm.es/info/antrosim/docs/Paolo_Viazzo_Anthropology_Ethnology_in_Italy.pdf

5

THE TRAJECTORY OF FRENCH
ANTHROPOLOGY, SEEN THROUGH A
RECENT TRANSFORMATIVE EPISODE

SOPHIE CHEVALIER

This chapter offers a panoramic view of contemporary French anthropology, partly following Robert Parkin's article on its history in the book *One Discipline, Four Ways* (Chicago University Press, 2005). Whereas Robert Parkin is an outsider, I actively engaged in building up the discipline, so that a measure of self-reflection is inevitable. My story takes off from an event in 2007 when an 'Assessment of Anthropology in France' bought together the anthropological community for three days in Paris. The reasons for this meeting, the debates that took place and the collective decision to form a new unified federation were a strong message sent to French anthropology.

While there is some truth to the image of French anthropology/ethnology as a fragmented discipline whose main institutions are subjected to endless and brutal interventions, this is only a partial account of what goes on in the name of anthropology today. In my review of the institutional field I consider the state of the discipline in the main national institutions and, more broadly, relations with the other social sciences, which were mostly inherited from the past; links to the museums, which, after a lapse, have been renewed recently; the main objects of study, methods and levels of observation and areas of geographical concentration; the prominent theoretical themes and their producers; the dissemination of anthropological knowledge and the language question; and professional career options. Does French anthropology retain its own specific identity when compared to the main Western traditions of anthropology, and also with regard to new directions for the discipline in the rest of the world?

In what follows, I will outline the French tradition of anthropology only briefly, concentrating rather on the present situation in some detail (see also Chevalier 2015a). Parkin's (2005) review offers a good guide to French anthropology's historical development. Whereas he is an outsider I, however, am actively engaged in organizing the discipline as a contemporary practitioner, so my account is inevitably more subjective.

Anthropology is unusual for the number of names it has assumed in different national traditions, in which relations with neighbouring disciplines vary considerably. At the same time, the recent emergence of a world anthropology, with English as its lingua franca, has introduced a degree of homogenization, including in France, despite a measure of cultural resistance. Like British social anthropology, the modern French discipline owes much to Durkheim's sociology project and has struggled institutionally with an ethnology focused on folklore, material culture and local traditions. But, unlike in Britain, an ecumenical version of sociology, including what might be taken elsewhere for anthropology, was institutionally dominant and *ethnologie* was retained as the normal description of what ethnographers do. Specialist study of small-scale rural cultures was as likely to be undertaken in rural France as in the colonies until Lévi-Strauss chose to label his structuralist project *anthropologie sociale*. Since then the two terms have coexisted with 'anthropology' now tending to prevail as the general term.

My point of departure is an insider's ethnographic account of very recent attempts to reorganize the plural organization of French anthropology in the context of threats to the discipline's integrity and indeed to higher education in general. As mentioned, in 2007, the anthropological community came together for a historical three-day event in Paris to make an 'Assessment of Anthropology in France'. I will explain the reasons for this meeting, the discussions held and the collective decision to form a new unified federation after years of internal division. I will add a sketch of the contemporary intellectual terrain, reflecting on theoretical approaches, methods and levels of inquiry, areas of geographical concentration and the main objects of study. Finally, I will examine the dissemination of anthropological knowledge and the language question. The chapter concludes by asking whether French anthropology has a specific identity any longer. For all the obstacles that it faces, a lot of exciting work is being carried out in its name.

A SPECIAL EVENT: THE NATIONAL ASSESSMENT
OF FRENCH ANTHROPOLOGY

In 2007, the two associations for general anthropology, the Association Française des Anthropologues (AFA) and the Association Pour la Recherche en Anthropologie Sociale (APRAS), co-organized a national assessment exercise for anthropology, the Assises de l'ethnologie et de l'anthropologie en France (note the use of both terms for the discipline).[1] This was meant to be an evaluation of the discipline carried out by its practitioners, as opposed to a government-sponsored ranking exercise. A number of smaller and more specialized groups joined these two main associations, many of them concerned with practising or disseminating anthropology outside universities and the principal research institutions.

This assessment exercise was made possible by a specific historical context. AFA was founded in 1979 and, due to conflicts over strategy and organization, a dissident part, APRAS, broke away to form a rival general association in 1989. When the older generation of anthropologists retired, the lines of division between these two associations became blurred and the two groups of members found that they could work together for this 2007 meeting, while still maintaining their distinct identities. APRAS had the reputation of being the more elitist of the two associations, being well-established in the CNRS (National Centre for Scientific Research) where it exercised its influence; it also played an active part in discussions over the foundation of the Musée du Quai Branly. It organized lectures and conferences that helped bring intellectual debates within anthropology to the attention of the French public. AFA had more flexible recruitment criteria, accepting members without professional institutional status, a move that the APRAS has copied only recently. AFA publishes the *Journal des Anthropologues* as a vehicle for an anthropology that is more involved in public debates and contemporary politics.

The other key factor was a series of reforms launched by the French administrations of the two institutions mainly responsible for academic anthropology, the CNRS and universities. These changes led to reductions in the number of jobs available to recent Ph.D. students and to a professional landscape where anthropologists were more numerous outside academia than within it. No previous generation had experienced anything like this. The assessment exercise thus provided an occasion on which the whole discipline, regardless of professional standing, could come together to discuss a critical situation.

This gathering of French anthropologists to discuss the discipline's present and future, while exploring possibilities for presenting a united front, was unprecedented in recent decades – the last one had taken place in 1977. Three decades later, for three days in December 2007, about 350 people met each day in Paris's two main anthropology museums, which had themselves been for several years a focus of considerable controversy between competing visions of the discipline – the Musée de l'Homme and the Musée du Quai Branly. (I will return to this point.) The sessions first took place in the empty and freezing halls of the former and then in the latter's luxurious Claude Lévi-Strauss amphitheatre.

Much of the discussion was concerned with French anthropology's current institutional difficulties and particularly with the almost exclusive focus on training for academic research. which had led to large numbers of doctoral students pursuing a handful of university or specialist research positions. Some participants felt that the development of training tracks geared to non-academic careers would offer an effective way to respond to student and public interest in anthropology, while also shoring up the discipline's future in French society.

More than this, it was widely recognized that new objects and methods for the discipline were needed and that the position of anthropologists in our own society should be reviewed. One session specifically addressed anthropology's relations with other disciplines. The challenge posed to French anthropology's international standing by the rising dominance of English in global scholarship also occupied their attention. This is particularly important for a discipline that (unlike other social sciences or some other national traditions of anthropology) is largely organized around specific geographical areas shared with international networks of peers from many countries. Of course, English is also strong in the rest of Europe, while the need for multinational collaboration is stressed by funding bodies.

It was somewhat disappointing that relatively few senior anthropologists attended the *Assises*, although some publicly indicated their support. Even so, the turnout was impressive and the level of enthusiasm high. The predominance of junior academics and students held out some hope for the future. The presence at these meetings of colleagues from the French regions served to remind everyone that anthropology in France is not exclusively a Parisian – or strictly academic – profession.

Other events since then have brought people together to discuss the state of the discipline, including a 2008 forum of anthropological associations in Aix that attracted representatives from some twenty associations (out of more than thirty who expressed an interest). These associations are based on geographical area (e.g. the Société des Océanistes), specialism (e.g. Applied Medical Anthropology for Development and Health, AMADES) or general anthropology but with regionally based practitioners (e.g. Rhône-Alpes).

Following these deliberations, a small group worked together assiduously for more than a year to build up a new national association, the Association

Française d'Ethnologie et d'Anthropologie (AFEA), which ended up admitting the members of associations like the APRAS and AFA and individual subscribers. This was the first step towards unity in a slow and difficult process that the protagonists hoped would give rise to a more effective public voice for the defence of the discipline. The first annual conference of AFEA was held in Paris during September 2011 at the Graduate School for the Social Sciences (EHESS). It was based on a model taken from other countries, such as that of the Association of Social Anthropologists of the UK and the Commonwealth or, on a much larger scale, of the American Anthropological Association (AAA). The organizers wished to allow participants to discover the range of topics covered by anthropologists around the country, including graduate students and recent Ph.D. students. Six hundred people attended, two-thirds of them as presenters, divided between forty-five panels and eleven round-table discussions.

SOME INSTITUTIONAL FEATURES
OF FRENCH ANTHROPOLOGY

The main feature of anthropology in France – and this is not new – is that the discipline's institutional position within French academia has been remarkably weak compared to its international standing. For historical reasons (Chevalier 2015b), sociology has always been stronger than anthropology, even though they were born together through the work of Durkheim and Mauss. Compared with other social sciences, anthropology has little presence in the French university system and depends disproportionately on research institutions for employment. By most accounts, there are about 350 professional anthropologists employed in France, with about half holding full-time research positions (160 in the CNRS, some in the Institute for Development Research (IRD) and the other half in university posts – of which the EHESS has a large share). The latter are evenly divided between anthropology appointments and positions in other departments (often sociology). All academics with combined responsibility for teaching and research and researchers in the CNRS have posts in academia and research institutions and promotions are made through national commissions comprised of their peers. CNRS researchers are appointed and controlled by a commission whose members are partly elected and partly appointed by the Ministry of Research. Academics who teach as well as do research are selected and promoted in two stages: first, a national commission vets candidates' eligibility, then the universities themselves make the actual appointments. CNRS researchers are even more subject to bureaucratic control, and also to national recruitment policies; for instance, positive discrimination favouring women in recruitment for senior research positions, which has proved on the whole beneficial. Changes in women's recruitment at the professorial level are slow (women account for 17% of full professors across all disciplines in France). Selection by one's peers may of course be problematic, and the rapid turnover of anthropologists serving on the commission ensures that most strands of the discipline are represented over time.

As I have already noted, French anthropology, in contrast with Britain for example, is not as strong or as well organized as sociology. Until the formation of the new federation of anthropological associations (AFEA), anthropologists did not have a national association to defend their interests, especially when it came to safeguarding the discipline's position at universities. Sociologists, on the other hand, have long had a national association, as well as a specific association for university teachers in sociology. In any subject – and anthropology is no exception – policymaking, research centres and training are centralized in Paris, despite consistent efforts to create centres in regional universities, such as the Centre for Research and Documentation on Oceania in Aix-Marseille. There are of course some dynamic university departments and small research laboratories in the provinces.

Anthropologists teach in a huge variety of academic contexts, mainly due to the shortage of full-time positions in anthropology departments but also because of the widespread demand for anthropologists' methodological competence in other social science departments. Today probably more anthropologists teach outside anthropology departments than in them. This means that teaching anthropology can no longer be just about training students to become professional anthropologists. Despite the discipline's relatively weak position within universities, the demand for anthropological teaching is strong.

The European Union's Bologna reform – the simplification of courses to three levels or 'LMD' (Licence/Masters/Doctorate) in order to harmonize university degrees across Europe – has not worked out well for anthropology in France. Indeed many anthropologists fear that anthropology could be further squeezed out of higher education as a result. In effect, the licence has become a necessary feeder for Masters' programmes. But relatively little undergraduate level anthropology training is available in French universities.[2] Anthropology programmes often do not really start until Master's level in many universities or at the EHESS, which trains the lion's share of graduate students. This leaves the pressing question of how to ensure that undergraduate students get initial exposure to the discipline, given that only a handful of universities offer degrees in Anthropology at this level. Moreover, anthropology training at Master's level is increasingly limited to multidisciplinary programmes, where it is often a marginal partner in a 'forced marriage' with other, stronger disciplines imposed by bureaucracy.

Doctoral programmes have been formed in some universities by faculties composed of several departments that share research grants for doctoral students, putting departments (and disciplines) in competition with each other. The time usually taken by anthropology students for completing a Ph.D. is a handicap for grant applications. Either grants are not awarded on these grounds or they do not cover the whole period needed for completing the Ph.D. In other words, the specific requirements of the discipline are not recognized. It is becoming ever more difficult to get state funding of anthropological research for a doctoral thesis. The Ministry of Research has tried to restrict university enrolments to students with public funding, but only some universities have obeyed this directive.

Research is carried out in universities but it has to be combined with teaching and administrative tasks. In the CNRS, researchers do not have to teach – they can do it as a sideline, and they usually do, but it is not compulsory. These researchers are organized in centres based on geographical or topical research interests. University teachers may be associated with one of these centres. Anthropology research centres are attached to section 38 of the CNRS as part of the Institute for Human and Social Sciences, which controls policy in this area and makes most final decisions, even if they go against the recommendations of the disciplinary commissions.

Until recently, people were quite free to choose their research topics, because everyone had a right to a share of the money available at their centre and these funds were redistributed internally. But recently the ministry has reduced the amount of money allocated to research centres and requires researchers to apply for specific projects run by a new body, the National Agency for Research (ANR). The social sciences are not a high priority for the ANR, which does, however, provide special funds for young researchers.

A special organization, the Agency for the Evaluation of Research and Higher Education (AERES, today HCERES), is in charge of evaluating research centres and university degrees. Every five years it reviews university curricula, research centre projects and all the individuals involved. Teachers and researchers are placed in two categories, those who publish and those who do not, according to criteria fixed by AERES, which evaluates the number of publications and the class of journal. HCERES has come under strong criticism for its lack of transparency. It is difficult, for example, to know who the evaluators are or how to contact them.

As far as the Ministry is concerned, 'big is beautiful'. Universities are encouraged to regroup as clusters known as Poles for Research and Teaching (PRES) and research is increasingly organized through enormous projects combining various partners (universities, research centres and museums) known as LABEX. The main aim is for these clusters to achieve economies of scale through collaborations that the bureaucracy considers profitable.

Anthropology enters this professional ladder principally at the stage of research training. Moreover, there is a huge discrepancy between the demand for anthropology professionals in universities or research centres and the supply of doctoral students and recent Ph.D. students. Anthropology's dependence on public institutions is linked to the weakness of applied anthropology in France. Anthropologists still train students as if they will get a job at the CNRS or at universities. Under pressure from the authorities, but also from postdoc students, who cannot find jobs in the traditional institutions, some curricula are now being developed at Master's level with an eye to providing anthropological training suitable for a wider range of professions. The most successful of these are in medical anthropology. However the University of Lyon 2 has a Master's degree in 'the anthropology of art and culture' and the University of Provence one in 'the anthropology of development' (which is also taught at Strasbourg and Paris 7, but not run by anthropologists there). Some anthropologists from outside the mainstream profession – working in private companies or as consultants – have started to pool their experience and skills by organizing meetings and discussion groups. This is still quite new and, for a long time, was dismissed as irrelevant by the custodians of the mainstream discipline. Even now some argue that the only point of these activities is to sustain the hope of one day returning to academia.

LINKS TO MUSEUMS

The museum landscape of anthropology in France has been transformed in the last decade, above all in Paris. This has given rise to an abundant literature, much of it critical, even polemical, but I do not want to get into all that here.[3] The Museum of Mankind (Musée de l'Homme) and the National Museum of Popular Arts and Traditions (MNATP) have undergone changes that involve much more than the removal of their collections elsewhere. These changes rather express a paradigm shift for anthropology museums, from a scientific model – artefacts are there to be studied as a means of acquiring better knowledge about the societies that produced them – to an aesthetic one – artefacts are there to be wondered at. The most prestigious objects previously held by the Musée de l'Homme made their way to the new Musée du Quai Branly (MQB), known as the 'Museum of the First Arts'. The objects held by the MNATP were taken to Marseille, where they awaited the construction of a new building known as the Museum of European and Mediterranean Civilizations (MuCEM), which opened in 2013.

This redistribution of artefacts perpetuates the divide between 'Us' and 'Them', although the inclusion of the Mediterranean in Europe (partly

France's response to Germany's rising dominance in Europe itself) could be considered a small improvement. The MQB's exhibits were arranged by the architect Jean Nouvel in a traditional pattern according to geographical area, featuring the natives of Africa, Oceania, some parts of Asia[4] and the Americas. Many French anthropologists believe that art curators and merchants have imposed their point of view on this display and that the architecture expresses a myth of the primitive that has long fascinated the Western imagination, as Nouvel himself has explained elsewhere. This plan makes nonsense of anthropologists' reflections on museography, especially when compared with the pioneering museum of Neuchâtel (Switzerland) and counterparts in North America. The fact is that Quai Branly represents a move from ethnology to aesthetics and it has been enormously successful with the public. Anthropologists, in their turn, were at first reluctant to embrace this project and some of them would say they were excluded from it. Although research is not central to the new museum, since 2005 the secondment of Anne-Christine Taylor-Descola[5] to head the department of research and teaching there has generated funding for a number of research projects undertaken by doctoral students and postdocs. Some of the temporary exhibits are the fruit of long-term anthropological research, such as Philippe Descola's 'The image Workshop' (2010–2011). The museum also hosts courses, seminars and conferences. In however limited a way, the MQB is starting to play a leading role in organizing anthropological practice.

It can be said that the museography of the MuCEM and its exhibition policy are quite similar to that of the Quai Branly. Temporary exhibits on fashionable topics are combined with a permanent collection displaying the best pieces arranged in traditional fashion.[6] Moreover, there is a serious shortage of material from the rest of the Mediterranean, which has still to be collected. Here political considerations (President Sarkozy's proposed Mediterranean Union) have trumped scientific knowledge in the decision to expand the museum's geographical scope. Its predecessor's principal aim (the MNATP) was to reveal the peasant side of France in the spirit of salvage ethnography, particularly given the decline of traditional rural culture since the 1950s. But the initial focus of the museum on research and teaching began to wither away from the 80s, leading to these functions being hived off elsewhere. As in Quai Branly, curators play a key role in the scientific management and the place of the researchers is marginalized.

To sum up, the relationship between museums and research has been weakened as a result of both these transformations of institutions central to the history of anthropology in France. The new successor museums are engaged in a project of cultural dissemination in which anthropological research plays little or, at best, a marginal part. Unsurprisingly perhaps, studying art is now one of the major preoccupations of young French anthropologists.

RELATIONS WITH OTHER DISCIPLINES

French anthropology has always been linked to the other social sciences and the humanities, but it also has links with the 'hard sciences', such as biology and medicine. Sociology, however, is the discipline with which it has been most closely entangled. We may recall that Mauss was a sociologist long before he took over the Institute of Ethnology. If anthropologists have always enjoyed an unchallenged monopoly for their studies of 'the other', the substantial number of those who worked in France not only had to compete with the more recognized exotic branch but also to distinguish themselves from sociologists. Sociology, with its powerful institutional establishment, has always been the stronger discipline in France, putting ethnology permanently on the back foot. Undergraduate teaching today usually combines sociology and anthropology, and anthropologists are found more often in sociology departments than in their own. So the two disciplines are joined at the hip, as it were, and individuals often move between them in their careers. Is Bruno Latour a sociologist or an anthropologist? What about Didier Fassin? One solution to the ambiguity has been to label departments (and one journal) '*socio-anthropologie*'. Many anthropologists consider this to be an abuse of language, an attempt by sociology to suck the lifeblood out of their discipline by borrowing their ethnographic method and claiming to study human ontologies.[7] Being so close to sociologists, yet needing to differentiate themselves from them, has made French anthropologists slow to address questions of social class and gender that they took up later than anthropologists elsewhere, towards the end of the 70s. Only from the early 80s did they begin to take an interest in cities, industrial life, immigrant groups, sport and complex organizations, in short the whole range of social life rather than just a part of it.

Along with these developments came a renewed interest in philosophy. It had long been a tradition for many leading French anthropologists to come to the discipline from a training in philosophy – Mauss and Lévi-Strauss of course, but also a good number of the sixties generation, such as Maurice Godelier, Philippe Descola and Marc Abélès. Although this path is less common for young anthropologists today, philosophy is still an important point of reference for them and is enjoying something of a rebirth in anthropology, as manifested in joint seminars. Being attracted to ideas is not necessarily to the detriment of empirical research. Indeed, newcomers to the discipline trained by the Ecole Normale have to adapt, for better or worse, to Malinowskian methods if they want to be taken seriously as anthropologists. This enduring familiarity of French anthropologists (and sociologists) with philosophy is distinctive when compared to their Anglo-Saxon brethren.

Historical anthropology, which has developed as something of an independent specialism in France, draws on the work of leading anthropologists like Lévi-Strauss and Goody but is practised mainly by historians rather than by anthropologists themselves.[8] The emergence of the history of colonialism, which came to French anthropology later than in the English-speaking world, has led some to take an interest in the intellectual history of their discipline, its precursors and discourses on alterity. More recently, a focus on the history of museums and their role in the development of French physical and social anthropology has been quite prominent.[9] Anthropologists have never stopped being interested in the history of their discipline, in kinship, for example. But history sometimes bites back and, like it or not, they have lately found themselves associated in the public imagination with the culture of racist imperialism, as for example when a series of publications, conferences and films was issued under the title of 'The Human Zoo'. This association with late nineteenth-century practices led to an exhibition at the Quai Branly in 2011–12, commissioned by the French football star and activist Lilian Thuram, called 'Exhibitions: The Invention of the Savage'. This was linked to calls for anthropologists to be more directly engaged with the predicament of black people in contemporary France.

Anthropologists have always been attached to the Museum of Natural History, but ethnobiology and ecological anthropology have recently emerged in response to both a new preoccupation with environmental policy and to the established preference of funding agencies for the natural sciences. This interest in the natural environment has drawn anthropologists into working with specialists in architecture and landscape, while other researchers collaborate with chemists, physicists and engineers on studying the industrial environment. These anthropologists often have to work outside their own departments in engineering schools and public works programmes. Gradually, however, anthropologists are beginning to take part in more balanced interdisciplinary research projects.

Interdisciplinarity is a hallmark of cognitive anthropology, which has developed slowly in France and remains marginal to the mainstream discipline. A research centre located at the Jean Nicod Institute explores the interface of the human, social and cognitive sciences. Dan Sperber, a pioneer in this field, used to work there, but surrounded by a few anthropologists. *Terrain* is the only anthropology journal that sometimes publishes articles inspired by this approach. The field's marginality in France is reflected in the use of English in communications between French practitioners of cognitive anthropology, despite the claim of some critics that cognitive science is the naturalization of culture carried out in the name of Lévi-Strauss's original project.

Though the cognitive turn has brought anthropology closer to psychology, including psychoanalysis, the two disciplines have long been linked in

French anthropological theory. Today there is some collaboration between anthropologists and psychologists, usually in a clinical context, with the former called in to help diagnose the mental problems of transcultural patients.[10]

Medical anthropology has advanced rapidly in France over the last decade, partly in response to a new demand for anthropology courses from nursing schools and medical faculties. AMADES, the Association for Applied Medical Anthropology, mentioned above, has encouraged a dynamic exchange between anthropologists and health professionals. It encourages research by offering a prize for the best thesis in this area and publishes many studies undertaken in Europe and elsewhere. This has probably been French anthropology's most successful interdisciplinary field; collaboration with sciences such as biology and chemistry is more problematic because it requires the development of a common language of communication.[11]

What conclusions can we draw regarding the relationship between anthropology and other disciplines? Anthropologists now address new questions in ways that extend the range of their traditional data sources. This has sometimes taken place within a genuinely interdisciplinary framework, but more often without anthropological theories and methods being granted their own say. In a report on restructuring the social sciences commissioned by the Gulbenkian Foundation, Immanuel Wallerstein (1996) made a plea for a single social science, giving reasons based on epistemology and scientific policy. In such a discipline, anthropology would not be just the prerogative of anthropologists nor would history belong to the historians, etc. We are far from that situation, but some anthropologists have begun to produce more synthetic forms of knowledge by engaging with members of other disciplines in pursuit of common ends.

THEORETICAL APPROACHES, METHODS AND OBJECTS

Uneasiness concerning disciplinary identity owes something perhaps to the disappearance of strong theoretical guidelines in French anthropology. Marxist anthropologists still sometimes apply a structuralist approach to their historical inquiries, but very few anthropologists claim to be structuralists these days, even those trained by Claude Lévi-Strauss. There has been a noticeable revival of interest in the work of the discipline's 'founding fathers' such as Marcel Mauss, Emile Durkheim, André Leroi-Gourhan and Maurice Merleau-Ponty. Rereading the classics is part of a greater openness to the anthropological literature produced by the English-speaking world, although the number of translations available is still small. At the same time, whatever the case may have been in the past, French anthropology could be said to have turned in on itself of late, a trend that may be observed more generally in contemporary France.

In short, two main trends may be identified in French anthropology today. The first and dominant approach is still concerned with trying to understand the properties of social and cultural groups through the articulation of individual actions with collective structures. The second, which has some affinity with a branch of French sociology, has entirely abandoned the ambition of locating its findings within any notion of social structure and is concerned with specific practices that individuals have in common, sometimes without even situating these in time or space, never mind in society. A third approach of growing importance for younger anthropologists, led by Philippe Descola and Bruno Latour, focuses on relations between human and non-human agents. The latter term includes animals, plants, technology and ideas. It is linked to a desire to treat objects of different scale – from elementary particles to collective abstractions – in the same way, with the consequence that human beings lose their unique political status. The adoption of a new vocabulary does not seem to have greatly changed empirical methods.[12]

The difficulties some of us have faced in identifying representative keynote speakers for large conferences, such as those organized by AFEA or EASA (the European Association), is another indication of the reduced prominence of particular theoretical approaches. The 2012 EASA conference, the first of its kind held in France, invited to a plenary panel on French anthropology Philippe Descola, who is well established in anthropology, with Bruno Latour and Didier Fassin, two figures who have links with other disciplines as well as with anthropology, even though they are well known abroad as anthropologists.[13]

Where do French anthropologists work these days? They were penned up in their rural worlds for much longer than elsewhere and were slow to spend time in the city. Field research has been carried out in cities only since the 1980s, first in France itself and latterly abroad. They have often worked there with geographers and other urban specialists. I did not mention geography in the previous section, since, although the two disciplines come together in fieldwork today, there is little intellectual exchange between them. Urban anthropology has overtaken the previous focus on rural life in recent years, despite the latter's centrality in the discipline's formation.

The rural-urban divide leads us to the question of research on specific geographical areas. Despite the prevalence of regionalism in the organization of research and employment, this is no longer strongly linked to what anthropologists actually do, even if language skills are involved. Sub-Saharan Africa still attracts many French anthropologists today,[14] but their fieldwork is no longer confined to the francophone areas once drawn by the colonial map. The same applies to Asia, where many researchers now go to China above all and also to India, without abandoning South East Asia. Research in North Africa and the Middle East includes new metropoles like Dubai. Anthropologists of Latin America no longer restrict their interests to indigenous peoples but, like their Brazilian counterparts, often engage with urban and industrial life. Oceania has its own self-contained research centre. French anthropologists are still reluctant to work in North America, with the exception of Québec, where exchange relationships exist. Such relationships are stronger in Europe. Much more research has taken place since 1989 in Central and Eastern Europe, including Russia (and not just Siberia, but Moscow and other places). Some younger researchers have taken an interest in the Indian Ocean, which is now a special area of sorts.[15]

Yet the majority of French anthropologists work in France or at least have carried out fieldwork there. Anthropology at home has a long and honourable history in France, which I have discussed elsewhere (Chevalier 2015c), but the difference between carrying out research at home and abroad is being elided. Whereas earlier generations often devoted their lives to working in a particular area, it is more common today for individuals to spread their activities between a number of field sites, simultaneously or over time. This is often for practical reasons: university teachers are not as free to move as their CNRS counterparts, and short bursts of local research can be combined with occasional trips abroad. But also research networks are now spread all over the world, so that multisited fieldwork is becoming commonplace, as in the English-speaking world. This adds a new twist to the classic rules of Malinowskian fieldwork – when anthropologists spread themselves across a number of field sites, they are less likely to speak the local language. In other words, French anthropologist are accommodating globalization.[16]

French anthropologists are still heavily committed to fieldwork-based ethnography as their core method, a requirement for a Ph.D. in the subject even if some topics allow a measure of flexibility. The term 'ethnography' is enjoying a tremendous vogue in the other social sciences these days. Most of the time this involves the collection of 'qualitative data' during a specific period of fieldwork, but without the aspiration to grasp the social whole, which is the hallmark of anthropological ethnography, when the results are written up. This is linked to a growing demand for courses on ethnography given by anthropologists outside their discipline and, indeed, outside universities. Everyone wants to get in on it – nurses, social workers, political scientists, architects and specialists in cities, communications, education and sport – and the list goes on. Some historians, demographers and geographers have taken it up, as have the sociologists who have coined the term 'sociography'. The classical distinction made by Lévi-Strauss between 'ethnography', the collection of field material for the purpose of describing and analysing a single society, and 'anthropology', a comparative exercise aimed at determining universals and differences, has gone. The term 'ethnology' is used less today, even though it found a place (rather than 'ethnography') in the name for the new French association, AFEA. A growing number of researchers outside the discipline now call themselves ethnographers or anthropologists, even social anthropologists.

This appropriation of anthropologists' professional labels by outsiders has provoked new theoretical reflections on the methods of ethnography.[17] The sociologists have done the same (Beaud and Weber 2003; Naudier and Simonet 2011; Barthélemy, Combessie, Fournier and Monjaret, 2014), with some of them striking out on their own against both quantitative sociology and anthropology. How have French anthropologists defended their turf in the face of such diffusion? Our main claim has been that observing a live phenomenon, however systematically, cannot generate the same knowledge that long-term immersion in the field provides. Individual interviews done by sociologists are not the same as informal two-way exchanges over a prolonged period. Without disparaging one approach at the expense of another, we must stress the importance of distinguishing between the various practices lumped together as 'ethnography', even while embracing an interdisciplinary approach to the social sciences. This infatuation with ethnography, however, ignores the question of its relevance to global phenomena: is fieldwork in a bank sufficient for us to understand the financial crisis? Does interviewing AIDS victims enable us to explain the disease's prevalence in a given society? Apart from the problem of choosing research tools, we still have to link the local and the global and, indeed, to study one world. French anthropology is slowly coming to terms with these issues.

This trend has been reflected in identification of new objects of research over the last two decades, such as national and international institutions, NGOs, corporations and refugee camps, for example. Other objects and themes have been taken up again after a period of neglect: engagement with the countryside has been renewed as one aspect of environmentalist concerns with nature, risk and new technologies. The body, inspired by Mauss's essay on the topic, is once more an important focus. The classic fields of kinship, religion, politics and economy have been recast in a global and comparative context through a focus on international adoption, new religions, indigenous movements, credit rating agencies, discrimination against minorities and so on. All these topics address questions of social structure in some way, but there is also a discernible trend to move inquiry onto a more intimate level, concentrating on personal behaviour by studying artistic creativity, emotions or political activists.

This review has shown that the interests of French anthropologists do not differ greatly from those of their colleagues elsewhere. They have just been somewhat slower to take up topics fashionable everywhere in the world today.

DISSEMINATION OF FRENCH ANTHROPOLOGY
AT HOME AND ABROAD

Despite the success of 'French theory' in parts of the Anglophone world and French anthropology's continuing ability to export some of its achievements, it is undeniable that the French language is becoming increasingly marginal and this has made it necessary to devise new means of disseminating our knowledge. Within France itself, anthropology has a prominent place in publishing and the media more generally. The latter make ample use of anthropologists as commentators on the news, whether it be the financial crisis or political change in some country or another. Anthropologists have been strangely silent on certain subjects, such as the troubles in the suburbs.

French anthropology sustains a large number of professional journals, given the size of the audience, ranging from general (*L'Homme*, *Terrain*, www.ethnographiques.org, and *Journal des anthropologues*) to more specialized publications (*Ethnologie française*, *Techniques et cultures*, *Etudes Rurales*, etc.). Most of them receive heavy subsidies from the state in the form of direct grants or salaries. But some, like *Ethnologie française*, are owned by private publishers and must sell copies for survival. Most journals now publish articles in English and other languages, less to attract new readers than to reduce their translation costs.

In order to increase their readership, many journals now publish online. There are two main platforms for online publications, a private one, www.cairn.info, which publishes over 200 journals – not only in the social sciences – making articles available free of charge after five years of restricted access. The other portal is www.revues.org, founded in 1999 as the first platform for the humanities and social science journals in French. While revues.org originally promoted only French journals, today it also welcomes journals from outside France and some produced partly or wholly in other languages. This policy has helped extend its international reputation. The platform is now run by the Centre for Open Electronic Publishing (CLEO), which brings together the CNRS, EHESS and the universities of Provence and Avignon and is based in Marseille.

CLEO also offers new tools and services for researchers including, since 2000, *Calenda*, which is becoming the most important French-language, open access, online calendar for the humanities and social sciences, and *Hypothèses* (2008), which is a publishing platform for research notebooks, often taking the form of a logbook or blog and enabling the 'notebooker' to generate a dialogue with readers. Another development in this direction has been the opening of an Archive for the Human and Social Sciences (HAL-SHS), where a growing number of researchers deposit their texts. French anthropologists have taken advantage of all these developments.

Apart from voluntary exchanges linking individual researchers in this way, some national institutions like the ANR require collaboration with research units outside the country. EU-sponsored research programmes are often comparative and necessitate anthropologists from different countries working together; these are often connected to policy issues and have had mixed results owing to their bureaucratic nature. The European Association of Social Anthropologists (EASA) was founded in 1989; it offers a meeting ground for all European anthropologists. For years the French tended to boycott it for linguistic reasons, but in 2012 the EASA biannual meeting took place in the Paris suburbs, at the University of Paris Nanterre. EASA also has its own bilingual English-French journal, *Social Anthropology*. The new generation of French anthropologists is unquestionably more at ease in English than its predecessors, is well versed in Anglophone literature and therefore more willing to participate in English language events and publications, such as those sponsored by the AAA. I should add that shared approaches to teaching across European countries are encouraged by the Bologna reform of universities and by programmes like ERASMUS, which allow students and some teachers to travel abroad.

So, although national anthropologies have by no means disappeared, a new anthropology in (and of) Europe is gradually coming into being, forcing researchers out of their national isolation and exposing them to the work of their colleagues elsewhere.

CONCLUSION

This review of French anthropology raises questions of a more general sort concerning the relevance of a national frame of reference for investigations of contemporary intellectual history. We might add the increasingly uncertain place of universities in the production of knowledge, when compared with their status in the previous century. The collapse of European empires and the challenge posed to Western dominance by the rise of emerging economies such as China, India and Brazil are just the headlines of a process that goes by the name of 'globalization'. France is experiencing these tectonic shifts acutely, given its erstwhile centrality in world developments and present reluctance to abandon global pretensions, while its language and civilization are being marginalized by the rise of English as the world language, especially for scientific communications.

Michel Foucault closed his 'archaeology of the human sciences' – originally *Les mots et les choses* (1966), published in English as *The Order of Things* (1973) – with some reflections on why psychoanalysis and 'ethnology' '... occupy a privileged position in our knowledge ... because, on the confines of all the branches of knowledge investigating man, they form a treasure-hoard of experiences and concepts, and above all a perpetual principle of dissatisfaction, of calling into question ... what may seem, in other respects, to be established' (1973 [1966]: 373).

> They are not so much two human sciences among others, but they span the entire domain of those sciences, they animate its whole surface ... They are 'counter-sciences'; which does not mean that they are less 'rational' or 'objective' than the others, but that they flow in the opposite direction, that they lead them back to their epistemological basis, and that they ceaselessly 'unmake' that very man who is creating and re-creating his positivity in the human sciences' (1973 [1966]: 379).

Foucault attributed anthropology's originality to its being both 'traditionally the knowledge we have of the peoples without histories' and 'situated in the dimension of *historicity*', by which he meant 'within the historical sovereignty of European thought and the relation that can bring it face to face with all other cultures as well as with itself' (ibid : 376–77). He was sure the human sciences had reached their limit and this was doubly true of a discipline whose premises were being undermined by the collapse of the European empire.

French anthropology thus finds itself in a 'perfect storm' of social transition. It has lost its traditional objects, whether these were 'peoples without history' who now produce postcolonial theory or a rural France that is being emptied by the rise of cities or partially filled by an influx of second homes. The main theoretical approaches of the 70s and early 80s, structuralism and Marxism, are long gone. 'Ethnography' is practised by nurses or, more ominously, by sociologists, often involving practices that anthropologists scarcely recognize as their own. French anthropology was always institutionally weak and now faces even more powerful threats to its right to occupy a place in the public sphere.

Is that all there is to it, then, doom and gloom all around? The short answer is definitely not. Recent events, such as the first AFEA congress, have shown that the situation in French anthropology is far from depressing: the very forces breaking down the discipline's insularity are bringing out its ability to respond creatively to the world in the making. First, young anthropologists are turning in ever larger numbers to professional areas beyond universities and academic research centres, proving anthropology's relevance as a source of intellectual vision and a toolkit of methods for a wide range of different work situations. Others are bringing the classic ethnographic approach to an extraordinary diversity of research objects, showing that long-term fieldwork and a focus on relations between individuals and groups at many levels of society, from the local to the global, may help us grasp the world that is moving beneath our feet.

Faced with the void left by the collapse of late twentieth-century grand theory, anthropologists are exploring new theoretical approaches in numerous conversations with scholars in the rest of Europe and even further afield. This development is taking place when the hegemony of a few leading imperial powers has given way to a much more diverse and egalitarian network of national anthropologies around the world. At the same time, French anthropology is rediscovering its own specific intellectual history in interesting and distinctive ways. This dialectic of renewal is fed by the great transformations of the early twenty-first century. The end of anthropology has been forecast often enough, but the evidence from France refutes any such prediction.

Sophie Chevalier is currently Professor of Anthropology at the University of Picardie Jules Verne in Amiens, and director of the research centre Habiter le Monde EA4287. Her main interests are economic life, consumption practices and a comparative history of anthropology at home. Her most recent book is *Anthropology at the Crossroads: The View from France* (2015).

NOTES

1. I served as the President of APRAS since 2008 and helped to organize the assessment exercise. APRAS terminated its activities in 2013.
2. So far there are only four three-year bachelor programmes, at the University of Lyon 2, University of Toulouse Jean Jaurès, University of Paris Nanterre and the University of Nice. Most undergraduate programmes allow specialization in anthropology only in their last licence year.
3. De L'Estoile (2007); Dupaigne (2006); Price (2007); Segalen (2005), just to list the most notable works on this subject. I must also pass over the reasons for the restructuring that has taken place.
4. The Musée Guimet is the specialist centre for Asian fine arts.
5. She is still paid by the CNRS. The MQB itself does not pay the salary of any researcher.
6. See Mazé, Poulard and Ventura (2013).
7. It is a pity that English does not have an equivalent to the French *vampiriser*.
8. One exception to this trend is the anthropologist Alban Bensa.

9. This theme has featured strongly in the work of the Laboratory for the Anthropology and History of Cultural Heritage (LAHIC).
10. The controversial ethnopsychiatrist Tobie Nathan, who claims Georges Devereux as a mentor, founded a centre in Paris VIII-Saint-Denis to provide clinical treatment with cultural diversity in mind.
11. I could mention the conference 'How Can the Social Sciences Help us to Understand the Nuclear World', Lyon, June 2012, which brought together people from different disciplines.
12. A conference, organized by the APRAS and the Laboratory for Social Anthropology, on 'An Animalist turn in Anthropology?' was held at the Collège de France in June 2011. See Houdart and Thiery (2011).
13. Women play a significant part in organizing and energizing the discipline, but none were invited to share the podium. Misogyny, including among women themselves, is still prevalent in French public life.
14. Thanks to Irène Bellier for this information collected at the first AFEA conference in September 2011.
15. As demonstrated by a recent Nanterre conference in April 2011 on the island societies of the Indian Ocean.
16. No one epitomizes this strategy more than Marc Abélès (2008 or 2011), whose research ranges between Europe, the United States and China, via the WTO.
17. See for example Ghasarian (2002); Leservoisier (2005); D. Fassin and A. Bensa (2008). The French Ethnological Society published its reflections on this topic under 'Multiple Ethnographies' (2013) and 'Ethnographers' Careers' (2014).

REFERENCES

Abélès, M. 2008. *Anthropologie de la globalisation*. Paris: Payot.

———. 2011. *Pékin,798*. Paris: Stock.

Barthélemy, T., Combessie, P. Fournier L.-S. and A. Monjaret. 2014. *Ethnographies plurielles* : Déclinaisons selon les disciplines. Paris: CTHS.

Beaud, S. and F. Weber. 2003. *Guide de l'enquête de terrain*. Paris: La Découverte.

Bensa, A. 2006. *La fin de l'exotisme: Essais d'anthropologie critique*. Toulouse: Anacharsis.

Bellier, I. and T.M. Wilson (eds). 2000. *An Anthropology of European Union: Building, Imagining and Experiencing the New Europe*. Oxford: Berg.

Bonté, P. and M. Izard (eds). 1991. *Dictionnaire de l'ethnologie et de l'anthropologie*. Paris: PUF.

Chevalier, S. 2015a. *Anthropology at the Crossroads: The View from France*, The Royal Anthropological Institute Country Series. Oxford: Sean Kingston Publishing.

———. 2015b. 'Anthropology in France today' with E. Lallement, in S. Chevalier (ed.), *Anthropology at the Crossroads: The View from France*, The Royal Anthropological Institute Country Series. Oxford: Sean Kingston Publishing.

_____.2015c. 'Anthropology at home', in James D. Wright (ed.) *International Encyclopedia of the Social and Behavioral Sciences*, vol. 1, Oxford: Elsevier, pp. 751–757.

Dupaigne, B. 2006. *Le scandale des arts premiers: la véritable histoire du musée du quai de Branly*. Paris: Mille et une nuits.

Fassin, D. and A. Bensa. 2008. *Les politiques de l'enquête*. Paris: La Découverte.

Foucault, M. 1973 [1966]. *The Order of Things*. New York and London: Pantheon Books.

Ghasarian, C. (ed.). 2002. *De l'ethnographie à l'anthropologie reflexive: Nouveaux terrains, nouvelles pratiques, nouveaux enjeux*. Paris: Armand Colin.

Houdart, S. and O. Thierry (ed.). 2011. *Humains, non humains*. Paris: La Découverte.

Leservoisier, O. (ed.). 2005. *Terrains ethnographiques et hiérarchies sociales: Retour réflexif sur la situation d'enquête*. Paris: Karthala.

L'Estoile, D.B. 2007. *Le goût des Autres: De exposition coloniale aux arts premiers*. Paris: Flammarion.

Mazé, C., Poulard, F. and C. Ventura (ed.). 2013. *Les Musées d'ethnologie: Culture, politique et changement institutionnel*. Paris: CTHS.

Naudier, D. and M. Simonet (ed.). 2011. *Des sociologues sans qualités? Pratiques de recherche et engagements*. Paris: La Découverte.

Parkin, R. 2005. 'The French-Speaking Countries', in F. Barth, A. Gingrich, R. Parkin and S. Silverman (eds), *One Discipline, Four Ways: British, German, French, and American Anthropology*. Chicago: University of Chicago Press, pp. 157–253.

'Pourquoi coopérer ?'. 2012. *Terrain* (58).

Price, S. 2007. *Paris Primitive: Jacques Chirac's Museum on the Quai Branly*. Chicago: University of Chicago Press.

Schmitt, J.-Cl. 2008. 'Anthropologie historique', *Bulletin du centre d'études médiévales d'Auxerre, BUCEMA* [online]. Retrieved 30 January 2017 from https://cem.revues.org/8862?lang=en

Segalen, M. 2005. *Vie d'un musée: 1937–2005*. Paris: Stock.

Sperber, D. 2011. 'A Naturalistic Ontology for Mechanistic Explanations in the Social Sciences', in P. Demeulenaere (ed.), *Analytical Sociology and Social Mechanism*. Cambridge: Cambridge University Press.

Wallerstein, I. (ed.). 1996. *Open the Social Sciences: Report of the Gulbenkian Commission on the Restructuring of the Social Sciences*. Stanford: Stanford University Press.

CHAPTER

6

THE INTELLECTUAL AND SOCIAL HISTORY OF FOLKLORISTICS, ETHNOLOGY AND ANTHROPOLOGY IN FINLAND

ULRIKA WOLF-KNUTS AND PEKKA HAKAMIES

From the late twelfth century until 1809, Finland was part of Sweden, a legacy reflected in the prevalence of the Swedish language and its official status till today. It then became an autonomous Grand Duchy within the Russian Empire until the Russian Revolution, which prompted the Finnish Declaration of Independence in 1917. Naturally the encounter of these three cultures stirred the anthropological curiosity.

During the Russian period in the middle of the nineteenth century, interest in Finnish identity with its particular Finno-Ugric language and extreme northern culture specificities raised and incited scientists to observe Finnish rural cultural expressions. Simultaneously, the Swedish minority prompted a complementary interest in Swedish and more generally Scandinavian culture. After the Second World War international – mostly British and North American – theoretical ideas from anthropology were accepted as starting points for scholarly work. Finnish and Finland-Swedish ethnologists and students of folklore deal with native topics and apply international theories and methods in order to position themselves within the worldwide network of colleagues. If little is known about Finland in anthropology today, it is because the major part of the rich local scientific production has been produced in the vernacular. This chapter makes up for this absence by drawing attention to the richness of Finnish folklore and ethnology production since early 1800.

In Finland, folkloristics, or folklore studies, and ethnology are two separate academic disciplines, demanding different kinds of knowledge and different skills from people involved in their activities. This fact should be interpreted in the context of Finland's geopolitical, cultural and historical background. When one ponders over why folklore studies are so strong in Finland today that the discipline has the power to stand alone, one should remember that during the nineteenth century both folkloristics and ethnology were strongly connected with the process of nation-building, language and identity. Folklore studies are generally regarded as more international than ethnology, which is more focused on regional studies (Siikala 2006: 155, 165).

FOLKLORISTICS

The Influence of National Romanticism on Folklore Studies in Finland

The documentation of Finnish folklore dates back to the late Middle Ages when, in 1544, the reformer Mikael Agricola published a weather rule: *Satehexi peijuen sappi/Poudixi Cuum kehä* (A parhelion predicts rain, a ring around the moon means dry weather) (Sarajas 1982: 4). In the seventeenth century, the Finnish and Sámi languages were found to be related and, during the following century, the affinity with other Finno-Ugric languages was increasingly asserted. The German philosopher Gottfried Wilhelm von Leibniz (1646–1716) promoted the need to demonstrate historical relations between peoples using a comparative method; his ideas reached Sweden and its Finnish regions and inspired scholarly thinking in a most remarkable way (Sarajas 1982: 82). The kin relation between Hungarian, Sámi and Finnish languages was proved by another German scholar, Martin Fogel, in 1669, and consequently Swedish scholars and intellectuals debated over the relationship between Finnish and Hungarian (Korhonen 1986: 28–29). The study of languages shifted its focus from classical languages and their relationship with the vernaculars to the comparison between different languages: the Finno-Ugric language family was 'discovered', with its special structure and independent vocabulary so different from Indo-European languages. The study of Finno-Ugric languages constituted a new field of research in several European universities, among them Göttingen, Germany and Uppsala, Sweden (Siikala 2006: 157). Antiquities were also of great interest to the Swedish King Gustavus II Adolphus. At the beginning of the seventeenth century, he prescribed that memories such as folklore, but also concrete artefacts and natural objects, should be collected through the Antiqvitetskollegium (College of Antiquities); this would have helped establish the contemporary period as a kingdom of great power. At the end of the seventeenth century, there were already collections of folklore and a theoretical base in folklore studies concerning the relationship between both languages and people.

During the eighteenth century, a national romantic wave swept over Europe. One of the prominent figures was the Prussian literary critic and philosopher Johann Gottfried von Herder (1744–1803). He disliked the French influence on German literature and, therefore, underlined the importance of national writing. To him the concept of *Volk* was central, for there one could find the authentic, distinctive soul of the Volk, the nation, which expressed itself in its own language about its own essential matters. He collected and annotated German folksongs. Herder also advocated the right for different nations to maintain and develop their distinctive culture (Wretö 1984).

At the same time, though probably not directly influenced by Herder, the librarian and later Professor of Eloquence at the Royal Academy in Åbo (in Finnish Turku, the administrative centre of the Grand Duchy of Finland) Henrik Gabriel Porthan (1739–1804) asserted similar ideas for Finland and for the Finnish language and culture. He had visited Göttingen and been influenced by Leibniz. He wanted to conduct comparative investigations into Finno-Ugric languages using empirical material (Siikala 2006: 157) and was the follower of a well-known learned tradition of making use of Finnish folklore and poetry for diverse purposes (Sarajas 1982: 2f). He tried to inspire the readers of his journal *Tidningar utgifne af et sällskap i Åbo* (News published by a society in Åbo) to gather proof of nationally interesting subjects, but without success (Andersson 1967: 34f). In his *De poësi Fennica* (1766–1778), he proclaimed the qualitative superiority of Finnish pagan songs over songs from the Christian era, but he also said that Finnish superstition had been borrowed from the Sámi population and the Swedes. In this way, he brought the scholarly issue of spontaneousness versus borrowing to the fore and, according to Otto Andersson, formulated 'the comparative folkloristics in nuce' (Andersson 1967: 32). Besides his concentrated efforts for Finnish culture and folklore, we can see how Porthan worked with issues such as diffusion and comparison.

Anders Johan Sjögren (1794–1855) was the first to conduct scholarly expeditions to the Finno-Ugric peoples in Russia. From several expeditions he brought back onomastic, ethnographic and linguistic material, which inspired other collectors to make equal contributions (Siikala 2006: 157).

His way of working, based on practical fieldwork, has been an influential model for Finnish folkloristics and ethnology ever since.

After the political changes of 1809, Finland, until then part of Sweden, became a Grand Duchy under the Emperor of Russia. Language became even more of an issue. Whilst Swedish was no longer the official language of the 'new' country, a large part of Finland's population did not wish to embrace Russian as their official language. A strong feeling of identification with the majority of the population – that is, the Finns and their language and culture, developed among the intelligentsia and students at the Royal Academy in Åbo (Honko 1987: 69). Finnish folklore started to be regarded as a means of creating the Finnish literary language and, consequently, a Finnish identity. However, a Finnish language was needed not only for the sake of literature, but also in order to maintain schools in Finnish and for state bureaucracy. In fact, Finnish became an official language in Finland only in 1863 (Siikala 2006: 158).

Students gathered around the topic of Finnish folklore and started to collect oral traditions among Finnish-speaking people in Finland and, to some extent, also in Sweden and Russia. Gradually, this effort resulted partly in the epic of *Kalevala* (1835, 1849), edited and written along traditional folklore patterns by Elias Lönnrot (1802–1884), and partly in one of the world's most valuable archives of folklore, the *Kansanrunousarkisto*, the Folklore Archives, run by Suomalaisen Kirjallisuuden Seura (The Finnish Literary Society) in Helsinki. The *Kalevala* is said to have played a large role in creating Finnish identity up until the Second World War (Wilson 1976). To a large extent, the ambition to call attention to Finnish culture was upheld by students whose main language was Swedish (cf. Honko 1980: 34). The Russian authorities found that the 'capital' Turku (in Swedish called Åbo) was situated too close to Sweden, their former enemy. So they moved the capital to Helsinki, some 170 km east of Turku, and when in 1827 Turku and the Royal Academy were devastated by a disastrous fire, the university was also moved to Helsinki. The new university was called the Imperial Alexander University and, due to countrywide political circumstances, the atmosphere there was pro-Finnish.

At the university, a group of students with a Finland Swedish background gathered around their teacher Axel Olof Freudenthal (1836–1911), who called the status of the Swedish language in Finland into question. He asserted that Finland was one country with two languages, Finnish and Swedish, and that the Finland Swedes formed a bridge between the Scandinavian and Finnish tribes. In order to demonstrate the Scandinavian bonds, Freudenthal established the Svenska Landsmålsföreningen i Finland (The Swedish Dialect Society) along the lines of parallel organizations in Sweden. The idea was to investigate the stock of folklore in every parish. Consequently, among other activities, he let his students tell stories and record them in their home variants of Swedish. Several other folklore genres were also collected in this society (Wolf-Knuts 1991: 19).

In Ostrobothnia, the school teacher Johan Oscar Immanuel Rancken had corresponding thoughts. He had studied at university and was inspired by the Finnish efforts. However, he realized that Swedish culture was valuable as well. Like Porthan once, he tried to raise people's interest in Swedish cultural matters in Finland, but without success. Therefore, he collected folklore himself, but in 1852, during the fire of Vasa, his collections were destroyed. In the 1860s, he asked his pupils to describe life in their home parishes, which resulted in a unique collection. He also employed some great collectors of prose folklore and folk songs (cf. Österlund-Pötzsch and Ekrem 2008: 20–40; Wolf-Knuts 2001).

At the end of the nineteenth century, language matters grew even more problematic. The Finnish endeavour was strong, whereas the authorities favoured a Russian advantage. The Finland Swedes looked to the Finnish ambitions for a strong identity and, among other things, they founded the Svenska litteratursällskapet i Finland (The Society of Swedish Literature) with aims corresponding to those of the Finnish Literature Society. Folklore was central and later the Folkkultursarkivet (The Archives of Folk Culture) was founded in Helsinki to take care of the collections.

The university in Helsinki was Finnish-minded. From this circumstance arose the idea of establishing a university for the Finland Swedish young in Turku. This was done in 1918, and in 1926 a professorship for the History of Music and for Folklore was founded. Otto Andersson (1879–1969) held the chair at the same time as being an important Finland Swedish politician and the Rector of Åbo Akademi University. The contrastive character of Åbo Akademi University as the Swedish University in Finland set the frame also for folklore studies. Andersson and his successors mainly dealt with Swedish folklore in Finland. For a long time, due to the complicated relationship between the language groups, there was practically no cooperation between the Swedish folklore department and its Finnish counterparts. Only after the Second World War did the mental borders start to crumble.

The influence of National Romanticism on folklore studies in Finland is characterized by the relationship between the two languages in the country, Finnish and Swedish, as identity markers. As a contrast to the reigning Swedish culture, and later on to the dominant Russian culture, folklore was collected by Finnish supporters but also by Swedish supporters at variance with Finnish efforts. Influences from Sweden and Scandinavia were obvious. Collecting itself can be regarded as the seed of museum collections, and thoughts about diffusion and comparison were predominant theoretical perspectives.

In the 1930s, the profound feeling of kinship with Finno-Ugric peoples in the Soviet Union influenced folklore studies in a political way due to the fact that university people such as Martti Haavio (1899–1973) and Matti Kuusi (1914–1998), professors of Finnish and Comparative Folklore Studies *(suomalainen ja vertaileva kansanrunous)*, were involved in a right-wing ideological organization called the Akateeminen Karjalaseura (the Academic Society for Karelia). The Second World War brought a serious break in academic work. After the resumption of normal life, international politics did not play a role in folklore studies.

The Finnish School, a Positivist Endeavour

Around the turn of the nineteenth century, the German Friedrich August Wolf (1759–1824) stated that Homeric poetry could hardly be considered the work of one single person and that comparison could be a serious philological method of research. Julius Krohn (1835–1888), a Finnish-minded folklorist of German descent, investigated the background to the *Kalevala* epic. He was influenced by contemporary philology and the historical paradigm dominating arts subjects at the time. Comparison became his tool and diffusion his theme of research. He tried to identify geographical roots and historical matters in the epic and, in the course of his investigations, it turned out that the *Kalevala* was neither particularly old nor particularly Finnish. The Finns had borrowed and adapted the themes (Hautala 1969: 67–71). He found Scandinavian and German traits in it. Julius Krohn worked out a research method for folklore studies, which dominated international research for more than a century. This is called the Finnish Research Method, or the historic-geographic method, and is built on the collection of variants and the comparing of them according to specific principles in order to demonstrate the original state of a folklore item and how it has changed.

This method was refined by Julius Krohn's son, Kaarle Krohn (1863–1933). He held the first chair for folklore studies in Finland. In 1918, he published *Kalevalankysymyksiä* (translated into German in *Die folkloristische Arbeitsmethode* (1926, English translation in 1971), in which he presented the different methodological conditions needed to conduct serious folklore research. Like his father, he found that parts of the *Kalevala* epic were from the Viking age and that the protagonists were historical people in real situations. The historic-geographic method was an answer to demands for a scientifically acceptable research method such as the positivist scientific methods of the time. The Finnish method was widely accepted and practised. Kaarle Krohn and several, mainly Nordic, folklorists founded the association of Folklore Fellows in 1908. Their dream was to investigate as many folklore items as possible according to the Finnish method in order to find the *Märchen*, the legend or original form of a folklore text, its time and place of origin, its original language and the ways it had circulated, both vertically and geographically. Genetic prerequisites were seen as the only explanation: 'every myth, tale or legend was invented only once' (Honko 1981: 18). Large amounts of recordings were needed. The Folklore Archive with the Finnish Literary Society and its Finland Swedish counterparts were extremely important when it came to the collecting of material and its retrieval. Antti Aarne (1867–1925) created a type catalogue, which, later on, Stith Thompson (1885–1976) and Hans-Jörg Uther (1944–) developed as an indispensable tool for this kind of research. The studies have been published since 1910 in the series 'Folklore Fellows' Communications', which published its three hundredth issue in 2010. Later the method was criticized for being Eurocentric and not considering possible changes in the bulk of material investigated, but at the time it put Finnish folklore studies on the map and even today some researchers accept it. Alan Dundes contextualized it as a counterpart to evolutionism through the concept of 'the devolutionary premise' (Dundes 1969).

Although he himself had written his doctoral dissertation partly by using the Finnish method, Lauri Honko (1932–2002) was another critic of it. He doubted the value of the method in the long run, but he would not deny its impact on folklore studies (Honko 1981).

The folklore studies of the Finnish School were a positivist endeavour. Thanks to the Krohns and their successors, Finland became internationally well known in folklore circles. Language was still important but not only for the sake of national identity. Comparison with folklore from other parts of the world diminished the importance of Finnish and Swedish. However, critical viewpoints characteristic of ongoing qualitative scholarly work arose. This happened along with the easing of Finland's political situation, as a neighbour of the Soviet Union, when international anthropologically accentuated influence, above all from the United States, was of current interest.

Fieldwork and Performance

The folklore research conducted using the Finnish method did not consider the active narrator of a story or song, nor even the listener. It was a text-centred type of folklore, which explained nothing about recent times and society or people's actual needs.

In the 1960s, with considerable and vital influence from American anthropology and with the help of the practical, portable tape recorder, fieldwork gained importance in the study of folklore. Certainly, fieldwork was an essential part of nineteenth-century folkloristics as well, but now, in the twentieth century, influenced by the interest in narrative, it was questioned in a more constructive way than ever before. Now the gathering of folklore was the kernel of a fairly lengthy research process. The performers' way of creating their pieces of folklore was focused on. The 'ethnography of speech' had arrived in Finland.

This current was heralded by Juha Pentikäinen (1940–). Inspired by the anthropology of religion, he wrote an investigation into Marina Takalo and her repertoire (Pentikäinen 1971), based on both archived and recorded material, but stricto sensu it was taken up by Annikki Kaivola-Bregenhøj (1939–) (Kaivola-Bregenhøj 1996 (1988)) and Anna-Leena Siikala (1943–2016) (Siikala 1990 (1984)). Both of them wanted to know how narrators construct their narratives when telling a story. The tape recorder allowed these scholars to listen again and again to the same story told by the same narrator and to find until then unnoticed details of highly significant meaning for the storyteller's message or for the listener. It was no longer the motifs in a classic understanding of a story that were central but the variation of the same story told many times by the same narrator or the narrative's underlying meaning. Both of these scholars preferred to analyse recordings in Finnish. A parallel investigation was conducted in Swedish by Lena Marander-Eklund (1958–), for whom life stories were of great interest (Marander-Eklund 2000). As a continuation of these performance-centred studies, several investigations on narratives and memory can be considered.

In the 1990s, Lauri Honko adopted a performance-centred perspective when he revitalized the long dormant *Kalevala* and epic research by long empirical fieldwork in Kerala, India, and described how the Siri epic was constructed. To all of these scholars, the concept of variation was central: how does a singer or narrator vary the same theme in different ways?

But fieldwork was also fruitful for other reflections. Suddenly the collector of folklore was just as important as the performer. Interviewer and interviewee were equal. It took two to create an interview. As a consequence thereof the role of the interviewer came to the fore. His or her influence on the material gathered was an important factor when trying to understand the meaning of a recording: reflexivity entered the scene. In this phase of folklore research in Finland, British and U.S. anthropology were the most influential. The ideas were partly provided by colleagues in Sweden. Therefore, the awakening interest in Finland as a multicultural society was now central.

Cultural-Historical Folkloristics

Perhaps it could be said that Finnish-method folkloristics and performance-based folklore studies are two opposite endeavours. One requires a lot of recordings, a wide geographical and historical angle of approach, a macro perspective and a positivist mind. The other is content with very limited material, analysed from a micro perspective in contemporary time with interpretation and understanding as the theoretical point of departure. However, all the time cultural-historical folkloristics also remained relevant. The amount of studies with a historical perspective produced is vast, so only a few examples will be mentioned below.

The historical perspective came to the fore through archived material analysed by other theoretical and methodological perspectives than that found in the Finnish Method school. In the 1970s, inspired by the Swedish folklorist Carl Wilhelm von Sydow, Lauri Honko started an international long-lasting debate about the value and reliability of, above all, folk belief genres. For years, this debate engaged Finnish, Nordic and U.S. folklorists. However, with the rising and gradually dominating interest in contemporary field material it faded away, though it was important for the psychological angles of incidence in the folk belief research conducted by Lauri Honko (Honko 1962), Juha Pentikäinen (Pentikäinen 1968) and Ulrika Wolf-Knuts (Wolf-Knuts 1991).

Seppo Knuuttila (1948–) (Knuuttila 1992) concentrated his studies of Finnish worldview matters on the history of mentality, and Pekka Hakamies (1953–) analysed proverbs (Hakamies 1986) from the perspective of cultural encounters, a perspective that, in recent times, has been popular in studies of ethnicity, multiculturalism and migration.

An important ramification is represented by the many studies conducted with the help of cultural analytical perspectives. Archived material from rural nineteenth-century Karelia was a special field of interest for Laura Stark (see, for instance, Stark 2006), to whom gender studies were extremely inspiring.

Ever since the beginning of the nineteenth century, the *Kalevala* and related topics have been central to Finnish folklore research. In 2005, Lotte Tarkka published her dissertation on *Kalevala*-like poetry, using theories about intertextuality (Tarkka 2005: 63–74). The Kalevala Institute (http://www.kalevalainstituutti.fi/en/) offers an international milieu for research on epics and other *Kalevala*-like poetry.

Recent Folkloristics

A salient fact about folklore studies in Finland is that language was important for the formation of identity. Still today, when folklore studies in Finland have become an eminently international discipline, Finnish folklorists tend to stick to material in Finnish or Finnic languages, be it in recently recorded or long-archived material. Hence, Finland Swedish folklorists mostly concentrate their studies on Finland Swedish material. However, there seems to be a gap between the two groups of folklore students, for, although they cooperate in meetings and projects, there is no comparative research on the similarity and difference between Finnish and Finland Swedish folk tradition. Finnish folklorists tend to be keener on making comparisons with their eastern neighbours.

However, international influence on folklore studies in Finland should not be underestimated. Since the political situation allows ongoing contact with colleagues all over the world, folklorists in Finland are extremely well aware of international research, its methods and theories, and this is very clearly demonstrated in contemporary research. Both written and oral folklore are of interest, both text-centred and performed folklore are investigated. Folklore in Finland today shows great variety, which is only right for research conducted in postmodern and poststructural society. Finnish participants were numerous at Nordic conferences for ethnologists and folklorists; Nordic cooperation was conducted through both the Nordic Institute of Folklore and its successor the Nordic Network of Folklore. Lauri Honko was active within UNESCO's work on the safeguarding of folklore. He was also the chair of the International Society for Folk Narrative Research from 1974 to 1989. New members join the Folklore Fellows (http://www.folklorefellows.fi/), which maintains the series 'Folklore Fellows' Communications' and 'Folklore Fellows' Network' and the internationally recognized FF Summer School.

ETHNOLOGY

The Five Ethnologies

According to Nils Storå, it is possible to trace the interest in Finnish ethnology back to the school of Åbo gymnasium, which in 1827, after the big fire, rose from its ashes and, in a way, was a substitute for the university, which had been transferred to Helsinki. There several pupils shared an interest in folk culture. In different ways, they contributed to the development of a Finnish national consciousness. For instance, Sven Gabriel Elmgren worked with the Finnish Literary Society; Antero Warelius is said to have invented the Finnish word for ethnology, *kansatiede*; the initiative to create a historical museum in Turku was an important task for Lars Wilhelm Fagerlund and Oskar Rancken was an important collector of folklore. In the course of time, their ideas spread along with the rising national endeavours and developed into academia. Storå enumerates five ethnologies: antiquarian ethnology, language-based ethnology, regional ethnology, cultural-historical ethnology and anthropological ethnology (Storå 1990: 1–2).

Antiquarian Ethnology

Antiquarian ethnology is characterized by an interest in collecting material folk culture. Two lines can be discerned. Firstly, one can say that scholarly archaeology has been practised since 1870, when J.R. Aspelin (1885–1915) took the initiative to found the Suomen muinaismuistoyhdistys – Finska fornminnesföreningen (The Finnish Antiquarian Society), whose aims were to create a system for the safeguarding of monuments of great value, to start research, to get lay people involved in these matters and, from the 1890s, to collect objects for a planned national museum. The latter activity was, among others, taken charge of by the students at the university. In this work, Aspelin and his co-workers were inspired by Swedish archaeologists and the typologies they had founded on evolutionistic thought. Comparative typology was a characteristic of the works on folk culture in Finland, Russian North Karelia and Russia of Uuno Taavi Sirelius (1872–1929), the first professor of what then was called Finno-Ugric Ethnography at the University of Helsinki.

Secondly, in 1891 Arthur Hazelius (1833–1901) established the Skansen open air museum in Stockholm, Sweden, an event that in many ways inspired Finnish ethnographers and students to make efforts of a similar kind. In 1900, in the country parish of Kimito, the teacher Nils Oskar Jansson (1862–1927) opened his Sagalund open air museum to demonstrate what the culture of his area was like. The Seurasaari open air museum in Helsinki was founded in 1909. Educative purposes lay behind the museums: it was regarded essential to know yourself in order to recognize your history.

Antiquarian ethnology was characterized by an ethnographic interest in the Finnish and Finnic peoples of Russia and by inspiration from Sweden. The purpose was to educate the Finnish people about their own culture through museum activities. The antiquarian interest resulted in the creation of several museums, among others the National Museum in Helsinki, and of ethnology as an academic discipline (cf. Storå 1990: 2–4).

Language-Based Ethnology

In the section about folklore studies, we saw how language was one of the reasons for collecting cultural evidence. The dialect societies were mentioned as one of the channels through which folklore was collected. From 1874, as in the dialect society of Uppsala, Sweden, Axel Olof Freudenthal arranged meetings with his students, in which the young men had to pronounce and name objects in dialect. His aim was to publish an ethnographical dictionary according to a principle concerning the close connection between an object and its designation, later to be developed in the idea of *Wörter und Sachen* (words and objects). When in 1904–1907 Herman Vendell (1853–1907) published his *Ordbok öfver de östsvenska dialekterna,* he took a large amount of the material from the dialect society's collection.

A corresponding activity in Finnish was supported by the Muurahaiset society (The Ants) founded at the university in 1886 by Theodor Schvindt (1851–1917). The aim of this society was, with the help of questionnaires, to collect concepts connected with objects in housing and labour processes. There was also a dialect society in Finnish, Kotikielen Seura, founded in 1876 by August Ahlqvist (1826–1889), as a parallel organization to the Swedish dialect societies. In 1914, Svenska litteratursällskapet i Finland (The Society for Swedish Literature in Finland) arranged the first ethnographical expedition among the Swedish-speaking population. As a result, the first issue of *Folkloristiska och etnografiska studier* was published in 1916 and included a couple of ethnological articles. Both N.E. Hammarstedt at the Nordic Museum in Stockholm and Wilhelm Mannhardt inspired the work. In 1937, the Folklore Archives of the Society were set up as an archive encompassing both dialect and ethnographic material. In Central Europe and Sweden, great atlases of linguistic matters and ethnographic information were compiled, which also inspired Finnish scholars to produce corresponding works (cf. Storå 1990: 4–7).

Regional Ethnology

In ethnology, description and comparison were the main methods of work. Objects from different regions were compared and systematized. Big collections were needed for solid scholarly work on diffusion and origin. Consequently, every region had to be investigated. This idea was meant to create an awareness of one's home district. Rural parish and village studies were completed by detailed in-depth investigations, a way of conducting research that led scholars to reflections about cultural areas and provinces. U.T. Sirelius was one of the representatives of this kind of ethnology. Deep, detailed village investigations suitable for a theoretical basis of cultural areas were conducted; for instance, by Sigurd Erixon in Stockholm, Sweden.

In 1894, the natural history and geography teacher Robert Boldt (1861–1923) started the first society for home district matters in Lohja. He was particularly keen on folklore, but material evidence of folk culture became central to his work. He also founded corresponding societies when he moved around the country. Moreover, he promoted research on home district matters, both by scholars and lay people. As a reaction to this interest in home district matters a number of local museums were established and, since 1910, two journals have been published, *Kotiseutu* and *Hembygden,* both meaning 'home district', in Finnish and Swedish respectively.

Inspired by these ideas, in 1906 Otto Andersson founded a society called Brage, whose purpose was twofold. On the one hand, it was to revitalize – or in fact partly even create – Swedish folk culture in Finland; on the other to sustain an interest in research. This society published the *Wörter und Sachen* (words and things) journal *Budkavlen* (The Fiery Cross), which still exists, however with a different orientation.

As a professor of Sociology and a director of the Institute for Nordic Ethnology at Åbo Akademi University, but educated by the anthropologist Edvard Westermarck, K. Rob. V. Wikman (1886–1975) devoted himself to research on folk beliefs and custom. In this respect, he combined folklore studies with ethnology. He was partly influenced by prevailing thought about diffusion but, more importantly, he made use of sociological and psychological issues in his research. He was inspired by British anthropology and German *Volkskunde*. He was the chief editor of the immense *Finlands svenska folkdiktning* (Finland Swedish folklore) collection, but diverging opinions with regard to his anthropological colleagues' views, especially concerning the volume on custom, complicated his work.

Regional ethnology left vestiges in the form of detailed descriptions, a growing lay interest in local culture and scholarly thought about cultural areas and regions. Influence came from Sweden for Western thinkers such as Wilhelm Mannhardt or Edward Burnett Tylor (cf. Storå 1990: 7–9).

Cultural-Historical Ethnology

It goes without saying that the historical perspective was important in ethnology, as in all other arts subjects. At Åbo Akademi University, the first relevant professorship was established in 1919 and was called the Chair for Nordic Cultural History and Folk Life Research. It was planned for Gabriel Nikander (1884–1959), who had a cultural-historical education. Nikander concentrated his research partly on the bourgeoisie and nobility, and partly on rural culture. Appointed to the Swedish university in Finland, he regarded Finland Swedish cultural issues his main field of interest. Consequently, he doubted the theory of cultural circles *(Kulturkreislehre)*, for, to his mind, it covered too wide a geographical perspective. Instead he was strongly influenced by the German historian Karl Lamprecht and the folklorist Hans Naumann's research on *gesunkenes Kulturgut* (sunken cultural materials). According to Nikander's thinking, the lower social strata were important as objects of research, for they comprised and made possible the understanding of the thoughts and customs of the higher social strata.

Rural culture from a historical perspective was central to the work of Albert Hämäläinen (1881–1949), Professor of Finnish Ethnology in Helsinki, who investigated Finnish culture both in Sweden and Russia among kindred people. Later, in 1985, his chair was changed to Chair for Cultural Anthropology. Ilmar Talve (1919–2007), Professor of Ethnology at Turku University, concentrated his research on urban ethnology with a historical perspective. Helmer Tegengren (1904–1974), Nikander's successor at Åbo Akademi University, continued the historically influenced research on ethnological matters. He took his models from Sweden in constructing questionnaires, and established the ethnological archives at Åbo Akademi University. Among other topics, his research concerned the history of the iron works in Billnäs and Oravais. His successor Nils Storå (1933–) wrote a thorough historical analysis of the parish of Kronoby.

Cultural-historical ethnology was based on history and combined studies of elite and folk culture and introduced urban topics (cf. Storå 1990: 9–13).

Anthropological Ethnology

Due to the geopolitical situation of Finland, the influence of ethnography was considerable. The interest in kindred peoples in Russia led many Finnish ethnologists to investigate the harsh conditions of their ways of life. One example is Albert Hämäläinen, who visited several Finno-Ugric peoples before the borders closed. Later, the harnessing of natural resources also fascinated ethnologists in Finland. In his doctoral dissertation 'Die Einleitung der Ehe: Eine vergleichend ethno-soziologische Untersuchung über die Vorstufe der Ehe in den Sitten des schwedischen Volkstums' (1937), K. Rob. V. Wikman combined 'wide comparative European views, social, historic-genetic and psychological aspects' (Storå 1990: 13). In his studies of Sámi culture, Helmer Tegengren handled nature and natural resources as objects of scholarly concern, and this continued with his successor Nils Storå (1933–), who carried on Sámi research but also studied the archipelago and its technologies and resources. The influence of Swedish ethnology was obvious.

Around the middle of the twentieth century, influence from British, theoretically more advanced, anthropology affected ethnologists in Finland. Description was not sufficient; more intriguing questions about the reason for cultural phenomena and their processes in society had to be formulated. Here K. Rob. V. Wikman was a prominent figure, for he saw that a combination of many different kinds of perspectives was needed.

Urban ethnology was certainly not new in Finland when in the 1960s it was reintroduced from an anthropological angle. Asko Vilkuna (1929–), Professor of Finnish and Comparative Folk Life Studies, introduced this area of research in Jyväskylä, inspired by developments in Sweden. Complexity came into focus in studies of small marginal groups or of how different groups in a pluralistic society managed to live together. It goes without saying that with the increasing industrialization of Finnish society questions about tradition as a remnant in relation to continuity and change were appreciated issues (cf. Storå 1990: 13–15; Korkiakangas 2010: 155–56).

Recent Ethnology

Of course, the fall of the Iron Curtain also influenced ethnology in Finland (cf. Åström 2005, which is the basis for the following survey). The country's population became more international due to political circumstances outside the country and the influence of European and U.S. modernity. A gradual growth of multiculturalism evoked topics concerning ethnicity, minorities and identity (cf. Korkiakangas 2010: 156). Migration and cultural encounters between the Finnish population and refugees or other immigrants came to the fore. Urban ethnology in all its complexity flourished. Reflections on *Alltagskultur* (everyday life) in eating habits, new and/or changing customs, new understandings of old concepts – for instance, the family – were fruitful. In the 1990s and 2000s, great interest was shown in memories of life after the last wars (1939–1940, 1941–1944). Today, one of the dominant theories concerns materiality, reviving the importance of objects and material culture in ethnology. These matters had been transferred to museology in the 1990s.

Anthropological influence is noticeable. Culture is regarded as a process in which the use of history is central. Power is an important analytical concept. Therefore, for instance, investigations of memory, of the process of gentrification seen in many towns or of the selection of elements of culture to be a heritage are often encountered in recent publications. Current research is pluralistic, characterized by questions about fragmentation and disintegration. The perspective is constructivist. Interpretative methods are widely used when scholars are searching for meaning in the cultural process under investigation. Gender is certainly an important theme and reflexivity with regard to fieldwork is evident. Kindred cultures are again of interest. Some researchers consider the European heritage among the nobility and bourgeoisie in Finland worthy of ethnological investigations. Bo Lönnqvist (1941–) and Anna-Maria Åström (1951–) have studied manor houses and bourgeois culture in detail. Historical anthropology has provided the theoretical background.

The ethnology dealing with natural resources and technology has certainly seen an upswing with the general interest in ecological matters. Studies of man and technology, or man and consumption, are self-evident topics in the ethnology of today, at all universities where the discipline is taught. Thoughts about deindustrialization are a consequence of ecological ethnology and a rising interest in matters of religion and the future of the individual accounts for a great deal of research.

Finland is sensitive to currents from different cultural sciences practised in Europe and the United States. Colleagues in the Nordic and Baltic countries, however, hold a prominent position not only as theoretically inspiring partners, but also as associates in practical work.

According to Ilmar Talve (Talve 1963: 23), ethnology in Finland is a historical discipline with a strong interest in regional and social matters. Storå (Storå 1990: 15) adds the psychological perspective as an important ingredient. Inspired by the Swedish ethnologist Nils-Arvid Bringéus's book *Människan som kulturvarelse* (Bringéus 1976), ethnology in Finland also defines itself as the discipline dealing with man as a cultural being in various kinds of societies.

The Influence from Anthropology

In both folklore studies and ethnology in Finland, anthropology is a bourdon tone in the background. Due to Finland's geopolitical position, Siberia and Northern Russia were early areas of interest. Anders Johan Sjögren, mentioned above, conducted his first expedition to Russia at the beginning of the 1820s. In the 1840s, inspired by the *Kalevala* epic, Mathias Alexander Castrén (1813–1852) visited Finno-Ugric peoples in Russia and Siberia. Henrik Holmberg (1818–1864) described the peoples in Russian America (i.e., Alaska), while at the beginning of the twentieth century Kai Donner (1888–1935) documented culture among the Samoyeds. This fascination for Finno-Ugric cultures has prevailed among Finnish ethnologists and folklorists until recent times. Even one of the Folklore Fellows' Summer Schools (2007) included a visit to Karelia and the important places in *Kalevala* research. Since 1980, there has been a department specifically for social and cultural anthropology at Helsinki University. Contrary to the other chairs mentioned here, it is not in the Faculty of Arts, but in the Faculty of Political Sciences.

In Jyväskylä, a professorship for Finnish and Comparative Folklife Studies was established in 1964. There ethnology was regarded on a very broad basis and, in fact, ethnology, folkloristics and cultural anthropology are combined. Anthropology was even considered more important than folkloristics by the first professor, Asko Vilkuna. In 1970, Veikko Anttila (1929–1990) was appointed Associate Professor of Ethnology. This chair is nowadays specialized in folkloristics and the holder is Professor Laura Stark (1966–). Since 1998, Ilmari Vesterinen (1941–) had held a Chair of Cultural Anthropology, which, however, was abolished in 2009.

Since 1980, cultural anthropology has been an independent discipline at Jyväskylä University, but closely connected with ethnology and folkloristics. The three are combined in one discipline called Ethnology (Korkiakangas 2010: 149–60).

The fascination with remote cultures also had an offspring in a Professorship in Moral Philosophy established in 1906 at the University of Helsinki and was given to Edward Westermarck (1862–1939). He was an empiricist and conducted several quite long field trips to Morocco. He had a comparative approach and published several important works on wedding ceremonies, sexuality, evil and the sacred. Westermarck was appointed Rector of Åbo Akademi University in 1918 (Lindberg 2008: 162–64). K. Rob. V. Wikman was Professor of Sociology at Åbo Akademi University. He studied marriage customs and ethnopsychology. His interest was in line with Gabriel Nikander's and Otto Andersson's.

The influence of anthropology can also be seen as part of the background to religious studies in Finland. The scholar of religion Uno Harva (Holmberg) (1882–1949), who was Professor of Sociology at Turku University, had a keen interest in the Finnish kindred peoples of northern Eurasia. In recent times, Juha Pentikäinen has shown interest in Siberian vernacular religions.

CONCLUSION

Finland's geopolitical and cultural-historical situation between, on the one hand, a tradition in the Swedish language with its roots in Greek and Latin and, on the other, a strong wish for an officially accepted Finnish language with its affinity to other Finno-Ugric languages, and completely different from the Indo-European languages, created an interest in scholarly ideas of comparison as a research method. Finnish and Swedish national identities were supported by the collection of numerous museum objects and vast amounts of archival folklore material from fieldwork within the country and in neighbouring countries. Finnish identity was formed in opposition to Russian efforts to make the inhabitants loyal to the Russian authorities. Museums and folklore archives exhibited Finnish culture. At the same time, however, museum and folklore archives also manifested a strong bond with Finno-Ugric cultures. Correspondingly, the Swedish population in Finland saw their kindred bonds in the Nordic, Scandinavian culture. Influence from Nordic, Scandinavian and, above all, Swedish ethnology and folkloristics with a cultural-historical style was extremely important. However, in the long run, international ideas about what folklore studies, ethnology and cultural anthropology could be like influenced research in Finland and nowadays international congresses, conferences, journals and the Internet connect Finnish scholars with colleagues all over the world. Methodologically and theoretically, Finnish scholarship follows international norms and standards. The material, however, often comes from the national field.

Ulrika Wolf-Knuts held a chair as the Professor of Folkloristics at Åbo Akademi University, Åbo, Finland. Since 2015 she has been the Chancellor of this university. Her specific field of interest is folklore, comprising minority studies (Swedes in Finland), folk religion, methodologies of folkloristics and the history of folkloristics.

Pekka Hakamies is Professor of Folkloristics at the University of Turku, School of History, Culture and Arts Studies. He has studied proverbs, Finnish-Russian relations in folk culture, identity issues in Karelia at the Finnish-Russian border area and the process of modernization. He is the editor of the series Folklore Fellows' Communications.

REFERENCES

Ahlbäck, R. 1945. *Kulturgeografiska kartor över Svenskfinland*. Helsingfors: Svenska litteratursällskapet i Finland. (Svenska litteratursällskapet i Finland. Skrifter 300.) (Folklivsstudier 1.)

Andersson, O. 1967. *Finländsk folklore: Tidig Kalevalaforskning, finlandssvensk insamlingsverksamhet*. Åbo: Åttas förlag.

Åström, A.-M. 2005. 'What is a Swedish Ethnology in Finland?', *Budkavlen*, special issue: 119–28.

Bringéus, N.-A. 1976. *Människan som kulturvarelse: En introduktion till etnologin*. Lund: LiberLäromedel.

Dundes, A. 1969. 'The Devolutionary Premise in Folklore Theory', *Journal of the Folklore Institute* 6(1): 5–19.

Hakamies, P. 1986. *Venäläisten sananparsien vaikutus karjalaiseen ja suomalaiseen sananparsistoon*. Helsinki: Suomalaisen Kirjallisuuden Seura. (Joensuun yliopiston humanistisia julkaisuja 6, Suomalaisen Kirjallisuuden Seuran toimituksia 451.)

Hautala, J. 1969. *Finnish Folklore Research 1828–1918*. [Helsinki:] Societas scientiarum Fennica. (The History of Learning and Science in Finland 1828–1918, 12.)

Honko, L. 1962. *Geisterglaube in Ingermanland 1*. Helsinki: Suomalainen Tiedeakatemia. (Folklore Fellows. FF communications 185.)

———. 1980. 'Upptäckten av folkdiktning och nationell identitet i Finland', in L. Honko (ed.), *Folklore och nationsbyggande i Norden*. Åbo: Nordiska institutet för folkdiktning, pp. 33–51. (NIF Publications 9.)

———. 1981. 'Forskningsmetoderna inom prosatraditionen och deras framtid', in G. Herranen (ed.), *Folkloristikens aktuella paradigm*. Åbo: Nordiska institutet för folkdiktning, pp. 15–54. (NIF Publications 10.)

———. 1987. 'The Kalevala Process', in A. Jabbour and J. Hardin (eds), *Folklife Annual 1986: A Publication of the American Folklife Center at the Library of Congress*. Washington, D.C.: Library of Congress, pp. 66–79.

Kaivola-Bregenhøj, A. 1988. *Kertomus ja kerronta*. Helsinki: Suomalaisen kirjallisuuden seura. (Suomalaisen Kirjallisuuden Seuran toimituksia 480.)

Kaivola-Bregenhøj, A. 1996. *Narrative and Narrating. Variation in Juho Oksanen's Storytelling.* Helsinki: Suomalainen tiedeakatemia. (FF communications 261.)

Knuuttila, S. 1992. *Kansanhuumorin mieli: Kaskut maailmankuvan aineksena.* Helsinki: Suomalaisen Kirjallisuuden Seura. (Suomalaisen Kirjallisuuden Seuran toimituksia 554.)

Korhonen, M. 1986. *Finno-Ugrian Language Studies in Finland 1828–1918.* Helsinki: Societas scientiarum Fennica. (The History of Learning and Science in Finland 1828–1918, 11.)

Korkiakangas, P. 2010. 'Ethnology in the 21st Century', in J. Lehtonen and S. Tenkanen (eds), *Transnational Reflection of Past, Present and Future.* Turku: Turun yliopisto.

Krohn, K. 1926. *Die folkloristische Arbeitsmethode begründet von Julius Krohn und weitergeführt von nordischen Forschern erläutert von Kaarle Krohn.* Oslo: Aschehoug. (Instituttet for sammenlignende kulturforskning B 5.)

Lindberg, C. 2008. 'Anthropology on the Periphery: The Early Schools of Nordic Anthropology', in H. Kuklick (ed.), *A New History of Anthropology.* Oxford: Blackwell.

Marander-Eklund, L. 2000. *Berättelser om barnafödande: Form, innehåll och betydelse i kvinnors muntliga skildring av födsel.* Åbo: Åbo Akademis förlag.

Österlund-Pötzsch, S. and C. Ekrem. 2008: *Swedish Folklore Studies in Finland 1828–1918.* [Helsinki:] Societas scientiarum Fennica. (The History of Learning and Science in Finland 1828–1918, 13b.)

Pentikäinen, J. 1968. *The Nordic Dead-Child Tradition: Nordic Dead-Child Beings: A Study in Comparative Religion.* Helsinki: Suomalainen tiedeakatemia. (FF communications 202.)

———. 1971. *Marina Takalon uskonto: Uskontoantropologinen tutkimus.* Helsinki: Suomalaisen Kirjallisuuden Seura. (Suomalaisen Kirjallisuuden Seuran toimituksia 299.)

Sarajas, A.M. 1982. *Studiet av folkdiktningen i Finland intill slutet av 1700-talet.* Stockholm: Almqvist & Wiksell International. (Kungl. Vitterhets historie och antikvitets akademiens handlingar, filologisk-filosofiska serien.19.)

Siikala, A.-L. 1990. *Interpreting Oral Narrative.* Helsinki: Suomalainen tiedeakatemia. (FF communications 245.)

Siikala, J. 2006. 'The Ethnography of Finland', *Annual review of anthropology* 35: 153–70.

Stark, L. 2006. *The Magical Self: Body, Society and the Supernatural in Early Modern Rural Finland.* Helsinki: Suomalainen tiedeakatemia. (FF communications 290.)

Storå, N. 1990: *Fem etnologier: Etnologin i Finland i finlandssvenskt perspektiv.* Åbo: Etnologiska institutionen vid Åbo Akademi.

Talve, I. 1963. *Suomalainen kansatiede.* Turku. (Reprint from Sananjalka 5.)

Tarkka, L. 2005. *Rajarahvaan laulu: Tutkimus Vuokkiniemen kalevalamittaisesta runokulttuurista 1821–1921.* Helsinki: Suomalaisen Kirjallisuuden Seura. (Suomalaisen Kirjallisuuden Seuran toimituksia 1033.)

Wilson, W.A. 1976. *Folklore and Nationalism in Modern Finland.* Bloomington, IN: Indiana University Press.

Wolf-Knuts, U. 1991. *Människan och djävulen: En studie kring form, motiv och funktion i folklig tradition.* Åbo: Åbo Akademis förlag.

———. 2001: 'Johan Oskar Immanuel Rancken – den finlandssvenska folkloristikens fader', in C. Bregenhøj (ed.), *Oskar Rancken: Pedagog och samlare, folklivsvetare och historiker.* Helsingfors: Svenska litteratursällskapet i Finland, pp. 9–23. (Meddelanden

ULRIKA WOLF-KNUTS AND PEKKA HAKAMIES

från Folkkultursarkivet 18. Skrifter utgivna av Svenska litteratursällskapet i Finland 632.)

Wretö, T. 1984. *Folkvisans upptäckare: Receptionsstudier från Montaigne och Schefferus till Herder*. Stockholm: Almqvist & Wiksell International. (Acta Universitatis Upsaliensis. Historia litterarum 14.)

7

THE POLITICS AND PRAXIS OF THE DISCIPLINE(S) OF 'STUDYING "OUR OWN" AND/OR "THE OTHER" PEOPLE IN LITHUANIA'

Vytis Ciubrinskas

Sociocultural anthropology, in the Western sense, is still little known in the Baltic states. The space usually covered by anthropology is filled by national ethnology, biological anthropology, sociology and other disciplines. Particular political, intellectual and academic factors stunted the growth of sociocultural anthropology in the Baltic states during the periods of major changes in the twentieth century. Meanwhile national ethnologies of the region are on the edge of scholarship and public interest in creating a repository for identity politics or at least folk heritage politics in a New Europe vis-à-vis the European Union. The most constant methodological challenge to Lithuanian ethnology during the different periods of its existence came from the powerful field of history, which incited ethnology towards 'owning the past' and providing meta-theories about it. And the main ideological frame, which characterized the discipline for decades, was nationalism, providing both resistant strategies during the Soviet period and methodological nationalism. Particular attention is paid in this chapter to the epistemological challenges that the discipline(s) faced when encountering the historical materialism of the Soviet period and methodological nationalism. The 'ethnic paradigm', still predominant in Lithuanian ethnology, and also its local version – the 'ethnic culture'– are denounced as producing 'monoculturalism – a strategic form of identity politics', and prescribed ethnic and institutionalized identities, thus running counter anthropology's vocation with the recognition of diversity.

As has been widely noticed by almost everyone who does research on the developments of social and cultural anthropology in Central and Eastern Europe (Hofer 1968, 2005; Stocking 1982; Gellner 1996; Skalník 2002; Hann 2003, 2007a; Hann, Sárkány and Skalník 2005; Verdery 2007; Lofgren 2008), in this part of the world there are two disciplines engaged in the field – sociocultural anthropology itself and European ethnology. The latter discipline had already been labelled 'national ethnography' by the end of the 1960s by Tamas Hofer, in his influential article 'Anthropologists and Native Ethnographers in Central European Villages: Comparative Notes on the Professional Personality of Two Disciplines' (1968: 311–15). Orvar Lofgren used to call it the 'ethnology of the nation' (Lofgren 2008: 119); Chris Hann proposed calling it 'nation-centred anthropology' (2007a: 9). Hann shows that this double disciplinarity of the field is rooted in the German tradition, going back to Herder's 'recognition of the unique spirit of each people, conceived of as a separate organism, developing according to its own specific trajectory' (ibid.). Such an early variant of cultural relativism had a lasting effect on scholarship in Central and Eastern Europe and the Soviet bloc during the era of nationalist mobilization (ibid.: 7), which followed the collapse of the region's empires in the nineteenth and twentieth century.

Historically speaking, German-language contributions played a major role in setting academic agendas for the development of anthropology in Central and Eastern Europe. Such terms as *Ethnographie, Ethnologie* and *Volkerkunde* are usually synonyms in Germany nowadays, while the field of inquiry covered by the former term Volkskunde is often divided into more or less autonomous subfields, such as folklore, material culture and museum studies, recently replaced by the term empirical cultural studies.

George Stocking (in Hann, Sárkány and Skalník 2005: 6) and Katherine Verdery (2007) point out that both disciplines – national ethnology and sociocultural anthropology – are influenced if not defined by colonialism, and the distinction between the two is made on ideological and political grounds: one is 'nation-building' and the other 'empire-building' anthropology. Even today the politics of the 'peoples studying' discipline(s) are shaped by ethnonationalist and postcolonial discourses. Verdery, after experiencing such discourses first hand (during her numerous fieldwork trips in Romania and elsewhere in Central and Eastern Europe), admits that postsocialist processes of nation and national culture (re)building are actually re-enacting the hundred year old – dating from the collapse of the empires period – rhetoric of 'looking to the folk to reveal the nation's original character' (2007: 49). As Central and Eastern Europe was, and in some respects still is, busy and preoccupied with identity politics, the region's national ethnologies suited the public interest in creating a repository for national culture politics or, at least, for folk culture heritage politics. So if postcolonial anthropology was the creation of overseas colonizers, Central and Eastern European ethnography was that of 'Europe's *colonized*, with expectable differences of emphasis' (ibid.). In regard to this emphasis, different epistemologies were employed, (re)producing, or at least leading to, 'hierarchies of knowledge' between Western (cosmopolitan) and Central and Eastern (national) scholarship (Buchowski 2004).

National ethnology and sociocultural anthropology, taken as separate disciplines, are of different natures and have different usages in ex-communist countries. In most cases, the former was (is) 'acting on behalf of nation' (Kaschuba 2006 [1999]), from 'a kind of salvage operation and cultural engineering' (Gellner 1996) during the period of nineteenth-century nation-building, through those of cultural-ethnic nationalist strategies of resistance to communism at the end of the twentieth century. The latter is a novelty, a 'product of Westernization', which in most cases came to the region through the postsocialist changes as post-communist era studies of the global human condition in comparative perspectives, 'untouched by Marxism or nationalism' (Buchowski 2007: 10). Eventually, it became a discipline that challenged the 'natural' order of the nationally established social sciences and humanities by introducing politics of knowledge beyond methodological nationalism or postcolonialism (Kelertas 2006) as well as providing new epistemologies. As Verdery pointed out, anthropology contrasted the salvage strategies of the (former) colonized to whom 'neither comparison nor theory creation was useful; it requested close description of local traditions, instead' (2007: 49).

Thus anthropology was at odds with 'home-bred' ethnology in the region. In Lithuania at least, the former was raised in the traditions of ethnocentric descriptivism and fired with cultural nationalism – a dominant feature of the recent Baltic revolution, the Singing Revolution[1] – as well as the ethnocultural politics of the post-revolutionary period (Ciubrinskas 2008). If in the Soviet period the politics of the discipline of ethnology were framed in ethnic (cultural) nationalism providing some sort of resistance or counter-establishment strategies against the Soviet regime, this changed into the ethnification of culture after the collapse of socialism.

Most attention in this chapter is paid to current disciplinary developments in Lithuania both in the field of studying 'our own' people as well as 'the other' peoples. How was the field influenced by ideologies and institutional policies? How were such analytically void terms like 'nation' or, over the last two decades, the severely criticized term 'culture' (cf. Gupta and Ferguson 1992; Fox and King 2002) used in the epistemology of the discipline(s) and manipulated by identity politics?

The chapter uses documentary sources but is primarily based on the data obtained from a few informants who were particularly close to, or even participants in, the events accompanying the growth and failure of anthropology as a discipline in Lithuania. My own experience of participation in the activities of institutes, museums and universities practising ethnology and anthropology research has enabled me to give an account 'from the participant's point of view'.

I will start from the development of the national ethnology discipline in Lithuania and continue with the 'post-revolutionary' emergence of the new field of sociocultural anthropology.

BUILDING THE *TAUTOTYRA* (NATIONAL ETHNOLOGY) DISCIPLINE

Historically speaking, as has already been pointed out, national ethnologies accompanied nation-state (re)building ideologies and national identity (re)formations or revivals in Central and Eastern Europe, including the last post-communist revival. Such national ethnologies limited themselves to their own nation-folk studies, following Herder's synonym made of the terms 'nation' and 'folk' (Hann 2007b: 261). Such an approach to 'studying peoples' often meant an interest in documenting a 'pristine' local/regional 'folk culture' found and described in rural hinterlands of the nation states. In Ernest Gellner's terms, nationalism began with ethnography, which in the region appeared first as a 'salvage operation', as he puts it:

> The interest of folklorists and ethnographers lay in the description, collection, study, preservation, and often exaltation of their national (peasant) cultures. This holds true particularly for the countries of the 'third time zone' of Europe, 'which presented the greatest problems from the viewpoint of the implementation of the nationalist principle of one culture, one state ... Many of the peasant cultures were not clearly endowed with a normative High Culture at all ... [As a consequence] ... nationalism began with ethnography, half descriptive, half normative, a kind of *salvage operation* [my emphasis] and cultural engineering combined. (Gellner 1996: 115–16)

This 'salvage operation' and 'cultural engineering' has been attributed to the nineteenth-century 'spring of nations' period but, in the Lithuanian case, it was also used in the interwar period, 1918–1940, of the first Lithuanian Republic to build a 'normative' image of traditional Lithuanian culture and heritage. It underwent a *tautotyra* (the local name for the Volkskunde type of national ethnology) shaping process that is to say predominantly descriptivist documenting of 'local/regional culture' and the cultural-historical paradigm in the analysis of data.

Jonas Balys, the most prominent Lithuanian ethnologist-folklorist of the interwar period, later part of the Lithuanian diaspora in the United States, took a major step in developing ethnology in Kaunas, the then capital city of Lithuania. He founded the Programme and Department of Ethnology *(Etnikos katedra)* in 1934 at Vytautas Magnus University and, a year later, the Lithuanian Folklore Archive, which became the leading centre for Lithuanian folklore studies, where he edited the international journal *Tautosakos Darbai* (Folklore Studies). Balys saw tautotyra first as 'one's own nation's folk studies' and considered it as equivalent to German Volkskunde or Swedish *folklivforskning*. As he wrote: 'The very name [etnika] already shows that it is a science about the peoples (*tautamokslis*), – the part of *etnika* that studies ourselves and our closest neighbors is *tautotyra*. *Tautotyra* aspires to provide a real picture of the life of the European peoples, to understand the external and internal essence of every nation in its historical development ...' (Balys 1934).

Balys was educated in, and became a typical practitioner of, Central North European Volkskunde. In 1932 he defended his Ph.D. at the University of Vienna, at the school of one of the founders of *Kulturgeschichte* in anthropology, Wilhelm Schmidt. Immediately after completing his postdoctoral studies in Helsinki, he became a proponent of the Finnish historical-geographical method. On coming back to Lithuania, he gained a reputation as an active opponent of evolutionism, at a time when it was nationally the prevailing epistemology in the field. Balys tried to set a new epistemological standard for Lithuanian etnika by criticizing evolutionism and promoting a cultural-historical perspective with a strong positivistic stance: 'As there are no "iron laws" in the spiritual sphere (neither are they absolute in the technical sphere), we therefore have to follow the historical method by, first, collecting facts, then evaluating them critically and only afterwards drawing conclusions' (cf. Ciubrinskas 2001: 102).

The polemics between epistemologies of evolutionism and cultural historicism could be considered a sign of the discipline's scientific maturity, although 'salvage ethnography' was still a main feature of the period. Descriptivism and museology dominated Lithuanian ethnology and its main journal *Gimtasai Krastas* (Native-Land), which was also a kind of local history studies review. Archives and museums were full of local culture (ethnographic) collections much used for the publication of a series of local history monographs.

SOVIET ETHNOGRAPHY

The Soviet occupation of Lithuania in 1940 brought particular changes to the social sciences and humanities. The field of ethnology was renamed *Etnografija*[2] and, along with archaeology, was defined as 'a branch of history which studies the peculiarities and development of the material, social and spiritual cultures of the peoples' (Vysniauskaitė 1964: 9). It was institutionalized in the major research establishments of the country as a subfield of history. Since the end of the 1940s, departments of archaeology and ethnography have been founded at the Faculty of History of Vilnius University and at the Institute of History of the Academy of Sciences.

At the time, the discipline of history, dominated by Marxian-Leninist historical materialism, was the strongest epistemological challenge to ethnology. It was a strict requirement of the regime that a Marxist type of historicism be followed, so that at best ethnologists could use the Soviet part of diffusionism to counteract evolutionism. This was called the typological method, based on the concept of economic-cultural types and historical-ethnographic areas, introduced by the Russian ethnologist Nikolaj Ceboksarov in the mid 1950s (Ceboksarovas and Ceboksarova 1977). It was a combination of unilinear evolutionism and a cultural-historical approach. 'Types' and 'areas' were understood as developmental stages determined by the mode of production.

From the late 1970s onwards, evolutionism and the local version of diffusionism turned into positivism. While still within the theoretical framework of historical materialism, positivism had a new research focus: 'everyday socialist lifestyles', studies of 'rural and urban inhabitance of Soviet Lithuania'. Most Lithuanian ethnologists formally fulfilled the epistemological requirements but at the same time resisted the 'cultural engineering' practices of the applied ethnology set by the regime.

In fact, ethnology, as an applied discipline, was serving two ideologies: the dominant ideology, which required the participation of local ethnologists in the 'creation of the new socialist traditions'. Here ethnologists were expected to take part in 'cultural engineering', by remodelling 'the old' feudal and religious traditions and creating new 'progressive' socialist ceremonials. And national identity politics, which implied taking a nonconformist stand and following patriotic research strategies as a professional mission.

COUNTER-ESTABLISHMENT RESEARCH STRATEGIES

Nonconformist ethnologists and Soviet-period folklorists saw their discipline as an instrument to 'nurture' the Lithuanian national folk (traditional) culture through participation in a 'salvage operation' (collecting cultural traditions) and in 'authentic genuine Lithuanian' folk-culture revivalist practices. Their professional promise was to perpetuate the discipline of Lithuanian ethnology and folklore by 'collecting traditions' and by analysing them as the authentic resource for the nation's folk culture and identity. As pointed out by James Clifford, culture-collecting that serves identity needs for 'collection and preservation of an authentic domain of identity cannot be natural or innocent. It is tied up with nationalist politics ...' (Clifford 1988: 218) and, from such an essentialist perspective, cultures become ethnographic collections:

> 'Cultures' are ethnographic collections ... Collecting ... implies a rescue of phenomena from inevitable historical decay or loss. The collection contains what 'deserves' to be kept, remembered, and treasured. Artifacts and customs are saved out of time. Anthropological culture collectors have typically gathered what seems 'traditional' – what by definition is opposed to modernity ... What is hybrid ... has been less commonly collected and presented as a system of authenticity. (Clifford 1988: 230–31)

Thus the 'culture collector', like the salvage ethnographer of the nineteenth century, could claim in Clifford's words to be the last to rescue 'the real thing' (ibid.: 228). This was the reification of 'traditional culture' into nineteenth century or turn of the twentieth century artefacts; so called 'traditional rituals' were 'collected in the field' of the rural hinterlands of Soviet Lithuania as 'typical and specific cultural traits' (using the terminology of the period) and were documented as 'real things' of an 'authentic Lithuanian past'.

At the same time, newly documented 'authentic traditions' became a major reference for identity politics and played the role of 'weapons of the weak', as an effective symbolic power against the 'inauthentic' – created by the establishment, thus supposed to be fake – Soviet traditions. The main moral imperative of ethnographers throughout the field was the urgency of 'traditional culture' collecting. As was pointed out by one of most influential ethnologists of the period, Vacys Milius: 'folklore antiquities are disappearing, old folk tradition performers are dying out, therefore there is an urgent need for the salvaging of what is left *in situ*, the analytic research meanwhile can be postponed for the following generations' (Milius 1992).

Such a culture-collecting urgency served also as a counter-establishment research strategy of the period. It was both a repetition of nineteenth-century salvage ethnography as well as the continuation of the 1920s to 1940s cultural-historical paradigm of documenting local history items for museum and archive collections.

Following the patriotic mission 'to collect the antiquities of our own culture', some ethnologists were busy finding traces of the most archaic past in the items collected, which was assumed to be the most authentic and genuine. Some of them ended up scrutinizing the pre-Christian Baltic past and, in doing so, paved the way for the movement of cultural revivalism of traditional (folk) culture.

CULTURAL REVIVALISM AND NORMATIVE 'LITHUANIAN FOLK CULTURE'

The traditional (folk) culture revivalist movement that emerged in the 1970s was particularly promoted during perestroika in the late 1980s and eventually grew into the 'Singing Revolution' of the early 1990s. The engagement with folklore was especially widespread among the younger generations. The new post-Stalin generation, mostly students, had had enough of the Soviet establishment's festive or parade-culture way of presenting 'folklore of soviet nations' on stage. Inspired by neo-romantic zeal, they developed an interest in reviving 'authentic Lithuanian' folklore by performing it 'not on stage'. In the words of Jonas Trinkunas, one of the leading figures of the movement, 'successful return to the traditional folk culture' was through 'creating spiritually charged territories – get-togethers' (1996). Acting as the head of one of the folklore clubs in Vilnius in the late 1960s and the 1970s, he describes the spirit of the time:

> It was 1968–1969, the beginning of the mass movement of [folklore] ensembles. The get-togethers and concerts of folk music would become a real festival: halls would be packed. The joy was not exclusively esthetic; a free spiritual territory that was not subordinate to anyone was discovered. In the get-togethers everyone sang and everyone danced – the boundary between the performers and the audience disappeared, and it testified to a successful return to the traditional folk culture. Requirements for professionalism was in second place; most important was authenticity and the songs of the people from their own region as well as the mood of nationhood affecting everybody. (Trinkunas 1996: 65–66)

Rather than openly resisting the regime, the dissident movement of the period, focusing on revivalism of human rights and especially those of the Catholic Church, took a somewhat conformist form.

Lithuanian national folk culture revivalism was a distinct form of the national identity politics in which Lithuanian folklore (folk culture) was not only enacted as 'ancient' and 'pristine', as an essential repository of the national folk culture, but also sought legitimization by the regime by conforming to the *liaudies kultura* form – a culture of the labouring masses/ folk. It was good for the Soviet term liaudies kultura to be presented as a substitute for 'traditional Lithuanian folk culture' and, consequently, liaudies kultura became a legitimized substitute for national culture and even for the nation itself. It was due to the Soviet Russian occupation and the statelessness of the Lithuanian nation and also to the reduction of the term nation *(tauta)* to ethnic or cultural nation (cf. Brubaker 1994, 1996) that the stage was set for nineteenth-century Herderian 'Volk' nationalism to be reused a hundred years later. So, under Soviet totalitarianism, the occupied Lithuanian nation and national culture had to be 'cultivated' as 'traditional culture', because 'any acts of devotion to the nation were banned, as were any attempts to "enact" it as a living entity' (Roepstorff and Simoniukstyte 2005: 180).

Thus, extreme importance was attributed to building a normative image of 'traditional folk culture' as a substitute for nation. The ethnologists' and folklorists' 'collected culture' items – with little criticism – were labelled 'authentic' and 'ancient' Lithuanian folk culture. These became for the revivalists the normative categories able to oppose the Soviet regime-imposed atheism, Russification and the Soviet festive, fake culture of communism. 'The ancient tradition' was claimed to be the core of nationhood along with the Lithuanian language and religion.

From the revivalist point of view, the ethnographic and folklore collections were viewed as repositories or 'treasuries of the nation', and ethnographers were encouraged to fill this 'treasury' with their own items collected in patriotic zeal. At the same time, those engaged in local history studies, folklore performers and other revivalists were expected to reflect upon the traditions (i.e., folk songs sung) performed with regard to the national/folk culture spirit, favouring ways that would inspire their audiences to retain traditions and facilitate their revival (Ciubrinskas 2000).

The popularity of the disciplines of ethnology and folklore studies grew significantly. They were sought after as disciplines able to prove the 'typical' and 'authentic' 'Lithuanian-ness', which became of core importance for ethnic national identity politics in the perestroika period. Ethnologists and folklorists, along with historians, linguists and literature specialists – employed at research institutions and universities or just research students – were supposed to be 'experts' in the field of 'Lithuanian traditional folk culture'.

It was hence high time for ethnologists to 'act publicly' and there were many offers from the increasingly open media to write an article or speak out on the issues of the so-called 'ethnic culture' – that is, on ancient Lithuanian mythology, rituals, symbols and traditions. Therefore the lectures and books of the leading ethnologists and Lithuanian traditional folk culture experts of the period, Norbertas Velius and Prane Dunduliene, became highly popular.

'Cultural engineering' was part of the revivalist reconstructions of the 'ancient tradition'. Eventually it combined with the 'invention of tradition', undertaken first by the neo-pagans, the most radical wing of revivalists, who used the resacralization of Lithuanian culture by recreating the pre-Christian rituals of the year and life cycles, in an attempt to revive [sic!] the whole system of the ancient Lithuanian faith (Trinkuniene 1994: 36). In general among the revivalists there was a deep interest not only in the traditions and archaic lifestyle but also in 'pagan beliefs, putting their reconstructions in opposition to militant atheism' (Apanavicius 1996: 59). For example, in the mid 1960s, the Rasa pagan midsummer solstice festival was reconstructed by the Vilnius local history club, which took the initiative of reconstructing the festival according to the ethnographic data collected by ethnologists and folklorists and stored in the archives. The pre-Christian summer solstice ritual was reinvented and first performed in Kernave (50 km northwest of Vilnius) in 1967 and since then has been celebrated every midsummer. The festival serves as an eloquent example of the 'reconstruction' or reinvention of tradition. As Apanavicius points out:

> Despite the persecution and disposition by the KGB, of this [folklore] movement and especially the St. John's day celebration in Kernave, which was viewed with suspicion ... there was a deep interest not only in the traditions and archaic lifestyle but also in pagan beliefs, putting their reconstructions in opposition to militant atheism. (1996: 59)

It embraced the idea of Lithuanian national culture and identity being rooted in traditional folk culture – in the ethnic culture of the Lithuanians, as descendants of the ancient Balts (Velius1989).

POLITICS IN THE FIELD: ETHNIC CULTURE STUDIES AND ETHNIFICATION OF NATIONAL CULTURE

The politics of rebuilding the Lithuanian nation state in the early 1990s promoted such national disciplines as Lithuanian language and history and national ethnology and folklore by reinforcing their role as 'identity cornerstones' while dismissing 'globalizing' ones, such as anthropology. 'Home-bred ethnology' against 'cosmopolitan' anthropology is a stance that enabled nationally well-established disciplines to monopolize certain basic social science categories, such as 'ethnicity' and 'culture', as well as to coin new terms like 'ethnic culture'.

The term 'ethnic culture' *(etninė kultura)* was coined by Velius, who was the most influential folklorist and ethnologist from the 1980s onwards and during the first decade of post-communist change. At one time, the term etninė kultura had a double meaning. Firstly it indicated the traditional Lithuanian folk culture; secondly it was understood as the subject of the discipline of Lithuanian ethnology.

This new term received mass approval during perestroika and even more so during and after the Singing Revolution. For a long time in Lithuanian ethnology, categories of 'ethnicity' and 'culture' were profiled into the rather monoculturalist framework of 'ethnic culture studies', which, in fact, became the most popular label in the ethnology and folklore field of expertise. Hence the actual profile of the disciplines of ethnology and folklore appeared to be 'ethnic culture studies'– that is, studying the culture that is locked in ethnicity.

In 1991, 'ethnic culture' was already approved in the new post-Soviet school manuals as a synonym for traditional Lithuanian folk culture: 'The new Lithuanian school faces the important task of nurturing ethnic culture, to encourage the recognition of its expressions by schoolchildren, to teach them values and perpetuate the ethnic culture traditions' (Cepienė 1992: 3). Furthermore, the term 'ethnic culture' became central in the dominant discourses on Lithuanian national culture and identity (Kuznecoviene 2007). This was particularly explicit in public narratives about the 'true Lithuanian' identity in the diaspora (Ciubrinskas 2009). The network of 'ethnic culture' institutions mushroomed in the country, especially after the Lithuanian parliament's Commission for the Safeguarding of Ethnic Culture was founded in 2000.

Nevertheless, social change and liberalism paved the way for social and cultural anthropology to appear on the Lithuanian academic scene. At first xenophobic and sometimes arrogant attitudes towards anthropology were predominant. According to Romas Vastokas, a well-known Lithuanian anthropologist from the diaspora, who has lived and worked as a university professor in Vilnius and Kaunas for the last twenty years, throughout the whole period of post-Soviet change, anthropology in Lithuania lacked conformity. These attitudes were rooted in the general perception that 'culture' is an intellectual achievement and/or in its confusion with a national 'ethnic culture' (Vastokas 2005). This was clearly visible in the institutionalization of the discipline of anthropology.

WAYS OF ESTABLISHING SOCIOCULTURAL ANTHROPOLOGY: XENOPHOBIA AND MANIPULATION OF THE NAME

A department of cultural anthropology was founded at Vytautas Magnus University (VMU) in Kaunas as early as 1990. The head of the department, Liucija Baskauskas, and three diaspora anthropologists from the United States and Canada started to give instruction in cultural anthropology. The role of the Lithuanian diaspora was central in the reopening of the University itself. After being closed down in the Stalinist period, it was reopened in 1989 as a modern Western university, becoming an example of the exporting of Western standards to postsocialist Lithuania. In fact, Lithuanian-American professors were an excellent example of 'missionary work for Lithuania', the identity politics and moral duty of those in the diaspora connected to the political wave of 'escaping communism' emigration in the 1940s 'to be of use to a communism devastated country' (see more in Ciubrinskas 2009).

However, before the programme in anthropology was fully established, after two years of operation, the Department of Cultural Anthropology ceased to exist due to its 'conversion' into the newly formed, but actually old-fashioned, *Volkskundliche* type Department of Ethnology and Folklore Studies (Anglickiene and Senvaityte 2001). This was a step towards conformity with the country's predominantly ethnoculturalist educational policies in the post-revolutionary period. One professor of Folklore commented on the decision suggesting that: 'We don't need to be taught about Africa: there is an urgent need to learn about our traditions instead. Even more so, we should learn more about our traditions because they are dying and the former, Soviet regime was not in favour of studying them' (Sauka 1999).

Another example of xenophobic attitudes comes from a round-table discussion held by the George Soros Foundation in Vilnius in 1999 and entitled 'Does Lithuania Need Sociocultural Anthropology?' The question put by the moderator: 'Couldn't Lithuanian ethnologists do what anthropologists do?' implied an equivalence between 'home-bred' ethnology and 'cosmopolitan' anthropology, with sociocultural anthropology being assumed a novelty, a field of scholarship without any 'tradition in the spectrum of national scientific development'. One of the participants, the head of the country's leading folklore research institution, asked the question: 'Do we really need this novelty? Are we not capable of achieving these proposed aims within existing research fields and institutions and within existing resources and research?' (Sauka 1999).

In fact, this pointed to a tendency to equate national ethnology with anthropology. While anthropology's identity is still to do with looking for otherness outside the world of one's own nation, it is quite easy to agree with Kirsten Hastrup, who states that 'native anthropology' is 'a contradiction in terms' (Hastrup 1993: 157). So by exploring their own (traditional) culture or 'their primitives within' (cf. Lofgren 2008: 119) in Hastrup's terms, East European ethnologists are actually doing 'native anthropology'. Thus, not surprisingly, such modern paradigms in anthropology, like 'anthropology at home' or 'anthropology back home', are not usually recognized by Central and Eastern European ethnologists as new (Godina 2002). The natural reaction of local researchers is that these innovations were already known.

Therefore in postsocialist countries this praxis is marked by a tendency to equate 'reclassified' ethnology with anthropology (ibid.: 9).

The most common way out of this was to add the fashionable label of 'anthropology' to the name of any *Volkskundian* department. In the era of postsocialism, a number of Central and Eastern European ethnological (former ethnographic) institutions changed their names to ethnology and cultural anthropology. The new label recognized the fact that anthropology had lately become fashionable along with other trends of Western scholarship. Folklorists and ethnographers gave up their identities overnight, calling themselves 'anthropologists'. Former departments of ethnology (or ethnography, Volkskunde, etc.) were now (re)named departments of ethnology and cultural anthropology (Godina 2002: 13).

It is easy to agree with Peter Skalník that the discipline of anthropology does not appear with a formal introduction of its name (for a wealth of examples, see Skalník 2002). He argues against that position by pointing out very clearly that there are significant differences between ethnology and anthropology: 'Those who maintain that ethnology(ethnography) is a synonym for anthropology and therefore anthropology is not actually needed, underestimate the strength of the historical sciences tradition, for they must know well that by making no distinction they automatically – in the specific conditions of Central/East Europe – help to preserve the *ancient regime*' (Skalník 2002: VII–VIII).

According to the Slovenian anthropologist Vesna Godina, who did research on the development and politics of the discipline, an attempt to merge ethnology with anthropology is directly linked to the 'money and power dilemma' (2002: 9). As it became both fashionable and fruitful to use the label of anthropology to attract prestige and raise funds, new establishments, departments, programmes, etc. provided a rare opportunity to attract new funding for research and teaching, as well as furnish new power bases in the positions of deans, heads and chairs (ibid.).

This is particularly true in the situation that arose at Vilnius University in Lithuania, where the interdisciplinary Programme of Cultural History and Anthropology was launched in 2000 in the School of History. It was supposed by the School's administrators that anthropology would take a small niche in the programme previously allocated to national ethnology, as a subfield of history. However the interest in the anthropology courses in the programme grew in comparison to those in history. In three years the programme became extremely popular and attracted some of the best students; it was found to be 'in competition' with history and the dean took the decision to reshape it so as to exclude almost all courses in anthropology but to leave the name of anthropology in the title. Since then the programme has, in fact, only been in history except for the single 'Introduction to Anthropology' course, but it continues to attract new students just because of its name. Thus the field of history at Vilnius University has gained new resources though it has cared little either for anthropology or, even, for ethnology.

THE SOCIAL ANTHROPOLOGY MASTER'S PROGRAMME
AND RESEARCH CENTRE IN KAUNAS

A crucial point in regaining the discipline occurred in 2003. During the very demise of sociocultural anthropology at Vilnius University,[3] the first Baltic anthropology conference was organized as a desperate step to call for international support for the field of anthropology in Lithuania. Appropriately titled 'Defining Ourselves: Establishing Anthropology in the Baltic States', it was attended by scholars from all the Nordic-Baltic rim countries as well as Germany, the United Kingdom, Canada and the United States. The topics ranged from the proper definition of the discipline, the subject matter of our enquiry here, to the urgency of understanding the post-Soviet 'transition'. Its participants, including keynote speakers Jonathan Friedman and Chris Hann, urged for the establishment of the sociocultural anthropology programme in the Baltic states. It was suggested that Lithuania take a lead. At the concluding round-table discussion, the representative of VMU, Jolanta Kuznecovienė, Chair of the Department of Sociology, proposed the programme be established in the Department of Sociology at VMU.

One year later, in 2004, an MA Programme in Social Anthropology was developed by Vaštokas, Kuznecovienė and myself (see more Ciubrinskas 2005) and launched there. It was registered in the study field of sociology and despite many efforts remained there until 2010, when anthropology finally entered the State's Register for Education as a separate social science discipline.

The profile of the programme's curriculum covers the anthropology of postsocialism and political anthropology, as well as the politics of identity and migration studies, regional emphasis being on Central and Eastern Europe. Since 2009, students have been given the possibility to enrol on the joint VMU and Southern Illinois University (SIU) certificate study four-course model of Intercultural Understanding, taught mostly by visiting faculty from SIU. Since 2006 – the first year of graduation – fourteen anthropology graduates have enrolled for doctoral studies at institutions including the universities of Cambridge, Queen's College in Belfast, the School of Oriental and African Studies (University of London), City University of New York and Martin Luther in Halle (Germany). Seven of them have already defended their Ph.D. theses.

The Centre for Social Anthropology (SAC) was established at VMU in 2005 as research unit. At present it runs international research projects and has half a dozen affiliated anthropologists with their own ongoing research projects, including guest researchers from the United States and the United Kingdom.

CONCLUDING REMARKS

In summing up, it is worth stressing that in the politics and praxis of the discipline of anthropology in Lithuania a clear difference remains between national ethnology and sociocultural anthropology. The former, throughout the periods of its existence, has functioned more or less as a branch of history and/or as an applied 'cultural tradition' engineering discipline. The latter, supposed to be cosmopolitan and a 'postsocialist novelty', has been met in Lithuanian academia with xenophobic if not arrogant attitudes.

The epistemological modus vivendi for these two 'peoples studying disciplines' is suggested by Hann as 'methodological pluralism' (Hann 2006). Such pluralism is noticeable and gains recognition in the recent fieldwork-based research conducted by Ullrich Kockel, in which Lithuania is portrayed as part of a 're-visioned' Europe (Kockel 2010), and also in the 'good life' studies of postsocialist Lithuanian society by Asta Vonderau (2009). It is also clearly seen in the scope of the journal *Lithuanian Ethnology: Studies in Social Anthropology and Ethnology*, published since 2001.

Vytis Ciubrinskas is an editorial board member of *Anthropological Journal of European Cultures* and an editor of *Lithuanian Ethnology*. He has authored, edited and co-edited volumes, journals and articles on transnationalism, identity politics, ethnicity, nationalism, anthropological theory and methodology, and postsocialist anthropology from the Central East European and North American perspective.

NOTES

1. On 23 August 1989, fifty years after the Molotov-Ribbentrop pact on the Nazi-Soviet occupation of the Baltic countries was signed, the Baltic Way – a human chain of joined hands from Vilnius to Tallinn via Riga – was organized by the National Fronts of all the free countries. It was the beginning of the Baltic countries' Singing Revolution, a newly adopted form of a one hundred year old tradition of mass singing, which had been performed during each of the National Folk Song Festivals organized regularly since the end of the nineteenth century. In 1990, Sajudis-backed

candidates won the elections to the Lithuanian Supreme Soviet and the restitution of Lithuanian independence was proclaimed, Lithuania becoming the first of the Soviet republics to declare separation from the USSR.

2. In this case, Russian anthropologists put it very clearly: 'The very fact that the discipline was invariably called "ethnografija" produced a "labelling effect". Indeed, it was mostly ethnography in its pristine sense – i.e., "description of the peoples" – rather than sociocultural anthropology. Most ethnographers mainly studied topics relating to material culture such as (ethnic) housing, food, clothing etc., in order to establish patterns of historic-cultural evolution (ethnogenesis, etc.)' (Bondarenko and Korotayev 2003: 235).

3. Despite the demise, some remarkable developments had taken place at Vilnius University a decade earlier. Already in 1991, the 'Introduction to Social Anthropology' course had been put into the curriculum of the history programme. In cooperation with the departments of anthropology at the Universities of Lund and Copenhagen, the first doctoral school – the International Nordic-Baltic School of Social Anthropology – was founded in 1996. In 2000 and 2001, the credit courses for doctoral students were given by Jonathan Friedman and Steven Sampson.

REFERENCES

Anglickiene, L. and D. Senvaityte. 2001. 'Etnines kulturos vagos gileja', *Darbai ir Dienos* 25: 292–94.

Apanavicius, R. 1996. 'Sovietizmas ir lietuviu etnine kultura', in A. Zalatorius (ed.), *Priklausomybes metu (1940–1990) lietuviu visuomene: pasipriesinimas ir/ar prisitaikymas*. Vilnius: Pasaulio lituanistu bendrija, pp. 53–60.

Balys, J. 1934. 'Lietuviu tautotyros reikalu', *Akademikas* 16.

Bondarenko, D. and A. Korotayev. 2003. 'In Search of a New Academic Profile', in D. Dracklé, I. Edgar and T. Schippers (eds), *Educational Histories of European Social Anthropology*. New York, Oxford: Berghahn Books, pp. 230–46.

Brubaker, R. 1994. 'Nationhood and the National Question in the Soviet Union and Post-Soviet Eurasia: An Institutional Account', *Theory and Society* 23(1): 47–78.

———. 1996. *Nationalism Reframed: Nationhood and the National Question in the New Europe*. Cambridge University Press.

Buchowski, M. 2004. 'Hierarchies of Knowledge in Central-Eastern European Anthropology', *Anthropology of East Europe Review* 22(1): 5–14.

———. 2007. 'Anthropology of European Post Socialism: Modes of Invention and Representation'. Retrieved 28 February 2011 from www.colbud.hu/apc-aa/img_ upload/.../Buchowski.pdf>

Ceboksarovas, N. and I. Ceboksarova. 1977. *Tautos rases, kulturos*. Vilnius: Mokslas.

Cepienė, I. 1992. *Lietuviu etnines kulturos istorija*. Kaunas: Sviesa.

Ciubrinskas, V. 2000. 'Identity and Revival of Tradition in Lithuania: An Insider's View', *Folk: Journal of Danish Ethnographic Society* 42: 19–40.

———. 2001. 'Challenges to Lithuanian Ethnology During the Soviet Period: The Discipline, Ideology, and Patriotism', *Lietuvos Etnologija/Lithuanian Ethnology* 1(10): 99–117.

————. 2005. 'The First Program in Anthropology in the Baltic States at Vytautas Magnus University in Kaunas, Lithuania', *EASA Newsletter* 39: 6–10.

————. 2008. 'Challenges to the Discipline: Lithuanian Ethnology between Scholarship and Identity Politics', in M.N. Craith, U. Kockel and R. Johler (eds), *Everyday Culture in Europe: Approaches and Methodologies*. Aldershot: Ashgate, pp. 101–18.

————. 2009. 'Diasporas Coming Home: Identity and Uncertainty of Transnational Returnees in Post-Communist Lithuania', in L. Kurti and P. Skalník (eds), *Postsocialist Europe: Anthropological Perspective from Home*. New York and Oxford: Berghahn Books, pp. 95–117.

Clifford, J. 1988. *The Predicament of Culture*. Cambridge, MA: Harvard University Press.

Fox, R.G. and B.J. King (eds). 2002. *Anthropology Beyond Culture*. Oxford and New York: Berg.

Geertz, C. 1994. 'Primordial Loyalties and Standing Entities: Anthropological Reflections on the Politics of Identity', *Public Lectures* 7. Collegium Budapest/Institute for Advanced Studies.

Gellner, E. 1996. 'The Coming of Nationalism and its Interpretations: The Myth of Nation and Class', in G. Balakrishnan (ed.), *Mapping the Nation*. London: Verso, pp. 98–145.

Godina, V. 2002. 'From Ethnology to Anthropology and Back Again: Negotiating the Boundaries of Ethnology and Anthropology in Post-Socialist European Countries', in P. Skalník (ed.), *A Post-Communist Millennium: The Struggles for Sociocultural Anthropology in Central and Eastern Europe*. Prague: Set Out, pp. 1–22.

Gupta, A. and J. Ferguson. 1992. 'Beyond "Culture": Space, Identity, and the Politics of Difference', *Cultural Anthropology* 7(1): 6–23.

Hann, C. 2003. 'The Anthropology of Eurasia in Eurasia', *Working Papers of the Max Planck Institute for Social Anthropology* 57.

————. 2006. 'Nations and Nationalism in Central Eastern Europe', in G. Delanty and K. Kumar (eds), *The Sage Handbook on Nations and Nationalism*. London: Sage, pp. 399–409.

————. 2007a. 'Anthropology's Multiple Temporalities and its Future in Central and Eastern Europe: A Debate', *Working Paper of the Max Planck Institute for Social Anthropology* 90.

————. 2007b. 'All Kulturvolker Now?: Social Anthropological Reflections on the German-American Tradition', in R.G. Fox and B.J. King (eds), *Anthropology Beyond Culture*. Oxford and New York: Berg, pp. 259–76.

Hann, C., M. Sárkány and P. Skalník (eds). 2005. *Studying Peoples in the People's Democracies: Socialist Era Anthropology in East-Central Europe*. Münster: LIT Verlag.

Hastrup, K. 1993. 'Native Anthropology: A Contradiction in Terms?', *Folk: Journal of Danish Ethnographic Society* 35: 147–61.

Hofer, T. 1968. 'Anthropologists and Native Ethnographers in Central European Villages: Comparative Notes on the Professional Personality of Two Disciplines', *Current Anthropology* 9(4): 311–15.

————. 2005. 'Anthropologists and Native Ethnographers in Central European Villages: Comparative Notes on the Professional Personality of Two Disciplines', in C. Hann, M. Sárkány and P. Skalník (eds), *Studying Peoples in the People's Democracies: Socialist Era Anthropology in East-Central Europe*. Münster: LIT, pp. 343–61.

Kaschuba, W. 2006 [1999]. *Einfuhrung in die Europeische Ethnologie*. Munich: Verlag C.H. Beck.

Kelertas, V. (ed.). 2006. *Baltic Postcolonialism*. Amsterdam and New York: Rodopi.

Kockel, U. 2010. *Re-visioning of Europe: Frontiers, Place Identities and Journeys into Debatable Lands*. Basingstoke: Palgrave Macmillan.

Kuznecoviene, J. 2007. 'Lithuanian National Identity: Dimensions of Closeness and Openness', *Filosofija: Sociologija/Philosophy: Sociology* 18(2): 1–13.

Lofgren, O. 2008. 'When is Small Beautiful? The Transformations of Swedish Ethnology', in M.N. Craith, U. Kockel and R. Johler (eds), *Everyday Culture in Europe: Approaches and Methodologies*. Aldershot: Ashgate, pp. 119–32.

Milius, V. 1992. 'Etnografijos pasiekimai ir rupesciai', *Liaudies kultura* 2(23):10–23.

Roepstorff, A. and A. Simoniukstyte. 2005. 'Cherishing Nation's Time and Space: The Tradition Maintaining Lithuanian Identity', in T. Otto and P. Pederson (eds), *Anthropology and the Revival of Tradition*. Aarhus: Aarhus University Press, pp. 157–92.

Sauka, L. 1999. 'Comment to the discussion "What is Contemporary Anthropology"'. The George Soros Foundation [Open Society Lithuania], Vilnius, May 1999.

Skalník, P. (ed.). 2002. *A Post-Communist Millennium: The Struggles for Sociocultural Anthropology in Central and Eastern Europe*. Prague: Set Out.

Stocking, G. 1982. *Race, Culture, and Evolution: Essays in the History of Anthropology*. Chicago and London: University of Chicago Press.

Trinkunas, J. 1996. 'Autentiskos liaudies kulturos paieskos septintajame – astuntajame desimtmetyje', in A. Zalatorius (ed.), *Priklausomybes metu (1940–1990) lietuviu visuomene: pasipriesinimas ir/ar prisitaikymas*. Vilnius: Pasaulio lituanistu bendrija, pp. 61–69.

Trinkuniene, I. 1994. 'Tradicines kulturos nykimo ir islikimo prielaidos', *Filosofija: Sociologija/Philosophy: Sociology* 3(15): 35–47.

Vastokas, R. 2005. 'From Glasnost to NATO: Retired and Restless in a Post-Soviet State', *Trent University Newsletters* 2: 14–16.

Velius, N. (ed.). 1989. *Lietuviu etnines kulturos draugijos istatai ir darbo programa*. Vilnius: Mokslinis metodinis kulturos centras.

Verdery, K. 2007. '"Franglus" Anthropology and East European Ethnography: The Prospects for Synthesis' [Comment on C. Hann, 'Anthropology's Multiple Temporalities and its Future in Central and Eastern Europe'], *Working Papers of the Max Planck Institute for Social Anthropology* 90, *Sociologicky Casopis/Czech Sociological Review* 43(1): 204–8.

Vonderau, A. 2009. 'Models of Success in the Free Market: Transformations of the Individual Self-Representation of the Lithuanian Economic Elite', in I. Schroeder and A. Vonderau (eds), *Changing Economies and Changing Identities in Postsocialist Eastern Europe*. Berlin: LIT Verlag, pp.111–28.

Vysniauskaitė, A. (ed.). 1964. *Lietuviu etnografijos bruozai*. Vilnius: Valstybine politines ir mokslines literaturos leidykla.

8

MOIETIES, LINEAGES AND CLANS IN POLISH ANTHROPOLOGY BEFORE AND AFTER 1989

Michał Buchowski

~~~⁀⁀⁀~~~

In the memory of Marian Kempny

The following chapter on anthropology/ethnology in Poland accentuates the plurality of the discipline both at the level of institutional segmentation and theoretical diversity up to the end of 20th century. The seemingly univocal domination of the Marxist paradigm during the socialist period has not been the rule for Polish ethnologists, while the predominance of fieldwork 'at home' made them more like their counterparts in other countries of the 'Eastern bloc'. Importantly, I – like several others in this volume – confirm that the socialist period has not been a monolith. In the 1950s and 1960s the need to reconcile a romantic world view about folk traditions with the modernist belief in science and social progress constituted a paradoxical specificity of Polish ethnology/anthropology; since the late 1970s important theoretical shifts have led anthropologists away from both preoccupations with folk life and with theoretical positivism. Well before the post-1989 transformation, Polish ethnology/anthropology had been able to build on various Western theories as well as produce its own. Yet, well after the 1989 transformation the discipline is still in search of its own identity, not least due to its institutional segmentation.

In this chapter I accentuate the emotional attachment to the discipline among its practitioners. This unexpectedly exposes the importance of 'other rationality' that guides the field, which emerges against the odds of its relatively weak institutional position and in the background of significant sociopolitical transformation. An exercise in mapping the 'tribal' structure of Polish anthropology allows me to articulate pressing issues that the discipline faces today – that is, the need to develop theory that is deeper embedded in fieldwork, and a culturalist perspective that would not overlook social, political and economic reality in its dynamics.

Most Polish anthropologists would agree with the Nietzschean statement, evoked also by Geertz (1986: 105), that anthropology is their *frohliche Wissenschaft*. Engagement in the discipline is to a large extent emotional. This passion translates into activity that we now reconstruct in terms of research paradigms. Born in the nineteenth century as a mixture of romantic ideas about folk customs, positivist endeavours to collect data and a general evolutionist concept of culture, the interpretive community of anthropologists embarked on a complicated trajectory of its own development intertwined with wider social and cultural transformations. Despite constant changes, the Polish 'sciences of Man and his culture' shared features similar to those identified as characteristic of American anthropology by Sherry Ortner:

> Although anthropology was never actually unified in the sense of adopting a single shared paradigm, there was at least a period when there were few large categories of theoretical affiliation, a set of identifiable camps or schools, and a few simple epithets one could hurl at one's opponents. Now there appears to be an apathy of spirit even at this level. We no longer call each other names. We are no longer sure of how the sides are to be drawn up, and where we would place ourselves if we could identify the sides. (1984: 126–27)

No doubt, there has always been a huge disproportion in the total numbers of Polish and American anthropologists. Nevertheless, in the last two or three decades, we can observe an analogous entropy in Polish anthropology and we need to ask ourselves what the historical reasons for this are. One may also wonder whether a diversification of the topics studied and theories applied goes together with a creation of discursive monads divided by walls of silence and a lack of intellectual exchange. There are complex reasons for the increasing pluralism of Polish ethnology. Changes in the discipline are a function of the external influences of the international community of anthropologists and its own internal dynamics. The diversification of paradigms also results from the fact that sociocultural anthropology in the country was until recently in the process of reconstituting itself and on an urgent quest for identity. As a matter of fact, these processes have never stopped. One might expect the radical political shifts ensuing after 1989 have decisively redirected the shaping of the discipline. Whether this is the case in Poland is one of the questions addressed in this chapter.

There is a problem in finding adequate categories to study these issues. Habitually, such terms as school, orientation or style are evoked and used interchangeably. *School* seems to be the most focused concept, since it implies a unity of views on the subject studied, methods applied and modes of explanation utilized. For example, in the history of anthropology we quite easily identify the Durkheimian or Malinowskian schools. The personality of the intellectual leader leaves its imprint on the way his or her followers conceptualize problems and think. *Orientation* assumes merely that several scholars share some scientific paradigm of interpretation without any particular adhesion to the same school. Therefore, we can refer to the notions of functionalism or structuralism without thinking of them as unified schools whose members strictly follow the same principles in their research practice. Thus, in the scholarly orientation known as anthropological functionalism, several schools can be distinguished, such as the Oxford and Manchester schools; or, in symbolic orientation, different modes of its application – e.g. Victor Turner's and Mary Douglas' – can be distinguished. A *style* in anthropology is produced by a combination of the following elements: belonging to a certain intellectual tradition; a significance ascribed to empirical materials in the overall reasoning; a more or less realistic status assigned to empirical facts; the interpretive or scientific character of the whole disciplinary practice; and, last but not least, a conscious ascription to a certain tradition of doing anthropology. In this way, one can discriminate realistic or constructivist approaches to anthropology as well as scientific and interpretive styles of doing anthropology. All these terms are useful in our view of the discipline's history, especially in its local national context, but leave virtually untouched such extra-intellectual and methodological factors as group or generation affiliation, disciplinary origins, local academic centres' traditions, personal ties and hierarchical dependencies. Taking them into account would bring us closer to the anthropology of anthropology or, at the very least, to the ethnography of the discipline. This is what I try to approximate here.

In order to grasp the situation in Polish anthropology, I metaphorically employ categories of *tribe, moieties, lineage* and *clan*. Anthropologists form, on the one hand, a kind of Michel Maffesoli's (1988: 141ff.) neo-tribe – that is, a group of people united by ideas, symbols and practices attractive to them. Membership of it is informal, voluntary, fluctuating and egalitarian. However, on the other hand, academic practice is at the same time institutionalized, exclusive, to a certain extent authoritarian and permeated with power relations. 'A moiety is one of the two complementary elements of a tribe which is divided into two organisations co-operating in ceremonial, social and political life' (Szynkiewicz 1987: 249). Moiety and lineage affiliation are defined by blood relationships, and in the case of anthropologists by their disciplinary training. Still, today one can distinguish ethnological and sociological moieties in the contemporary Polish anthropological tribe[1] that were even more separated and conspicuous at the turn of the millennium. Both have their own genealogy, mythology and organizations – the Polish Ethnological Society and the Social Anthropology section within the Polish Sociological Society. Dual membership is very rare and communication between members for a long time was really poor – mostly ceremonial. Within these two moieties, several clans can be found. The classification I offer does not pretend to cover all major events in Polish anthropology or to delineate precisely the discipline's borders. The existence of tricksters whom it is difficult to classify in the clans listed must be mentioned.[2] The cartography of anthropology at the beginning of the 1990s is a starting point for the discussion on its transformations in the last decade of the twentieth century. The ethnographic paradigm, characteristic of the discipline in Poland in the 1960s and partially in the 1970s, represents a useful point of reference for a description of its further developments.

'ETHNOGRAPHISM' OF THE ETHNOGRAPHIC PARADIGM

The paradigm that dominated the Polish 'sciences concerned with culture and local traditions' can be called ethnographic for several reasons: it was an officially used nomenclature of the time;[3] it mostly represented a sort of descriptive practice and, as such, this paradigm could be easily contrasted with those that emerged in opposition to it.

Up to the 1970s, independently of all theoretical nuances, most scholars shared a kind of positivist view of science.[4] Positivism is the twin brother of modernism and socialism; at the same time, it is a product of it (Bauman 1992: 156–74). Science had an assigned function in the huge project of modernizing and rationalizing society. The role of ethnography in this project was to describe 'the world on the wane' of folk culture at home and, relatively seldom, abroad. The accepted method was intermittent fieldwork, mostly in rural communities, and a kind of eyewitness description of its results, sometimes phrased in terms of the rudimentary theory of (socialistic) transition from tradition to modernity. 'Being there' and witnessing certain events was sufficient to put forward 'objective' judgements on material, social and spiritual 'facts'. However, despite these positivist assumptions, scholars were caught in an ideological conundrum. Besides, folk culture was seen as a relic of the old times, permeated with superstitions to be devoured by the inevitable progress of history. On the other hand, peasant tradition was a root of 'the working people of towns and the countryside', a culture that should be valued and praised. Holding a romantic world view of both folk traditions and modernist convictions on science and social progress, ethnographers made an effort to register rational elements and unique inventions in folklore that could be adopted by contemporary society. Such elements were found in agricultural practices, construction techniques, a variety of useful tools and skills, the use of natural materials, native medicine, knowledge about the world and, last but not least, diet.[5] Descriptivism was a ruling method. Perhaps also in order to avoid any political implications, ethnographers were practising what I called 'ethnographism' (Buchowski 2011: 160), a combination of empiricism, historical sociology, as well as the standardized monograph of a village or region, devoid of any risky theoretical conceptualization – with the exception of rather crude assumptions about the modernization processes taking place, such as industrialization and migration from the countryside to the cities. This was a sort of ethnography that 'investigates culture by means of objects' (Kaniowska 1984: 61). In an attempt to represent culture, the ethnographic monograph was perceived as 'documentary photography of past and contemporary culture', or even an 'album of photographic snapshots' (Kaniowska 1984: 67–68).

Remarkably, Polish ethnographers, in contrast to many representatives of other social sciences, were seldom directly politically involved or ideologically motivated, and the prosocialistic cause merely coincided with their combined modernism and romanticism. On the one hand, and probably also due to the ethnographers' self-restraint in developing any grand theory, 'Polish authorities showed remarkably little interest in the choice of issues researched by anthropologists' (Sokolewicz 2005: 299). On the other hand, 'Polish anthropology ... was not strongly influenced by Marxism-Leninism or by Soviet anthropological models' (Posern-Zieliński 2005: 110). This view has been common for a long time and as Krzysztof Piątkowski noticed, 'historical materialism was not creatively and consistently applied in ethnographic work' (1985: 42). I would add that Polish ethnography in socialist Poland was anything but Marxist, and ethnographers, more or less consciously, were generally immune to political pressure (Buchowski 2011: 158–59). The stereotypical attribution of Marxism to ethnographers in Eastern Europe under communist regime – still widespread in Western academia – is a result of erroneous generalization that assumes that authoritarian ideology had to leave its imprint on every single aspect of life.

Although Poland probably remained the country in the communist bloc most open to Western influence, no doubt the authoritarian system hindered the free flow of scientific ideas between East and West. Translations of then the most recent anthropological works, with the exception of Claude Lévi-Strauss's, were virtually non-existent, but one has to keep in mind that several more classical anthropological works were available in Polish.[6] Isolationism contributed to the perpetuation of the ethnographic paradigm (Burszta and Kopczyńska-Jaworska 1982: 51) of which the huge, monumental two-volume monograph *Ethnography of Poland: Changes of Folk Culture* (Biernacka, Frankowska and Paprocka 1976, 1980) appears today as representative for the post-war generation, and, at the same time, is the swan song representative of its generation.

BREAKING THE TRADITIONAL PARADIGM

Thus, it looks as if Polish ethnography dealt with changes in culture and society, but was itself resistant to change for a long time. However, transformations in the social sciences and humanities in Poland in the 1970s, related to the country's opening up and relaxation of the system, inevitably affected ethnography. The espousal of the label ethnology was the epitome of the process and a symbol of a break with the previous mode of practising the subject. Czesław Robotycki distinguished three styles of doing ethnology in the 1980s. First, it was the continuation of traditional, positivist ethnography. Second, it was 'ethnology based upon world trends and literature – first of all Anglo-Saxon'. The third style referred, according to him, to 'the achievements of French and Russian structuralism, French "new history", phenomenology, and it takes into account the insight of Polish classics dealing with culture, such as J.S. Bystroń and S. Czarnowski' (1992: 5). As a representative of the latter, Robotycki focuses virtually only on this trend. He does not analyse the divisions within other styles and omits anthropological orientations beyond the ethnographic tradition, which makes his picture partial. Nevertheless, his point of departure, namely the contrast between traditional and post-traditional paradigms, seems appropriate, since it defines the actual battlefield between the older and younger generations in the 1980s.

A NEO-TRIBE OF ANTHROPOLOGISTS BY THE END OF THE 1980S

As I mentioned at the beginning, already in the 1980s ethnology comprised just one moiety within the wider anthropological neo-tribe. Its counterpart consisted of a perhaps smaller but significant moiety of declared anthropologists who had their roots in sociology. The two moieties often mutually ignored each other's existence, both in their writings (by neglecting the existence of the other's publications in their own works) and in academic rituals (by lack of collaboration in or invitations to scientific events). Here, in order to present a perspective of Polish anthropology in the 1980s and the beginning of the 1990s wider than that of Robotycki, both groups must be taken into consideration.

ETHNOLOGICAL MOIETY

Scientific Ethnology

I include in this clan all those who were trained in ethnography but had systematically transformed the traditional paradigm into a more theoretically sound and sophisticated one. This was done by the application of modern, updated anthropological concepts to specific subjects studied. The group was often spurned in the accounts of contemporary Polish anthropology, which might be caused by the fact that scientific ethnologists were scattered across the country, and failed to create a unified formation or a particular manifesto. Their existence and theoretical assumptions were implicit in their works on 'traditional' and more modern anthropological topics, such as folk and alternative medicine (Penkala-Gawęcka 1988), social life and kinship (Szynkiewicz 1981, 1992), ethnic minorities (Mróz 1992), rituals and customs (Maj 1986; Kabzińska-Stawarz 1991), cultural identity, or work and festivity (Zadrożyńska 1983). Quite often, scholars tackled extra-European problems, such as Polish migrants in the United States (Posern-Zieliński 1985), or the folk economy in Central Asia (Gawęcki 1983) and Africa (Vorbrich 1989).[7] Improvement of the discipline was understood as 'giving [it] dynamics and looking after (including borrowings) more subtle theoretical foundations for previous and new research topics and methods of their realisation' (Szynkiewicz 1992a: 24). This modernization is visible in an important and original undertaking entitled *Ethnological Dictionary* (Staszczak 1987). Scholars of this breed were not particularly concerned with the philosophical background to their practice and the status of their statements. They focused on interpretations of given phenomena in terms of handy, reasonable anthropological concepts. Implicit rationalism and assumed objectivism combined with realism. This justifies the label 'scientific' that I have invented in order to describe this clan.

New Polish Ethnology

The mythical forefathers of this clan have been partly enumerated above by Robotycki. No doubt, access to the translated works of Lévi-Strauss,

Otto, Eliade, Barthes, Dumézil, Mauss as well as such schools as *La nouvelle historie* and the Tartu School in semiotics prompted the emergence of this group that was concentrated in Warsaw and Cracow, and around the journal *Konteksty: Polska Sztuka Ludowa*. The lineage had its manifesto in which we can see that from the beginning it was divided into smaller clans: orthodox-structural, structural-historical, structural-mythological and phenomenological (cf. Benedyktowicz et al. 1980: 47). Later publications indicate that this lineage transferred into more autonomous sub-lineages: phenomenological (Benedyktowicz 1992), studies of contemporary myths in popular culture (Robotycki 1992) and a structuralist one. Within the latter, at least three caucuses should be distinguished: first, structuralism deeply concerned with the mythical nature of any cultural creation (Stomma 1981, 1986); second, that inspired by the British version of structuralism (Wasilewski 1976, 1989); third, that strongly influenced by Russian semiotics and Eliade's morphology of the sacred (Tomicka and Tomicki 1975; Tomicki 1976, 1981).

New Polish ethnology was generated by open opposition to 'ethnographism', the major factor uniting the clan. Its main aims, articulated by Ludwik Stomma, were to abandon the positivistic paradigm and develop a systematic view on culture based on categories of culture themselves; to pay special attention to the semantics of culture; to focus on mental culture; to reject the classificatory approach in favour of inherent and eternal (*longue durée*) systemic features of culture; and to utilize insights of akin disciplines – linguistics, cultural history, mythology, art and literature (Benedyktowicz et al. 1980: 47). This group consciously created an aura of uniqueness; it had a set of classical works its members referred to in their publications and they tried to include their own works in this canon by citing each other and exchanging public letters in their journal. In practice, it became obvious that the range of ideas its advocates wanted to embrace made them methodologically incompatible. Phenomenology and structuralism were particularly conspicuous. Some efforts to historicize structuralism also seem misplaced. How can one talk about social agents changing history, if their thinking represents exactly the same structural pattern that sails through time independently of 'external', superfluous historic events?

Socio-pragmatic Anthropology

This clan was territorially concentrated in the Departments of Ethnology, and of Cultural Studies at Adam Mickiewicz University in Poznań. Its members, particularly in the 1980s, were attracted by the so-called socio-regulative (known also as socio-pragmatic) theory of culture and historical epistemology elaborated by the philosopher Jerzy Kmita (cf. 1985). In many respects, Kmita's approach was similar to that elaborated by Maurice Godelier and Marshall Sahlins, as well as that of Pierre Bourdieu. The concept of social practice was at the heart of this theory. It was understood as a historically transformed realization of social reality. Social practice is an 'objective' functional structure; however, it is enacted by the people operating within it. In their daily practices, individuals pursue their own beliefs about the world. In fact, these individuals have an influence on the shape of social practice, but one should keep in mind that they continuously act within the framework of the fixed functional determination of practice.

The school worked out its own language of epistemological analysis (perceived as hermetic by some) of various theories in the social sciences and humanities, especially anthropological ones. Through this critical reading of ideas and practices, the traditional ethnographic paradigm would be overcome. In their interpretations, socio-pragmatists accepted several principles, some of which sound obvious today, but were not so almost four decades ago. First, that science is a domain of culture, like language, art, religion and several other distinguishable domains. Thus anthropological theories should not be seen merely in terms of their logical connections, but also in a wider social and cultural context. Science, born in sixteenth- and seventeenth-century Europe, is a specific kind of practice regulated by an evolving set of values (goals to be achieved) and norms (prescribed means of how to realize these values). Scientific images do not reflect reality, as positivists believed, but are a part of the 'cultural dimension of the human objective world' (Pałubicka 1990). The latter statement corresponds with Ortner's opinion that 'there exits only one reality and it is constituted by culture from top to toe' (1984: 153). Second is the double principle of historicism. Not only cultures but also our images of these cultures are constantly evolving. Therefore, anthropological descriptions present changing constructs of assumed cultural phenomena, which, in fact, are permeated with our own views of them. Moreover, they are inherently infused with the intentions of actors living in a given culture and this 'emic' aspect should always be taken into account. While the view about the cultural dimension of social life unifies epistemologists with the 'new Polish ethnologists', historicism is what divides them. For the first, there are no invariant features of cultures and people create history; they are not simply subjected to predetermined structures. Motivated by these major principles, socio-pragamatists tried to relativize commonly shared and universally applied anthropological categories such as magic, religion, ritual, language, etc. Thus reinterpretation addressed various spheres of culture: linguistic (Burszta 1986), customary and moral (Grad 1993), magical, religious and ritualistic (Buchowski 1986, 1993). Issues of cross-cultural analogy (Gierszewski 1987), relativism, rationalism and cross-cultural translations were also discussed (Buchowski 1990, 1997; Buchowski and Burszta 1992; Burszta 1992). They emphasized the ethnocentric character of anthropological concepts, their evolution and the cognitive implications for our view of cultures, the 'other's' cultures in particular. Most members of the lineage limited themselves to an epistemological analysis of exiting anthropological theories. A few also tried to go further and offer their own interpretations of specific subjects, based on the critical epistemological elucidation of prior theories and assumptions of the socio-pragmatic theory of culture.

THE SOCIOLOGICAL MOIETY

This moiety had its own disciplinary genealogy and consciousness, different from that of ethnologists. Ethnologists had no doubts about their tribal anthropological membership. Rebellion against traditional ethnography meant for them a change of theoretical orientation and, in fact, an attempt to catch up with their kin abroad. However, the sociological moiety was sensitive to anthropology but, at the same time, belonged institutionally to another powerful tribe. Their spirit was anthropological while their flesh was sociological. This moiety arose also from the reaction to the positivistic paradigm. Sociology's anthropological dissenters were disappointed, on the one hand, with the results of scientific, quantitative sociology and, on the other, with the poor quality of the ethnographic practice of the times. A false image of hibernating ethnography for a long time caused sociologists to consider themselves the only real alternative to it and to ignore ethnologists. This was reciprocal!

Social Anthropology

This clan, ideologically and socially integrated, was located in the Social Anthropology Unit of the Department of Sociology at Jagiellonian University in Cracow. Its mythical father, Bronisław Malinowski, was born in this city; its founding father was Andrzej Waligórski (1973) and its father in the 1970s and 1980s was Andrzej Paluch. This group developed international relations, propagated a myth of its uniqueness, and for some time actually appeared to some Western scholars as the only anthropological caucus behind the Iron Curtain (cf. Holy 1987).

The Malinowskian heritage and its analysis, particularly shedding light on his Polish intellectual background unknown to the Western public, defined this clan's interests for years (Paluch 1976; Flis and Paluch 1985; Kubica and Mucha 1985; Ellen et al. 1988). Critical interpretation of various theories, starting with that of structural functionalism (Flis 1988), via the American 'culture and personality' school (Mach 1989), and a general outline of anthropological theories (Olszewska-Dyoniziak 1991) comprised a major part of this clan's interests. At the beginning of the 1990s, Zdzisław Mach (1993) published a book on political protest in communist Poland, which was in fact the first major attempt to interpret some empirical material in this school. Paluch consequently emphasized the sociological nature of anthropology, although most of the masters of anthropology discussed in his book (1990) called themselves, and are considered today, cultural anthropologists (eight out of ten). No doubt this was related to the issue of emblematic identity in this clan, and the social anthropologists wanted to establish a realm that would distinguish them from ethnologists, who, as I mentioned, they ignored.

Sociological Anthropology

The centre of this clan was Warsaw. Its intellectual roots reach back to the humanistic sociology of Stanisław and Maria Ossowski and of Zygmunt Bauman (1966), who, already in the 1960s, had tried to take cultural aspects into account in social studies. In the 1970s, this tradition was continued in the innovative studies on lifestyles by Andrzej Siciński (1978) and on the theory of contemporary culture by Marcin Czerwiński (1971, 1988). On the one hand, for this clan's members, traditional sociology, which still dominated the Polish scene, was too scientific, locked in grand theories and statistical data management that could say nothing about daily life and practices. On the other hand, the philosophy of culture was too detached from the problems of real life. In order to render the condition of society, actors should be seen as enacting cultural patterns. Therefore, members of this clan accepted the view that culture matters. In a sense, they wanted to combine the best achievements of the sociology of culture, philosophy and anthropology in order to interpret social life and its human dimension. Like both the socio-pragmatists and new ethnologists, they believed that culture should be understood as identity and not be identified with society. Sociological analyses blind to the phenomenon that culture powerfully shapes social practice are like an attempt to paint a rainbow in black and white.

Work on 'grand anthropological narratives' comprised an important part of this clan's activity. A thorough study on sociological and anthropological theories of exchange was carried out by Marian Kempny (1988), a scholar transferred from Cracow. An attempt to include a cultural dimension in sociological analysis did not mean that members of the clan shared the same methodological approach. The methods varied from more sociological, qualitative interpretations of data on typical ethnological topics, such as ethnic prejudices (Nowicka 1990), through multifarious sociological and

cultural interpretations of the contemporary social perception of time
(Tarkowska 1992), to the cultural interpretation of alternative theatre in an
authoritarian system (Jawłowska 1988). Perhaps because of the sociological
influence, the members of this clan addressed more often than ethnologists
the social processes taking place in Polish society. The first real initiatives
to unite the anthropological tribe in Poland were also undertaken by the
representatives of this circle. The Social Anthropology Section within the
Polish Sociological Association, open to ethnologists, was created there and
Kempny became its first leader. A conference designed to indicate shared
topics and methodology, as well as to integrate leading scholars, was also
organized by this group (Tarkowska 1992a). Common interests with certain
members of socio-pragmatic anthropology resulted in joint publications
(Buchowski and Kempny 1992; Kempny and Burszta 1994).

A NEW FORMATION

By the end of the 1980s, Polish anthropology formed a self-conscious
discipline. Although comprised of two major pillars, who partly ignored
each other, it underwent development from implicitness to explicitness and
scholars increasingly called themselves anthropologists. This identity was
not clear and did not mean that scholarship genealogy was forgotten or put
aside. It meant that ethnologists and some sociologists also felt themselves to
be anthropologists. This phenomenon had several reasons. Partly, it was an
attempt to become part of a worldwide anthropological neo-tribe to which
many scholars 'naturally' gravitated. The sociological and socio-pragmatic
clans were particularly influenced by the Anglo-Saxon intellectual tradition,
different from the continental practice of *Volkskunde*. Opposition to the
'ethnographic paradigm' – that is, the way the latter was exercised in the
post-war period – motivated unsatisfied rebels to seek new inspirations and
made them stick together. Despite all the differences, anthropology began
to function as a label to which new generations could subscribe. And, last
but not least, the term itself started to become fashionable and by the end of
1990s one could count declared anthropologists in hundreds. However, one
can ask if they met disciplinary minimal standards.

It is noticeable that in the 1980s many anthropologists were concerned
primarily with theoretical and historical issues. Fieldwork had not been
given much prominence in many declared anthropologists' considerations,
with the exception of 'scientific ethnologists', who practised it mostly in an
intermittent fashion. Vital at that time, issues such as social protests and
movements, martial law, the self-organization of society, the functioning
of the authoritarian system and its symbolic universe had not been

addressed at all.[8] Ethnologists remained focused on traditionally defined topics. However, they at least knew what it meant to do fieldwork, while many self-declared anthropologists, even today, have not undergone this rite of passage. Interest in theory can be explained in several ways. After years of intellectual isolation, anthropologists wanted to 'catch up' with contemporary developments in the discipline. Critical accounts of both historical and contemporary theories were meant to fill the gap and build bridges. Stipends abroad facilitated this form of anthropological enterprise and the publications that followed attracted the attention of Polish readers. 'Working in theory' suited local intellectual practice in the related fields of sociology, philosophy and the then emerging cultural studies. It seems that it was easier to pursue an academic career in theory than to bother with the interpretation of strenuously collected empirical data. Perhaps traditional or theoretical issues also comprised a kind of political 'safe haven' for scholars wanting to express themselves fully and freely under a still – at least to some extent – authoritarian regime. Whatever the case, this complex constellation of factors led to Polish anthropology being largely theoretical in the last decade before the collapse of communism.

CHANGE AFTER THE BREAKTHROUGH?

The year 1989 brought enormous political and economic change that affected the situation of science and scientists in the region in many ways. Science's mode of operation changed and the status of scientists in society evolved. Competitive standards were applied in the hunt for grant funding and freedom in public life eliminated the remainders of taboo topics. More scholarships abroad opened further possibilities to strengthen the already deep (by regional standards) ties with the international community of scholars. Hundreds of new titles in the social sciences and humanities were translated into Polish. In such a context, scholarship in the country had to change and anthropologists could not evade these shifts.

However, I hold that, with respect to the transformation of anthropological paradigms, the political change in the 1990s only partially influenced the course of their developments in the country. One might have expected a radical reformation in the topics studied and methodology used. However, at the beginning of the decade, a visible continuity of the problems discussed can be observed. The references already cited show that several theoretical issues started and cultivated in the 1980s were still on board in the first half of the 1990s. Theory of anthropology was predominantly present in the writings of anthropologists from the sociological moiety in Cracow and Warsaw and that of the ethnologists from Poznań. Anthropologists also became involved in

making the Polish public more informed about world trends in the discipline
by translating contemporary classics in symbolic, interpretive, cognitive and
postmodern anthropology. Many, particularly in Poznań, engaged in work
on entries or popularizing articles for encyclopaedic editions that started to
thrive on the market. In addition, several handbooks were written (Nowicka
1991; Olszewska-Dyoniziak 1994; Burszta 1996). Most of these theoretical
works published in the last decade of the twentieth century were definitely
more sophisticated and up to date than before. More articles, and even a
few books, were accepted by international journals and foreign publishers.
Easier access to world publications meant that merely summarizing the
achievements of classics and some new orientations in anthropology was
no longer viable or, at least, respected. An 'account period'– that is, a stage
during which one of the main tasks of an anthropologist was to acquaint
Polish readers with the discipline itself – gradually became outdated. This
does not mean, however, that, in some cases at least, a 'recycling' mode of
writing 'anthropology' totally faded away.

Therefore, for those who continued the practice of doing anthropology
understood predominantly as a philosophy of anthropology or philosophical
and cultural reflection on anthropological issues, only the content had
changed. Invented by the 'continental tyrants', new issues, trends and
theories were integrated into local discourses. Subsequently, the issues of
postmodernism, the literary turn in anthropology, reflexive anthropology,
globalization and multiculturalism, the media and popular culture problems
(Kempny 1994; Wyka 1994; Burszta and Piątkowski 1994; Burszta and
Kuligowski 1999; Kempny, Kapciak and Łodziński 1997), the status of
ethnographic description from a post-structural perspective (Kaniowska
2000), semiotics in ethnology (Piątkowski 1993) and controversies over
modes of contemporary anthropological interpretation (Buchowski
1997), have replaced previous concerns with methodology, rationality
and relativism, or language and cognition. So far, so good. Conceptual
considerations are vital for any discipline. However, to a large extent,
several scholars assumed that it is enough to reflect on these topics merely
in theoretical terms. For them the anthropologist was/is like a flâneur
wandering in the library and searching for ideas. Fieldwork was not an
integral part of this kind of project nor, to put it more radically, did it have
to be. This view continued an influential tradition of pre-1989 anthropology.
It probably stemmed from a too literally understood postmodern tenet, an
implicitly shared conviction that 'reality' is constructed anyway, so why
bother about it? Therefore, ideas can be built on ideas. The topics addressed
made these writings attractive for readers, but had simultaneously made
relations with the internationally recognized practice of anthropology
questionable, placing it closer to theoretical cultural studies. No doubt, a

changing world makes us transform our understanding of the way fieldwork is done, but in this paradigm, fieldwork, even if discussed, was in fact denied and for many constituted a purely virtual reality.

The development described above did not mean that other ways of practising anthropology disappeared. Clan heritage still played some role in the scholars' affiliations in the 1990s, but its role significantly diminished. Scientific anthropologists continued their research projects (Schmidt 1996), many of them abroad, in Africa (Vorbrich 1989) or Latin America (Kairski 1999). Tomicki (1990) started a new kind of historical anthropology. New Polish ethnologists (by that time a bit older) cultivated their interests in structures of long duration or popular culture analysed from the related perspectives of phenomenology and hermeneutics (Czaja 1994; Benedyktowicz 2000), Barthian analysis of mythical thinking in popular culture (Robotycki 1998; Nowina-Sroczyńska 1997; Sznajderman 1998) and the historical analysis of ideas on certain subjects (Libera 1997). These attempts were meant to show how universal our modes of thinking are. However, the social context in which these mental structures operate was in fact totally neglected. I identify this style of reasoning with the ethnological style of interpretation of contemporary culture. Socio-pragmatists have gradually shifted to new fields of postmodern and contemporary culture issues (see above) or transition studies (see below), but their followers published a new generation of books referring to a similar theoretical framework (Kowalski 1999). Social anthropologists from Cracow became involved in political anthropology (Mach 1993), research on identity and minorities, initially theoretical (Mach and Paluch 1992) and gradually based on fieldwork (Mach 1998). Studies on theories in anthropology in selected fields had also been done (Romaniszyn 1994; Flis 2000). As already indicated, sociological anthropologists, partly like epistemologists, pursued their interest in the theory of anthropology but, as I will show, were one of the first to make attempts to wrestle with new socio-economic change.

To characterize these developments, seen from the perspective of moieties and clans, in a few words is not an easy task. Some new names appeared on the scene, since a younger generation of scholars entered the field. The disciplinary map became much more complex as new alliances, based on common interests crossing territorial boundaries and affiliations, were formed. A shift towards more 'earthly' and current topics is noticeable, but concern with theoretical issues remained strong, especially if one puts it in the context of what has been said about theoretical anthropology above. To a considerable extent, the practice of a social anthropology detached from the grass roots of life has followed the 'pre-revolutionary' pattern. The same applied, at least at the beginning of the 1990s, to anthropological attempts to study postsocialist change that started with its theoretical conceptualization.

It is difficult to identify who among those considering themselves anthropologists first attempted to conceptualize the change itself, since their articles were published in Poland and abroad right from the beginning. However, what is certain is that the first books concerned directly with change were edited by social anthropologists from Warsaw (Jawłowska and Kempny 1993, 1994). Contributions to these books presented theoretical considerations on the character of transition: What does the same concept of transformation mean in the Central European context? How are postsocialism and postmodernism related? How can anthropology study transition? Despite this theoretical inclination, anthropologists from the field of sociology seemed much keener to deal with current events than be oriented towards the ethnologists' 'deeper mental and *long durée* structures'. The latter remained almost helpless when it came to the issue of 'transition to democracy' studies (cf. Tarkowska 1994) and had given up this subject to sociology, which, in general, dominated the field. That sociological anthropologists became more involved in the study of change than ethnologists may also be a direct result of the sociologists' constant interest in current social issues. Ethnologists treated most sociological effort as superfluous, quantitative and politically substantiated. They preferred to keep a distance from developments in which they felt involved personally, but not interested analytically. Instead, many focused on topics that appeared curious and marginal for the public interested in big structures and models: vamps, coats of arms in advertisement, folk art, movie heroes, cartoons, etc.

Only after some time were these general efforts to conceptualize transformation followed by research and works on the topics related to them. They were/have been written in different fashions and many of them bear the signature of sociological reasoning. Dominated groups of various social status and origin, from religious and ethnic to sexual, in a Polish society in the process of transformation were studied in this manner by Mucha et al. (1999). Youth culture has been a subject of continuous research for Barbara Fatyga, which resulted in a work that presents an interesting mixture of sociological data and anthropological interviews (1999). The 'new' issue of poverty has become a focus of attention (*Kultura* 1998). Among ethnologists, Buchowski (1997a) conducted research through fieldwork on the adaptation of a rural community to the changing structural framework and the transformation of its social relations at the grass roots level. He also outlined a historical conditioning of the meaning of civil society in Poland (1996) and analysed the transition as an invented concept denoting particular change at a particular time and place that in a specific way affects social life in local communities in Poland (2001).

CONCLUSION

In my view, a significant theoretical transformation of Polish ethnography and part of sociology into anthropology had started more than a decade before the 1989 revolution occurred. The event itself did not radically change the discipline's paradigms for several years. Anthropology, though there is without doubt more and more of it and it is increasingly interesting, mature and sophisticated, has followed, to a large extent, patterns of practice elaborated in the 1980s. Thus, progress with respect to the level of scholarship has been made. The particularity of Polish anthropology in the 1990s can be reduced to two features: keeping distance from fieldwork understood in the classical, established by Malinowski, Anglo-Saxon or French manner, and an inclination to study culture as detached from social relations. I would say that 'ethnologists' and theoretical 'cultural anthropologists' were in fact doing what they used to do in the previous decade. They covered new and more current phenomena in their considerations, many of them generated by the 1989 events. However, this 'ideational' approach meant that the Change (die Wende in German), and the social and cultural problems related to it, were rarely addressed. The change was not anthropologically conceptualized and no significant anthropological theory of the postsocialist change has been elaborated. Only a small group of local, let us say, 'social anthropologists' (mostly those who were also concerned with the social and cultural transformations after 1989 itself) alongside a group of Western scholars[9] have tried to fill this gap. In this sense, the Change, 'zmiana' in Polish, did not radically change anthropology in the first decade after it. A certain discrepancy between historical events and a readiness to conceptualize them took place. No doubt, in this period, more extensive contacts with the world enabled further openness, intellectual imports and opening to the West, but for those concerned with this issue of how anthropology managed to deal with enormous social and cultural transformations resulting from the expansion of neoliberal capitalism to the region, it was to a large extent dissatisfying. In this respect, the Nietzschean and Geertzean call could be paraphrased in the lament: *Anthropologie, meine traurige Wissenschaft* (anthropology, my sad science). The state of affairs began to change in the following decade, which saw several critical works on multiple consequences of neoliberalism for various social classes in postsocialist societies, and Polish anthropology entered a period of its interesting, cosmopolitan development.

Michal Buchowski is Professor of Anthropology at University of Poznan and European University Viadrina. He lectured as a Visiting Professor at Rutgers, Columbia and Warsaw Universities. His scientific interests com-

prise postsocialism, migration and multiculturalism. He served as President of the European Association of Social Anthropologists and chair of the
World Council of Anthropological Associations. Currently he is a president
of the Polish Ethnological Society.

NOTES

This chapter is based on an article published as Buchowski (2002). I would like to thank
the Institut für Europäische Ethnologie at Vienna University for permission to publish
it again, even though in a modified form. Those interested in a deeper history of Polish
ethnology can read Buchowski (2011). I have finalized this text as a Visiting Overseas
Professor at National Museum of Ethnology in Osaka, Japan, in the academic year 2016–
2017. I thank my hosts for their support of my research.

1. I do not engage in a discussion on the distinction between cultural or social
    anthropology and ethnology. In the Polish context they are often used interchangeably.
    Here, I use the term anthropology as the most generic one for 'sciences of woman/man
    and her/his culture', encapsulating both ethnology and social/cultural anthropology.
    This multiplicity is reflected in the names of the various anthropological academic
    institutions, such as the departments of ethnology and cultural anthropology –
    today in Cieszyn (Upper Silesia), Cracow, Gdańsk, Łódź, Poznań, Szczecin, Toruń,
    Warsaw, and the social anthropology units within the department of sociology at
    several universities, but notably strong in Cracow and Warsaw.
2. As for the 1990s, let me merely indicate here the very anthropologically minded
    works of folklorists (Jerzy Bartmiński, Piotr Kowalski and Dorota Simonides),
    archaeologists (Andrzej Kowalski, Jerzy Ostoja-Zagórski), physical anthropologists
    (Jan Strzałko, Janusz Piontek) and historical anthropologists working mainly on
    pre-Columbian American cultures (Andrzej Wierciński, Mariusz Ziółkowski).
3. In the interwar period, the discipline that embraced both the *Volkerkunde* and
    Volkskunde distinguished in the German tradition was called ethnology. After the
    Second World War, following in the footsteps of the Soviet science, Poles, as well
    as other nations in the region, adopted the term 'ethnography', to emphasize that
    empirical (-graphy) and theoretical (-logy) aspects of research are dialectically
    intertwined (see Wróblewski 1967; Posern-Zieliński 1973: 96). The term 'ethnology'
    started to be used again, first in publications and then in the official nomenclature, in
    the 1970s; 'cultural anthropology' was added at the break of the 1980s and 1990s.
4. For a much more extensive characteristic of a problematized history of Polish post-
    war ethnography and the ethnographic paradigm that dominated until the 1970s,
    see Buchowski (2011: 147–59).
5. This attitude recalls that of Bronisław Malinowski, who wanted to make Trobrianders
    as empirical and rational as British logicians (cf. Leach 1957: 128–31).
6. Interestingly enough, Lévi-Strauss was translated thanks to the effort of a group of
    sociologists and philosophers. By 1970, his *Totemism, Savage Thought, Structural
    Anthropology* and *World on the Wane* had been published in Poland. Among the
    classics translated by the beginning of the 1970s one can name, for example, James
    G. Frazer, Edward B. Tylor, Bronisław Malinowski, Alfred Kroeber, Ruth Benedict,

Margaret Mead, Ralph Linton, Benjamin Whorf, Edward Sapir and Raymond Firth. A similar principle applies to many works in the related fields of psychology, history of religions, sociology and philosophy.

7. Here, as well as in what follows, I cite merely exemplary works illustrating the argument. In most cases there were several publications that could be mentioned.

8. The only exception I am aware of is Robotycki (1990). This article was written after strikes in the Gdansk Shipyard, but was refused publication by the censor. In the United States, Jan Kubik (1994), who studied in Cracow, published a book on Polish social protests in the 1970s and 80s and wrote about the 'Solidarity' movement.

9. One can list such names as Elizabeth Dunn, Deborah Cahalen, Lisa Gurr, Elizabeth Vann, Christie Long, Marysia Galbright, Carole Nagengast (all of them American scholars), Chris Hann, Frances Pine, Edouard Conte and François Bafoil.

REFERENCES

Bauman, Z. 1966. *Kultura i społeczeństwo* [Culture and Society]. Warsaw: Państwowe Wydawnictwo Naukowe.

———. 1992. *Intimations of Postmodernity*. Routledge: London.

Benedyktowicz, Z. 1992. 'Widmo środka świata: Przyczynek do antropologii współczesności' ['A Spectre of the Centre of the World: A Contribution to the Anthropology of Contemporary Life'], *Polska Sztuka Ludowa* 46(1): 16–32.

———. 2000. *Portrety 'obcego': od stereotypu do symbolu* [Portraits of 'Alien': From Stereotype to Symbol]. Kraków: Wydawnictwo Uniwersytetu Jagiellońskiego.

Benedyktowicz, Z., C. Robotycki, L. Stomma, R. Tomicki and J.S. Wasilewski. 1980. 'Antropologia kultury w Polsce – dziedzictwo, pojęcia, inspiracje: Materiały do Słownika' ['Anthropology of Culture in Poland – Heritage, Concepts, Inspirations: Materials for the Dictionary], *Polska Sztuka Ludowa* 34, part I (1): 47–60; part II (2): 117–25.

Biernacka, M., M. Frankowska and W. Paprocka (eds). 1976/1980. *Etnografia Polski: Przemiany kultury ludowej* [Ethnography of Poland: Changes of Folk Culture], vol. 1 and 2. Wrocław: Ossolineum.

Buchowski, M. 1986. *Magia: Jej funkcje i struktura* [Magic: Its Functions and Structure]. Poznań: Wydawnictwo Naukowe UAM.

———. 1990. *Racjonalność, translacja, interpretacja* [Rationality, Translation, Interpretation]. Poznań: Wydawnictwo Naukowe UAM.

———. 1993. *Magia i rytuał* [Magic and Ritual]. Warsaw: Instytut Kultury.

Buchowski, M. (ed.). 1996. *Oblicza zmiany: etnologia a współczesne transformacje społeczno-kultusrowe* [Faces of Change: Ethnology and Contemporary Social and Cultural Changes]. Miedzychód: Eco.

———. 1997a. *Reluctant Capitalists: Class and Culture in a Local Community in Western Poland*. Berlin: Centre Marc Bloch.

———.1997. *The Rational Other*. Poznań: Humaniora.

———. 2001. *Rethinking Transformation: An Anthropological Approach*. Poznań: Humaniora.

———. 2002. 'Main Currents in Polish Anthropology: Continuity in Change Before and After 1989', in K. Köstlin, P. Niedermüller and H. Nikitsch (eds), *Die Wende als Wende? Orinetirungen Europäischer Ethnologien nach 1989*. Vienna: Verlag des Instituts für Europäische Ethnologie, pp. 63–82.

———. 2011. 'Polish Ethnology in the Periods of "Early" and "Late" Socialism: From Non-Marxist Orthodoxy to Post-Ethnographical Pluralism', in U. Brunnbauer, C. Kraft and M. Schultze Wessel (eds), *Sociology and Ethnography in East-Central and South-East Europe: Scientific Self-description in State Socialist Countries*. Munich: Oldenbourg Verlag, pp. 147–72.

Buchowski, M. and W. Burszta. 1992. *O założeniach interpretacji antropologicznej* [On the Assumptions of Anthropological Interpretation]. Warsaw: Wydawnictwo Naukowe PWN.

Buchowski, M. and M. Kempny. 1992. 'Antropologia i socjologia wobec problemu racjonalności (uwagi na temat unifikacji teorii społecznej)' ['Anthropology and Sociology vis-a-vis the Problem of Rationality'], in E. Tarkowska (ed.), *Socjologia i antropologia*. Wrocław: Wiedza o kulturze, pp. 125–37.

Burszta, J. and B. Kopczyńska-Jaworska. 1982. 'Polish Ethnography after World War II', *Ethnos* 47(1–2): 50–63.

Burszta, W. 1986. *Język a kultura w myśli etnologicznej* [Language and Culture in Ethnological Thought]. Wrocław: Polskie Towarzystwo Ludoznawcze.

———. 1992. *Wymiary antropologicznego poznania kultury* [Dimensions of Anthropological Cognition of Culture]. Poznań: Wydawnictwo Uniwersyteckie UAM.

———. 1996. *Czytanie kultury: pięć szkiców* [Reading Culture: Five Essays]. Łódź: LodArt.

Burszta, W. and W. Kuligowski. 1999. *Dlaczego kościotrup nie wstaje?* [Why the Skeleton Does not Rise?]. Warsaw: Sic!

Burszta W. and K. Piątkowski. 1994. *O czym opowiada antropologiczna opowieść?* [What Tells the Anthropological Story?]. Warsaw: Instytut Kultury.

Czaja, D. (ed.). 1994. *Mitologie popularne* [Popular Mythologies]. Universitas: Kraków.

Czerwiński, M. 1971. *Kultura i jej badanie* [Culture and Research on It]. Warsaw: Instytut Filozofii i Socjologii PAN.

Czerwiński, M. 1988. *Przyczynki do antropologii współczesności* [Contributions to Contemporary Anthropology]. Warsaw: Państwowy Instytut Wydawniczy.

Ellen, R., E. Gellner, G. Kubica and J. Mucha (eds). 1988. *Malinowski Between two Worlds: The Polish Roots of an Anthropological Tradition*. Cambridge: Cambridge University Press.

Fatyga, B. 1999. *Dzicy z naszej ulicy: Antropologia kultury młodzieżowej* [Wild People from Our Street: An Anthropology of Youth Culture]. Warsaw: ISNS UW.

Flis, M. 1988. *Teorie struktury społecznej w antropologii funkcjonalnej* [Theories of Social Structure in the Functionalist Anthropology]. Wrocław: Ossolineum.

———. 2001. *Antropologia społeczna Radcliffe'a-Browna: Z wyborem pism* [Social Anthropology of Radcliffe-Brown: With Selected Writings]. Kraków: Nomos.

Flis, M. and A.K. Paluch (eds). 1985. *Antropologia społeczna Bronisława Malinowskiego* [Social Anthropology of Bronisław Malinowski]. Warsaw: Państwowe Wydawnictwo Naukowe.

Gawęcki, M. 1983. *Wieś środkowego i północnego Afganistanu: tradycja i próby modernizacji* [Village in Central and Northern Afghanistan: Traditions and Attempts at Modernisation]. Wrocław: Polskie Towarzystwo Ludoznawcze.

Geertz, C. 1986. 'The Uses of Diversity', *Michigan Quarterly Review* 25: 105–23.

Gierszewski, Z. 1987. *Problem analogii międzykulturowej: z dziejów badań antropologicznych* [Problems with Cross-cultural Analogy: From the History of Anthropological Research]. Poznań-Warsaw: Państwowe Wydawnictwo Naukowe.

Grad, J. 1993. *Obyczaj i moralność* [Custom and Morality]. Poznań: Wydawnictwo Naukowe UAM.

Holy, L. 1987. 'The Podhale School of Anthropology', *Anthropology Today* 3(3):18.

Jawłowska, A. 1988. *Więcej niż teatr* [More than Theatre]. Warsaw: Państwowy Instytut Wydawniczy.

Jawłowska, A. and M. Kempny (eds). 1993. *Kulturowy wymiar przemian społecznych* [A Cultural Dimension of a Social Change]. Warsaw: IFiS PAN.

———. 1994. *Cultural Dilemmas of Post-communist Societies*. Warsaw: IFiS Publishers.

Kabzińska-Stawarz, I. 1991. *Games of Mongolian Shepherds*. Warsaw: Instytut Historii Kultury Materialnej.

Kairski, M. 1999. *Indianie Ameryki Środkowej i Południowej: Demografia, rozmieszczenie, sytuacja etno-kulturowa* [Indians of Central and South America: Demography, Settlement and Ethno-cultural Situation], vol. 1–2. Poznań-Warsaw: Centrum Studiów Latynoamerykańskich/Instytut Etnologii i Antropologii Kulturowej UAM.

Kaniowska, K. 1984. 'Tradycja metodologiczna powojennej etnografii polskiej' ['Methodological Tradition of Postwar Polish Ethnography'], *Lud* 48: 51–69.

———. 2000. *Opis: Klucz do rozumienia kultury* [Description: The Key for Understanding Culture]. Łódź: Polskie Towarzystwo Ludozanwcze.

Kempny, M. 1988. *Wymiana i społeczeństwo* [Exchange and Society]. Wrocław: Ossolineum.

———. 1994. *Antropologia bez dogmatów – teoria społeczna bez iluzji* [Anthropology without Dogma – Social Theory without Illusion]. Warsaw: IFiS PAN.

Kempny, M. and W.J. Burszta. 1994. 'On the Relevance of Common Sense for Anthropological Knowledge', in K. Hastrup and P. Hervik (eds), *Social Experience and Anthropological Knowledge*. London: Routledge, pp. 121–38.

Kempny, M., A. Kapciak and S. Łodziński (eds). 1997. *U progu wielokulturowości* [At the Threshold of Multiculturalism]. Warsaw: Oficyna Naukowa.

Kmita, J. 1985. *Kultura i poznanie* [Culture and Cognition]. Warsaw: Państwowe Wydawnictwo Naukowe.

Kowalski, A. 1999. *Symbol w kulturze archaicznej* [Symbol in the Archaic Culture]. Poznań: Instytut Filozofii UAM.

Kubica, G. and J. Mucha (eds). 1985. *Między dwoma światami – Bronisław Malinowski* [Between Two Worlds: Bronisław Malinowski]. Warsaw-Kraków: Państwowe Wydawnictwo Naukowe.

Kubik, J. 1994. *The Power of Symbols against the Symbols of Power: The Rise of Solidarity and the Fall of State Socialism in Poland*. University Park: The Pennsylvania University Press.

Kultura. 1998. *Kultura i Społeczeństwo* 37(2) [Special Issue on Poverty and Suffering].

Leach, E. 1957. 'The Epistemological Background to Malinowski's Empiricism', in R. Firth (ed.), *Man and Culture*. London: Routledge and Kegan Paul, pp. 119–37.

Libera, Z. 1997. *Mikrokosmos, makrokosmos i antropologia ciała* [Microcosmos, Macrocosmos and the Anthropology of the Body]. Tarnów: Liber novum.

Mach, Z. 1989. *Kultura i osobowość w antropologii amerykańskiej* [Culture and Personality in American Anthropology]. Warsaw, Kraków: PWN.

————. 1993. *Symbols, Conflicts and Identity: Essays in Political Anthropology*. New York: SUNY Press.

————. 1998. *Niechciane miasta* [Unwanted Cities]. Kraków: Universitas.

Mach, Z. and A. Paluch (eds). 1992. *Sytuacja mniejszościowa i tożsamość* [A Status of Minority and Identity]. Kraków: Wydawnictwo Uniwersytetu Jagiellońskiego.

Maffesoli, M. 1988. 'Jeux de masques: Postmodern Tribalism', *Design Issues* 4(1–2): 141–51.

Maj, M. 1986. *Rola daru w obrzędzie weselnym* [A Significance of Gift in a Wedding Ceremony]. Wrocław: Ossolineum.

Mróz, L. 1992. *Geneza Cyganów i ich kultury* [A Genesis of Gypsies and their Culture]. Warsaw: Wydawnictwo. Fundacji 'Historia pro futuro'.

Mucha, J. (ed.). 1999. *Kultura dominująca jako kultura obca: mniejszości kulturowe a grupa dominująca w Polsce* [Dominant Culture as Alien Culture: Cultural Minorities and Dominant Group in Poland]. Warsaw: Oficyna Naukowa.

Nowicka, E. (ed.). 1990. *Swoi i obcy* [Ours and Aliens]. Warsaw: Instytut Socjologii UW.

————. 1991. *Świat człowieka – świat kultury: systematyczny wykład problemów antropologii kulturowej* [World of Man – World of Culture: A Systematic Lecture on Cultural Anthropology Issues]. Warsaw: PWN.

Nowina-Sroczyńska, E. 1997. *Przezroczyste ramiona ojca: Studium etnologiczne o magicznych dzieciach* [Transparent Father's Arms: An Ethnological Study on Magical Children]. Łódź: Wydawnictwo Uniwersytetu Łódzkiego.

Olszewska-Dyoniziak, B. 1991. *Człowiek – kultura – osobowość* [Man – Culture – Personality]. Kraków: Universitas.

————. 1994. *Społeczeństwo i kultura: szkice z antropologii kulturowej* [Society and Culture: Essays in Cultural Anthropology]. Kraków: Universitas.

Ortner, S.B. 1984. 'Theory in Anthropology Since the Sixties', *Comparative Studies in Society and History* 26: 126–66.

Pałubicka, A. 1990. *Kulturowy wymiar ludzkiego świata obiektywnego* [A Cultural Aspect of the Human Objective World]. Poznań: Wydawnictwo Naukowe UAM.

Paluch, A.K.1976. *Konflikt, modernizacja i zmiana społeczna: analiza i krytyka teorii funkcjonalnej* [Conflict, Modernization and Social Change: An Analysis and Critique of the Functional Theory]. Warsaw: Państwowe Wydawnictwo Naukowe.

————. 1990. *Mistrzowie antropologii społecznej* [Masters of Social Anthropology]. Warsaw: Państwowe Wydawnictwo Naukowe.

Penkala-Gawęcka, D. 1988. *Medycyna tradycyjna w Afganistanie i jej przeobrażenia* [Traditional Medicine in Afghanistan and its Transformations]. Wrocław: Polskie Towarzystwo Ludoznawcze.

Piątkowski, K. 1985. Problematyka teoretyczna w powojennej etnografii polskiej [Theoretical Problems in Postwar Polish Ethnography], *Lud* 69: 35–62.

————. 1993. *Semiotyczne badania nad kultura w etnologii* [Semiotic Studies on Culture in Ethnology]. Toruń: Uniwersytet Mikołaja Kopernika.

Posern-Zieliński, A. 1973. 'Kształtowanie się etnografii jako samodzielnej dyscypliny naukowej' ['Creation of Ethnography as an Independent Scientific Discipline'], in M. Terlecka (ed.), *Historia etnografii polskiej* [The History of Polish Ethnography]. Wrocław: Ossolineum, pp. 115–67.

————. 1985. *Tradycja a etniczność: przemiany kultury Polonii* [Tradition and Ethnicity: Transformations of the Polish Americans Culture]. Wrocław: Ossolineum.

————. 2005. 'Polish Anthropology under Socialism: Intellectual Traditions, the Limits of Freedom, and New Departures', in C. Hann, M. Sárkány and P. Skalník (eds), *Studying Peoples in the People's Democracies: Socialist Era Anthropology in East-Central Europe*. Münster: LIT Verlag, pp. 109–28.

Robotycki, C. 1990. 'Sztuka a vista: Folklor strajkowy' ['A Vista Art: Strike Folklore'], *Polska Sztuka Ludowa* 44(2): 44–49.

————. 1992. *Etnografia wobec kultury współczesnej* [Ethnography vis-a-vis Contemporary Culture]. Kraków: Wydawnictwo Uniwersytetu Jagiellońskiego.

————. 1998. *Nie wszystko jest oczywiste* [Not Everything is Obvious]. Kraków: Wydawnictwo Uniwersytetu Jagiellońskiego.

Romaniszyn, K. 1994. *Świat gospodarek ludzkich* [A Universe of Human Economies]. Kraków: Wydawnictwo Uniwersytetu Jagiellońskiego.

Schmidt, J. 1996. *Granica i stereotyp* [Border and Stereotype]. Miedzychód: Eco.

Siciński, A. (ed.). 1978. *Styl życia. Przemiany we współczesnej Polsce* [Lifestyle: Changes in Contemporary Poland]. Warsaw: Państwowe Wydawnictwo Naukowe.

Sokolewicz, Z. 2005. 'Polish Expeditions Abroad, 1945–1989', in C. Hann, M. Sárkány and P. Skalník (eds), *Studying Peoples in the People's Democracies: Socialist Era Anthropology in East-Central Europe*. Münster: LIT Verlag, pp. 289–301.

Staszczak, Z. 1987. *Słownik etnologiczny: Terminy ogólne* [Ethnological Dictionary: General Terms]. Warsaw-Poznań: Państwowe Wydawnictwo Naukowe.

Stomma, L. 1981. *Słońce rodzi się 13 grudnia* [Sun Birth on 13 December]. Warsaw: Ludowa Spółdzielnia Wydawnicza.

————. 1986. *Antropologia kultury wsi polskiej XIX wieku* [Anthropology of the Polish Countryside's Culture of 19th Century]. Warsaw: Ludowa Spółdzielnia Wydawnicza.

Sznajderman, M. 1998. *Biblia pauperum*. Kraków: Wydawnictwo Uniwersytetu Jagiellońskiego.

Szynkiewicz, S. 1981. *Rodzina pasterska w Mongolii* [Pastoral Family in Mongolia]. Wrocław: Ossolineum.

————. 1987. 'Moiety [Moieties]', in Z. Staszczak (ed.), *Słownik etnologiczny: Terminy ogólne* [Ethnological Dictionary: General Terms]. Warsaw-Poznań: Państwowe Wydawnictwo Naukowe, pp. 249–50.

————. 1992a. 'Po co nam antropologia?' ['What for Anthropology?'], *Etnografia Polska* 36(1): 21–24.

————. 1992. *Pokrewieństwo: studium etnologiczne* [Kinship: An Ethnological Study]. Warsaw: Wydawnictwo Uniwersytetu Warszawskiego.

Tarkowska, E. 1992a. *Socjologia i antropologia: stanowiska i kontrowersje* [Sociology and Anthropology: Standpoints and Controversies]. Wrocław: Wiedza o Kulturze.

————. 1992. *Czas w życiu Polaków* [Time in Poles' Life]. Warsaw: IFiS PAN.

————. 1994. *Antropologia wobec zmiany* [Anthropology and Change]. Warsaw: IFiS PAN.

Tomicka, J. and R. Tomicki. 1975. *Drzewo życia: Ludowa wizja świata i człowieka* [A Tree of Life: Folk Image of the World and Man]. Warsaw: Ludowa Spółdzielnia Wydawnicza.

Tomicki, R. 1976. 'Słowiański mit kosmogoniczny' ['Slav Cosmogonic Myth'], *Etnografia Polska* 20(1): 47–97.

————. 1981. 'Religijność ludowa' ['Folk Religiosity'], in M. Biernacka, M. Frankowska and W. Paprocka (eds), *Etnografia Polski: Przemiany kultury ludowej* [Ethnography of Poland: Changes of Folk Culture], vol. 2. Wrocław: Ossolineum, pp. 29–70.

———. 1990. *Bogowie i ludzie* [Gods and People]. Wrocław: Ossolineum.

Vorbrich, R. 1989. *Daba – górale północnego Kamerunu* [Daba: Mountaineers of Northern Cameroon]. Wrocław: Polskie Towarzystwo Ludoznawcze.

———. 1996. *Górale Atlasu marokańskiego: Peryferyjność i przejawy marginalizacji* [Moroccan Atlas Mountaineers: Peripheral Status and Marginalisation]. Wrocław: Polskie Towarzystwo Ludoznawcze.

Waligórski, A. 1973. *Antropologiczna koncepcja człowieka* [An Anthropological Idea of Man]. Warsaw: Państwowe Wydawnictwo Naukowe.

Wasilewski, J.S. 1976. *Podróże do piekieł: Rzecz o misteriach szamańskich* [Flights to Hell: On Shamanistic Mysteries]. Warsaw: Ludowa Spółdzielnia Wydawnicza.

———. 1989. *Tabu a paradygmaty etnologii* [Taboo and the Paradigms of Ethnology]. Warsaw: Wydawnictwa Uniwersytetu Warszawskiego.

Wróblewski, T. 1967. *Wstęp do etnografii* [An Introduction to Ethnography]. Poznań: Wydawnictwo Naukowe UAM.

Wyka, A. 1994. *Badacz społeczny wobec doświadczenia* [Social Scientists vis-a-vis Experience]. Warsaw: IFiS PAN.

Zadrożyńska, A. 1983. *Homo faber i homo ludens* [Homo Ludens and Homo Faber]. Warsaw: Państwowe Wydawnictwo Naukowe.

Zowczak, M. 2000. *Biblia ludowa* [Folk Bible]. Wrocław: Fundacja Nauki Polskiej.

9

BETWEEN ETHNOGRAPHY AND ANTHROPOLOGY IN SLOVAKIA
Autobiographical Reflections

Alexandra Bitušíková

This chapter, devoted to the past and present developments of the discipline in Slovakia, is written as an auto-ethnography. Having studied the *národopis* (description of the nation, also called 'ethnography and folklore studies') at university at the turn of the 1970s and 1980s and having later observed the change of ethnography into ethnology and anthropology as an insider of the academy, I offer my personal take on the defining features of the discipline in earlier periods and nowadays. I draw attention to the fact that in the pre-socialist period ethnology/anthropology in Slovakia was primarily interested in national culture and thus came hand in hand with folklore studies. The dominant position of folklore was maintained in the Soviet era, while the stifling dominance of the Marxist paradigm caused many discipline practitioners – if they were not embarking on the prevailing paradigm – to refrain from providing any theoretical commentary to their data. I consider that this caused major damage to the theoretical development of the discipline. Thus the sociopolitical transformation at the turn of the 1980s and 1990s can overall be seen as a welcomed change that opened the discipline to the intellectual influence of its Western counterparts. Still, I assert that an ethnologist/anthropologist from postsocialist Europe is bound to grapple with paradoxes, since the welcoming of the tradition of sociocultural anthropologies in this part of the world came exactly at the time when the West announced the end of the discipline.

One may add that the need to learn Western theories came alongside the emergence of theories that denounced the domination of Western approaches. I attempt to see crisis not only as limiting but also as enabling: while I acknowledge that the rivalry between anthropology and ethnology is rather about form not substance, and although I see the call for deeper cooperation between the two as slightly utopian, I am also hopeful that cross-fertilization is possible, and that the actual issues (such as the need to strengthen the traditional fieldwork component in ethnologists' university curriculum or the necessity for a more complex use of history in the discipline) have to be addressed in order for the discipline to develop in the future.

The objective of the chapter is to reflect on past and present developments of the discipline in Slovakia, while the discipline tries to find its way from the národopis of the pre-socialist and socialist periods to the ethnology and social and cultural anthropology of the present day. In this chapter, I use the terms ethnography, ethnology and social and cultural anthropology in line with their use in Slovakia at the time.

The main term for the discipline in the pre-socialist period (before 1948) was národopis. The term ethnography became dominant under the Soviet influence after 1948 (Kiliánová 2005b: 258). It was used as a name for the scientific discipline dealing with research on national (folk) culture, not as a name for the research method or results of ethnographic research, as is commonly understood in British or American anthropology. Ethnography was considered a close sister of folkloristics (folklore studies). They grew up and worked together, as they stemmed from the same root: the folk culture heritage, which is considered to be the only true foundation of national culture. The chapter proposes a personal and non-systematic reflection based on my own professional life story, my experience, observations, doubts, questions, challenges and opportunities. It is written as an autobiographical ethnography (auto-ethnography) of Central and Eastern European ethnology/anthropology that may hopefully reflect the feelings of other scholars of the same generation from Central and Eastern Europe.

A large amount of scholarly literature has been written about the history and recent development of ethnography/ethnology/social and cultural anthropology in Central and Eastern Europe in the last two decades, mainly because of the birth or rebirth of these disciplines since 1989 (see, for instance, Bitušíková 2002, 2003; Buchowski 2004; Dracklé, Edgar and Schippers 2003; Hann 1993, 1995, 2002, 2005, 2007; Hann et al. 2007; Hann, Sárkány and Skalník 2005; Kiliánová 2005a, 2005b; Podoba 2005,

2007b; Skalník 2002, 2005; Tužinská 2008). We have read opinions from both Western and Central and Eastern European scholars, from those who escaped communism by emigration and those who stayed at home, from critics and supporters as well as from representatives of the older and younger generations. Their works deal with institutional, methodological, conceptual, epistemological and thematic changes in Central and Eastern European ethnography, ethnology and social and cultural anthropology, with the dichotomies and battles between 'old' (often understood as bad) ethnography or ethnology and 'new' (understood as good) anthropology and their relation to other disciplines and with changes in curricula and research. It is paradoxical that this rejection of national ethnographies in favour of the transition to international social and cultural anthropology in postsocialist Europe should happen at a time of intense debate about the death of anthropology in the Anglo-American world (see, for instance, Comaroff 2010; Gingrich 2010; Hannerz 2010a).

Despite diverse opinions on anthropology in postsocialist countries (the negative ones coming mostly from native scholars in these countries) and the 'threat' of the end of anthropology, the promise of the discipline in Central and Eastern Europe cannot leave us pessimistic. Here is a discipline that has been in transition since its beginnings – both in the centre and at the periphery, in democracies and totalitarian regimes. However, the reasons for these continuous changes vary. They can be 'natural', as new theories and knowledge develop, or imposed by various ideologies. As Andre Gingrich says, 'sociocultural anthropology represents a complex web of intellectual and social processes that interact with their respective contexts of political economy and society' (Gingrich 2010: 553). Like other social sciences and humanities, anthropology has never been totally independent of politics. There is no doubt that four decades of forced intellectual isolation from Western anthropology created a wide, deep crack in the development of the discipline in Central and Eastern Europe that cannot be repaired overnight. But, to quote Andre Gingrich again, '... not every transition needs to turn into crisis, nor is every crisis in itself a catastrophe ... In fact, a number of good reasons for cautious and realistic optimism emerge if we briefly contrast some features of the current transition "out of" national traditions with those of the historical transition "into" the era of national traditions' (Gingrich 2010: 553). This quote will constitute the main hypothesis for my reflections.

BACK TO SOCIALISM: PERSONAL MEMORIES

In order to draw an ethnographic picture of the discipline in Slovakia (different from that which I formally and chronologically described in Bitušíková 2003), I have travelled back to the pre-1989 period to deliver an eyewitness account of the discipline at the time.

In the late 1970s and early 1980s, I was a student at the Department of Ethnography and Folkloristics of Comenius University in Bratislava. This was a period of late normalization following the Soviet invasion in 1968. Let us not forget that the forty years of state socialism in Czechoslovakia were not a homogeneous historical era. Národopis, or ethnography, was under the permanent influence of the ruling Marxist ideology, but the level of this influence varied significantly during the four decades. The 1950s put strong political pressure on institutions and people. Several leading scholars were accused of bourgeois nationalism and expelled from academic or research institutions. The new ideology caused a major shift from theoretical and methodological pluralism (mainly functionalism and functional structuralism applied in research in the 1930s and 40s) to the only 'right' theory – Marxism-Leninism and methodology based on dialectical and historical materialism.

The 1960s period was one of growing political relaxation and liberalization that had a short-term, but significant, impact on the discipline. It was in this era that the term ethnology was officially introduced for the first time and appeared in the names of the Institute of Ethnology (Kabinet etnológie, 1968) at Comenius University, of the yearly journal *Ethnologia Slavica – An International Review of Slavic Ethnology* (1969), a student international seminar with fieldwork trips (the Seminarium ethnologicum (1968)), and the resource centre Archivum ethnologicum. By bringing the term ethnology into official structures, a new orientation towards Western ethnology and anthropology was quietly introduced. These activities led to intense international networking and collaboration and to promising new theoretical and methodological discourses. For instance, in folklore studies, a structural, synchronic approach to the interpretation of various genres of folklore was instituted by some scholars (e.g. Mária Kosová). In addition, the first independent department of ethnography and folkoristics was established at Comenius University in 1969 as a result of a split in the Department of Archaeology, History of Arts, Ethnography and Folkloristics. However, this positive development did not last long. The Soviet occupation in August 1968 ended all hopes for any democratic change and what followed during the 'normalization' period was a slow return to socialist ethnography and to further and deeper isolation from Western anthropological theories (for more about these periods, see, for instance, Bitušíková 2003; Podoba 2005;

Kiliánová 2005a; Kiliánová and Popelková 2010, but also works by Czech authors Kandert 2002, 2005; Skalník 2002, 2005; Lozoviuk 2005).

I started my university studies at Comenius University in the late 1970s. Studying ethnography during socialism was a sort of privilege. Only ten to fifteen students were admitted to studies each year. The number of candidates who applied was always far greater than the number of those that could be admitted. In addition, priority was given to candidates with a 'good cadre profile'. These were students with a working-class family background and active in the Socialist Youth Union, whose parents were members of the Communist Party and presented a positive oral or written statement on Soviet 'brotherly aid' in August 1968 (the official term for the military invasion by the Soviet army and its allies). Open access to university studies was given to a special category of students who were young people from working-class backgrounds (workers) who were offered a fast secondary education and a degree allowing them to enter university education ('maturita') because of their Communist Party membership. As I did not fulfil any of these required criteria (except for a successful result in the entrance exams), I was not admitted to university studies. But this was socialist Czechoslovakia: I appealed to the Rector and with the help of a distant relative who happened to be a director of the Evening University of Marxism-Leninism and who made a quick phone call to him, and with the 'good' profile thus acquired, I was finally enrolled at Comenius University as a full-time student in ethnography and folkloristics.[1]

Some old notes and textbooks from my university period retrieved from the cellar testify to the content of the ethnography curricula; in particular a small notebook marked Index, with a list of courses, lectures and seminars that I attended during my university studies and all the marks (now credits) I received. This small Index gives a precise picture of curricula of the time. The majority of subjects were obligatory; students could rarely select an optional course. The list of subjects included: an Introduction to Ethnography; an Introduction to Folkloristics, Theory and Methodology; the History of Ethnography and Folkloristics; the Ethnography of Slavic People; Fieldwork Techniques; Material Culture; Social Culture; Spiritual Culture (Rituals); Comparative Folklore Studies; Prosaic Folklore; Folk Arts; the Folklore of European Nations; Museology; Ethnomusicology; Ethnochoreology; Ethnicity and Ethnic Processes; Fieldwork Praxis; Excursion (a ten to twelve day tour of Slovakia and specific places of interest); and Museum Internship. Fieldwork was a significant component of the curricula. All students had to spend several weeks during the summer period (and also at later stages of the year) in the field in Slovakia doing research related to the topic of their thesis. In addition to specialist courses, students had to take general courses and courses in neighbouring disciplines (e.g. Foreign

Language; Statistics; Latin; Historic Geography; History of Czechoslovakia; Sociological Methods; Art History; and even Physical Exercise). A separate group of subjects formed the obligatory ideological 'package', composed of Political Economy; Marxist-Leninist Philosophy; Scientific Communism; Cultural Politics and the History of the Communist Party; and International Workers' Movement.

THE MARRIAGE OF ETHNOGRAPHY/ETHNOLOGY AND HISTORY

Unlike Western anthropology, which has remained partially or completely autonomous from history, Central and Eastern European ethnography was considered a historical discipline (even a subdiscipline of history or 'an auxiliary historical science'). Understanding the discipline in this way is still quite common, especially among historians. The roots of a close relationship between ethnography/ethnology and history can be found in the beginnings of the discipline under the Austro-Hungarian monarchy and are related to the National Revival, the Enlightenment and the formation of the Slovak nation in the nineteenth century (see, for instance, Kiliánová 2011). Since then, ethnography has evolved as a national discipline, with the main focus on research (collection, description, classification and preservation) into the culture and way of life of 'the folk' (the lower socio-economic strata in rural areas, especially peasants) in a diachronic perspective, showing changes of folk culture phenomena throughout history.

Folk culture was considered the essence of the nation (Podoba 2005: 247). By researching into and preserving folk culture and by supporting a romantic public view of 'the folk' (singing and dancing Slovaks dressed in folk costumes), ethnography and folkloristics were expected to contribute to the strengthening of national awareness and identity. Research was oriented towards archaisms, collecting and documenting traditional 'old' customs, rituals, songs, dances, narratives, costumes, architecture, art, etc. that were about to disappear during the modernization and industrialization of the country. In addition to the focus on traditional pre-socialist rural culture, new research inspired by Soviet ethnography in line with the motto 'Soviet ethnography – our model' (also the title of a study written by Andrej Melicherčík in 1951) came into being in the early 1950s. Its key objective was to study social and cultural changes (of course only the positive ones) in 'new-born' socialist villages and in industrial areas. The hero and model respondent in this kind of research was the new farmer – member of a cooperative farm – or the worker (often a miner, the most glorified representative of the working class).

Soon after the communist takeover in 1948, a few Czech and Slovak ethnographers published first books and papers that became the manifesto of a 'new style', Soviet-type Marxist ethnography, considered 'the best, most progressive and most humane in the world' (Nahodil and Kramařík 1951, quoted in Scheffel and Kandert 1994). The title of the guiding book, *J.V. Stalin a národopisná věda (J.V. Stalin and the Ethnographic Science)* written by Czech ethnographers Otakar Nahodil and Jaroslav Kramařík, founders of a so-called Marxist circle, with a contribution by J.V. Stalin (1952), speaks for itself (for more details see Scheffel and Kandert 1994; Skalník 2005; Skalníková 2005). In this book, Nahodil and Kramařík call for a relentless battle against any expressions of the bourgeois nationalism and cosmopolitan ideology that are the foundation stone of Western bourgeois ethnography (Nahodil and Kramařík 1952: 89).

In Slovakia, Andrej Melicherčík, a leading personality in ethnography and the author of a fundamental theoretical book of the pre-socialist period, inspired by functionalism and structuralism, *Teória národopisu (Theory of Národopis*, 1945), was also quick to recognize the need to reconsider his previous theoretical and methodological views and to acknowledge his commitment to Marxist ethnography and its historicism (see also Skalník 2005). Although the majority of scholars in Slovakia were not sympathetic towards the new ideological rhetoric, they did not find the courage to oppose it openly. I fully agree with Josef Kandert, who says that 'such scholars retreated into the niche of pure positivism and tended to publish their field data without commentary. This strategy, understandable in personal terms, hindered the intellectual development of the discipline' (Kandert 2005: 238).

The marriage between ethnography/ethnology and history has remained strong throughout the entire history of the discipline in Slovakia. It was the result firstly of a Germanic legacy of *Volkskunde*, which had an impact on academic and research development in the whole of Central and Eastern Europe and, secondly, of historical materialism as the only method permitted for the study of society under socialism. Even today, more than twenty five years after the fall of the Iron Curtain, historical methods in ethnology/ anthropology have their strong advocates. I will discuss the reasons later.

ANTHROPOLOGY DURING SOCIALISM AND ITS TRANSFORMATIONS

The term 'anthropology' in socialist Slovakia (Czechoslovakia) stood officially only for physical anthropology, which was studied at faculties of science and had no connection with ethnography, ethnology or social and cultural anthropology. This disciplinary division corresponded to the Soviet model. Ernest Gellner in the preface to the book *Soviet and Western Anthropology* (1980), a unique set of contributions both from Western and Soviet scholars, drew attention to the difficulty of reading this book in which either the authors or the translator adjusted their phrasing to the terminological expectations of Western readers, which caused some confusion of meanings (Gellner 1980: x). Indeed, the translation of terms used differently in the West and in Central and Eastern Europe can lead to misinterpretations of theoretical assumptions even these days.

However, my first encounter with social and cultural anthropology and with Western anthropological schools, theories and methods took place during the first year of my university studies back in the socialist period. Anthropology was hidden under the course named Theory and Methodology. The lecturer, a distinguished professor, Emília Horváthová, presented a good, non-ideological overview of the complex history and development of anthropology, but any deeper insights were impossible because of the total absence of any available anthropological literature. Scientific literature from Western Europe or the United States was neither imported nor translated (with a few exceptions of Czech translations, such as Frazer's *Golden Bough*). The only way of obtaining key anthropological books was to smuggle them from Poland, where collaboration and contacts with Western social sciences were much more open and translations of anthropological publications more readily available. Yet, without any intellectual stimulation at lectures, seminars or conferences and with no opportunity to learn and to apply anthropological concepts and methods in research, the Slovak ethnography of the socialist era remained relatively untouched by any anthropological theories and stayed locked in its own little world of a positivist, historicist science. Probably the only major theoretical revolution in ethnography during socialism was caused by the work of the Soviet ethnographer Yulian Bromley *Etnos and Ethnography* (1973), based on a primordialist concept of ethnos that inspired several Slovak researchers to apply ethnic theories in their work.

Despite the very limited theoretical contribution of Slovak ethnography to social and cultural anthropology, it would be unfair to omit or ignore some positive contributions, especially the numerous results of empirical ethnographic research that should be praised for their complex description and summarization of various aspects of the traditional culture of Slovaks living in Slovakia or abroad, ethnic minorities living in Slovakia or even comparative Slavic studies in the Carpathian and Balkan regions. These research outcomes are also a good source of data for present anthropological analyses. Ethnography (understood in a 'Western' way) remains an important part of social and cultural anthropology and the discipline's identity.

A number of regional monographs and large-scale synthetic publications such as the *Ethnographic Atlas of Slovakia* (1990), the *Folk Culture Atlas of the Slovaks in Hungary* (1996), the *Folk Culture Atlas of the Slovaks in Romania* (1998), the *Encyclopaedia of Folk Culture in Slovakia* (1995, now available also in an open access online version on www.ludovakultura.sk) or *Slovakia – The European Context of Folk Culture* with a comparative European perspective (1997, 2000) that were published after 1989 as a result of long-term, extensive research under socialism may not represent a theoretical breakthrough in anthropology, but remain a significant source of information for the understanding of the European cultural heritage now and in the future. In addition to 'traditional' topics, here and there several scholars attempted to apply new methodological and theoretical approaches to their research and the outcomes of it (e.g. Soňa Švecová, Zora Apáthyová-Rusnáková, Emília Horváthová, Adam Pranda or Milan Leščák; see Podoba 2005). In the late 1970s and the 1980s, a slow liberalization away from Marxist ethnography encouraged Slovak ethnographers to open up new topics, especially urban themes (research on diverse urban environment phenomena). To begin with, urban research was focused on the study of the cities of the first democratic Czechoslovak Republic from 1918 to 1938 (mainly Bratislava, later Banská Bystrica, Trenčín, Skalica, Nitra and others). On the basis of interviews, oral histories, memoirs, archive documents or local newspapers, urban researchers demonstrated the diversity of pre-socialist democratic urban life, stressing (often idealistically) the multicultural and tolerant character of cities in those days.

I consider myself a member of this group of urban scholars. Urban ethnology/anthropology has been my main research interest since the early 1990s. From the 'urban romanticism' (Podoba 2005) of the 1980s, documenting a harmonious coexistence of diverse ethnic, religious, social and other groups in an interwar Slovak city, based on non-critical analysis of collected narratives, my urban-oriented colleagues and I gradually 'matured', embraced and developed a broader, deeper, more critical and more anthropologically comparative perspective on contemporary sociocultural processes and on the symbolic and social production of urban space in Slovak cities within the context of Central Europe, Europe or the world (e.g. Bitušíková 2009, 2010; Bitušíková and Luther 2010a, 2010b; Luther 2010; Darulová 2010 and others). This development has not been primarily the result of a desperate desire to practise a more Western-like anthropology but of a new post-1989 opportunity to reflect on social processes in an open, critical way, taking into account numerous aspects of the postsocialist transformation. And last but not least, it has been the fruit of new collaboration without borders, access to a literature that we were deprived of in the past, opportunities to travel to international conferences and to meet colleagues who used to be on the other side of the 'wall'.

POST-1989 ETHNOLOGY AND SOCIAL AND CULTURAL ANTHROPOLOGY

The collapse of the communist regime in 1989 opened doors to 'everything', the good and the bad. The first changes were related to the physical demolishing of old symbols of communism: the renaming of streets and squares and the introduction everywhere of new institutions, concepts, ideas, symbols, images, words, terms ... Ethnography as a term for a science quickly became an anachronism. Everyone felt that something needed to be changed. Numerous debates about the future of the discipline were taking place in every institution, especially at the leading research institution Národopisný ústav (Institute of Ethnography) of the Slovak Academy of Sciences and the Department of Ethnography and Folkloristics at Comenius University. The key points of the debates were related to the re-evaluation of methodological and theoretical approaches, the introduction of new topics, changes of institutional names and the transformation of the journal *Slovenský národopis*. Contacts with Austrian ethnologists from neighbouring Vienna started immediately after 1989 and contributed to these debates.

A cosmetic change of renaming ethnography ethnology was considered to be the first step towards the 'anthropologization' of the discipline in the region. I have critically discussed the transition from ethnography to ethnology and social and cultural anthropology elsewhere (Bitušíková 2002, 2003), and so have other colleagues (for instance Podoba 1991, 1994, 2005, 2007a, 2007b; Kiliánová 2002, 2005a, 2005b; Tužinská 2008). In all previous studies we documented the development of ethnography/ethnology/anthropology departments in Slovakia: the transition of the oldest Department of Ethnography and Folkloristics at Comenius University in Bratislava through the Department of Ethnology and Cultural Anthropology to the present Department of Ethnology and Museology, and the establishment of three other departments – the Department of Ethnology and Folklore Studies at Constantin Philosopher University in Nitra, the Department of Ethnology and Extra-European Studies at SS. Cyril and Method University in Trnava and the Department of Social Sciences and Ethnology at Matej Bel University in Banská Bystrica. All these departments offer a mixture of old (ethnographic and folkloristic, historically-oriented) and new (anthropologically-oriented) subjects and courses. The department in Nitra offers specialization in ethnomusicology; the Trnava department focuses on the ethnology of extra-European cultures; and the one in Banská

Bystrica on applied ethnology. Despite these specializations, the study programmes of the four departments are similar and can be described more as ethnological studies. The teaching staff consists of ethnologists trained before and after 1989; therefore the curricula reflect a mixture of 'old' and 'new', with an increasing tendency towards social anthropology. The thematic scope of Bachelor dissertations and Master's and Ph.D. theses shows a much broader list of topics than in the past and most of them concern research on contemporary phenomena and social and cultural changes in postsocialist societies or (less often) in other parts of the world. In addition to these four departments, The Institute of Ethnology of the Slovak Academy of Sciences provides doctoral education in ethnology/social anthropology that requires international mobility as part of the studies.

Chris Hann, in his debate with a number of anthropologists mainly from Central and Eastern Europe published as a working paper of the Max Planck Institute for Social Anthropology (2007) and as a monothematic issue of the *Czech Sociological Review* (2007), calls for the integration of ethnology and anthropology into existing institutes and departments. He argues: 'I think that it is generally a mistake to attempt to create a separate discipline called Social Anthropology, as a rival and competitor to the established intellectual communities. A genuinely comparative and cosmopolitan anthropology department would be able to integrate colleagues working on contemporary transformations with those specialized in other periods of history, and the integration should be mutually beneficial' (Hann et al. 2007: 3). Most anthropologists from Central and Eastern Europe active in this debate have been rather sceptical about this proposal. I myself would tend to agree with Chris Hann, and would like to see better collaboration between ethnologists and anthropologists. But as Juraj Podoba says, Hann's vision of institutional unification is more utopian than realistic (Podoba 2007a: 33). I cannot see any mature, confident, 'genuinely comparative and cosmopolitan anthropology departments' in the region that would be able to do it. Not yet.

In Slovakia, the rivalry between the two professional 'tribes' led to the establishment of an Institute of Social Anthropology at the Faculty of Social and Economic Sciences of Comenius University in Bratislava in 2002. Since 2005/2006 the institute has opened its Bachelor Study Programme in Social Anthropology, followed by Master's and Ph.D. programmes. Study has been oriented towards cognitive, economic and political anthropology, with additional courses in Anthropological Theories and Methods, the Anthropology of Postsocialist Societies, Roma Studies, Jewish Studies, Urban Anthropology and others. The institute puts strong emphasis on fieldwork. The staff consists of a younger generation of scholars, some of them trained abroad. The members of the institute have also founded the Slovak Association of Social Anthropologists as an alternative to the

Ethnographic Society of Slovakia *(Národopisná spoločnosť Slovenska)* that had been a voluntary professional association of ethnographers and ethnologists (both academics as well as those working in museums and cultural institutions) since 1958.

Despite rather limited collaboration between the new institute and the four older departments, there are no reasons for being pessimistic about future developments, even if they may take a while to materialize. Older ethnographers/ethnologists continue to carry out their research, some of them trying to apply more anthropological approaches and studying contemporary societal and cultural changes, while a young generation of anthropologists is gradually developing new understandings of the discipline. For this reason, we may wonder as Chris Hann does: 'Why this lack of solidarity with those who belong to my own professional tribe and wish to expand its history?' (Hann et al. 2007: 9). We know that ethnology and anthropology are not identical twins, but they are the closest of blood relatives. They both investigate the diversity of human ways of life, the differences and similarities between cultures and societies. Why not embrace diversity, differences and similarities within the discipline itself? The 'anthropological' versus 'non-anthropological' debate should move on to be gradually replaced by a debate on good versus bad research.

'WHO AM I?': THE DOUBTS OF A PRESENT DAY SLOVAK ETHNOLOGIST

This may be a strange subtitle when playing the game of auto-ethnography, but hopefully it may strike a chord with other Slovak (or even Central Eastern European) scholars. This question relates to my previous doubts about the gap between ethnology and anthropology, which has an impact on my own professional identity. Am I an 'old' ethnographer, a 'more advanced' ethnologist or even a social anthropologist? The most influential experience in my professional career and a real cultural (academic) shock happened during the summer of 1994 when I was a visiting research fellow at the University of Cambridge, United Kingdom. Spending two months in the university library and having an opportunity to touch and read anthropological books that I only knew from my university lectures opened my eyes but, at the same time, made me doubt whether I would ever be able to overcome a theoretical, methodological and intellectual gap caused by the politically enforced academic and research division between 'us and them', 'East and West', or 'the periphery and the centre'.

Since then, after twenty years' hard work of trying to overcome the methodological and theoretical gap, I still feel confused and uncertain about who I am. I will always hesitate between my traditional ethnographic education and newly adopted anthropological knowledge. I will probably never have a chance to carry out long-term research in a distant foreign destination and will remain an 'anthropologist at home'. In Slovakia, I rarely dare to say that I am a social anthropologist. It would be considered an overestimated or arrogant statement by both old ethnographers and young anthropologists. It seems as if we all suffered from a complex about the superiority of anthropology and a lack of self-confidence about national ethnography/ethnology.

Having developed broad international collaboration in several areas of anthropological interest, I prefer to publish the results of my research in foreign books or journals. This means that my publications are almost unknown in Slovakia because my Slovak colleagues do not have access to them. In addition, these works can hardly compete with anthropological publications written by Western colleagues. Most of my Central and Eastern European colleagues try to reinvent themselves in different ways. Despite some difficulties, I feel lucky and privileged to have had a chance to develop a substantial part of my professional career in a free society, but it is sometimes difficult to get rid of the burden of the socialist past. On our shoulders we carry all kinds of discontinuities that have an impact on our work. We often feel alone or unrecognized. In the end, this is probably a feeling shared by most national ethnologists/anthropologists from the 'periphery'. We all want to be an equal part of the global anthropological research community because we pursue the same curiosity and desire to find out more about the world we live in and to understand humanity and its diversity of ways of life and cultures. Therefore, it is positive to see, using Ulf Hannerz's words, more bridges and more frequent ferries, more interactions and linkages between the mainland of British, American and French anthropologies, and an archipelago of large and small anthropological islands (Hannerz 2010b: 16–20). New collaborations bring anthropological centres and peripheries closer and contribute to better mutual understanding without blunting awareness of existing differences caused by different histories of academic and research traditions.

THE FUTURE?

In thinking about what can and should be done for the future of teaching and research in ethnology and social and cultural anthropology in Slovakia, there are several points that need to be mentioned. I will start with education. My thoughts have been inspired by Andre Gingrich's reaction to the 2009 AAA (American Anthropological Association) conference on the end of anthropology (Gingrich 2010). In order to raise the level of theoretical anthropological knowledge among Slovak scholars, it is crucial to improve international collaboration and combat academic inbreeding, which is still a common practice at Slovak universities (students getting all degrees from the same university and the best ones also being hired by it). National recruitment works against the diversity of academic staff and students as well as against that of opinions, and of methodological and theoretical approaches. Spending part of the studies abroad, at least at the doctoral level, is an essential condition for the career development of every young scholar but also for the future of the discipline. Numerous policy papers and institutional, national and European strategies support this view and my own experience proves that doctoral candidates and young researchers who spent part of their studies abroad show a significant difference in their professional development when compared with those who only studied 'at home'.

Other possible ways of building international bridges are co-supervision (a local and international supervisor), joint doctoral programmes and schools, and short-term mobility, leading to closer collaboration in research and thus to the enhancement of research and the empowerment of less advanced institutions. Although we all face global societal and economic challenges, each country also has its own specific problems that are best understood by local researchers and can be best studied and solved by mixed teams of local and international scholars in the place of origin and not only in those institutions that appear in the top 100 or 500 rankings. Only true international two-way collaboration and mobility leads to the understanding of different ethnological and anthropological traditions across the globe.

The second condition relevant for the development of social and cultural anthropology in Slovakia is a good source of literature, a good library. Without classic and recent texts written by leading world anthropologists, it is impossible to grow and develop. And although our libraries still own only a very limited amount of anthropological works, all Slovak university libraries offer open access to dozens of online databases (as part of a European project). Unfortunately, not many scholars know this or use it (often because of language limitations).

My third point addresses the need for proper ethnographic fieldwork, which remains the keystone of our methodological pool. From discussions with colleagues from all Slovak ethnology and anthropology departments, it seems that today's students prefer to choose research topics concerning the study of contemporary cultural and societal phenomena using a synchronic approach and to do research from the comfort of their home via the Internet instead of carrying out long-term fieldwork. I am not against using tools and methods offered by new technologies, but I do believe that they should remain only additional, alternative methods to participant observation.

The generational gap between ethnography/ethnology and anthropology scholars in Slovakia is also increasingly reflected in the use of literature sources. Reading postmodern anthropology is a way of distinguishing oneself from 'the old school' and of being part of the Western anthropology tribe.

In the past twenty years, ethnological research in Slovakia has diversified rapidly and moved towards social and cultural anthropology in a number of ways (especially in the application of anthropological theories, concepts and methods, and in more comparative approaches). Although it remains mostly 'at home', its thematic scope has broadened and is mainly oriented towards contemporary societal and cultural changes. Each thematic specialization finds its own inspiration in anthropological theories. For instance, the development of urban ethnology in Slovakia since the 1990s can be considered a good example of a transition from positivist ethnographic research to anthropological research, inspired by various urban theories (from poststructuralist studies of ethnicity, class or gender in the urban context to studies of global and globalizing cities and of the production of urban space and planning, see, for instance, Low 2005). Similarly, research into ethnicity and ethnic relations, identity, memory, values, the impact of social, political and economic changes on local communities and social groups or even folklore has undergone a radical change in Slovakia, being inspired and influenced by social and cultural anthropology, mostly of Anglo-American origin.

But do Slovak ethnologists want this total 'anthropologization' of ethnology in Central and Eastern Europe? Do they want to abandon all traditions of the discipline in the region? Do they want to say goodbye to the historical contextualization of research that has been so often criticized by Western colleagues? Maybe we would rather like to see in turn a slight 'ethnologization' or 'historization' of anthropology. As early as 1980, Ernest Gellner wrote: 'It is ironic that at the very moment at which anthropology in the West is finding its way back to history, not without difficulty, Soviet anthropology is in part practicing a mild detachment from it' (Gellner 1980: x). Similarly, Chris Hann calls for the use of historical methods in studying postsocialist transformations (Hann et al. 2007). I would even argue that the close relationship of ethnology and history in Central and Eastern Europe is not a sign of the discipline's backwardness but of its maturity. In this region with so many historic ruptures and discontinuities, it would be impossible and irresponsible to study societal and cultural transformations without taking into account historical and political contexts while also applying other anthropological methods and theories.

Another criticism of Central and Eastern European ethnology concerns its inward-looking perspective and national orientation towards the folk culture heritage. This research focus has become very marginal in recent years, although the topic remains important and relevant if we think of the influence of globalization upon cultures, which, on the one hand, may lead to cultural homogenization but, on the other, also to the mobilization of local and regional cultures and a growing awareness of cultural differences and action to preserve them. UNESCO's Universal Declaration on Cultural Diversity (2001), the Convention for the Safeguarding of the Intangible Cultural Heritage (2003) and the Convention on the Protection and Promotion of the Diversity of Cultural Expressions (2005) – all summarized in Tevje's statement on the importance of tradition in the famous musical *Fiddler on the Roof* ('Without our traditions, our lives would be as shaky as a fiddler on the roof') – strongly support preservation and the sustainable utilization of the folk culture heritage in regional development.

From their beginnings, ethnography and ethnology in Central and Eastern Europe had developed broad expertise in all aspects of cultural heritage in the European context, but this expertise has been diminishing. Young scholars show no interest in research on 'traditional' national cultural phenomena. In some areas, the expertise is already disappearing as the old scholars retire. Again I must mention Chris Hann's note that British anthropology students have limited opportunity to engage with their own traditions and could benefit from some engagement with the social transformation of their own country (Hann et al. 2007: 11). Can we, postsocialist scholars, learn from this lesson? Can we let all categories of scholars in our tribe work in what they are good at without categorizing them and putting them into new/good and old/bad boxes? Every transition takes time. A little anthropologization of ethnology and a little ethnologization of anthropology could be beneficial for the development of our discipline, and not only in Central and Eastern Europe. It only requires less professional arrogance, more understanding, solidarity and professionalism in whatever we do.

Alexandra Bitušíková is Associate Professor at Matej Bel University in Banská Bystrica. She received her Ph.D. from Comenius University in Bratislava. She participated in several European research projects and is author of over 100 publications on urban anthropology, social and cultural change in Central Europe, gender and doctoral education in Europe.

NOTE

1. Though I still feel bad about the way I became a student on the strength of a single phone call, I am happy about the Rector's final decision: I am one of the three graduates (out of thirteen in my class) who are still in the field and happy to be there.

REFERENCES

Bitušíková, A. 2002. 'Anthropology as a Taboo: A Few Comments on Anthropology in Slovakia', in P. Skalník (ed.), *A Post-Communist Millennium: The Struggles for Sociocultural Anthropology in Central and Eastern Europe, Prague Studies in Sociocultural Anthropology 2*. Prague: Set Out, pp. 141–46.

———. 2003. 'Teaching and Learning Anthropology in a New National Context: The Slovak Case', in D. Dracklé, I.R. Edgar and T.K. Schippers (eds), *Educational Histories of European Social Anthropology*. New York and Oxford: Berghahn Books, pp. 69–81.

———. 2009. 'Post-Socialist City on the Way to Diversity: The Case of Banska Bystrica', in M. Janssens et al. (eds), *Sustainable Cities: Diversity, Economic Growth and Social Cohesion*. Cheltenham and Northampton, MA: Edward Elgar Publishing, pp. 108–21.

———. 2010. 'Public Spaces in the Marketing of the City', in A. Bitušíková and D. Luther (eds), *Cultural and Social Diversity in Slovakia III: Global and Local in a Contemporary City*. Banská Bystrica: Univerzita Mateja Bela, pp. 48–55.

Bitušíková, A. and D. Luther. 2010a. 'From Uniformity to Sustainable Diversity: Transformations of a Post-Socialist City', in M. Janssens et al. (eds), *The Sustainability of Cultural Diversity: Nations, Cities and Organizations*. Cheltenham and Northampton, MA: Edward Elgar Publishing, pp. 178–206.

Bitušíková, A. and D. Luther (eds). 2010b. *Cultural and Social Diversity in Slovakia III. Global and Local in a Contemporary City*. Banská Bystrica: Univerzita Mateja Bela.

Buchowski, M. 2004. 'Hierarchies of Knowledge in Central-Eastern European Anthropology', *Anthropology of East Europe Review* 22: 5–14.

Comaroff, J. 2010. 'The End of Anthropology, Again: On the Future of an In/Discipline', *American Anthropologist* 112 (4): 524–38.

Darulová, J. 2010. 'From Localism to World Cultural Heritage', in A. Bitušíková and D. Luther (eds), *Cultural and Social Diversity in Slovakia III: Global and Local in a Contemporary City*. Banská Bystrica: Univerzita Mateja Bela.

Dracklé, D., I.R. Edgar and T.K. Schippers (eds). 2003. *Educational Histories of European Social Anthropology*. New York and Oxford: Berghahn Books.

Gellner, E. 1980. 'Preface', in E. Gellner (ed.), *Soviet and Western Anthropology*. New York: Columbia University Press, pp. ix–xvii.

Ghosh, Y.A., J. Grygar and M. Skovajsa (eds). 2007. 'Sociální antropologie v postsocializmu', *Sociologický časopis/Czech Sociological Review* 43(1).

Gingrich, A. 2010. 'Transitions: Notes on Sociocultural Anthropology's Present and its Transnational Potential', *American Anthropologist* 112 (4): 552–62.

Hann. C. 1993. 'Introduction: Social Anthropology and Socialism', in C. Hann (ed.), *Socialism: Ideals, Ideologies, and Local Practice*. London: Routledge, pp. 1–26.

———. 1995. *The Skeleton at the Feast: Contributions to Eastern European Ethnography*. Canterbury: University of Kent at Canterbury. Centre for Social Anthropology and Computing Monographs 9.

———. 2007. 'Rozmanité časové rámce antropologie a její budoucnost ve střední a východní Evropě', *Sociologický časopis/Czech Sociological Review* 43(1): 15–30.

Hann, C. (ed.). 2002. *Postsocialism: Ideals, Ideologies and Practices in Eurasia*. London: Routledge.

————. 2003. *Socialism: Ideals, Ideologies, and Local Practice*. London: Routledge.

————. 2005. *The Skeleton at the Feast: Contribution to East European Anthropology*. Canterbury: University of Kent.

Hann, C., M. Sárkány and P. Skalník (eds). 2005. *Studying Peoples in the People's Democracies: Socialist Era Anthropology in East-Central Europe*. Münster: LIT Verlag.

Hann, C. et al. 2007. 'Anthropology's Multiple Temporalities and its Future in Central and Eastern Europe: A Debate', *Working Papers of the Max Planck Institute for Social Anthropology* 90: 1–13.

Hannerz, U. 2010a. 'Diversity is Our Business', *American Anthropologist* 112(4): 539–51.

————. 2010b. *Anthropology's World: Life in a Twenty-First-Century Discipline*. London and New York: Pluto Press.

Kandert, J. 2002. ⊠The Czech School in Social Anthropology ', in P. Skalník (ed.), *A Post-Communist Millennium: The Struggles for Sociocultural Anthropology in Central and Eastern Europe*. Prague: Set Out, pp. 43–48.

————. 2005. 'The Unchanging Praxis of "Home" Anthropology: Positivists and Marxists in the Czech Case', in C. Hann, M. Sárkány and P. Skalník (eds), *Studying Peoples in the People's Democracies: Socialist Era Anthropology in East-Central Europe*. Münster: LIT Verlag, pp. 237–44.

Kiliánová, G. 2002. 'Etnológia na Slovensku na prahu 21.storočia: reflexie a trendy', *Slovenský národopis* 50(3–4): 277–291.

————. 2005a. 'Ethnology in Slovakia at the Beginning of the 21st Century: Reflections and Trends', in G. Kilánová et al. (eds), *Ethnology in Slovakia at the Beginning of the 21st Century: Reflections and Trends*. Bratislava and Wien: Institut für Europäische Ethnologie der Universität Wien, Band 27 and Institute of Ethnology of the Slovak Academy of Sciences in Bratislava, pp. 16–35.

————. 2005b. 'Continuity and Discontinuity in an Intellectual Tradition under Socialism: The "Folkloristic School" in Bratislava', in C. Hann, M. Sárkány and P. Skalník (eds), *Studying Peoples in the People's Democracies: Socialist Era Anthropology in East-Central Europe*. Münster: LIT Verlag, pp. 257–72.

————. 2011. 'Kolektívne výskumy ľudovej slovesnosti v druhej polovivi 20. Storočia. Príspevok k dejinám etnológie na Slovensku', *Etnologické rozprawy (Ethnological disputes)* 18(1–2): 24–35.

Kiliánová, G. and K. Popelková. 2010. 'Zavádzanie marxistickej etnografie v národopise na Slovensku: zmena vedeckého myslenia?', *Slovenský národopis* 58(4): 410–24.

Low, S.M. 2005. *Theorizing the City*. New Brunswick, NJ and London: Rutgers University Press.

Lozoviuk, P. 2005. 'The Pervasive Continuities of Czech Národopis', in C. Hann, M. Sárkány and P. Skalník (eds), *Studying Peoples in the People's Democracies: Socialist Era Anthropology in East-Central Europe*. Münster: LIT Verlag, pp. 227–36.

Luther, D. 2010. 'Citizens, Developers and a Globalising City', in A. Bitušíková and D. Luther (eds), *Cultural and Social Diversity in Slovakia III: Global and Local in a Contemporary City*. Banská Bystrica: Univerzita Mateja Bela, pp. 31–39.

Melicherčík, A. 1945. *Teória národopisu*. Liptovský Svätý Mikuláš: Tranoscius.

————. 1951. 'Sovietska etnografia – náš vzor', *Národopisný sborník SAVU* 10: 5–23.

Nahodil, O. and J. Kramařík. 1951. 'Práce J.V. Stalina o marxizmu a jazykovědě a některé otázky současné etnografie', *Český lid* 6: 6–17.

————. 1952. *J.V. Stalin a národopisná věda*. Praha: Nakladatelství Československo – sovětského Institutu.

Podoba, J. 1991. 'Diskusia o našej vede', *Národopisné informácie* 2: 124–29.

————. 1994. 'Dva modely výučby vedy o vývoji kultúry a spoločnosti', *Etnologické rozpravy* 1(2): 79–86.

————. 2005. 'On the Periphery of a Periphery: Slovak Anthropology behind the Ideological Veil', in C. Hann, M. Sárkány and P. Skalník (eds), *Studying Peoples in the People's Democracies: Socialist Era Anthropology in East-Central Europe*. Münster: LIT Verlag, pp. 245–56.

————. 2007a. 'Social Anthropology in East-Central Europe: Intellectual Challenge or Anachronism?', in C. Hann et al., 'Anthropology's Multiple Temporalities and its Future in Central and Eastern Europe: A Debate', *Working Papers of the Max Planck Institute for Social Anthropology* 90: 28–33.

————. 2007b. 'Sociálna antropológia v stredovýchodnej Európe: intelektuálna výzva alebo anachronizmus?', *Sociologický časopis/Czech Sociological Review* 43(1): 175–82.

Salner, P. (ed.). 1991. *Taká bola Bratislava*. Bratislava: Vydavateľstvo Veda.

Scheffel, D. and J. Kandert. 1994. 'Politics and Culture in Czech Ethnography', *Anthropological Quarterly* 67(1): 15–23.

Skalník, P. (ed.). 2002. *A Post-Communist Millennium: The Struggles for Sociocultural Anthropology in Central and Eastern Europe*. Prague: Set Out.

————. 2005. 'Czechoslovakia: From Národopis to Etnografie and Back', in C. Hann, M. P. Sárkány and P. Skalník (eds), *Studying Peoples in the People's Democracies: Socialist Era Anthropology in East-Central Europe*. Münster: LIT Verlag, pp. 55–86.

Skalníková, O. 2005. 'The Foundation of the Czechoslovak Academy of Sciences in 1952 and its Importance for Czech Národopis', in C. Hann, M.P. Sárkány and P. Skalník (eds), *Studying Peoples in the People's Democracies: Socialist Era Anthropology in East-Central Europe*. Münster: LIT Verlag, pp. 171–82.

Tužinská, H. 2008. 'How Far Have We Gone with Being Applied? From Národopis to Antropológia, Curricula Heterogeneity and Public Engagement in Slovakia', *Studia ethnologica Croatica* 20: 193–209.

GROUNDING CONTEMPORARY CROATIAN CULTURAL ANTHROPOLOGY IN ITS OWN ETHNOLOGY

JASNA ČAPO AND VALENTINA GULIN ZRNIĆ

This chapter assesses the Croatian scientific tradition of ethnology and cultural anthropology from the national (folk) ethnology of the late nineteenth century and the beginning of the twentieth century, through the dominance of the cultural-historical paradigm during the twentieth century, and the transformation of ethnology in cultural anthropology since 1970. It also devotes substantial space to the actual trends in anthropological research, to the educational status of anthropology in Croatian universities and to the place of the discipline in the Croatian society. Finally, the positioning of Croatian ethnology/cultural anthropology in the international academic community is thoroughly discussed: to what extent is there a genuine dialogue between domestic and outside ethnologists/cultural anthropologists? Authors argue that it is not only the synergy of so-called national ethnologies and anthropology that should be developed but a powerful hybridity that would create a 'third space', in Homi Bhabha's terms, by radically questioning both – domestic and 'foreign', ethnological and anthropological – intellectual traditions as the ground for future European research in the discipline(s).

Officially, there have been no cultural anthropologists in Croatia until recently. The only academic programme for the education and training of students in the discipline during the whole twentieth century was the Department of Ethnology at the Faculty of Humanities and Social Sciences of the University of Zagreb. Notwithstanding the research paradigm adopted, theories favoured or methodology applied, we all had the professional title of ethnologist. It was not until 2004 that the Department changed its name to the Department of Ethnology and Cultural Anthropology, indicating significant changes in the programme and courses that had actually started a decade before in the Department, and even four decades earlier in another research centre, the Institute of Ethnology and Folklore Research, where theoretical strands and the methodology of cultural anthropology had been domesticated in the study of our own past and contemporary culture. Thus, a recent change in the departmental curriculum and name only acknowledged, albeit somewhat belatedly, previous disciplinary dynamics.

In assessments of Croatian ethnology in general reviews, it is regarded as being one of the 'national ethnologies', a term often used to denote the development of twentieth-century Central, East and South-East European ethnologies. The term itself dates from 1955 and denotes disciplines dealing with 'national folk culture'.[1] The definition could have been applied to Croatian ethnology until the first half of the twentieth century, but, for the major part of the following fifty years, it was only barely applicable: the 'national' – Croatian was not a central issue – ethnologists actually held back from research into their own (ethnic, national) culture during the socialist regime of multinational Yugoslavia (Rihtman-Auguštin 2004). Moreover, 'folk' and 'tradition' as fundamental concepts were deconstructed in the 1970s and 'culture' was dragged from remote past times into the present with all the theoretical, epistemic and methodological issues implied in that situation. Therefore, the above-mentioned definition of 'national ethnology' does not recognize certain inner, interdisciplinary dynamics and conflicts and/or the parallelism of paradigms and restatements of the discipline's subject matter in Croatia over the course of the second half of the twentieth century.[2]

It might be more appropriate to call the Croatian ethnology of the last fifty years a 'two-pronged' ethnology, since it has embraced both 'cultural-historical' and 'cultural-anthropological' perspectives and agendas. The latter were introduced into Croatian ethnology in the 1970s, when the theoretical, methodological and analytical apparatus of cultural anthropology had been adopted and used in research for decades, ranging from structuralism to symbolic and postmodern anthropology and from participant observation to discourse and phenomenological analyses. It is a 'two-pronged' ethnology, since, at its core, it is basically one discipline with two strands or two bodies of knowledge: 1) ethnological knowledge – referring to folk culture – which for the major part of the second half of the twentieth century was in search of its (South) Slavic origins and not of ethnic, national or Croatian culture exclusively (it was in fact supranational, Čapo 1991) and 2) cultural anthropological knowledge – which, paradoxically, could be said to have been 'more' national, since, in dealing with contemporary everyday life, it focused on the domestic field of contemporary Croatian culture. In fact, the overall development of Croatian ethnology over at least the last thirty years, in its theoretical, methodological, analytical and interpretive aspects, could be best referred to as 'anthropology at home' or 'auto-anthropology'.

In order to pinpoint what has been said, we shall present developments in Croatian ethnology and comment on them from a historical and contemporary perspective[3] – that is, in terms of the continuity and ruptures in disciplinary history that significantly influence the discipline's standing in Croatia today.

NATIONAL ETHNOLOGY: 'THE SCIENCE OF PEOPLE' (1890S–1930S)

The beginning of Croatian ethnology as a discipline is intermingled with a national movement of the late nineteenth century and its reverberations (particularly under the Austro-Hungarian Monarchy Croatia was part of until 1918) and based on the romanticist's idea of folk. The new discipline aimed at the documentation of folk (peasant, rural) culture in its entirety; peasant culture was conceived of as the source of national identity. In contrast, the culture of Croatian society's elite (aristocracy) was thought of at the time as being under the centuries-old influence of foreign cultures and thus estranged from its own national culture.

Antun Radić (1868–1918), the founding father of Croatian ethnology and proponent of the above-mentioned view, called it 'the science of people' (*narodoznanstvo*, Radić 1936–38). He was active in the former Yugoslav Academy of Sciences and Arts and was significantly inspired by the French intellectual tradition (Jules Michelet in particular). Radić prepared a detailed questionnaire on material and social life, including customs, beliefs and folk poetry and prompted the writing of detailed local ethnographies on Croatian villages throughout the first half of the twentieth century; their comprehensiveness provided a backdrop for numerous later analytical approaches. Radić's way of conceiving ethnology was in several respects quite ahead of its time: his plea was that the aspects of a culture be studied within the entire cultural context or, to use anthropological terminology, holistically. He insisted on detailed synchronic description of culture.

Furthermore, his aim was not so much to study culture as to understand people and their way of life or, in other words, not only to establish the material appearance of cultural facts but also to incorporate them into their local context and knowledge, to provide an interpretation of people's life (Čapo Žmegač 1995). His concept of the discipline was national ethnology in the proper sense of the word. The above-mentioned aspects of his work notwithstanding, he remained a peripheral influence on later developments.

REGIONAL EUROPEAN ETHNOLOGY: THE 'CULTURAL-HISTORICAL APPROACH' (1920S–1990S)

The Department of Ethnology was founded at the Faculty of Humanities and Social Sciences in Zagreb in the 1920s. Closely connected to Slavic philology from its beginnings and under the (German) influence of cultural diffusionism, a new approach developed in Croatian ethnology – later known as the 'cultural-historical approach'. It was akin to (European) diffusionist and (American) culture area approaches, had an overriding diachronic perspective and an itemized notion of culture. It would become the dominant ethnological paradigm, especially after the Second World War, prevailing both in research and teaching for decades.

Ethnologists focused on the history of culture, which carried them beyond the national (Croatian) cultural past into the depths of the (South) Slavic past. Although national orientation persisted during the interwar period, the focus on South Slavic culture was more congruent with the current circumstances – for after the First World War Croatia entered a state formation with some of the other South Slavic nations – and, after the Second World War, it became the most appropriate framework for ethnology in a multinational socialist Yugoslavia (1945–1991). Firmly adhering to 'cultural genetic' and 'cultural geographic' research – that is, research into the origins and geographic distribution of cultural elements – Milovan Gavazzi (1895–1992) focused on defining the historical cultural strata of traditional peasant culture as well as spatial cultural areas in South Eastern Europe.[4] Thus national ethnology became something like regional European ethnology. That this was a culturalist rather than a nationalist paradigm is shown by the kind of knowledge that it produced – long inventories of cultural items typical of a certain area in the region (Čapo 1991; Čapo Žmegač 1995).

Well into the socialist period, the majority of ethnologists studied exclusively peasant culture and opposed a change in either the cultural-historical paradigm or the subject matter of research. There are certain paradoxes involved in this: on the one hand, a discipline dealing with the peasantry – the 'authentic' representative of the nation according to nineteenth-century Central European conceptions, while at the same time a class judged hostile to communist ideology and socialist society – was potentially subversive for the Yugoslav authorities. On the other hand, since it entrenched itself in historical and culturalist research – in a search for Slavic rather than national roots of peasant culture – it managed to survive and acquire its own, unobtrusive and invisible societal niche. It has been argued that this was its way of safeguarding the freedom of scholarly writing and escaping the ideological trap of communism, which left an imprint on other social sciences (e.g. sociology) (Čapo Žmegač 1999; Rihtman-Auguštin 2004). From such a position, as the socialist grip on society became weaker in the 1980s, ethnology began to thrive but still remained in its marginal position with regard to other sciences as well as to public recognition and influence.

The cultural-historical orientation introduced ethnological cartography as its basic methodology, with questionnaires on some 150 topics related to the 'material', 'social' and 'spiritual' elements of folk culture and data gathered in more than 3,300 locations throughout Yugoslavia. This was part of the Ethnological Atlas of Europe project, whose most prominent figure was Branimir Bratanić (1910–1986), a professor at the Department of Ethnology in Zagreb. The Atlas project was based on then dominant positivistic thought and the tendency towards objectivity, classification and exactness: it was never completed and only part of the material was published (*Etnološki atlas Jugoslavije* 1989). Today, its methodology is still part of the Department's ethnological curriculum; it is also employed in a project to digitalize the archived research material.

The strong domination of the cultural-historical paradigm in the Ethnological Department probably influenced the fact that in the mid 1960s an anthropological course introduced by Vera Stein Erlich could not be taught there but in the Department of Sociology.[5] Educated in the United States, Erlich promoted a sociocultural agenda, a synchronic approach and research into recent changes; she also wrote an introductory textbook on cultural and social anthropology (Erlich 1966, 1968) but could not penetrate the diachronic and 'salvage' approach of Gavazzi's and Bratanić's ethnology.

From the 1920s onwards, the Department of Ethnology's curriculum was based on the cultural-historical paradigm and this orientation remained more or less unchanged for the next seventy years. For a long time, it was petrified and resisted all intellectual 'provocations' from related sciences abroad (cultural/social anthropology) or at home (Institute of Ethnology and Folklore Research in Zagreb). Since it was the only department that educated ethnologists, the very fact that just one type of knowledge – that of cultural-historical ethnology – was reproduced for decades, thus ignoring the existing alternative ethnologies and new vistas developing at another institutional centre, meant that it was not without a great deal of influence.

CULTURAL ANTHROPOLOGICAL INPUTS:
'TWO-PRONGED' ETHNOLOGY (1970S–1980S)

Another niche for ethnological research was developing at today's Institute of Ethnology and Folklore Research, founded in 1948. The critique of the cultural-historical paradigm, which developed at the Institute, mostly following the German critical ethnology of Hermann Bausinger in the 1970s, pointed out that by treating the 'cultural element' as an ahistorical and isolated item, cultural-historical methodology led to the 'canonization' of customs and neglect of context and change. The second major critique was aimed at the atheoretical orientation of ethnology. Structural and communicational definitions of culture were introduced and ethnology's potential to be a critical science of contemporary society and culture was promoted. A new paradigm appeared on the horizon, which was called (retrospectively in the late 1980s) 'the ethnology of our everyday life' (Rihtman-Auguštin 1988). The personal pronoun 'our' indicates a radical shift with regard to temporal, spatial, thematic and contextual dimensions of ethnological research. The Institute's project in the 1970s had a cultural anthropological agenda: it dealt with tradition (folklore, customs) in contemporary urban and socialist contexts and raised the issues of continuity and change. The idea of 'folk = original = ancient' was deconstructed as a romantic canon used in the nationalizing context of the nineteenth century, and the concept of 'the people' identified with peasants alone (thus ignoring all other social groups) was demystified. Folk culture was gradually conceptually upgraded into popular culture, mass culture, culture of the 'ordinary man' and of 'our everyday life'. These new trends resulted in structural and symbolic interpretations of culture – both traditional and modern – offering significant revisions of cultural-historical interpretations (for example, of the extended family, *zadruga*; Rihtman-Auguštin 1984). They dealt with the deconstruction of fundamental ethnological concepts (e.g. 'customs'), opening up everyday life as an ethnological niche for doing research into the contemporary world.[6] In order to make a distinction between so-called 'old' and 'contemporary' trends, the term 'ethnoanthropology' was used occasionally for the 'anthropologized' strand of Croatian ethnology at the Institute. It is also interesting to note that this radical disciplinary shift and the whole 'important and characteristic period of the "initialization" of Croatian ethnology as a modern(istic) European discipline' was marked by the authority of female ethnologists (Prica 2004: 42), both in intellectual and institutional terms (i.e., Dunja Rihtman-Auguštin (1926–2002), then the director of the Institute and others).

What was actually at stake in the 1980s was defining the subject matter of ethnological research: was it ethnos ('the people', with the goal of ethnology being the reconstruction of ethnic history through research into culture) or culture (including the synchronic perspective of Croatian society and without exclusively ethnic references) (Rihtman-Auguštin 1988; Belaj 1989; Čapo 1991)? Therefore, the term 'two-pronged' ethnology refers to institutional as well as to conceptual matters. The division it pinpoints was most evident in the 1980s and 1990s.

A THRIVING DISCIPLINE AT THE TIME OF RADICAL CHANGES (1990S)

This issue of a two-pronged discipline was still present in the 1990s. A significant number of articles written during that decade dealt with the state of crisis in Croatian ethnology regarding its subject matter and its twofold traditions (ethnological vs. anthropological, European vs. American) and their relationship in terms of open debate, conflict, compatibility, power relations, potential synergy, etc.

However, a true crisis was unfolding in real life: the break-up of Yugoslavia and the establishment of the Croatian state (1991) were followed by war. Against the background of state and national insecurity, everything that ethnologists of either orientation were studying as their subject matter – 'the people', 'the nation', 'the culture', 'everyday life' – was viewed in a new dimension. Both kinds of Croatian ethnologies reacted to the contemporary political and societal turmoil. The situation brought to the fore issues of national (Croatian) tradition (which lost its South Slavic aura), and those dealing with peasant culture, in the cultural-historical vein, studied specific topics concerning Croatian customs and beliefs. Some colleagues retained an interest in traditional culture but questioned the petrified models of cultural-historical research and anthropologized their analyses, making them more socially, contextually and diachronically nuanced: monographs on 'suppressed' traditions (Christmas, Easter) as well as on Croatian peasant culture in general were published (Rihtman-Auguštin 1997; Čapo Žmegač 1997; Vitez and Muraj 2000). In some of these monographs, the authors are more or less conscious of the role of ethnologist/anthropologist in the production of identity in the nascent Croatian state. This strand of research and writing was therefore called the (critical) ethnology of identity (Čapo Žmegač 2002; see also Prica 1995).

Another strand of research developed at the Institute focused on everyday war experiences, traumas and refugees and broached the issues of subjectivity, partial truths, insider positioning, the ethics of research and the commitment and responsibility of the researcher in the postmodern epistemic vein, thus building a corpus of the so-called 'ethnography of war'

(Čale Feldman, Prica and Senjković 1993; Jambrešić Kirin and Povrzanović 1996). The practitioners mostly grounded their interpretations in American anthropological postmodern theory and the 'literary turn' stressing that rhetoric and subjectivity are part and parcel of the ethnological enterprise. Their objective was to describe aspects of wartime as perceived and lived by individual actors (ordinary citizens, soldiers, Croats, Serbs, children, refugees). The insistence on fragments generated a certain experimentation with the ethnographic text, which allegedly changed 'the face of Croatian ethnographic writing' (Čale Feldman 1995: 81). This stream of research brought about an internationalization of Croatian ethnology/cultural anthropology until then unseen. Though it was praised by some (Johler 1998), it was met with suspicion by others and judged as subjective, biased, partial, solipsistic and politically or nationalistically committed writing (Greverus 1996), so that the ethnographers of war had to defend the potential and convincing nature of their writing; to fight for their texts to be recognized not just as native narratives about life in war but as ethnological analyses of it (Povrzanović 1995). The problem of the author's positioning in the construction of knowledge was already discernible then and remains relevant today.

The history of ethnology became another relevant topic in the 1990s. The opuses of the leading figures in Croatian ethnology were critically reread; some ethnologists went in search of the reasons for the atheoretical orientation of cultural-historical ethnology; the political context of Croatian ethnology's development was suddenly recognized and interpreted in the context of the political agenda of 'nationalizing' the Croatian peasantry in the late nineteenth century; issues of ethnologists' self-censorship during socialism were discussed as was how the system of political power limited scholarly perceptions, topics and outputs (Rihtman-Auguštin 2004). Another strand in dealing with the history of Croatian ethnological thought, methodology and ethnographic writing was based on postmodern critique and discursive deconstruction. This developed into a strong postmodern theoretical position, which dealt with issues of representation, 'exoticization' of the research subject – the domestic Other (the peasants) – power relations and postcolonial critique. It revisited the whole corpus of ethnographies from the proto-ethnological period to the most recent ethnographic writings and ethnological input and included a critique of the 'ethnology of our everyday life', the approach that had suggested the limits of the discipline in the 1970s (Prica 2001).

Besides the kinds of research mentioned above, from the late 1980s, and even more so in the 1990s, new issues, approaches and subdisciplines flourished at the Institute. These included gender issues, identity and ethnicity issues, historical demography, contemporary popular culture and youth culture, the anthropology of food, visual anthropology, media anthropology, economic anthropology, political anthropology, anthropology of migration and the cultural studies approach. All these trends are also evident in current research.

With so many developments in various directions, it is obvious that at least one 'prong' of ethnology – that practised at the Institute of Ethnology and Folklore Research – lost its sharpness. In spite of, or maybe precisely because of, the challenges experienced by the society, nation and state in the 1990s, ethnological and anthropological production was opening up in different directions and rapidly modernizing to the point at which, via the ethnography of war, a significant epistemological and topical rupture with the totality of Croatian ethnology occurred. In short, the difficult 1990s resulted in flourishing, self-conscious and assertive ethnology – both domestically and internationally. These trends continued into the next decade, in which the two prongs of the discipline characteristic of the 1980s and 1990s began to lose their edge.

A DIVERSIFIED DISCIPLINE IN THE 2001-2010 DECADE

The profile of current research projects[7] combines both the ethnological and cultural anthropological streams of the discipline, thus ending the previous rather sharp division between the two. Projects are more diversified than ever before and communicate with contemporary European and American strands of the discipline. There is research dealing with contemporary identities (regarded as situational, fluid, partial, deterritorialized) and processes of identification within globalization theories of culture and society and supported by various subdisciplines such as the anthropology of migration and transnationalism, of the city and of religion, the ethnography of the Internet, etc. Another set of research topics is to do with the anthropology of postsocialism, namely with the transitional character of Croatian modernity, the cultural mechanisms of hybridization, new strategies of everyday resistance to the experience of deprivation, exclusive world views, cognitive innovations and inversions of social values. The research on contemporaneity is also grounded on influential epistemologies derived from postcolonial and feminist critique and cultural studies. Another area of research deals with traditional culture. A few rare projects are still inspired by the cultural-historical paradigm (both in terms of topics and methodology) and study ethnic cultural history. Most, however, focus on traditional culture while putting Croatian identity in the context of European integration processes; still others deal with the usage of traditional culture in contemporary cultural tourism and local cultural politics (with an orientation towards the application of ethnological knowledge to the creation of local cultural development). Others are more interested in studying the impact of global cultural politics (e.g. UNESCO) on local, regional and national heritage protection. There are also some professional projects dealing with the editing, publishing and digitalizing of ethnographic manuscripts and material gathered from the late nineteenth century onwards. Participation in international projects has been rather modest (FP6-KASS project, COST, bi- and trilateral projects) but there is an increase in international institutional cooperation (with Austria, the United Kingdom, Finland, Germany and other countries).

Structure and Numbers

As far as numbers are concerned, there are approximately forty ethnologists/cultural anthropologists involved both in higher education and institutional research at present. During the twentieth century, the number of professional ethnologists was less than half of today's; the number has risen mainly in the past fifteen years thanks to the state policy of financing young researchers. The amount of researchers has certainly contributed to diversification and transformations in the discipline.

Beside those following an academic career, professional ethnologists are also employed in museums, conservation departments and various other institutions. The main professional organization is the *Croatian Ethnological Society*,[8] founded in 1959, and numbering some two hundred members. The Society organizes annual conferences and occasional round tables on current topics such as 'ethnology and economy' or 'ethnology as an ethical and committed discipline', and publishes the journal *Etnološka tribina*. There are two other influential journals: *Narodna umjetnost: The Croatian Journal of Ethnology and Folklore Research* (published by the Institute of Ethnology and Folklore Research) and *Studia Ethnologica Croatica* (published by the Department of Ethnology and Cultural Anthropology in Zagreb), which publish both in Croatian and English. The articles can be accessed via the web page for scientific journals in Croatia.[9]

The rising number of professionals is also due to the proliferation of graduate and postgraduate courses and studies in ethnology and cultural/social anthropology in the past decade. The Department of Ethnology in Zagreb was renamed in 2004 when the term Cultural Anthropology was added,[10] following which the Department grew rapidly. A new Department of Ethnology and Cultural Anthropology was founded at the University in Zadar in 2004. Curriculums in Zagreb and Zadar combine the two disciplinary traditions – the cultural-historical and the cultural anthropological. Both departments have adopted the Bologna process and offer a three-year (BA) and a two-year (MA) programme. Although there was interest in introducing an MA programme in Cultural Anthropology at other Zagreb faculties and/or Croatian universities, they have not yet been established due to financial and organizational problems. The Department in Zagreb also offers a doctoral programme (with the participation of colleagues from the Institute of Ethnology and Folklore Research and the universities of Ljubljana and Bergen). A novelty is the Department of Anthropology, introduced a decade ago at the Faculty of Humanities and Social Sciences in Zagreb (which also hosts the Department of Ethnology and Cultural Anthropology). The programme promotes the American model of anthropology as 'the science of man' (combining the natural and social sciences) with biological anthropology and archaeology dominating cultural anthropology.[11]

Discipline and the Society

A major contemporary issue is the status of the discipline and its societal presence. To understand its status one has to plunge once more into the history of ethnology and be aware of certain facts that have interacted over time. Firstly, during the twentieth century, the field of applied ethnology in Croatia developed mostly in relation to public presentation of tradition (at folklore festivals), the preservation of traditional architecture or participation in the revival of local customs. Secondly, as already mentioned, the dominant paradigm taught at, until recently, the sole Department of Ethnology was cultural-historical, dealing with the origins and distribution of the cultural elements of traditional folk culture. This influenced the fact that ethnologists were trained in only one type of ethnological knowledge, which also affected public cognizance of the discipline – as the discipline concerning the peasantry and its traditions. Thirdly, marginalization of the discipline is also a result of its relations with the socialist regime. As already argued, a new socialist, worker state pushed the peasant population onto the margins of social interest and the same fate befell ethnology (Rihtman-Augustin 2004). Moreover, prominent figures in ethnology during socialism 'voluntarily came to anchor on that very same margin' – neither criticizing nor supporting the system – and in that way Croatian ethnology managed to resist 'the ideological indoctrination that the discipline capitulated to in certain other socialist countries'.[12] Detachment from politics and power relations 'did make possible fairly unrestricted scholarly work, but with the application of considerable self-control (self-censorship) and the accompanying relatively low level of funding. Ignoring politics and avoiding involvement had its price: ethnology languished without influence on either politics or the public' (Rihtman-Augustin 2004: 50).

The issue in the 1990s became how to get out of the societally marginal status. Ethnology achieved this to a certain extent by a committed ethnography of war and by producing (critical) ethnologies of identity, as previously mentioned. Another avenue was proposed: the pursual of a constant 'critical dialogue with those in power' (Sklevicky 1991). It was Dunja Rihtman-Auguštin who most of all engaged in research on power relations in cultural phenomena, political ideologies and rituals in the 1990s. She convincingly argued that such critical writing was a means of social, intellectual and political commitment that ethnology needed if it wanted to gain public recognition (Rihtman-Auguštin 2004: 54, 86). Today, there is a vast array of possible arenas of activity for a committed and critical ethnology/cultural anthropology in, for example, multicultural, multi-ethnic and migration projects, cultural tourism, regional developmental projects, etc. By participating in these projects, the discipline's responsibility remains double, since ethnologists/cultural anthropologists are in the role of both social actors and self-reflexive social commentators and critics of what they themselves and others are doing. Such a commitment could change the discipline's societal recognition and status only if ethnologists/cultural anthropologists take a more proactive societal role and manage to impose a different image of their discipline and the manifold areas of their expertise. Otherwise, the gap between what we actually do (or could do) – studying contemporary social and cultural processes, intra- and transnationally as well as globally – and what we are perceived as doing – for example, studying historical forms of peasant culture – will widen.

In Dialogue with Sister Disciplines

Finally, one of the current issues is also the positioning of Croatian ethnology in the international academic community. It could be said to be somewhat invisible due to the language barrier. The main strategy for overcoming the problem is to publish in foreign publications and/or to publish in English in domestic journals. However, in spite of a wide exchange network established with institutions abroad and worldwide web distribution of information, the reception of these domestic publications is modest and, not unexpectedly, as one of us witnessed, they find their way to library shelves filled with books and journals in Slavic languages, though they are published in English or another language.

Croatian ethnologists/cultural anthropologists are members and regularly attend the conferences of prominent professional associations (International Society for Ethnology and Folklore (SIEF), European Association of Social Anthropologists (EASA), International Association for Southeast European Anthropology (InASEA), American Anthropological Association (AAA) and others). International conferences are also organized at home; for instance, those on higher education and curriculums in Europe (Studia ethnologica Croatica 2008), on the anthropology of space and place (Čapo and Gulin Zrnić 2011) or the cultural practices of postsocialism (Prica and Škokić 2011).

These activities notwithstanding, the debate remains open as to what extent there is a genuine dialogue between domestic and foreign ethnologists/cultural anthropologists. As was seen in relation to the ethnography of war in the 1990s, ethnologists working 'at home' are too easily defined as mere 'natives' rather than 'native ethnologists', especially if they come from and work in the countries that have traditionally been the terrain of cultural anthropology. Croatia is such a fieldwork site, which attracted numerous American and European cultural anthropologists both in the pre- and post-1990 period. Not only are 'native ethnologists/cultural anthropologists' identified with the culture they come from, they are also identified with the powerless, marginal and dubious position of their State, a process through which the ethnologist becomes equally powerless, marginal and ambiguous, as argued by Ines Prica (1995).[13] The same author claimed that there is a lack of communication in the relations between cultural anthropology (that of the Other) and Croatian ethnology (and national ethnologies more generally) and even contempt and prejudice on the part of anthropology towards so-called national ethnologies. This is even more pronounced when a 'native ethnologist' dares question the authoritative voice of anthropologists working from the centres of anthropological production. The situation is quite different from the viewpoint of domestic ethnology. Prica (ibid.) stated that the latter is willing to engage in dialogue with anthropology, through which it strengthens the identity features of its discipline while at the same time striving to remain faithful to its own specific cultural situation and disciplinary anchorage. A decade later the issue of the 'hierarchies of knowledge' is revisited in postsocialist studies (cf. Prica 2006, 2007).

We argue that the prospect for Croatian ethnology in international forums lies in the scope of the anthropology at home/*ethnologie du proche*[14] practised in Croatia and that a more committed participation of Croatian ethnology in the academic ideoscape could develop on that very platform. Our basic subject – folk – was not remote in space (as in anthropology) but in time. In a way, it was the domestic or autochthonous yet temporally distant Other that Croatian ethnologists were dealing with, and the development from the 1970s onward was an effort to bring it (temporally) closer. In that effort, all aspects of theoretical, methodological and epistemic issues that sprang from such a radical shift in subject matter from 'then' to 'now' (e.g. in the domestic 'ethnology of our everyday life') are similar to that which sprang from the shift in subject matter from 'there' to 'here' (e.g. in British 'anthropology at home'). The latter shift – towards *here* – is also evident in the concept of 'anthropology of Europe':[15] here, in Europe, we – the ethnologists and anthropologists – finally meet!

In this meeting, the most potent issue may be that on reflexivity – in epistemic, methodological, interpretive and ethical terms. The complex issue of reflexivity, which has been discussed extensively in Croatian ethnology/cultural anthropology, represents a genuine potential for the convergence of the different European intellectual traditions of ethnology and anthropology. By putting self-reflexivity at the forefront of ethnological endeavour, we do not take our own society as a specific place of research but as, primarily, a common horizon, a state of knowledge *(Wissenszustand)*, which is the product of modernity (Niedermüller 2002). By participating in the constitution of the same society, the researched and the researchers share a common view of the world, and common – although not homogeneous – knowledge (common-sense understanding) (ibid.). In other words, together with the author, we claim that all research in European ethnology is based on the cognitive assumption that researchers share a significant part of their non-ethnological knowledge, social commitments and moral attitudes with the researched (ibid.: 59). Thus, research in which the researcher is a part of the society and culture that she/he studies is characterized by 'basic insidedness', in the sense of sharing some basic knowledge, the sense of belonging and emotions with the researched (Povrzanović Frykman 2004: 87–90). It is because of this interiorization that the anthropologist at home studying what is close to him *(chez soi)* will need a more vivid anthropological imagination of or estrangement ('autocultural defamiliarization') from what is known in order to distinguish the researched processes, topics and practices. As a result, the anthropologist will be faced with her/his personal attitudes and views directly or indirectly connected to the topic. Thus, anthropology at home/ethnologie du proche would seem to be a radical practice where the space and time of the field coincide with home. This coincidence goes beyond the mere overlap of otherwise separate locations: it refers to interweaving personal and professional life, roles, time and social activities, with strong mutual influence and shaping, and the field is inevitably located 'between autobiography and anthropology' (Hastrup 1992: 119). Anthony Cohen says: 'As an anthropologist, I cannot escape myself; nor should I try', but I '[use] myself to study others' (1992: 224). It is this fact that some describe as the 'fundamental principle' of fieldwork in research conducted in one's own culture and society (Pink 2000). From this point of view, the traditional canon of anthropology, 'the others – elsewhere – different', is dismantled and the creation of knowledge discussed in a new three-dimensional prism of 'us – here – similar' (Gulin Zrnić 2005; Čapo Žmegač, Gulin Zrnić and Šantek 2006).

There are two further comments we would like to make. Firstly, we argue that the potential of ethnologies/anthropologies lies in their sensibility to contexts, self-reflexivity and critical stances, which make them genuinely humanistic sciences. It is in these aspects, rather than in methodology per se (e.g. fieldwork), that European ethnologies/cultural anthropologies can posit themselves as distinctive in interdisciplinary academic forums. Furthermore, these aspects constitute strong grounds for the discipline(s') being open to diverse intellectual traditions in flux, which form its/their vibrant character.[16] It is not only the synergy of so-called national ethnologies and anthropology that should be developed but, as we would argue from the Croatian case, a powerful hybridity that creates the 'third space', in Homi Bhabha's terms, by radically questioning both – domestic and foreign, ethnological and anthropological – intellectual traditions as the grounds for future European research in the discipline(s).

Secondly, although doing fieldwork in a foreign community is still a hallmark of anthropology, it seems that doing fieldwork in one's own community will become ever more a reality given increasing budgetary restrictions in project funding. However, one could argue that one's own – namely European – society has become so diversified and multicultural that fieldwork at home might be no less instructive and revealing than fieldwork abroad. No matter where fieldwork takes place, the discipline's potency lies in the above-mentioned reflexivity (most importantly with regard to the production of knowledge), openness to multiple intellectual traditions and hybridity – by which anthropology at home/ethnologie du proche becomes cosmopolitan anthropology. The latter has been defined in ontological terms as 'the cornerstone of a future-directed anthropological ethic' as well as in terms of its 'transformative capacity' (Wardle 2010: 381).

In the end, and without considering the internal dynamics of the discipline, a powerful factor in shaping the destiny of ethnologies/anthropologies in Europe is not only financing per se, but the legal framework within which the discipline exists. Currently there is a public academic debate in Croatia on the new regulation of universities and public scientific institutes: the new law proposes the introduction of market-oriented rules of the game and a profit orientation. That alone, more than the intellectual and methodological core of the discipline, could affect its shaping, choice of topics, orientation of projects, ethics and its overall public presence.

Jasna Čapo is a Senior Research Fellow at the Institute of Ethnology and Folklore Research and adjunct professor at the University of Zagreb. She studied in Zagreb before doing her Ph.D. at the University of California at

Berkeley. Her research interests are in the anthropology of migration and the politics of identity construction in diaspora settings.

Valentina Gulin Zrnić is a Senior Research Fellow at the Institute of Ethnology and Folklore Research in Zagreb. Her research interests include the anthropology of city, anthropology of place and space, identity studies, Mediterranean studies, history of Croatian ethnology and qualitative methodological issues.

NOTES

The chapter was written in 2010; part of the chapter was published (with permission granted by the editors of the volume) in: Jasna Čapo and Valentina Gulin Zrnić: 'Croatian Ethnology as Cultural Anthropology at Home'. Ethnologia Balkanica vol. 17, 2014.

1. In order to define uniform international terminology, the conference of the European 'folk ethnographers' in Arnhem in 1955 introduced the notion of 'national ethnology' for disciplines dealing with national folk culture (Hofer 1968, in Prica 2001: 17).
2. One might say that to use the term today, at least in relation to Croatian ethnology, is not to acknowledge the diversification of the disciplinary development and to adhere to a certain idea of developmental fixity, which is – as critics and theoreticians have warned so many times – 'in the eye of the beholder': paradoxically, due to the changed thematic scope of Croatian as well as many other European ethnologies in the 1970s and 1980s from folk/rural interest to contemporaneity, 'it is actually those Western anthropologists who did their fieldwork in Central and Eastern Europe who appear to be fixated on peasants (cf. Prica 2004)' (Buchowski 2007: 21). The recognition of the multiple developments of 'national' ethnologies, of course, leads to the issue of the (power) relationship of 'small European ethnologies' and 'colonial anthropology' (Prica 2001), which also resonates in the debates of the last decade.
3. In this review, we have decided to present the history of the discipline in Croatia, since it seems that a better knowledge of particular intellectual contexts and practices of the discipline might improve the dialogue and possible rapprochement of diverse European ethnologies/social and cultural anthropologies, as well as decrease generalizations and broad evaluations such as, for example, that Central and Eastern European ethnologies have studied exclusively national folk culture. The debate concerning ethnological and social anthropological traditions of research (Hann et al. 2007) shows that some European ethnologies have been inspired by anthropological knowledge for decades; however, the contrary has not been the case.
4. Cultural areas were defined as regions with identical natural conditions in which different human groups live in a similar manner – that is, share a considerable number of specific cultural elements (Gavazzi 1978).

5. Although Croatian sociology has never developed an anthropologized stream, the Social Anthropology course is still on the curriculum today.

6. With such a reorientation towards contemporary life, ethnology stepped onto the terrain of sociology but did not overlap with its subject of research at the time. Sociology was dealing with contemporary society in terms of socialist ideology, models and government; ethnology focused on the ordinary, trivial and ephemeral aspects of the everyday in search of cultural processes and practices, continuity and change, strategies of resistance, etc.

7. This review refers to the state of projects in 2010.

8. http://www.hrvatskoetnoloskodrustvo.hr/

9. The address: http://hrcak.srce.hr/. Professional journals are also published by museum institutions: *Etnološka istraživanja* is published by the Ethnographic museum in Zagreb and *Studia Ethnologica Dalmatica* by the Ethnographic museum in Split.

10. In comparison with some other Central and Eastern European ethnologies, the change of departmental name was neither sudden nor premature after the collapse of socialism. It merely acknowledged the internal dynamics of the discipline over a period of forty years in which cultural anthropological knowledge had been contained in domestic ethnology; indeed the change of name came tardily. Since the constitutive influences shaping Croatian ethnology have come from (American) cultural anthropology – for example, semiotic anthropology and postmodern criticism – it is understandable that cultural and not social anthropology was eventually added (social anthropology in fact left no significant mark on Croatian ethnology, except in the last decade, when some of its practitioners acknowledged anthropology at home as a comparatively interesting development within British social anthropology). Croatian ethnology has incorporated other influential ethnological and anthropological streams over the decades: German criticism of the 1970s, French structuralism, Italian studies on ideology, the Scandinavian turn towards studies of ethnicity and historical anthropology, the deconstructivism and poststructuralism of the 1980s and 1990s, feminist anthropology, etc.

11. This anthropology programme is mostly taught by colleagues from the Institute of Anthropology in Zagreb (founded in 1992). A decade ago, anthropology was classified as a humanistic science in Croatia, sharing the same branch of science as ethnology. However, since biological, demographic, genetic and forensic research dominates at the Institute of Anthropology, some argue that anthropology should be reclassified as a natural science.

12. The discipline in Croatia has neither been renamed 'ethnography' nor indoctrinated by Marxist theory.

13. One could further argue that some kind of imagining of the Other must remain in order to legitimize anthropology as such. This is an implicit disjuncture where the Other – for example 'former socialist countries' – is precluded from the privileged domain and the notion of her/his own society, and thus subtly nativized, 'located in a separate framework of analysis' (Gupta and Ferguson 1992: 13–14) or more radically, as Arjun Appadurai (1988) put it, 'spatially incarcerated'.

14. The term 'ethnologie du proche' or 'ethnology of proximity' was inspired by the title of Marc Augé's text (1989), in which he describes the path of French ethnology (social anthropology) from research into spatially remote others towards 'ethnology

at home' *(ethnologie chez soi)* and research into spatially close others. See Čapo Žmegač, Gulin Zrnić and Šantek 2006.

15. An anthropology of Europe posits Europe as a meaningful object of study: it would be 'an anthropology that acknowledges the plurality and diversity of this *sui generis* entity (Europe) and its constituent parts' (Barrera-González 2005: 14; cf. Goddard, Llobera and Shore 1994). See Hann (2005) for the concept of Eurasia. See also, on quite another foundation not derived from the concept of a unified anthropology of Europe, case studies on Europe's reterritorialization published in *Ethnologia Europaea* (32(2) 2002). Another attempt at summarizing European ethnological and anthropological research is Martine Segalen's article on 'les études européanistes': rather than proposing directions for a unified anthropology of Europe, the article questions 'the conditions of a genuine ethnology of Europe' (2001: 253).

16. In our view, the openness of Croatian ethnology to diverse influences in the last forty years (see endnote 10) and the creative incorporation of manifold theoretical, methodological, analytical, interpretive and reflexive perspectives into the research of one's own culture make the discipline much more intellectually potent than its possible grounding in a single paradigm.

REFERENCES

Appadurai, A. 1988. 'Putting Hierarchy in its Place', *Cultural Anthropology* 3(1): 36–49.

Augé, M. 1989. 'L'autre proche', in M. Segalen (ed.), *L'Autre et le Semblable: Regards sur l'Ethnologie des sociétés contemporaines*. Paris: CNRS.

Barrera-González, A. 2005. 'Towards an Anthropology of Europe: Outline for a Teaching and Research Agenda', in P. Skalník (ed.), *Anthropology of Europe: Teaching and Research*. Prague: Set-Out, pp. 3–25.

Belaj, V. 1989. 'Plaidoyer za etnologiju kao historijski znanost o etničkim skupinama', *Studia Ethnologica* 1: 9–13.

Buchowski, M. 2007. 'Some Lessons from the Importance of History in the History of Central European Ethnology', in C. Hann et al. (eds), 'Anthropology's Multiple Temporalities and its Future in Central and Eastern Europe: A Debate', *Max Planck Institute for Social Anthropology, Working Paper* 90: 18–22.

Cohen, A. 1992. 'Self-conscious Anthropology', in J. Okely and H. Callaway (eds), *Anthropology and Autobiography*. London and New York: Routledge, pp. 221–41.

Čale Feldman, L. 1995. 'Intellectual Concerns and Scholarly Priorities: A Voice of an Ethnographer', *Narodna umjetnost* 32(1): 79–90.

Čale Feldman, L., I. Prica and R. Senjković (eds), 1993. *Fear, Death and Resistance: An Ethnography of War in Croatia 1991–1992*. Zagreb: Institut za etnologiju i folkloristiku.

Čapo, J. 1991. 'Hrvatska etnologija: znanost o narodu ili o kulturi', *Studia Ethnologica* 3: 7–15.

Čapo Žmegač, J. 1995. 'Two Scientific Paradigms in Croatian Ethnology: Antun Radić and Milovan Gavazzi', *Narodna umjetnost* 32(1): 25–38.

———. 1997. *Hrvatski uskrsni običaji: Korizmeno-uskrsni običaji hrvatskog puka u prvoj polovici XX: stoljeća: svakidašnjica, pučka pobožnost, zajednica*. Zagreb: Golden marketing.

————. 1999. 'Ethnology, Mediterranean Studies and Political Reticence in Croatia: From Mediterranean Constructs to Nation-building', *Narodna umjetnost* 36(1): 33–52.

————. 2002. 'Petrified Models and (Dis)Continuities: Croatian Ethnology in the 1990s', in K. Köstlin et al. (eds), *Die Wende als Wende? Orientierungen Europäischer Ethnologien nach 1989*. Vienna: Institut für Europäische Ethnologie, pp. 94–109.

Čapo Žmegač, J., V. Gulin Zrnić and G.P. Šantek. 2006. 'Ethnology of the Proximate: The Poetics and Politics of Contemporary Fieldwork', in *Etnologija bliskoga: Poetika i politika suvremenih terenskih istraživanja*. Zagreb: Institut za etnologiju i folkloristiku and Jesenski i Turk, pp. 261–310.

Čapo, J. and V. Gulin Zrnić (eds). 2011. *Mjesto/nemjesto: Interdisciplinarna promišljanja prostora i kulture*. Zagreb: Institut za etnologiju i folkloristiku.

Erlich, V.S. 1966. *Family in Transition: A Study of 300 Yugoslav Villages*. Princeton, NJ: Princeton University Press.

————. 1968. *U društvu s čovjekom, tragom njegovih socijalnih i kulturnih tekovina*. Zagreb: Naprijed.

Etnološki atlas Jugoslavije: Maps and Comments. 1989. Vol. 1, Zagreb.

Gavazzi, M. 1978. *Vrela i sudbine narodnih tradicija*. Zagreb: Liber.

Goddard, V.A., J.R. Llobera and C. Shore (eds). 1994. *The Anthropology of Europe: Identities and Boundaries in Conflict*. Oxford and Providence, RI: Berg.

Greverus, I.-M. 1996. 'Rethinking and Rewriting the Experience of a Conference on "War, Exile, Everyday Life"', in R. Jambrešić-Kirin and M. Povrzanović (eds), *War, Exile, Everyday Life: Cultural Perspectives*. Zagreb: Institute of Ethnology and Folklore Research, pp. 279–86.

Gulin Zrnić, V. 2005. 'Domestic, One's Own, and Personal: Auto-Cultural Defamiliarisation', *Narodna umjetnost* 42(1): 161–81.

Gupta, A. and J. Ferguson.1992. 'Beyond "Culture": Space, Identity, and the Politics of Difference', *Cultural Anthropology* 7(1): 6–23.

Hann, C. 2005. 'The Anthropology of Eurasia in Eurasia', in P. Skalník (ed.), *Anthropology of Europe: Teaching and Research*. Prague: Set-Out, pp. 51–66.

Hann, C., et al. (eds). 2007. 'Anthropology's Multiple Temporalities and its Future in Central and Eastern Europe: A Debate', *Max Planck Institute for Social Anthropology, Working Paper* 90.

Hastrup, K. 1992. 'Writing Ethnography: State of the Art', in J. Okely and H. Callaway (eds), *Anthropology and Autobiography*. London and New York: Routledge, pp. 116–33.

Jambrešić Kirin, R. and M. Povrzanović (eds). 1996. *War, Exile, Everyday Life: Cultural Perspectives*. Zagreb: Institute of Ethnology and Folklore Research.

Johler, R. 1998. 'Was war da eigentlich? – "War. Exile. Everyday Life. Cultural Perspectives": Notizen zu einem ethnologischen Forschungsprojekt in Kroatien', Österreichische Zeitschrift für Volkskunde 101(1): 69–80.

Niedermüller, P. 2002. 'Europäische Ethnologie: Deutungen, Optionen, Alternativen', in K. Köstlin et al. (eds), *Die Wende als Wende? Orientierung Europäischer Ethnologien nach 1989*. Vienna: Institut für Europäische Ethnologie der Universität Wien, pp. 27–62.

Pink, S. 2000. '"Informants" Who Come "Home"', in V. Amit (ed.), *Constructing the Field: Ethnographic Fieldwork in the Contemporary World*. London: Routledge, pp. 96–119.

Povrzanović, M. 1995. 'Crossing the Borders: Croatian War Ethnographies', *Narodna umjetnost* 32(1): 91–106.

Povrzanović Frykman, M. 2004. '"Experimental" Ethnicity: Meetings in the Diaspora', *Narodna umjetnost* 41(1): 83–102.

Prica, I. 1995. '"To Be Here – to Publish There": On the Position of a Small European Ethnology', *Narodna umjetnost* 32(1): 7–23.

———. 2001. *Mala europska etnologija*. Zagreb: Golden marketing.

———. 2004. 'Žene obavljaju muški posao: Rod i autoritet u hrvatskoj etnologiji', in R. Jambrešić Kirin and T. Škokić (eds), *Rod i narod*. Zagreb: Institut za etnologiju i folkloristiku, pp. 33–48.

———. 2006. 'Etnologija postsocijalizma i prije. Ili: Dvanaest godina nakon "Etnologije socijalizma i poslije"', in L. Čale Feldman and I. Prica (eds), *Devijacije i promašaji: Etnografija domaćeg socijalizma*. Zagreb: Institut za etnologiju i folkloristiku, pp. 9–24.

———. 2007. 'In Search of Post-socialist Subject', *Narodna umjetnost* 44(1): 163–86.

Prica, I. and T. Škokić (eds). 2011. *Horror-porno-ennui: Kulturne prakse post-socijalizam*. Zagreb: Institut za etnologiju i folkloristiku.

Radić, A. 1936–1938. *Sabrana djela*. Zagreb: Seljačka sloga.

Rihtman-Auguštin, D. 1984. *Struktura tradicijskog mišljenja*. Zagreb: Školska knjiga.

———. 1988. *Etnologija naše svakodnevice*. Zagreb: Školska knjiga.

———. 1997. *Christmas in Croatia*. Zagreb: Golden marketing.

———. 2004. *Ethnology, Myth and Politics: Anthropologizing Croatian Ethnology*. Aldershot: Ashgate.

Segalen, M. 2001. 'Les Études Européanistes', in M. Segalen (ed.), *Ethnologie: Concepts et Aires Culturelles*. Paris: Armand Colin, pp. 253–71.

Sklevicky, L. 1991. 'Profesija etnolog: analiza pokazatelja statusa profesije', in D. Rihtman-Auguštin (ed.), *Simboli Identiteta*. Zagreb: Biblioteka Hrvatskog etnološkog društva, pp. 45–72.

Vitez, Z. and A. Muraj (eds). 2000. *Croatian Folk Culture at the Crossroads of Worlds and Eras*. Zagreb: Golden marketing – Tehnička knjiga.

Wardle, H. 2010. 'Introduction: A Cosmopolitan Anthropology?', *Social Anthropology* 18(4): 381–88.

CHAPTER

11

ANTHROPOLOGY IN GREECE

Dynamics, Difficulties and Challenges

ALIKI ANGELIDOU

INTRODUCTION

During the last twenty years an important amount of texts have been written in English, French and Greek regarding the history of anthropology in Greece, a discipline that has a recent institutional presence but a long intellectual trajectory in this country. This chapter provides a synthesis of the above-mentioned research, pointing out their main contributions. Most of these publications question the reasons why although Greece has been an emblematic object of anthropological investigation within the Mediterranean paradigm after the Second World War, it is only in the late 1980s and early 1990s that anthropology got institutionalized in Greek universities. They come across the strong influence of folklore in Greek academia as a nation-building science and the resulting 'hellenocentrism' of Greek academic institutions, which made difficult the establishment of anthropology as a 'cosmopolitan' discipline oriented towards the study of 'cultural differences'. They also consider the heavy influence of the Anglo-Saxon, and to a lesser extent French, tradition in the anthropological study of Greek society, questions raised by the practice of 'anthropology at home' and the relationship between local and foreign scholars. Less attention has been given to issues such as the contrast between the academic proliferation of the discipline and its weak reception in Greek society, the lack of research institutions and funds, of periodicals and public debates dedicated to anthropology, staff and student demographic trends or career paths in academic and non-academic professions, which could question the position and role of Greek anthropology in a national, European and international level.

This chapter counterbalances this absence by providing recent data and reflections placed in a historical framework. After a brief overall presentation of the conceptual and institutional history of anthropology in the country, this chapter explores its academic establishment and its development during the last three decades, which represent its most flourishing period in Greek academia. Moreover, the chapter addresses, from the perspective of a native scholar working at a Greek university, certain less discussed issues, such as the teaching of anthropology. Finally, it deals with some of the challenges the discipline is facing today, which have become more prominent in the ongoing socioeconomic and political crisis of the last three years: the predominance of 'home anthropology', the contrast between the discipline's academic proliferation and its weak reception in Greek society, the media and the labour market, and the current threat represented by the neoliberal measures that have been implemented in the West as well as East European universities since the 1990s, and which have called into question the meaning and role of the social sciences at the beginning of the twenty-first century.

THE EPISTEMOLOGICAL AND INSTITUTIONAL BACKGROUND

The Difficult Development of the Social Sciences and the Hegemony of Folklore

During the last twenty years, a significant number of texts, in English, French and Greek,[1] regarding the development of anthropology in Greece have been published. Most of them take as a starting point the aftermath of the Second World War, when the first foreign anthropologists conducted fieldwork in Greece.[2] They also address the much earlier development of folklore in Greek academia but, in most cases, they do not perceive folklorists' work as a kind of 'home anthropology' and a relevant precursor of Greek anthropology. Additionally, some more recent texts examine the occasional, fragmentary efforts, not forcibly identified with one specific discipline, of a handful of prominent individuals to conduct field research and study cultural difference in Greek society before the institutionalization of anthropology.[3]

More specifically, most publications question the reasons anthropology has been established only recently, in the late 1980s and early 1990s, in Greek universities although Greece has been an emblematic object of anthropological investigation in the Mediterranean paradigm since the aftermath of the Second World War. Most authors relate the late appearance of anthropology in Greek academia to the country's sociopolitical and scientific history: in Britain, France or the United States, social and/or cultural anthropology was developed as a 'cosmopolitan' science (Hann 2003) and a colonial empire-building discipline in search of a distant Other. In Greece, however, since the late nineteenth and early twentieth century, other scientific fields, such as folklore, history or archaeology, have predominated; these had national orientations and were more focused on the study of the Self.[4] The strong influence of folklore in Greek academia as a nation-building science and the resulting hellenocentrism of Greek scientific institutions are thus considered the main reasons for the difficulty anthropology faced in establishing itself as a comparative discipline oriented towards the study of 'cultural differences'.

These tendencies can be better understood if we consider the historical conditions under which these local scientific traditions were founded in order to serve social and political purposes different from those of West European or American anthropology. Since the nineteenth century, not only Greece but all south-eastern European societies have been involved in a double political and mental modernization enterprise: the construction of a state on the one hand and nation-building on the other. These two projects have been combined and each one has been given priority in different historical periods and by different political regimes, orienting to a large extent the directions of scientific work. In this sense, the late presence of anthropology in Greek academia is related to the fact that 'national' disciplines (history, folklore, ethnography, philology, archaeology) were supported by the new states, as they had a certain political usefulness for them, whilst anthropology – and other social sciences – with its critical, comparative and extraverted approach was considered of little use. As Herzfeld (1982) has shown for the Greek case, these 'national' disciplines were designated to contribute to the construction of national identities in the young Balkan states, which had been recently created after the dissolution of the regional empires (Ottoman, Russian, Habsburg), with still many disputed territories and minorities in most of the neighbouring countries. This construction was not only an internal process but also an external issue, related to the search for recognition and support from their French, British or Russian protectors that had contributed to the creation and further expansion of these nation-states (ibid.).

More precisely, the term *laografia* was introduced in 1884 by the founding father of the discipline of folklore Nikolaos Politis in the first volume of the Historical and Ethnological Society of Greece, which had been inaugurated two years before with the goal of studying contemporary Greek history and culture. In 1909, Politis gave a definition of and some guidelines to the topics that should be studied by this discipline in the first volume of *Laografia*, the new journal he had launched. Politis had studied philology and law in Athens and Munich. He combined the English terms 'folklore' and 'ethnography' and privileged the ancient Greek term laografia (Toudasaki 2003: 38) for the new discipline he wished to establish and which he viewed as equivalent to British folklore or German *Volkskunde*, focused on the study of the Greek people. In the same text, he distinguished laografia from ethnology, the equivalent of *Völkerkunde*, concerning more distant people living 'in a state of nature'. Following these ideas, in 1908 Politis founded the Greek Folk Society and in 1918 the Folk Archive, which in 1926 were incorporated into the Greek Academy of Sciences, where again folklore studies, history and archaeology were dominant.

'Folk', equivalent to 'rural', culture was always studied in its relationship to and as a continuation of the ancient Greek civilization and went hand in hand with the development of archaeology, philology and history. Laografia placed emphasis on the common elements of ancient Greek culture and the 'folk culture' of its time and tried to prove the continuation of a homogenous Greek culture through the ages. Most of the first Greek *laografoi*, such as S. Kyriakidis or G. Megas, had a degree in Philology and/or Archaeology in Greece and Germany, but also solid knowledge of anthropological literature. They were influenced by evolutionist and diffusionist theories, especially by Frazer's works and Tylor's views on cultural survivals.[5] Nevertheless, as Toudasaki remarks, in their writings they did not seem to wish to identify the practice of laografia with the anthropological approach but preferred to use it in a selective way, 'in order to respond to the ideological request of reconstruction of the historical continuity' (2003: 44).

Following Politis, most folklorists intended to cover the whole spectrum of 'expressions' of the traditional way of life. Their material was mostly limited to rural Greece and they rarely gave any comparative perspective to their work. Although based in empirical collection of data, Greek folklorists did not consider systematic and in-depth field research an obligation (Nitsiakos 2008), fieldwork practice being reserved for local intellectuals, especially teachers, or students. Furthermore, despite their focus on the study of the countryside, they were not interested in studying a rural community as a social unit and in producing a monograph. Instead, they collected artefacts that remained decontextualized and whose aim was to prove the linear continuity of Greek (folk) culture from ancient days until the present. As

Nitsiakos notes, it took many years for the discipline of folklore to 'deny its philological past and to acquire a social and historical orientation' (2008: 20). It was in fact with the work of Kyriakidis's daughter, A. Kyriakidou-Nestoros, that Greek folklore studies started to catch up, thanks to her enthusiasm for Lévi-Strauss and her sometimes contentious involvement with American-based social and cultural anthropologists.

From the very creation of the Greek state ethnocentric folklore, positivistic history and archaeology were established in universities and scientific academies.[6] According to Politis' vision, laografia was a science that gave emphasis to language, to what he called 'oral monuments' *(mnemeia tou logou)*[7] – songs, tales, proverbs, wishes, narratives, etc. As a consequence, the discipline was introduced at the University of Athens, at the School of Philology in the Faculty of Philosophy (today the Department of Byzantine Philology and Folklore) in 1890. Later on, laografia would also be established in two other important Greek universities, but this time affiliated to history and archaeology instead of philology: in 1926 at the University of Thessaloniki, at the School of History and Archaeology in the Faculty of Philosophy (today in the Section of Modern and Contemporary History, Folklore and Social Anthropology) and in 1967 with the Chair of Folklore (today Section of Folklore) at the University of Ioannina, at the School of History and Archaeology in the Faculty of Philosophy. In all cases, as Nitsiakos (2008) remarks, laografia has remained until recently a discipline with little social orientation, thus making its inclusion in the social sciences difficult.

In parallel, a Greek Anthropological Society was founded in 1924 related to the development of physical anthropology at the University of Athens, where a Chair of Physical Anthropology was established from 1925 to 1970.[8] The scholars involved were mostly Professors of Medicine, such as C. Stéphanos and I. Koumbaris. Influenced by the racial theories of interwar German physical anthropology and British evolutionism, they used biological data to promote the continuity of Greek national identity (Trubeta 2009, 2010). The works of the physical anthropologist Aris Poulianos continued in the same spirit during the military junta years. Interestingly, despite its ethnocentric orientation, the Greek Anthropological Society developed a wide spectrum of anthropological debates and made possible dialogue between diverging scholars, from intellectuals such as K. Karavidas or the anthropologist J. Peristiany to numerous folklorists (Agelopoulos 2013).

These nation-building oriented processes went hand in hand with the rather limited presence of the social sciences in academia during the same period. As Gefou-Madianou remarks, 'whatever discipline did not openly support the historic myths through which the national identity has been constructed was considered suspect and therefore branded as unnecessary'

(Gefou-Madianou 1993: 164). Nonetheless, in the interwar period some interesting intellectual and research processes took place. On the one hand, during the 1920s and early 1930s sociological courses were introduced at the Universities of Athens, Thessaloniki and Panteion in the School of Political Sciences in the context of Philosophy, Law and the Classics (Gefou-Madianou 1993). Additionally, the Society of Social and Political Sciences was founded in 1916 and some social research journals published up until the Metaxas dictatorship in the mid 1930s. In the very first years of its introduction in Greece, sociology had been a critical and politically committed discipline. However, gradually, especially after the Second World War, many of the scholars involved in the above initiatives began to associate with the conservatives. Furthermore, social theory was introduced into Greek academic and broader intellectual life, but theoretical debates were rarely based on empirical research (Agelopoulos 2013).

On the other hand, as Agelopoulos (2010) explains, in the 1920s the agenda of some individual researchers became more society-oriented and focused on both modernization questions and on the study of the Others inside the national territory – that is, minority populations. Because of the geographical expansion of the Greek state and the inclusion of non-Greek speaking peoples, some outstanding personalities developed fieldwork practices in the newly acquired territories. The most prominent example is the lawyer Konstantinos Karavidas. Employee in different important state offices (Ministry of Foreign Affairs, Ministry of Agriculture, Agricultural Bank of Greece) and a close assistant of the Greek prime minister Venizelos, Karavidas conducted systematic demographic and sociological field research among the rural populations in the Smyrna region,[9] Thrace and Greek Macedonia. His surveys focused on Muslims and the Slavic extended family, the so-called *zadruga*, and had an applied political orientation in search of ways to better integrate the Muslim and Slavic populations of Northern Greece into the Greek state. He also devoted himself to the conceptualization of alternative ways of organizing the rural sector, based on existing social structures (the local community – *koinotita*), that would enable its development and adaptation to the modern capitalist economy. This 'quest for ethnology' (ibid.) in the 1920s lost its use value after the exchange of populations and the stabilization of the Greek borders in the late 1920s. From the early 1930s onwards the study of otherness turned into the study of sameness at the hands of ethnocentric folklorists and physical anthropologists.[10]

More generally, for almost a century – from the end of the nineteenth century until the 1980s – a local comparative and extraverted science based on the concepts of 'otherness', 'difference' and 'distance', on systematic fieldwork and the study of contemporary social and cultural processes, was not established in Greek academia. The 'national' sciences of folklore, archaeology, philology and history, focused on the veneration of the ancient past and giving emphasis to the study of Greek peasant life and to the construction of the national Self, overshadowed it. In this sense the late arrival of anthropology in Greek universities is related to the fact that 'national' disciplines were supported by the local elites and the new state, as they were politically useful to them, whilst anthropology – and other social sciences – with its critical, comparative and extraverted approach was considered of little use, if not dangerous (Gefou-Madianou 1993).

Observed from the Outside:
Greece as an Object of Anthropological Investigation

It is well known that after the Second World War, in the framework of the decolonization and rapid modernization of the societies that anthropology used to study as 'distant' and 'exotic' Others, anthropologists started to 'return home' and become interested in the study of European and American cultures, beginning with the peripheral and less industrialized societies of southern Europe and Latin America. In addition, due to the Cold War divisions, Greece, which was the sole country in south-eastern Europe to remain outside the socialist bloc, was perceived mainly as a 'Mediterranean' and no longer as a 'Balkan' society, and anthropology in Greece came under the strong influence of the Anglo-American (Papataxiarchis 2005) and, to a lesser extent, French epistemological paradigms (Toudasaki 2003; Tsibiridou 2003).

All historical accounts of the discipline start with the two seminal works that made Greece an object of systematic anthropological investigation: the famous monographs of the British John K. Campbell on the Sarakatsani, a pastoral-nomadic people in the Zagori region (1964) and of the American Ernestine Friedl on the village of Vassilika in central Greece (1962). Both researchers conducted fieldwork in the mid 1950s and made Greece one of the eminent paradigms of Mediterranean anthropology. Following the model of the holistic monographs produced on non-European societies and under the influence of the structural-functional paradigm, they are oriented towards small, isolated rural communities or populations. They put emphasis on kinship and gender roles, on political relations as well as on cultural values and patterns such as 'honour' and 'shame'.[11] More precisely, although focusing on a very specific ethnographic example, they depicted what they saw as characteristic features of Greek culture that could be generalized, and showed both the 'simplicity' and homogeneity of Mediterranean culture and its difference from those of Western Europe and North America (Bakalaki 1993). Their theoretical and methodological orientations would be followed

– with numerous combinations and variations – throughout the 1960s, 1970s and early 1980s by a growing number of their students and other young anthropologists, who would conduct research in Greece.[12]

Both Friedl and Campbell made little reference to politically sensitive questions of their times – such as the traumatic aftermath of the Second World War and the civil war in the countryside, the politics of national identity or the Greek state's position concerning minority groups. These silences are, however, understandable if we consider the political context in Greece but also the theoretical priorities of British and American anthropology at this time. In addition, they did not put their analysis into a historical perspective and based it mainly on oral sources. As a result, they presented a rather static image of Greece. Finally, although they were aware of the locally produced works of laografia they had but slight interest in them and cited little or no work in Greek.[13] Nevertheless, many of the above issues would be covered by their successors, some of whom would turn towards the study of social change and urban or semi-urban settings and be more open to local scientific production.

Similar topics would be elaborated too by French ethnologists, such as C. Piault, B. Vernier and M.-E. Handman, who also arrived in Greece in the late 1960s but mostly in the 1970s. Based on a different theoretical tradition, in which structuralism and Marxism were dominant, they did not focus on the role and function of social institutions and their interrelation in a functioning unit, but both on the reproduction and change of social structures through local resistance, challenges and negotiations. Emphasis was also given to the ways social groups and individuals seek to satisfy their material and symbolic interests, to family strategies and marriage exchanges, to strategies of inheritance and property as well as to symbolic and material forms of dominance. The French scholars were keener to integrate history into their writings and therefore showed interest in written sources and social history. They thus concentrated on recording the different structures and forms of the rural family household in various regions of Greece through archival historical demographic research (Toudasaki 2003). Nonetheless, following their Anglo-Saxon colleagues, they paid most attention to local rural communities.[14]

Despite their common interests in the ethnography of Greece, scientific contacts and exchanges among French and Anglo-American scholars were not very intensive. In fact, there was little dialogue either between them or with local scholars, each remaining focused on their respective scientific traditions. However, their studies contributed to the evolution and institutionalization of the social sciences in Greece. At the time, only a few courses and no departments of sociology or anthropology existed in Greek universities. More generally, the 1950s and 1960s were periods during which systematic modernization efforts were made by successive governments, especially regarding the countryside, which had been devastated by war and the country's industrialization. The 1960s also saw the start of a democratization process in political life that would soon be interrupted by the military junta in 1967. Part of these processes was the inauguration by UNESCO in 1959 of the Athens Centre for Social Research (Lampiri-Dimaki 2003). Directed by the anthropologist John Peristiany, the Centre played the role of an intermediary training a first generation of Greeks with critical instruction in the social sciences and hosting foreign scholars.[15] As Papataxiarchis (2003) remarks, a stimulating intellectual environment developed in this research institution, where anthropologists could meet with rural sociologists or human geographers who all came to study Greek society in the aftermath of the Second World War. These scholars were also connected to foreign institutions, such as the British and American School of Athens or the French Archaeological School (Couroucli 2007), which also created a stimulating intellectual environment concerning mainly the study of ancient but also of contemporary Greece.

The prolific activity of the Athens Centre for Social Research stopped when it was suddenly closed by the military junta in the late 1960s. The authorities perceived it as a locus for the production of 'dangerous' ideas. More generally, the political situation in Greece during the junta years slowed down the first successful efforts to establish the social sciences. On the one hand, it made the presence of foreign researchers in Greece difficult. On the other, a significant number of Greek intellectuals either left for north-western European countries[16] or were imprisoned and/or forced into exile. According to Papataxiarchis (2003), these processes impeded for another decade the establishment of the social sciences in Greek universities and the diffusion of critical social thinking in the public sphere. The social sciences would remain excluded from Greek academia until the end of the military dictatorship in the mid 1970s, when a new phase in the modernization of Greek society and academia began.

GREEK ANTHROPOLOGY GOES HOME: THE DYNAMICS OF A NEW DISCIPLINE

The Academic Establishment of Greek Anthropology

The institutionalization of anthropology is related to larger processes of democratization in Greek society and to the liberalization of academic life that took place after the fall of the junta in 1974 and the integration of the country into the European Union. The first Department of Sociology was inaugurated at Panteion University in 1981–82. After the coming to power of the Socialist Party and a new law on universities, adopted in 1982, other important transformations followed. This law introduced new social science departments, sections and curriculums in many newly created universities, usually those located close to national borders (Crete, the Aegean, Thrace).[17] The first anthropology departments were founded at the University of the Aegean on the island of Lesvos (1987–88)[18] and then in Athens,[19] at Panteion University of Social and Political Sciences (1990–91).[20] However, as Gefou-Madianou notes, 'the reasons for the creation of these new departments did not come about in response to identifiable needs within the society but as a consequence of the geopolitical concerns of the Greek state, through the promptings of the European Community as part of its goals towards "harmonization" and "standardization" and in response to the desire of the established academic community to become more westernized' (Gefou-Madianou 1993: 165).

Until then, Greeks who wanted to study anthropology were usually trained in various fields such as economy, law, history, philology, political sciences, folklore or sociology, and were obliged to go to the United States or to Western European universities for their undergraduate studies. A vast majority returned to Greece for fieldwork; a few conducted fieldwork elsewhere.[21] This trajectory was considered pioneering – following the latest theoretical and methodological trends of the time – 'indigenous anthropology' or 'anthropology at home'. After graduation, many of these Western-trained scholars returned to Greece and founded and/or staffed anthropology departments.[22]

Since its institution as a university discipline, anthropology has expanded rapidly within academia. According to Papataxiarchis (2005), the 1990s constituted a period of unique prosperity and growth for European and, more particularly, Greek anthropology, in terms of new departments, teaching, student numbers and research. Nowadays three departments, all in public universities, deliver a degree in Anthropology: the Department of Social Anthropology at Panteion University, Athens; the Department of Social Anthropology and History at the University of the Aegean, Mytilene; and the Department of History, Archaeology and Social Anthropology at the University of Thessaly, Volos.[23] Anthropology courses are also offered in various other departments or departmental sections (of Sociology, Folklore, Balkan Studies, Political Sciences, Law, Education, History and Ethnology) in numerous universities all around the country. The three above-mentioned departments also have MA programmes in Anthropology and a growing number of Ph.D. students.[24]

As Papataxiarchis (2005) remarks, the institutionalization of Greek anthropology parallels some important changes in the theoretical and methodological orientation of the discipline, which was facing at the time profound criticism, from postmodernism, postcolonial studies, cultural critique and feminist theories. He discerns three fundamental changes that took place in Greek anthropology at that period. First, Greek anthropologists adopted a critical distance from 'objectivism' and from essentializing discourses and focused on the study of subjectivity, conceptualizations of the self and on different identities, individual and collective. Second, there was a shift towards the 'ethnography of the particular' (ibid. 2005: 219), a turn from generalization to the acceptance of the particularity of each ethnographic field. Third, from the mid 1980s, Greek ethnography participated in the 'experimental moment' (ibid. 2005: 219), which implied a critique of ethnographic realism, which had been dominant until then.[25] Combined with the theoretical turn towards reflexivity, the theories of practice or constructivism, subjectivity was not relevant only for the objects of research (the observed) but also for the researcher him/herself (the observer) as a constitutive part of the ethnographic construction. The reflexive presence of the ethnographer in the process of knowledge, in relation to his own identity and experiences, is therefore necessary.

In addition, Greek society was no longer perceived as homogeneous and emphasis was given to its complexity and to the multiplicity of analytical and methodological tools that could be used in studying it. There was a shift from holistic to partial approaches, a restoration of the relationship between anthropology and history and an interest in social transformations. There was also a turn from rural to urban areas, a shift of interest from social to cultural processes and to a balanced inclusion of social and cultural dimensions of Greek society. According to the same author, specific themes such as kinship, family or religion no longer dominated and therefore researchers working in Greece were concerned with a variety of topics. As a result, Greek anthropology today is a polyphonic and diversified field (Papataxiarchis 2005).

Moreover, since the 1990s students have been graduating from the anthropological departments in Greece. Among them, some have continued their studies in French, British, American and, to a lesser extent, German-speaking universities, which enabled them to start doing fieldwork outside Greece, in near or distant places.[26] Other graduates have pursued doctoral studies in a Greek university on new topics such as migration, nationalism and ethnicity, gender and sexuality, urban cultures, medical anthropology, memory and many others, related to the ongoing changes of Greek society in the new Balkan, European Union and global context. During the same period, a considerable number of important anthropological texts were translated into Greek and numerous ethnographies of Greece written both by indigenous and foreign scholars were published.[27] In addition, anthropology courses were given in a growing number of departments of Hellenic studies in many West European countries and the United States. All these processes represented a new era in Greek anthropology and a shift away from the interest in the Self to that in the internal or external Other, as Papataxiarchis (2005) has noted.

Learning Anthropology in Greek Academia

A more recent theme discussed among Greek anthropologists is the teaching of anthropology (Bakalaki 1993, 1997, 2006; Dalkavoukis, Manos and Veikou 2010). There is no systematic statistical demographic data about students, teaching staff or researchers. The entrance of large numbers of students to university is, however, a general trend, promoted by the Greek Ministry of Education over the last two decades.[28] This has been part of the general democratization of higher education in the last twenty years, during which many new universities have been opened and free higher education has become accessible to many students from different socioeconomic backgrounds, offering possibilities for upward mobility. A side effect of this democratization process is that many young people are just eager to get a university degree no matter what its content and choose the social sciences either because they are not sure about what profession to follow or because they do not have the grades for a discipline in greater demand. Thus entrance to anthropology departments is for the large majority not a choice but the result of a perverse system of university admission: oriented towards more job-promising disciplines, candidates 'end up' in anthropology because of their low grades in the entrance exams.[29] Having failed to follow the discipline of their first choice, they are therefore often frustrated and worry about their future professional prospects. In many cases, they have little knowledge of what anthropology is about and most of the time they are ill-prepared to follow anthropology curriculums, as they lack general knowledge and have no background in social theory, since this is not systematically taught in secondary schools.[30] As a result, they are not motivated. However a considerable number of students become attracted by the discipline during their studies.[31]

The teaching curriculums in all anthropology departments cover a large spectrum of topics, from the classics to the latest tendencies, and give a good overview of all anthropological theories and methods. However, most courses are focused on Europe, as the research and teaching interests of the majority of the teaching staff are concentrated on Greece and the European continent. Additionally, because of the high number of students and the lack of resources, passive methods of teaching predominate in which students do not actively participate. Moreover, they have few possibilities for ethnographic observation and training in ethnography outside the class, for camera use or for other more hands-on means of learning. Consequently, there is often a gap between what students hear in the classroom and their everyday experiences, which prevents them from developing a self-reflexive way of thinking and theorizing (Dalkavoukis, Manos and Veikou 2010) and from connecting theory with their everyday lives.[32] In addition, there are few courses with an applied orientation and only one nationwide training programme co-funded by the EU that enables students to work for a limited period of time (three months) in a private or public institution related to their field of studies. Despite these difficulties, there is a very clear internationalization of Greek anthropology regarding both teaching and research. All departments are active in Erasmus exchanges and student exchange programmes with the United States or international summer schools.

Both BA and MA programmes are general, with only slight specialization in the different departments.[33] The lack of specialization, especially in postgraduate programmes, results in a lack of motivation among students to circulate between departments. As a consequence, they do not diversify their experiences. Another common practice is for anthropology graduates to leave Greece for an MA abroad and to return to a Greek university for their Ph.D.[34] In parallel, many graduates from a wide spectrum of other disciplines choose one of the Anthropology MA programmes.[35] This is again part of a larger phenomenon of the overcrowding of MA studies during the last two decades.[36] Students' orientation towards a Master's degree in Anthropology is often motivated by an interest in the specific discipline and also by their desire to acquire an extra diploma that they consider will give them a better chance of finding a job or a better salary, and/or an upgrade in jobs they already have, principally in the public sector. The number of Ph.D. students is increasing too. The majority are anthropology graduates; more rarely, they have another scientific background. For the moment, there have been few postdoctoral programmes developed in anthropology departments.

An important problem regarding Ph.D. studies and research more generally is the lack of a state research policy and of research institutions.[37] An interrelated problem is the lack of research funding both for Ph.D. students and for senior scholars.[38] During the last few decades, the most substantial funding has come from EU programmes. The latter are often thematically oriented [39] and usually have no space for the slow, immersed kind of ethnographic field research. However they take on researchers of various levels (Ph.D., postdoc and senior) to work together, a practice not so common among Greek anthropologists, who usually conduct research on an individual basis. There is only one scholarship for graduate studies delivered by the State Scholarships Foundation (IKY).[40] A number of private scholarships are also available, but they do not involve a strategic vision of research and follow personal criteria set up by the donors.[41] Moreover, research outside the country is poorly funded by Greek institutions, as an ethnocentric vision prevails that sees no reason to fund research that does not concern Greece, Greek diasporas or, more recently, south-eastern Europe.[42] Finally, scholars usually look for individual fellowships and grants or participate in EU and bilateral programmes. In many cases, they end up providing the funding for their research themselves, choosing therefore a nearby field site in order to limit expenses. Apart from money, departmental staff also lack the time to do long-term distant fieldwork, as there are often difficulties replacing them in their teaching duties and hence in obtaining research leave.

It becomes obvious that the development of anthropology in Greece has not been the result of any internal social or policy demand. Even after the fall of the military junta and the normalization of political life, the state apparatus still did not use the social sciences, and anthropology in particular, in order to organize and reproduce itself. On the contrary, it undertook several reforms in order to harmonize with and conform to European standards and look more 'modern' and 'European'. As a result, anthropology has been institutionalized as a new and fashionable science in relation to the 'modernization' and 'democratization' processes that have taken place during the last few decades, particularly since the integration of Greece into the EU. Despite this background, anthropology has started to systematically formulate a critical discourse concerning the social and cultural practices as well as the ethnocentric ideas that have dominated the conceptualization and production of Greek identity for more than a century. In parallel, imported and modelled by foreign scholars and concepts, and only slightly related to state policy, with an exclusively theoretical and academic orientation, anthropology today still has a weak connection with the Greek state and society and faces several challenges.

FUTURE CHALLENGES

Anthropology 'at Home' and Abroad

The first question raised concerns the dominance of 'home anthropology'. According to Papataxiarchis (2005), over the last three decades the number of local scholars studying Greek society has been constantly increasing. Although a growing number of Greek anthropologists conduct fieldwork outside Greece, they are still a minority. These facts are probably indicative of certain general tendencies in anthropology, which increasingly addresses questions about contemporary global phenomena and does not always encourage the taste for research in a society other than one's own. In the case of Greece though, where there is no long tradition of interest in 'otherness', these tendencies constitute a risk of an unbalanced predominance of 'indigenous anthropology'.

Many authors have signalled this danger. As Gefou-Madianou notes, a major issue for the first Greek anthropologists was the fact that, as Greece had never possessed colonies, it was difficult to identify an anthropological object of study outside national boundaries or find any funding for fieldwork research outside Greece. So Greek scholars were obliged to look inward, to establish their 'colonies' within (Gefou-Madianou 1993: 165–66), and remained close to the objectives of the other local disciplines: the search for their own cultural identity. The danger of such a methodological attitude was the potential reproduction of hellenocentric introversion and the lack of cross-cultural comparisons. The solution found was the connection of Greek anthropology to Western anthropological theoretical literature, which became its main frame of reference, allotting a secondary role to systematic field research.

In addition, during the last twenty years the strong influence of American postmodernist orientations has accentuated this dislike for fieldwork. Postmodern critique of closed, localized ethnographic studies and the development of multisited ethnography, urban anthropology, emphasis on subjectivity and a self-reflexive orientation have thus been applied in the Greek context. As a result, many Ph.D. students do not feel enthusiastic about launching themselves into the adventure of non-Greek fieldwork. Generally, they are much more attached to a theoretical endeavour than to a study based on systematic ethnography. The overall situation does not help, as it is difficult for them to get funding for training in specialized languages or courses on non-European societies. In addition, Ph.D. students have no opportunity to undertake teaching tasks in the university during their studies, as there are no funds for this. As a consequence, they lack any teaching experience and often do not imagine themselves in an academic career. The contribution of Greek anthropology to the study of the 'others' within Greece (minorities and migrants) during the last two decades has been remarkable. This cannot, however, be the sole orientation to give a future perspective to Greek anthropology.

Another, interrelated issue has to do with the connection between anthropology and folklore. Today, the borders between the study of the Self and the Other are no longer clear and unquestioned. As a result, the relationship between 'home/native/indigenous anthropology' and disciplines such as folklore and ethnography remains an open question. It is now commonplace that anthropology no longer has the monopoly on the study of 'otherness', whilst folklore is no longer devoted to the construction of the national Self. In Greece, as Nitsiakos (2008) remarks, since the 1970s laografia has broadened its fields of enquiry and taken on a more historical and social dimension, becoming an indigenous ethnographic science specialized in the study of Greek society and culture. Consequently, today the limits between folklore, ethnology, ethnography and anthropology are less clear than ever, especially when it comes to the question of studying a certain culture 'from inside'. Yet folklore studies have been in continuous decline during the last few decades and several research or academic institutions still bearing the name 'folklore' are gradually being staffed with anthropologists. The relation between these two disciplines remains complicated. Most often their rivalry is expressed as a competition for funding and academic positions and a struggle for legitimacy inside and outside academia. However, lately there has also been more collaboration between anthropologists and folklorists in common educational and research programmes.

In all cases, the more Greek anthropologists feel confident about their professional identity the more they critically distance themselves from readings of Western literature, base their work on solid field research and open up to other scientific traditions such as those developed in the neighbouring Balkan countries. Under these circumstances, the vindication of an anthropological identity does not run the risk of becoming a struggle for legitimacy inside academia or an imitation of foreign concepts and practices. Moreover, the search for a balance between fieldwork practices and theory, local legacies and new trends, and research inside and outside national borders becomes beneficial not only for a better understanding of Greek society but also for the production of an indigenous discourse that can enrich anthropological theory, linking local to global issues.

Anthropology Outside Academia

Most authors who address the history of Greek anthropology focus mainly on what is happening within academia, revealing significant transformations over the past thirty years. Less attention has been paid to the contrast between the academic expansion of the discipline and its weak reception in Greek society. In fact, anthropology has little visibility and recognition outside academia and is to a large extent unknown even among the country's elites. Whereas sociologists, philosophers or political scientists often participate in public debates and systematically write or appear in the media, few anthropologists do so, as they are rarely invited by the media to comment on topics, even on those in which they have expertise. Furthermore, the analytical tools specific to anthropology – that is, the questioning of common states through comparative analysis and systematic fieldwork practice, its 'bottom up' approach and its view 'from afar' – seem to be of little interest to the state or other policymaking instances, who often do not search for data, methods and approaches that could assist them in resolving specific social questions. Additionally, employers and policymakers both in the public and private sector usually ignore anthropology's potential contribution, and when hiring specialized staff they prefer, for example, psychologists, sociologists or social workers. The latter are organized in strong professional associations that consolidate their rights and have better recognition in the labour market.[43]

For their part, Greek anthropologists have not until today been so very eager to promote their professional skills outside the university and to participate in public debates or affairs. Most of them are members of important international associations such as the European Association of Social Anthropology (EASA), the Association of Social Anthropologists of the United Kingdom and Commonwealth (ASA), the American Anthropological Association (AAA) or the Modern Greek Studies Association (MGSA). There are, however, few active Greek scientific and/or professional anthropological associations that could contribute to the promotion of anthropological research and professional rights.[44] As a consequence, professional rights are relatively restricted, mostly assuring recruitment in public administrations or education.[45] As has been mentioned above, university curriculums have no applied orientations. Additionally, national and international conferences are systematically organized on various topics but rarely address the question of the discipline's professionalization.

The emphasis given to critical engagement and the reluctance to participate in social affairs puts theory and practice in conflict, isolates anthropologists from the public sphere, calls into question the extroverted character of the discipline and does not help to popularize it. As a result, Greek anthropology is nowadays much appreciated by the international anthropological community as well as in Greek universities, where it has established a dialogue with the most avant-garde trends in other scientific fields. At the same time, it is still little known outside academia, either in the labour market or among a non-specialist public. As pointed out above, the demand for anthropology studies is quite high. Until the recent economic crisis, the main reasons for this were the absence of fees for both undergraduate and graduate studies[46] and the possibility of pursuing a career in the public sector.[47] It is questionable, though, whether the demand for anthropological studies will continue in the years to come. Employment in the public sector has been drastically restricted due to severe budgetary cuts and radical downsizing.[48] As a consequence, university studies, which have always been seen by students and their parents as a personal and family 'investment' that will 'pay back' later in a good job, may have to face the challenge of either becoming more oriented to fields that can guarantee a job in the private sector and thus change to more 'profit-making' disciplines or vanish.

There is thus constant tension between students' demands for a more applied and job-related education and the professionals' vision that favours a more theoretical and academic approach to anthropology (Bakalaki 2006). As a result, the more anthropology is distanced from public debates and the job market, the more it attracts students with low motivation, for it is perceived as a 'light' or 'easy' discipline. This vicious cycle puts its future under threat. As has been argued by many anthropologists,[49] strong political and economic pressures tend to transform higher education into a series of institutions producing specialized knowledge able to solve concrete problems defined by the market. Nevertheless, the role of scientific thought is not only to give answers to problems but also to reflect upon the very existence and formulation of these problems. For the moment, anthropology departments are struggling to find a balance between these two different visions of what anthropology is about in the Greek case.

Neoliberal Education Policies

More generally, the high quality and dynamic profile of Greek anthropology is nowadays endangered by the neoliberal policies implemented in education at a European level (Shore and Wright 1999, 2000) and worldwide (Wright and Rabo 2010). Protests of students and teaching staff have been part of the social and political mobilization against neoliberal policies in Greece during the last years.[50] This mobilization has so far allowed higher education to curb the implementation of policies promoted by European governments and the EU. Similar reforms have already transformed numerous European universities over the last decades (Strathern 2000) and changed the conception of the role of (social) science and knowledge in the contemporary world (Shore 2008). Nevertheless, after several unsuccessful attempts, since August 2011 the Ministry of Education has succeeded in passing two laws (4009/2011 and 4076/2012) that are about to drastically transform higher education, following the main guidelines of the Bologna convention.

More precisely, the conception of the above-mentioned laws goes in the opposite direction to the previous law (1268/1982). The main changes introduced are similar to those observed elsewhere in the world (Shore 2007): on the one hand, less state funding and the commodification of knowledge and its market orientation, and, on the other, less democratic administration of universities and maintenance of state control. Although in Greece private universities are forbidden by the Constitution,[51] state universities are led to function with private corporate criteria, in which competition (among students and universities), excellence and financial 'autonomy' prevail. Fees are not introduced by the new law, except for MA studies. However, as state funding is radically diminishing, in the years to come universities will be obliged to impose fees in order to cover their expenses.

These radical changes have to be implemented within a short period of time and coincide with ongoing budgetary restrictions related to the economic crisis. As a result, most universities lack funds for basic needs, such as heating or the organization of academic activities. Academics' salaries are constantly being reduced.[52] In addition, whilst professors near retirement age are leaving universities to avoid severe pension cuts, there are few prospects for new recruitments. Many departmental programmes are threatened because of lack of teaching staff, and the existing staff is suffering from overload. Moreover, during the last reform the humanities were the first to be severely attacked with a plan to merge many foreign language and area studies departments as not career-promising.[53] There is no doubt that in an educational system that intends to make knowledge countable, 'useful' and connected to the market, the social sciences will also gradually have more difficulties justifying their raison d'être.

Furthermore, the new laws introduce a very hierarchical and corruption-friendly administrative system through boards of governors, where decisions are made by a restricted number of people, some of whom are not elected. This contradicts more democratic mechanisms of university administration developed over the last thirty years. Until now Greek scholars have participated actively and equally – that is, independently of their grade, in the administration of the department and university. This has meant a heavy administrative load but also relative independence in their work. Additionally, the Ministry of Education still maintains control in many academic issues, such as the number of students entering each department or the decision to merge departments. It thus effectively diminishes the 'autonomy' given to the universities by the new law, which in practice is restricted to the economic disengagement of the state from universities that must now provide a substantial part of their financing through private funds. Finally, the new legislation diminishes the role of the department as an administrative and pedagogical unit in favour of the school and guarantees no professional rights to graduates.

More generally speaking, the democratic and open character of the Greek university is under threat. Not only is administration becoming more centralized but the number of students is also falling. This is for economic reasons, as less people can afford higher education, but is also part of the reforms promoted by the Greek Ministry of Education. Moreover, as a result of the crisis, conservative ideas and a return to national ideals have gradually become popular for larger strata of the population. Such ideas get greater political representation in extreme right-wing parties that attack verbally and/or physically all kinds of 'otherness' in Greek society (migrants, homosexuals, leftists) as responsible for its current decline. The escalating aggressiveness towards progressive opinions critical of ethnocentric points of view threatens anew the very existence of the social sciences. As the discipline dealing with 'others' and with the vast majority of anthropologists associating themselves with progressive ideas and the left, anthropology is particularly exposed to these threats.

Furthermore, because of the crisis, Greece is re-emerging as a 'fashionable' object of investigation for a growing number of foreign – especially younger – anthropologists, with the risk, however, of its 're-exoticization'. At the same time, living and working conditions for Greek anthropologists are constantly deteriorating. The latter are gradually becoming part of the crisis phenomena they observe and are facing ongoing problems in the exercise of their teaching and research duties. Moreover, due to funding restrictions, they are starting to meet difficulties in participating in international scientific forums and in conducting field research outside Greece. All these phenomena remind older scholars of how things were before the 1980s, when universities in Greece were far less independent, extroverted and open to critical political thinking and when the social sciences had difficulties finding their place in academia.

CONCLUSION

As this chapter shows, after a long absence anthropology has evolved as a particularly dynamic field that has expanded in Greek universities over the last three decades. This was a period of economic prosperity, democratization and tighter adherence of the country to the European modernization project. Anthropology has thus established itself in the Greek scientific arena as a new, reflexive discipline and as a front line scientific field of international renown. However, despite its extensive proliferation, Greek anthropology has also confronted several difficulties related to its weak connection to both society and the state. The challenges the discipline faces are expected to grow rapidly in the years to come: in a period of ongoing political, socioeconomic and ideological unrest where the European character of Greek institutions is being called into question and the public sector is encountering severe budgetary cuts, the social sciences, and anthropology in particular, which have flourished during the last decades, are under threat. Nowadays, many critiques in Greece and abroad concern the superficiality of the Greek economic – and university – boom of the previous years. Is the expansion of anthropology since the 1990s also part of this 'bubble'? Will the discipline be able to find its way within the global transformations in economy, knowledge and university restructuring? Is anthropology relevant for tackling questions and for helping Greece face its current difficulties? These are some of the issues that will be addressed in the near future and that will determine its further orientations.

Aliki Angelidou is Assistant Professor at Panteion University, Athens. She conducted fieldwork in rural Bulgaria exploring postsocialist transformations. She published on migrants' mobility from Eastern Europe to Greece and on the comparative history of anthropology in Southeast Europe. Currently, she carries out research on household economy in a Greek agrotown.

NOTES

1. There are significantly fewer texts published in German, Italian and other languages but these have not been considered here.
2. For example, the works of Bakalaki (1993), Couroucli (1978), Gefou-Madianou (1993, 2000, 2010), Panopoulos (2003), Papataxiarchis (2003, 2005, 2013), Toudasaki (2003) or Tsibiridou (2003).
3. See Papataxiarchis (2003) and Agelopoulos (2010, 2013).
4. Interestingly, although a lot has been written about the relation between anthropology and folklore, the equally uneasy relation between anthropology and history in Greece has gone more unquestioned. It would be worth, for example, investigating why in most cases, Panteion University excepted, anthropology is part of the same department as history and archaeology, and not as sociology or geography. For some elements of discussion on the institutional relation between history and anthropology, see Panopoulos (2003). For some theoretical points on the relation between the two disciplines in the case of Greece, see Papataxiarchis (1993).
5. For an enlightening introduction to Greek folklore see Kyrakidou-Nestoros (1978).
6. The National Archaeological Museum and the Museum of Greek Handicrafts (today the Museum of Greek Folk Art) were founded on the same principles in the Greek capital in 1889 and 1918.
7. The transliteration from Greek has been made according to a simplified version of the Library of Congress system, except from names of institutions, disciplines or individuals already established in the bibliography with a different transliteration.
8. However, this Chair would remain vacant from 1950 to 1970 (Trubeta 2009).
9. At the same period, a School of Ethnology was to be inaugurated in Smyrna. The first university of the Greek state had been founded in Athens in 1837. Then, in 1920, Venizelos planned, for geopolitical reasons, to establish the second Greek university in the lands acquired in Asia Minor after the First World War, in Smyrna. The defeat of the Greek army in 1922 changed these plans and the second university was founded

in Thessaloniki in 1926. For an extensive analysis of the School of Ethnology at the University of Smyrna, see Agelopoulos (2010).

10. From the interwar years to the 1970s there were some scattered and fragmentary efforts to introduce anthropology in Greece, with prominent examples being the studies of the Marxist P. Lekatsas or the ethnographies of Prince Peter of Greece. For a detailed analysis of the various attempts to promote anthropology in Greece during this period, see the overviews of Agelopoulos (2013) and Papataxiarchis (2003, 2013). For the presence of foreign scholars, mostly geographers and (rural) sociologists, in Greece before the anthropologists' arrival, see Couroucli (1978).

11. For a critical approach of the main literature on the 'honour and shame' syndrome see Pina-Cabral (1989) and Herzfeld (1980).

12. Such as J. du Boulay, R. Hirschon, M. Herzfeld, J. Dubisch, M. Kenna, P. Allen, L. Danforth, C. Stewart or J. Cowan.

13. Campbell did engage, however, with the Greek scholar George Kavadias, a specialist on the Sarakatsani, with whom he had a critical disagreement about the nature and significance of Sarakatsan kinship patterns.

14. Foreign researchers, such as C. Piault or S. Hoffman, R. Cowan, and P. Aratow, produced during this period the first ethnographic films on (rural) Greece.

15. As Agelopoulos (2013) notes, rural development was one of the main reasons UNESCO promoted the Athens Centre for Social Research, the other being the inclusion of Greece in a larger project for re-establishing the social sciences in various countries and promoting independent, critical thinking.

16. Most of them went to France where they were influenced by progressive political ideas, Marxism and structuralism, that were dominant in French universities at the time.

17. At the same time, in the older central universities of the country (Athens, Thessaloniki, Ioannina) laografia and other 'national' sciences still prevailed.

18. First an MA programme was inaugurated in 1987–88 and then a BA programme two academic years later.

19. Its initial full name was the Department of Social Policy, Geography and Social Anthropology. However, a year later, Geography disappeared from both the title and the analytical programme. Then the other two disciplines split into two independent departments in 2004–5.

20. A Department of History and Ethnology was also founded during the same period (1990–91) at the University of Thrace, Komotini, where courses on both physical and social/cultural anthropology are taught but no degree in Anthropology is delivered.

21. For example, G. Makris did fieldwork in the Sudan or L. Economou in the United States.

22. Many others took positions in foreign universities with contemporary Greece as their field of research, such as M. Couroucli in France, N. Seremetakis, N. Panourgia and A. Karakasidou in the States or D. Theodossopoulos and E. Kirtsoglou in the United Kingdom.

23. A Department of History, Archaeology and Folklore was founded in 1999–2000 and was renamed in 2002 the Department of History, Archaeology and Social Anthropology.

24. In all the anthropology departments MA programmes started in the early 2000s.

25. For the role contemporary Greece could play as a mirror in the self-reflexive anthropological endeavour of that period, see also Herzfeld (1987).

26. Some of them have already taken positions in foreign universities, no longer as specialists of Greece. For example K. Retsikas is a specialist on Java or D. Dalakoglou on Albania.

27. Several publishing houses such as Alexandria, Plethron, Ellinika Grammata, Patakis, Kritiki or Gutenberg made an important contribution to this proliferation of anthropological texts in Greek.

28. For example, at Panteion University almost 200 students are admitted every year to the Department of Anthropology.

29. Disciplines such as journalism or psychology are much in demand because they are supposed to offer better professional prospects and attract students with higher grades.

30. No anthropology courses and only one sociology course are offered in secondary education. However, as this course is not included in the entrance exams programme, many pupils do not pay much attention to it.

31. In the case of mixed departments, such as that at the University of Thessaly, up to 70 per cent of students choose a major in history or archaeology, considering these disciplines have better professional prospects and more established professional rights than anthropology. However, they systematically attend the anthropology courses, as they find them interesting. As a result, they usually acquire an interdisciplinary approach to their specialization.

32. In some cases though, especially in universities located in smaller towns, anthropology departments or individual scholars and students are involved in common projects with local authorities and institutions, regarding, for example, the organization of local museums, of scientific conferences and other events that connect academia to local societies.

33. At Panteion University for example, emphasis is put on non-Greek ethnography. At the University of the Aegean, there is a focus on the ethnography of Greece and a special MA programme on gender studies.

34. Those who can afford it leave for MA and Ph.D. studies in the United Kingdom, France, Holland, Switzerland and, increasingly during recent years, in the United States.

35. This choice is made despite the fact that MA graduates in Anthropology that do not have a BA in Anthropology have no professional rights. According to Greek legislation, only BA and Ph.D. holders in Anthropology have such professional rights. MA graduates can, however, get a higher salary or job promotion with their degree no matter the discipline.

36. The proliferation of Master's degrees is both the result of a high demand on the part of students and a practice encouraged by the Ministry of Education, who has approved numerous new MA programmes during the last two decades.

37. There are a few research institutions, both private and public, where anthropologists are employed, such as the National Centre for Social Sciences, the Hellenic Folklore Research Centre of the Academy of Athens or several museums.

38. As a rule, public funding for education is very low and is diminishing even more nowadays (2.9% of the GDP). This is also the case for research in general and for the social sciences more specifically, which are even more at a disadvantage.

39. More precisely, during the last few years most funds were for research on migration and gender.

40. This state scholarship has existed since the early 1990s, but because of cuts in funds the grant for anthropology studies was suspended for several years whilst the grant for folklore studies was maintained. It is only in the last two years that the anthropology scholarship has again been attributed.

41. For example, stipends are often given to young scholars from the donor's home town or region or for a topic favoured by him/her – that is to say, with strong personal, emotional criteria.

42. This interest in the Balkans is related to the hegemonic role that Greek governments and entrepreneurs have attempted to play in the region during the last two decades.

43. There exists no official data regarding anthropology graduates' employment, so we can only provide some tendencies. In their majority, they are oriented towards jobs not related to their field of study. Among those who have a job related to the discipline, most are employed in different (social) services and administrative positions in the public sector, at a central and local level. During the last decade, NGOs, International Organizations, hospitals, museums and the media have also become important employers of anthropologists. Few work in education, in the business sector or in consultancy. Generally, during recent years the number of unemployed graduates has escalated due to the overall crisis.

44. A Society of Greek Anthropologists was founded in the 1990s but has been virtually inactive for many years now. The Greek Society for Ethnology is a much more active association, organizing regular seminars and book presentations and publishing the Journal *Ethnologia*. It is, however, open not only to anthropologists but also to other scholars from the humanities and social sciences and has a more scientific than professional character.

45. In secondary education, anthropologists can be hired only as sociologists, since no anthropology courses are included.

46. Although, as Bakalaki notes (2006), the cost of going to university in Greece is quite high in terms of preparatory courses for the entrance examinations and expenses related to accommodation and maintenance of students when they are studying away from home.

47. In comparison to other disciplines such as law or medicine.

48. Recently, in an effort to reduce the number of public servants, the government has adopted a rule of one recruitment for every ten retirements in the public sector.

49. See, for example, Shore and Wright (1999), Strathern (2000), Shore (2007).

50. Since the junta years and until today, Greek students have been relatively politicized. They actively take part in student associations and until the vote of the law 4009/2011 their participation was important, with elected representatives in the administration of their department and the university. Students' political activism deserves more analysis; however, such an analysis is beyond the aims of this chapter.

51. According to article 16 of the Greek Constitution, the development and advancement of the arts and sciences is an obligation of the State. Also, higher education is provided exclusively by institutions that are public corporations with full self-administration and that are under the supervision of the State. An attempt to change this article during the last revision of the Constitution in 2008 failed after the reactions and massive demonstrations of students and teaching staff all over Greece.

52. It is difficult to find exact data but generally academics' wages have decreased between 30 per cent and 40 per cent during the last three years.
53. This plan has been finally withdrawn due to the mobilization of students and departments against it.

REFERENCES

Agelopoulos, G. 2010. 'Contested Territories and the Quest for Ethnology', in N. Diamandouros, T. Dragona and C. Keyder (eds). *Spatial Conceptions of the Nation*. London: Tauris, pp. 181–191.

———. 2013. 'Multiple Encounters: Attempts to introduce Anthropology in Greece during the 1940s–1960s', in A. Bošković & C. Hann (eds). *The Anthropological Field on the Margins of Europe, 1945–1991*. Münster: LIT-Verlag, pp. 65–84.

Bakalaki, A. 1993. 'Anthropologikes prosegiseis tes sychrones ellinikes koinonias' ['Anthropological Approaches of Contemporary Greek Society'], in E. Papataxiarchis (ed.), *Diavazo, Afieroma sten Koinonike Anthropologia* [Diavazo, special issue 'Social Anthropology'] 323: 52–58.

———. 1997. 'Students, Natives, Colleagues: Encounters in Academia and in the Field', *Cultural Anthropology* 12(4): 502–26.

———. 2006. 'A Different Kind of Knowledge? Learning Anthropology in the Greek University System', *Journal of Modern Greek Studies* 24(2): 257–83.

Campbell, J.K. 1964. *Honour, Family and Patronage*. Oxford: Oxford University Press.

Couroucli, M. 1978. 'Oi anthropologikes ereunes sten agrotike Ellada' ['Anthropological Studies in Rural Greece'], *Sychrona Themata* [Contemporary Issues] 2: 83–90.

———. 2007. 'Identity, Nationalism and Anthropologists', in P. Sant Cassia (ed.), *Between Europe and the Mediterranean*. London: Palgrave Macmillan, pp. 73–87.

Dalkavoukis, V., I. Manos and C. Veikou (eds). 2010. *Anypopsiastoi Anthropologoi Kachypoptoi Foitetes: Didaskodas Anthropologia s' Autous pou 'Den te Chreiazodai"* [Unsuspecting Anthropologists, Suspicious Students: Teaching Anthropology to Those Who 'Do Not Need It']. Athens: Kritiki.

Friedl, E. 1962. *Vassilika: A Village in Modern Greece*. New York: Holt, Rinehart and Winston.

Gefou-Madianou, D. 1993. 'Mirroring Ourselves through Western Texts: The Limits of an Indigenous Anthropology', in H. Driessen (ed.), *The Politics of Ethnographic Reading and Writing: Confrontations of Western and Indigenous Views*. Saarbrücken and Fort Lauderdale: Verlag Breitenbach Publishers, pp. 160–81.

———. 1999. *Politismos kai Ethnographia: Apo ton Ethnographiko Realismo sten Politismike Kritike* [Culture and Ethnography: From Ethnographic Realism to Cultural Critique]. Athens: Ellinika Grammata.

———. 2000. 'Disciples, Discipline and Reflection: Anthropological Encounters and Trajectories', in M. Strathern (ed.), *Audit Cultures: Anthropological Studies in Accountability, Ethics and Academy*. London: Routledge, EASE Series, pp. 256–78.

———. 2010. 'Culture in the Periphery: Anthropology in the Shadow of Greek Civilization', in D. James, E. Plaice and C. Toren (eds), *Culture Wars: Context, Models and Anthropologists' Accounts*. New York and Oxford: Berghahn Books, pp. 57–72.

Hann, C. 2003. 'The Anthropology of Eurasia in Eurasia', *Max Planck Institute for Social Anthropology, Working Paper 57*.

Herzfeld, M. 1980. 'Honor and Shame: Some Problems in the Contemporary Analysis of Moral Systems', *Man* 15: 339–51.

———. 1982. *Ours Once More: Folklore, Ideology and the Making of Modern Greece*. Austin: University of Texas Press.

———. 1987. *Anthropology Through the Looking Glass: Ethnography at the Margins of Europe*. Cambridge: Cambridge University Press.

Kyrakidou-Nestoros, A. 1978. *E Theoria tes Ellenikes Laografias: Kritike Analyses* [The Theory of Greek Folklore: A Critical Analysis]. Athens: Etairia Spoudon Moraiti.

Lampiri-Dimaki, I. (ed.). 2003. *Koinonikes Epistemes kai Protoporia sten Ellada (1950–1967)*[Social Sciences and Vanguard in Greece (1950–1967)]. Athens: EKKE and Gutenberg.

Nitsiakos, V. 2008. *Prosanatolismoi: Mia kritike eisagoge ste Laografia* [Orientations: A Critical Introduction to Folklore]. Athens: Kritiki.

Panopoulos, P. 2003. 'Between Self and the Others: The Academic Establishment of Greek Anthropology', in D. Dracklé, I.R. Edgar and T. Schippers (eds), *Educational Histories of European Social Anthropologies*. New York: Berghahn Books, pp. 193–205.

Papataxiarchis, E. 1993. 'To parelthon sto paron: Anthropologia, istoria kai e melete tes neoellenikes koinonias' ['The Present in the Past: Anthropology, History and the Study of Contemporary Greek Society'], in E. Papataxiarchis and T. Paradellis (eds), *Anthropologia kai Parelthon: Symvoles sten Koinonike Istoria tes Neoteres Elladas* [Anthropology and the Past: Contributions to the Social History of Modern Greece]. Athens: Alexandria, pp. 13–74.

———. 2003. 'E Koinonike Anthropologia ste Metapolemike Ellada: Ta Prota Vemata' ['Social Anthropology in Post War Greece: The First Steps'], in I. Lampiri-Dimaki (ed.), *Koinonikes Epistemes kai Protoporia sten Ellada (1950–1967)* [Social Sciences and Vanguard in Greece (1950–1967)]. Athens: EKKE and Gutenberg, pp. 115–14.

———. 2005. 'Un moment pluriel: l'ethnographie grecque au tournant du siècle', *Ethnologie française* XXXV(20): 213–27.

———. 2013. 'From 'National' to 'Social Science': Politics, Ideology, and Disciplinary Formation in Greek Anthropology from the 1940s till the 1980s', in A. Bošković & C. Hann (eds.). *The Anthropological Field on the Margins of Europe, 1945–1991*. Münster: LIT-Verlag, pp. 31–63.

Pina-Cabral, J. 1989. 'The Mediterranean as a Category: Regional Comparison: A Critical Review', *Current Anthropology* 30: 339–406.

Shore, C. 2007. '"After Neoliberalism"? The Reform of New Zealand's University System', Copenhagen, Danish University of Education, Working Paper on University Reform 6. Retrieved 24 March 2017 from http://edu.au.dk/fileadmin/www.dpu. dk/forskning/forskningsprogrammer/epoke/workingpapers/om-dpu_institutter_ institut-for-paedagogik_20100127132545_wp-6-ny.pdf.

———. 2008. 'Audit Culture and Illiberal Governance: Universities and the Politics of Accountability', *Anthropological Theory* 8(3): 278–99.

Shore, C. and S. Wright. 1999. 'Audit Culture and Anthropology: Neo-Liberalism in British

Higher Education', *The Journal of the Royal Anthropological Institute* 5(4): 557–75.

————. 2000. 'Coercive Accountability: The Rise of Audit Culture in Higher Education', in M. Strathern (ed.), *Audit Cultures: Anthropological Studies in Accountability, Ethics and Academy*. London: Routledge, EASE Series, pp. 523–26.

Strathern, M. (ed.). 2000. *Audit Cultures: Anthropological Studies in Accountability, Ethics and Academy*. London: Routledge, EASE Series.

Toudasaki, I. 2003. 'Anthropologia kai Laografia: apo ten ekaterothen adiaforia sten ypo orous anagnorise amoivaion ofelematon' ['Anthropology and Folklore: From Both Sides Indifference to the Under Conditions Recognition of Mutual Benefits'], *Dokimes* 11–12: 7–63.

Trubeta, S. 2009. 'Physical Anthropology, Race and Eugenics (1880s–1970s): The Science – The Actors – The Ideas', Habilitation thesis. Eingereicht an den Fachbereich Geschichts- und Kulturwissenschaften der Freien Universität Berlin.

————. 2010. 'The "Strong Nucleus of the Greek Race": Racial Nationalism and Anthropological Science', *Focaal – European Journal of Anthropology* 58: 63–78.

Tsibiridou, F. 2003. 'Anagnoseis toy 'koinonikou' apo ten anthropologia sten Ellada tes metapoliteuses' ['Anthropological Readings of the "Social" in Post-junta Greece'], *Mnemon* 25: 185–202.

Wright, S. and A. Rabo. 2010. 'Anthropologies of University Reform', *Social Anthropology* 18(1): 1–14.

INDEX OF SUBJECTS

INDEX OF NAMES

www.ingramcontent.com/pod-product-compliance
Lightning Source LLC
Chambersburg PA
CBHW070912030426
42336CB00014BA/2381